Security sector reform and post-conflict peacebuilding

In memory of Rocky Williams

Security sector reform and post-conflict peacebuilding

Edited by Albrecht Schnabel and Hans-Georg Ehrhart

United Nations University Press

TOKYO · NEW YORK · PARIS

United Nations University Press
United Nations University, 53-70, Jingumae 5-chome,
Shibuya-ku, Tokyo, 150-8925, Japan
Tel: +81-3-3499-2811   Fax: +81-3-3406-7345
E-mail: sales@hq.unu.edu
General enquiries: press@hq.unu.edu
www.unu.edu

United Nations University Office at the United Nations, New York
2 United Nations Plaza, Room DC2-2062, New York, NY 10017, USA
Tel: +1-212-963-6387   Fax: +1-212-371-9454
E-mail: unuona@ony.unu.edu

United Nations University Press is the publishing division of the United Nations University.

Cover design by Marie Sese-Paul

Printed in the United States of America

ISBN 92-808-1109-6

Library of Congress Cataloging-in-Publication Data

Security sector reform and post-conflict peacebuilding / edited by Albrecht Schnabel and Hans-Georg Ehrhart.
   p.   cm.
Includes bibliographical references and index.
ISBN 9280811096 (pbk.)
1. National security. 2. Peace-building. 3. Civil-military relations.
4. Peacekeeping forces. 5. United Nations—Peacekeeping forces. I. Schnabel, Albrecht. II. Ehrhart, Hans-Georg, 1955–
UA10.5.S3735   2005
327.1′72—dc22   2005024342

Contents

Acknowledgements

A number of individuals and organizations have provided invaluable assistance and support at various stages of this book project.

First of all, we are grateful to the United Nations University, the Japanese Ministry of Foreign Affairs, and the German Ministry of Foreign Affairs for providing the funding for our work. We are grateful to the Swiss Peace Foundation (swisspeace) and the Institute for Peace Research and Security Policy at the University of Hamburg for offering us the time and opportunity to work on this project. We thank the latter for hosting a most stimulating author meeting in November 2001, and particularly Bernt Berger for his assistance during the workshop. We greatly appreciate the logistical and administrative assistance offered for the entire duration of this project by Yoshie Sawada of the Peace and Governance Programme of the United Nations University. We are grateful to Monica Blagescu for assistance during the early stages of the project. We thank UNU Press, particularly Gareth Johnston and Scott McQuade, for patiently supporting us in preparing and improving the manuscript for publication. We are grateful to two anonymous peer reviewers, whose comments allowed us to make important improvements over the initial draft manuscript; and we greatly appreciate the work of Cherry Ekins for copyediting the volume and for producing the index.

This book grew out of an international research project on "The Role of the Military in Post-Conflict Peacebuilding" jointly initiated in 2001 under the aegis of the United Nations University and the Institute for

Peace Research and Security Policy at the University of Hamburg. The project focused on two main issues: the role and conduct of international peace operations in the post-war transition phase, and security sector reform as a contribution to post-conflict peacebuilding efforts. Contributions on the first theme (by Anthony Anderson, Karin von Hippel, Ho-Won Jeong, Stephen Blackwell, Karen Guttieri, and Ann Fitz-Gerald) were published in the journal *S+F: Sicherheit und Frieden/Security and Peace* (Vol. 22, Nos 1/2), while the studies undertaken on the second theme culminated in this book. As those responsible for the overall project, we thank all project participants for sharing their insights with us and the readers of the *S+F* articles and this book.

We dedicate this volume to Rocky Williams, who contributed a chapter to the book and who passed away in January 2005. Rocky's contributions to the debate on security sector reform and its implementation in his home country of South Africa and throughout the African continent have been immense. Those lucky enough to have known, worked with, and learned from him miss him greatly. His legacy will motivate us to continue the important work he has begun.

Albrecht Schnabel
Hans-Georg Ehrhart
Bern and Hamburg

Acronyms

ACSS	Africa Center for Strategic Studies (USA)
ARENA	Alianza Republicana Nacionalista (El Salvador)
ARM	Army of the Republic of Macedonia
ASEAN	Association of South-East Asian Nations
AUC	Autodefensas Unidas de Colombia
CCMR	Center for Civil-Military Relations
CEE	Central and Eastern Europe
CFSP	EU Common Foreign and Security Policy
CIS	Commonwealth of Independent States
CNI	Central National Intelligence (Chile)
CNR	National Reconciliation Commission (Guatemala)
CNRT	Conselho Nacional da Resistencia Timorense (East Timor)
CONACOM	National Congress of Democratic Movements (Haiti)
CPAF	Cambodian People's Armed Forces
CPP	Cambodian People's Party
CSSDCA	Conference on Stability, Security, Development, and Cooperation in Africa
DAC	OECD Development Assistance Committee
DAO	defence attaché officer
DDR	disarmament, demobilization, and reintegration (of former combatants)
DINA	National Intelligence Directorate (Chile)
DPA	UN Department of Political Affairs
DPKO	UN Department of Peacekeeping Operations
DFID	Department for International Development (UK)
DUP	Democratic Unionist Party (Northern Ireland)

EAF	Entity Armed Forces (Bosnia)
EAPC	Euro-Atlantic Partnership Council
ECOWAS	Economic Community of West African States
ELN	Ejercito de Liberacion Nacional (Colombia)
EMERCOM	Ministry for Civil Defence, Emergencies, and Elimination of Consequences of Natural Disasters (Russia)
EU	European Union
EUPM	EU Police Mission in Bosnia and Herzegovina
FAD'H	Forces Armées d'Haiti
FAO	UN Food and Agriculture Organization
FARC	Fuerzas Armadas Revolucionarias de Colombia
FDI	foreign direct investment
FDNG	New Guatemala Democratic Front
F-FDTL	Falintil-Force Defence Timor-Leste (East Timor)
FMLN	Frente Farabunmdo Marti para la Liberacion Nacional (El Salvador)
FMS	Federal Migration Service (Russia)
FOM	freedom of movement
FRG	Guatemalan Republican Front
GANA	Grand National Alliance (Guatemala)
GEL	Georgian lari
GFAP	General Framework Agreement for Peace (Bosnia)
GTZ	Deutsche Gesellschaft für technische Zusammenarbeit
HNP	Haitian National Police
IC	international community
ICISS	International Commission on Intervention and State Sovereignty
ICRC	International Committee of the Red Cross
ICTY	International Criminal Tribunal for the former Yugoslavia
IDA	International Development Association
IDP	internally displaced person
IFI	international financial institution
IFOR	Intervention Force (Bosnia)
IICD	Independent International Commission on Decommissioning
IMET	US International Military Education and Training programme
IMF	International Monetary Fund
INTERFET	International Force for East Timor
IPAP	Individual Partnership Action Plan (Georgia)
IPTF	International Police Task Force
IRA	Irish Republican Army
ISAF	International Security Assistance Force (Afghanistan)
ISAP	International Security Advisory Board
JCO	joint commission observer (Bosnia)
KFOR	Kosovo Force
KPNLF	Khmer People's National Liberation Front (Cambodia)
MIA	Ministry of Internal Affairs (Georgia)
MICAH	International Civilian Support Mission (Haiti)

MINUGUA	UN Verification Mission in Guatemala
MINUSTAH	UN Stabilization Mission in Haiti
MND(N)	Multi-National Division North (Bosnia)
MNF	multinational force
MOD	Ministry of Defence (various countries)
MOI	Ministry of the Interior (Cambodia)
MOND	Ministry of National Defence (Cambodia)
MP	member of parliament
MSS	Ministry of State Security (Georgia)
MUP	Interior Police (Bosnia)
MVD	Ministerstvo Vnutrennikh Del (Ministry of Internal Affairs, Russia)
NATO	North Atlantic Treaty Organization
NEPAD	New Partnership for Africa's Development
NGO	non-governmental organization
NLA	National Liberation Army (Macedonia)
NSC	National Security Council (Georgia)
OAS	Organization of American States
OAU	Organization of African Unity
OCHA	UN Office for the Coordination of Humanitarian Affairs
OECD	Organization for Economic Cooperation and Development
OGV	Federal Group of Forces (Russia)
OIG	Office of the Inspector General (Bosnia)
OMON	militia unit of special detachment (Russia)
ONUSAL	UN Observer Mission in El Salvador
OPL	Organization of People in Struggle (Haiti)
OSCE	Organization for Security and Cooperation in Europe
PAC	civil defence patrols (Guatemala)
PAN	National Advancement Party (Guatemala)
PfP	Partnership for Peace programme
PIFWC	person indicted for war crimes
PKO	peacekeeping operation
PLA	People's Liberation Army (China)
PNTL	Policia Nacional de Timor-Leste (East Timor)
PolRI	Indonesian police force
PRK	People's Republic of Kampuchea
PRT	provincial reconstruction team (Afghanistan)
PSNI	Police Service of Northern Ireland
PSO	peace support operations
PUP	Progressive Unionist Party (Northern Ireland)
RCAF	Royal Cambodian Armed Forces
RDP	reconstruction and development programme
REMHI	Recovery of Historical Memory project (Guatemala)
ROE	rules of engagement
RS	Republika Srpska
RUBOP	regional unit on combating organized crime (Russia)

RUC	Royal Ulster Constabulary
SADC	Southern African Development Community
SAPS	South African Police Service
SCMM	Standing Committee on Military Matters (Bosnia)
SDLP	Social Democratic and Labour Party (Northern Ireland)
SEECP	South-East European Cooperation Process
SEPAZ	Secretariat of Peace (Guatemala)
SFOR	Stabilization Force (Bosnia)
SHIRBRIG	UN Standby High Readiness Brigade
SNI	National Information System (Brazil)
SOBR	special rapid-reaction unit (Russia)
SOC	State of Cambodia
SRSG	special representative of the Secretary-General
SSR	security sector reform
SST	security sector transformation
TNI	Indonesian military
UCK	Ushtria Clirimtare e Kosoves (Kosovo Liberation Army)
UDA	Ulster Defence Association
UDT	União Democratica Timorense (East Timor)
UDP	Ulster Democratic Party
UFF	Ulster Freedom Fighters
UNAMET	UN Mission in East Timor
UNCOHCHR	UN Cambodia Office of the High Commissioner for Human Rights
UNDP	UN Development Programme
UNDPKO	UN Department of Peacekeeping Operations
UNHCR	UN High Commissioner for Refugees
UNICEF	UN Children's Fund
UNMIH	UN Mission in Haiti
UNMISET	UN Mission of Support in East Timor
UNSG	UN Secretary-General
UNSOM II	UN Operation in Somalia II
UNTAC	UN Transitional Authority for Cambodia
UNTAET	UN Transitional Administration in East Timor
URNG	Guatemalan National Revolutionary Unity
UUP	Ulster Unionist Party
UVF	Ulster Volunteer Force
VMRO	Vnatresna makedonska revolucionerna organizacija (Internal Macedonian Revolutionary Organization)
WFP	World Food Programme
WHO	World Health Organization
YPA	Yugoslav People's Army

Contributors

Thomas C. Bruneau is Professor of National Security Affairs at the Naval Postgraduate School in Monterey, California. Between 1989 and 1995 he was chairman of that department. Since 1996 he has been programme manager for Latin America at the Center for Civil-Military Relations located at the Naval Postgraduate School, and was director between 2000 and 2005. He makes frequent trips to deliver seminars on civil-military relations to Latin America, Asia, and East/Central Europe. He has published extensively on Latin America and Portugal, and has two books appearing in 2006 on key issues in civil-military relations, including democratic control of intelligence agencies. He received his PhD from the University of California, Berkeley, and served 18 years on the faculty of the Department of Political Science at McGill University, Montreal, Canada.

David Darchiashvili is head of the Research Department of the Parliament of Georgia and a lecturer at the International Relations Department at Tbilisi State University. He is also the director of the Center for Civil-Military Relations and Security Studies, and a researcher at the Caucasian Institute for Peace, Democracy, and Development in Tbilisi.

Hans-Georg Ehrhart is a senior research fellow and lecturer at the Institute for Peace Research and Security Policy at the University of Hamburg (IFSH). He is a member of "Team Europe" of the European Commission's representation in Germany and previously served as a visiting research fellow with the Foundation for National Defence Studies, Paris, the Centre for International Relations, Queen's University, Kingston, and the EU

Institute for Security Studies, Paris. He received his MA and DPhil from the University of Bonn. Dr Ehrhart has published widely on issues such as disarmament, peacekeeping, conflict prevention, international organizations, post-Soviet politics, and German-French relations as well as German and European security politics.

Andrés Fontana is Professor, Dean of Graduate Studies, and director of the international relations major at the Universidad de Belgrano, Buenos Aires. He also holds professorships at the Catholic University of Cordova, the National University of Buenos Aires, and the Institute of National Foreign Services. From 1998 to 2000 he served as undersecretary for strategic policy in the government of Argentina. He received his PhD in political science from the University of Texas in Austin, USA.

Nibaldo H. Galleguillos is an associate professor in the Department of Political Science at McMaster University, Hamilton, Ontario. Before receiving his PhD from the University of Toronto he was a human rights lawyer in the Committee for Cooperation and Peace and an attorney at law in Santiago, Chile.

Dylan Hendrickson is a research fellow at the Centre for Defence Studies, King's College, London. Previously he was an independent consultant working for the Disasters Management Committee and the International Institute for Environment and Development in London, for UNHCR and UNICEF in Geneva, and for

Care International UK, among others.

Fernando Isturiz is currently working for the Association for Cultural Promotion, Argentina. He was most recently a senior associate for training at the International Peace Academy in New York. Colonel Isturiz was the director of the Argentine Armed Forces Joint Staff Center of Strategic Studies. He was also commanding officer of the Argentine Peace Operations Training Center (CAECOPAZ) and Argentina's contingent commander with the UN peacekeeping force in Cyprus.

Andrzej Karkoszka is a senior political adviser to the director of the Geneva Centre for the Democratic Control of Armed Forces (DCAF). Previously he held appointments with the Marshall Center in Garmisch-Partenkirchen, Germany, the Chancellery of the President of Poland, the Polish Ministry of National Defence, the Polish Institute of International Affairs, Warsaw, the Stockholm International Peace Research Institute, and the Institute for East-West Security Studies (now EastWest Institute), New York. He received his PhD in political science from the Polish Institute of International Affairs in 1977.

Chetan Kumar is an interagency specialist in the Political and Strategic Planning Unit of the Bureau for Crisis Prevention and Recovery, UNDP, New York. Previously he was a programme officer in the Office of the Special Representative of the UN Secretary-General for Children and Armed

Conflict, and a senior associate at the International Peace Academy, both in New York. He received his PhD from the University of Illinois at Urbana-Champaign.

William Maley is Professor and Foundation Director, Asia-Pacific College of Diplomacy, Australian National University. He was previously an associate professor of politics at the University of New South Wales. In 1998 he was appointed to the Australian Foreign Affairs Council. Dr Maley served as authorized international observer of elections with the UN Transitional Authority in Cambodia (UNTAC), and has field experience on several Afghan refugee projects with AUSTCARE.

Sophie Richardson is a consultant on Cambodia with the International Crisis Group, currently enrolled in a doctoral programme in the Department of Government and Foreign Affairs at the University of Virginia. Previously she worked for the National Democratic Institute for International Affairs, Washington, DC, where she served as senior programme officer for Asia.

Allison Ritscher is an intelligence officer at the Naval Special Warfare Command in San Diego, California. She was previously a reports/operations officer with the Joint Interrogation Center in Vaihingen, Germany, and a squadron intelligence officer in Virginia. She has received her MA in national security affairs from the Naval Postgraduate School in Monterey, California.

Peter Sainsbury is a freelance journalist with extensive field experience in Thailand and Viet Nam. He has also worked as managing editor and reporter for the *Phnom Penh Post* in Cambodia and as news and audio editor for *Radio New Zealand*.

Albrecht Schnabel is a senior research fellow at swisspeace – the Swiss Peace Foundation in Bern, Switzerland – where he is responsible for a research programme on human security and the coordination of swisspeace's early warning programme, FAST. He teaches in the Institute of Political Science at the University of Bern. He previously served as an academic officer in the Peace and Governance Programme of the United Nations University and held teaching positions at the American University in Bulgaria, the Central European University, and Aoyama Gakuin University. He has been a visiting research fellow at the Institute for Peace Research and Security Policy at the University of Hamburg (IFSH), and currently serves as a trainer on early warning and prevention for the UN Staff College, Turin. His research and publications focus on conflict and security studies, with an emphasis on conflict prevention and post-conflict peacebuilding. He holds a PhD in political studies from Queen's University, Canada.

Andrés Serbin is a professor at the Central University of Venezuela. He is president of Concertacion Centroamericana, a Central American network of non-governmental organizations. Between 1991 and 1993 he served as adviser to the Ministry of Foreign Affairs of Venezuela.

Ekaterina A. Stepanova is a senior researcher at the Center for Political and Military Forecasts of the Institute of World Economy and International Relations (IMEMO), Russia. Previously she was a MacArthur individual research fellow and research associate on foreign policy and security issues with the Carnegie Moscow Center. Dr Stepanova received her PhD from Moscow State University.

Biljana Vankovska is a senior fellow at the Geneva Centre for Democratic Control of Armed Forces (DCAF), Switzerland. Previously she was the head of the Institute of Defence at the University of Skopje, Macedonia, and a scientific adviser at DCAF. Dr Vankovska received her PhD in political science from the Department of Political Studies, University of Skopje.

Rocky Williams (d. January 2005) was director of the African Security Sector Transformation Programme at the Institute for Security Studies, Pretoria, South Africa. Previously, Colonel Williams served as the director of operations policy at the South African Ministry of Defence.

He was a former commander in Umkhonto We Sizwe – the guerilla army of the African National Congress. He held a PhD from the University of Essex, England, and was a member of the faculty of the School of Public and Development Management at the University of Witwatersrand.

Stefan Wolff is Professor of Political Science in the Department of European Studies, University of Bath, England. He is also a senior non-resident research associate at the European Centre for Minority Issues, and a professorial lecturer at the School of Advanced International Studies, Johns Hopkins University, Bologna Center. He has done consulting work for the Canadian Immigration and Refugee Board on the situation of ethnic minorities in Central and Eastern Europe and the former Soviet Union. Dr Wolff holds a PhD in political science from the London School of Economics, UK, and has published widely on German minorities in Europe, ethnopolitics, and the management of ethnic conflict.

1

Post-conflict societies and the military: Challenges and problems of security sector reform

Albrecht Schnabel and Hans-Georg Ehrhart

In post-conflict societies, the remnants of wartime military and security apparatuses pose great risks to internal security: inflated armies with little or no civilian control; irregular and paramilitary forces; an over-abundance of arms and ammunition in private and government hands; weak internal security forces; and a lack of trust in and legitimacy of the government's control over police and military forces.[1] Peacekeeping troops from other nations, regional organizations, and the United Nations attempt to support political and economic transition processes and the transition of wartime security systems. Without a secure environment and a security system that ensures security even after the departure of international peace operations, political, economic, and cultural rebuilding are impossible. The latter can take place only in an environment where the local security sector is subjected to a rigorous democratization process, putting the security forces in the service of society's safety, not its destruction, and where both internal and external security forces are contributing constructively to the rebuilding of process.

Reflecting on the experiences and analyses of an international group of academics and practitioners from various educational and professional backgrounds and diverse cultures of analysis and reflection, this book examines the role of local and external actors – with a focus on military forces – in meeting the challenge of sustainable post-conflict security sector reform.[2] Following analyses of the key challenges of security sector reform and the roles particularly of international peace operations in addressing the security needs of post-conflict societies, case studies

1

from Europe, Africa, Asia, and Latin America put these discussions in a regional and global context.

Post-conflict peacebuilding and the military

In a historic perspective, people directly concerned in violent conflict had to bear the consequences and the burden of reconstruction primarily on their own. In the post-international world a new understanding is emerging that it is in the very interest of the world society – for moral reasons, but more so for strategic and security reasons – to care about violent conflicts and their devastating consequences for regional, international, and human security. Not only the termination of war but also the rebuilding of post-war societies have become both livelihood and security issues. It was former UN Secretary-General Boutros Boutros-Ghali who, in his *Agenda for Peace*, introduced the concept of post-conflict peacebuilding as an important step in the sequence of preventive diplomacy, peacemaking, and peacekeeping.[3] He briefly defines post-conflict peacebuilding as "action to identify and support structures which will tend to strengthen and solidify peace in order to avoid a relapse into conflict".[4] The concept has become an inherent component in the UN's efforts to prevent and resolve conflicts, and to preserve peace. According to UN Secretary-General Kofi Annan:

By post-conflict peace-building, I mean actions undertaken at the end of a conflict to consolidate peace and prevent a recurrence of armed confrontation. Experience has shown that the consolidation of peace in the aftermath of conflict requires more than purely diplomatic and military action, and that an integrated peace-building effort is needed to address the various factors that have caused or are threatening a conflict. Peace-building may involve the creation or strengthening of national institutions, monitoring elections, promoting human rights, providing for reintegration and rehabilitation programmes, and creating conditions for resumed development. Peace-building does not replace ongoing humanitarian and development activities in countries emerging from crisis. It aims rather to build on, add to, or reorient such activities in ways designed to reduce the risk of a resumption of conflict and contribute to creating the conditions most conducive to reconciliation, reconstruction and recovery.[5]

Post-conflict peacebuilding is a complex and multidimensional, genuinely political process of transformation from a state of war or violent conflict to one of stability and peace, requiring, according to Kofi Annan, "a multifaceted approach, covering diplomatic, political and economic factors".[6] It embraces security, political, social, economic, and psycho-social dimensions, and it aims at the installation of both negative and, in the longer run, positive peace. While it is necessary to define appropriate measures and timetables (including exit strategies) and, in the interest of sustainability, to ensure transfer of ownership to local actors, this becomes a particularly difficult and cumbersome undertaking when the required multifaceted approach is not paralleled by "high-level strategic and administrative coordination" among the different actors involved in post-conflict peacebuilding tasks.[7] Moreover, in the interest of sustainability, coordination with local partners has to lead towards transfer of responsibilities. As the International Commission on Intervention and State Sovereignty (ICISS) notes, "the long-term aim of international actors in a post-conflict situation is 'to do themselves out of a job'... by creating political processes which require local actors to take over responsibility both for rebuilding their society and for creating patterns of cooperation between antagonistic groups".[8]

The roles of security forces – external and internal – and the process of security sector reform are key ingredients of the post-conflict peacebuilding agenda. Among the primary conditions for starting a process of conflict transformation and the rebuilding of political institutions, security, and economic structures is a secure environment.[9] That is the point where external military forces must be at hand to cope with such diverse tasks as the reinstallation of order, support for local security forces, disarmament of combatants, facilitation of security sector reform, protection of elections, demining, and securing the repatriation of refugees and protection of human rights. This is only possible if the activities of external military forces are integral parts of the overall transformation process of the post-conflict society concerned.

Military forces in even the most advanced democracies are themselves in a process of change. We are witnessing the emergence of a postmodern military that is characterized by six challenges. First, the traditional values of honour and fatherland are increasingly challenged by universal values such as freedom, democracy, and justice. Second, although fighting capacities remain important, other tasks – so-called missions other than war – are gaining relevance. The postmodern soldier is not only a fighter but also a peacekeeper, policeman, diplomat, social worker, and Peace Corps worker. Third, the example of the 2003 Iraq war and the wider war on terrorism notwithstanding, there is growing pressure for international legitimization of any kinds of external intervention. Fourth, the military is increasingly becoming internationalized. Multinational forces such as NATO's Allied Rapid Reaction Corps, the EU's Eurocorps, and the UN Standby High Readiness Brigade are examples for this process. Fifth, an ongoing "revolution in military affairs" is changing the way of war fighting and of intervention. Sixth, postmodern soldiers are confronted with a growing privatization of violence and the looming security dilemma this produces.[10]

The military is an institution of the state, and as such primarily an instrument to assure external security for the state and its society. Since the Kellogg-Briand Pact and the UN Charter, international law prohibits states from using the military as an aggressive instrument to exert state power within or outside of its borders. Since then two main concepts circumscribe the role of the military: defence (of national territory) and deterrence (of potential aggressors). Although these concepts will continue to play a significant role in military planning, they are becoming less relevant in a changing security environment in which, as already mentioned, international security threats are increasingly defined by intrastate, not interstate, conflicts. Internal conflicts have the potential to destabilize entire regions. In some regions (including Africa) such conflicts have become a permanent feature, similar to military dictatorships and *coups d'état* in the past. More developed, supposedly more peaceful regions of the world, such as Europe, are certainly not excluded from such threats. Ethnic and territorial conflicts have become commonplace events since the end of the Cold War. The disastrous consequences of these conflicts, including humanitarian catastrophes, massive refugee movements, regional destabilization, and organized crime and terrorism – and particularly the latter – have triggered not only political but increasingly military responses by the international community.

Leaving the legitimacy of the international war on terror aside, the success of humanitarian interventions (or, according to the ICISS, "interventions for human protection purposes") and complex peace operations in the post-Cold War years has been mixed. The UN's report on reforming UN peace operations offered a wide range of proposals to plan, implement, and train for future peace missions.[11] In general, the United Nations and regional groupings are beginning to show serious concern as to how to prepare for improved and more effective operations that support both negative peace (i.e. the absence of direct violence) and positive peace (i.e. the creation of political, economic, and social conditions to support sustainable justice and security).[12] Moreover, since the terrorist attacks on 11 September 2001 (9/11), the international war on terrorism has left a strong imprint on international involvement in post-war peace-building engagements, given the fear that unstable states and post-war societies provide an ideal breeding ground for terrorist training and activity.[13]

Militaries of troop-contributing countries to peace operations are faced with the following challenges. Traditional functions of national defence and deterrence give way to, or are complemented by, capacities to engage in conflict prevention, peace enforcement, peacekeeping, and the restoration of security and order. The main goal of military activities is no longer exclusively the defeat and elimination of an adversary, but the creation of a safe environment for a comprehensive and inclusive post-conflict political and social order. The deployment of intervention forces is often the first step towards the consolidation of peace. Soldiers must not think and act primarily in military categories, but must consider the political consequences of their actions and act as mediators and negotiators. Military personnel must cooperate intensively with both police and civilian components of today's complex peace operations.[14] Nevertheless, in the case of post-Taliban Afghanistan, the International Security Assistance Force (ISAF) supports the consolidation of peace while – on a different front – Operation Enduring Freedom engages in military combat against remnant Taliban forces as part of the war on terrorism. Thus separating the tasks of defeating and eliminating an adversary and creating a safe environment for the consolidation of a comprehensive and inclusive post-conflict political and social order – as mentioned above – confronts both internal and external military and other security forces with a difficult challenge: to establish and maintain "in the security sector institutions and procedures that are both effective in carrying out their missions and consistent with democracy and the rule of law".[15]

Intervening troops operate in an environment of fragile peace and order. They are confronted by military and paramilitary troops who must be integrated into post-conflict society after months or years of engagement in violent struggles against each other and the civilian population. In most post-conflict societies political institutions are absent or greatly weakened, there is an overabundance of war ordnance and weaponry, there is little or no civilian control over military and police, and mistrust and economic scarcity determine political and social relations. Both external and domestic actors are expected to cooperate in an effort to transform this delicate and fragile environment into sustainable peace. The gradual creation of democratic and legitimate state institutions and a functioning civil society is a key task on this road towards stability. And so are efforts to ensure that civil-military relations are restructured and are based on democratic principles, so that military and police forces enhance, not threaten, the security of state and society.

We are faced with a twofold transformation process. On the one hand military forces of troop-contributing third-party countries must address and meet the new challenges of peacekeeping, peace support, and peace-building tasks. On the other hand military, paramilitary, and police forces in war-torn societies must be transformed and integrated into acceptable, legitimate, and democratic security structures and actors. This book addresses these challenges as they concern both external and internal military forces, as well as their interaction, in the creation of an enabling environment for broader and sustainable peacebuilding performance.

The role of the military in security sector reform: Providing and receiving assistance

As noted in the preceding section, militaries have a crucial role to play in post-conflict peacebuilding. External militaries help facilitate the political, economic, and social transformation from a society that has been at war to a society that is able to follow a path towards long-term peace. The sheer presence of military forces might discourage the return to violence. Also, troops are engaged in active rebuilding tasks. Yet local militaries must continue to provide these security tasks on the ground once external forces return home; thus inadequate security sector reform will put post-conflict societies back on the slope towards violence and disintegration.

Effective peacebuilding requires a thorough reform of a society's security sector – a process that requires active involvement of military, economic, and political actors.[16] The "security sector" includes "all those organizations that have the authority to use, or order the use of, force or threat of force, to protect the state and its citizens, as well as those civil structures that are responsible for their management and oversight".[17] It includes military and paramilitary forces; intelligence services; police forces, border guards, and custom services; judicial and penal systems; and respective civil structures that are responsible for their management and oversight.[18] The OECD DAC Guidelines on Security System and Governance Reform define the broader security system, "which includes all the actors, their roles, responsibilities and actions – working together to manage and operate the system in a manner that is more consistent with democratic norms and sound principles of good governance, and thus contributes to a well-functioning security framework" as consisting of the following key elements.[19]

- Core security actors: armed forces; police; gendarmeries; paramilitary forces; presidential guards; intelligence and security services (both military and civilian); coastguards; customs authorities; and reserve or local security units (civil defence forces, national guards, militias).
- Security management and oversight bodies: the executive; national security advisory bodies; legislature and legislative select committees; ministries of defence, internal affairs, and foreign affairs; customary and traditional authorities; financial management bodies (finance ministries, budget offices, financial audit and planning units); and civil society organizations (civilian review boards and public complaints commissions).

- Justice and law enforcement institutions: judiciary; justice ministries; prisons; criminal investigation and prosecution services; human rights commissions and ombudsmen; and customary and traditional justice systems.
- Non-statutory security forces with whom donors rarely engage: liberation armies; guerilla armies; private bodyguard units; private security companies; and political party militias.[20]

In post-conflict situations internal and external actors must cooperate in mutually reinforcing the socio-economic, governance, and security dimensions of a highly fragile environment. The result must be an integrated approach to development, the strengthening of structures that allow for the peaceful resolution of disputes, and the prevention of violent conflict. Thus security sector reform has to be seen within the larger, multidimensional, political, economic, and societal framework of post-conflict peacebuilding. While the contributions to this book refer to this broader context, the focus is on the role and challenge of security sector reform as a contribution to peacebuilding. Furthermore, while the studies realize that the security sector (or security system) encompasses a much wider range of actors that are necessary to sustain successful reform efforts, the focus in the case studies presented in this book is on what the OECD Guidelines consider primarily the "core security actors" within the security system. The same applies to the role of external actors: the focus is on military contributions, as well as civilian partners in military peace support operations.

What are some of the key tasks for internal and external actors when reforming a society's security sector?[21]

- The peacetime capacity of military forces must be strengthened. There is a need for clear mechanisms for accountability; for a shift from being a threat to society to being a provider of security, and balancing resources spent on military compared to overall security sector spending; for reorientation of the military away from domestic politics; for overcoming ethnic and other divisions within the military; and for adjustment of training and education.
- The peacetime capacity of police forces must be strengthened. Police forces are important for community security, and thus economic and social development; they must overcome their bias towards certain parts of the population; police must serve the entire population, without preferences; human rights abuses by police forces must be checked and eliminated; and there must be support for border guards and customs services to prevent corruption, criminalization, and illicit trade.
- The peacetime capacity of judicial and penal systems must be strengthened. There is a need for investment in courts and prisons; prevention of the politicization of judicial appointments, delays of trials, and corruption; and the creation of an effective and impartial judicial system.

- Civilian management and review and evaluation must be strengthened. The goals here are to strengthen civilian expertise in defence, justice, and internal ministries; to establish independent audit offices; to establish civilian review boards for police forces and penal institutions; and to create parliamentary committees to cover defence, policing, and internal affairs.
- Respect for human rights and the rule of law must be promoted and guaranteed. It is important to instil respect for fundamental human and legal rights of citizens; to strengthen public legitimacy by making security forces trustworthy; and to make security forces focus on their central task, which is provision of security, not involvement in the political process and governance.
- Monitoring of security sector policy must be implemented and maintained. There is a need to build and strengthen a well-informed and independent civil society sector (NGOs, professional associations, independent media, and research and advocacy institutions); to review accountability and efficiency of the security sector; and to ensure that security sector monitoring is maintained after external assistance has been withdrawn.
- Transparency must be strengthened. It is crucial to strengthen effective oversight of the security sector by making their activities more transparent; to develop and publish regular official statements on security policy; to increase transparency in budgeting, accounting, and auditing; and to reduce corruption and waste in security sector programmes and activities.
- Regional confidence-building mechanisms must be promoted. It is important to encourage the establishment and strengthening of sub-regional organizations; to encourage external commitment to funding these organizations and strengthening their conflict prevention and mediation and resolution mechanisms; to include civil society in regional dialogues; and to promote and support regional civil society development and dialogue.
- Demobilization and long-term reintegration must be prioritized. This includes demobilization and disarming; reintegration of ex-combatants; reintegration of child soldiers; job training and creation; and long-term reform programmes to ensure security for ex-combatants and their families.
- Proliferation of small arms must be limited. In this context it is important to collect arms; to initiate buy-back programmes; and to enhance border control and internal security mechanisms to avoid the spread of small-arms.
- Finally, security sector reform must be integrated and mainstreamed into political dialogue and cooperation. This includes mainstreaming

security sector reform in development schemes and programmes,[22] and mainstreaming security sector reform in military and political post-conflict presence, including protectorates and quasi-protectorates. It also requires the provision of financial assistance conditional on successful security sector reform; the provision of external assistance limited to non-military use, or limitation of such spending on military forces; and the provision of clearly accounted, transparent, and audited defence budget requirements for political dialogue and development assistance.

Many of these tasks are part and parcel of post-conflict peace settlements and operation mandates (for example, the General Framework Agreement for Bosnia and Herzegovina). The challenge is to integrate them in all peace operations *and* to create mechanisms to ensure their functioning beyond the presence of foreign/international troops. All of these tasks are crucial components of a peacebuilding mission; crucial for short-term stabilization and long-term conflict prevention. All of these tasks highlight the interphase between human security principles; the social, economic, and political dimension of post-conflict peacebuilding; and security sector reform. The focus on the security needs of individuals and communities in post-conflict peace missions requires the linkage of political, economic, legal, social, and security sector reform. None of them can be advanced in isolation of the others.

External actors are tasked with two important issues. First, putting security sector reform on the right path during the period of external presence; and second, ensuring that local actors are efficiently trained and resourced to continue that work. At the same time, internal actors must collaborate with external security providers and deliver noticeable results – otherwise external actors lose interest and political and financial backing. Key obstacles in this process are that internal élites are often not interested in transparency, accountability, and legitimacy, while external actors are often not interested in long-term commitment.

As primarily non-military actors provide political, economic, and social assistance, military actors must respect the "do no harm" principle; that is, avoid making things worse than they already are.[23] They provide internal security to facilitate economic and political normalization (such as the return of refugees or preparation for elections). They disarm warring parties and neutralize peace spoilers who threaten to reignite the flames of war and intergroup hatred. External militaries secure the post-conflict environment; assist in reforming the security sector; and contribute to reconstruction. This is the main domain of their post-conflict activities, which, at the pre-conflict stage, affect the key sovereign rights of states and are virtually impossible to address without the consent of a reform-oriented government.

Structure and contents of the book

In summary, the aims of the book are to assess the role and place of military forces in post-conflict peacebuilding activities. This is done through thematic and country case studies that draw on primarily post-Cold War experiences in different regions of the world, and assessments of the opportunities, flaws, and challenges for internal and external militaries involved in post-conflict situations. The book concludes with an assessment of general and case-specific recommendations for improved performance in security sector reform.

The contributors to this volume agree that military forces have critical roles to play in the short- and long-term success of post-conflict peacebuilding, while they can be highly counterproductive if not tied into overall peace processes. External militaries must create a basic security environment to allow other peacebuilding efforts to succeed and to prevent internal forces from spoiling the fragile stability created in most post-conflict environments. Internal forces must be put under democratic control, and restructured and retrained to become an asset, not a liability, in the long-term peacebuilding process. The contributions to this book explore these issues by analysing the role of external forces (as part of peacekeeping/peace operations); of internal forces (in the context of security sector reform efforts); and of the interaction of external and internal forces.

The first part of the volume focuses on the record and challenges of security sector reform, as well as training requirements for peace operations in the post-conflict environment. In Chapter 2, "Security sector reform and donor policies", Dylan Hendrickson and Andrzei Karkoszka offer a comprehensive account of the challenges of security sector reform, with a particular focus on the role of the international donor community. They note that the importance of security sector reform for not only national but also regional and international security has only slowly been appreciated by international security assistance providers and recipient societies. Still, recipients of such assistance are sceptical concerning the conditions attached to reform efforts, and attempts by external actors to force their own institutional and structural preferences on societies in post-conflict transition. As Hendrickson and Karkoszka argue, "Past security assistance programmes were often ill-conceived and poorly implemented." Successful security sector reform ensures that weak, fragile states will not descend into violence and disorder. In addition, it helps consolidate good, responsible, and accountable governance. They emphasize that close cooperation between local stakeholders and the international donor community is crucial in ensuring successful reform efforts, irrespective of who has initiated and pressed them. They also caution us about the potentially detrimental effects of the war on terrorism on security sector reform in countries where state compliance is needed to suppress terrorist elements. In some such cases, repressive states and security apparatuses will be strengthened as their authoritarian grip on power is considered to be useful in fighting terrorism.

In Chapter 3, "African armed forces and the challenges of security sector transformation", Rocky Williams discusses the broader concept of security sector transformation in the African context. He shows that while in some cases externally encouraged and driven security sector reforms have increased political stability, in other cases the exact opposite happened. Security sector transformation can only be accomplished if it reaches far beyond the military security context: an entire array of institutional, economic, social, and political factors affect the impact that security sector reform might have on a country's internal and external stability. Thus, assistance strategies have to be highly contextual, "thoroughly indigenized and imbued with practical, local content", otherwise they will merely result in ill-suited imitations of non-African systems.

In Chapter 4, "Military forces training for post-conflict peacebuilding operations", Fernando Isturiz focuses on the particular training requirements for military personnel participating in multinational peace support operations. He notes that peacebuilding entails tasks that are not adequately addressed by conventional military doctrine and training. While he acknowledges that some troop-contributing nations are wary of the negative impact that peacebuilding might have on the combat-readiness of their troops, he also emphasizes that peacebuilding missions offer unique opportunities to expose military troops to varied in-theatre environments that generate useful skills even for conventional warfare. Moreover, participation in multinational operations offers direct experience with the challenges inherent in coalition warfare efforts. Thus, participation in post-conflict peace support operations is in fact a win-win situation – for the contributing troops and their militaries, as well as for the receiving societies whose security can be maintained in part only by the presence of international military forces. However, as Isturiz cautions, the unique challenges posed by post-conflict peace operations have to be recognized in national military training. Not doing so, and sending troops unprepared for peacebuilding environments, would be irresponsible, as post-conflict societies deserve, in Isturiz's words, "much more than amateur peacekeepers".

The remainder of the book engages in many of the issues raised in the preceding, primarily conceptual, chapters and reflects on these in the context of specific cases of post-conflict transition societies. The second part of the book focuses on experiences from Europe: the chapters reflect on post-conflict experiences in Macedonia, Bosnia, Russia, Georgia, and

Northern Ireland. In Chapter 5, "Ethnic-military relations in Macedonia", Biljana Vankovska shows that security sector reform in Macedonia has been driven largely by ethnic-military relations, as opposed to democracy building and civil-military relations. Interethnic reconciliation processes were thus initially more important, as they created the basic foundation on which to build security sector reform. In Chapter 6, "Democratization in Bosnia: A more effective role for SFOR", Allison Ritscher discusses the role of SFOR, and particularly American forces, in democratization efforts in Bosnia. When "post-conflict peacebuilding is no longer a charitable act but a strategic necessity", the military's role must be redefined not only to secure a negative peace but to build a positive peace. It is this expanded role that should, according to Ritscher, guide American approaches to future peacebuilding missions. In Chapter 7, "The use of Russia's security structures in the post-conflict environment", Ekaterina Stepanova examines the roles that non-military security components, such as the Ministry of the Interior's troops and special units, played in post-conflict missions within Russia. She argues that, while there is much that can be done to reform the Russian security sector, Western models and approaches are not always applicable. While external support and advice are welcome, they would resonate more effectively with Russian decision-makers if they came from the United Nations, rather than NATO in particular. In Chapter 8, "Civil-military relations and security sector reform in a newly independent transitional state: The Georgian case", David Darchiashvili analyses Georgian efforts towards security sector reform. Similar to Vankovska's findings, he argues that long-standing issues of national security and internal conflicts are crucial prerequisites to meaningful reform. At the same time, external support and encouragement cannot replace the need for societal consensus and widespread internal agreement on the structure and nature of the country's security structure. The final European case study is offered by Stefan Wolff. In Chapter 9, "The politics of fear versus the politics of intimidation: Security sector reform in Northern Ireland", he shows that in the case of a peace process hampered by what he calls the politics of fear and intimidation, security sector reform has little chance to take firm hold. Two issues have been particularly important in this context for Northern Ireland: the importance of broadly accepted peace agreements that address both security needs and political aspirations of all conflicting parties; and the presence of positive and strong leadership capable of generating a broad consensus on the peace process and efforts to marginalize spoilers set on derailing such public support.

The third part of the book features experiences from Latin America, including El Salvador, Guatemala, Columbia, Chile, and Haiti. In Chapter 10, "Civil-military relations in Latin America: The post-9/11 scenario and the civil society dimension", Andrés Serbin and Andrés Fontana discuss the challenges of building a consensus on the role of the military within and among Latin American countries, and on their relations with the USA, particularly in the context of redefined regional security priorities after 11 September 2001. Their chapter highlights the regional and international dimensions of domestic security sector reform, and the importance of close and interactive dialogue between the military and civil society to preserve Latin America's young and fragile democracies despite the USA's sudden shift of focus away from democratization to the promotion of strong security structures. In Chapter 11, "The military in post-conflict societies: Lessons from Central America and prospects for Colombia", Thomas C. Bruneau analyses post-conflict El Salvador and Guatemala and draws lessons for the current situation in Colombia. The former two have experienced relative peace and relative success in democratization, although El Salvador's progress in reforming its security sector has been by far more positive than the experience in Guatemala. Despite Columbia's much longer experience with democracy, its society has not been able to secure basic domestic peace. Bruneau would agree with Vankovska and Darchiashvili that ongoing conflicts must be resolved before security sector reform can be pursued with a modicum of success. Thus, first military might has to create peace, which will then allow the renegotiation of a less prominent role of the military in society. In Chapter 12, "Civil-military relations and national reconciliation in Chile in the aftermath of the Pinochet affair", Nibaldo H. Galleguillos shows that national reconciliation (in the form of the arrest of the former dictator Augusto Pinochet in 1999) was a basic prerequisite for political negotiations on civil-military reform. Nevertheless, although the chance existed to capitalize on this opportunity to come to terms with the past, including the armed forces' role during Pinochet's oppressive regime, continuing protection of the armed forces by national political and judicial élites has so far prevented meaningful reconciliation and thus meaningful and popularly supported and acceptable security sector reform. In Chapter 13, "The role of the military in democratization and peacebuilding: The experiences of Haiti and Guatemala", Chetan Kumar argues that, drawing on observations from those two case studies, post-conflict peacebuilding cannot take place – or succeed – without the military and supportive social classes, particularly if they have been highly dominant political actors during much of these countries' histories. Similar to Wolff's assessment of Northern Ireland, Kumar argues that "there is a need to bring the traditional backers of the military into a wider intersectoral consensus on the broad parameters of peaceful change".

The final part of the book offers experiences from Asia, with case studies from Cambodia, East Timor, and Afghanistan. In Chapter 14, "Security sector reform in Cambodia", Sophie Richardson and Peter Sainsbury offer their account of a mostly mixed security sector reform effort in Cambodia. Along the lines of Kumar's assessment, they come to the conclusion that the military has to be integrated into the broader reform process, otherwise the former military élite will sabotage reforms. In addition, security sector reform alone is a mute exercise without further political and social reforms. In Chapter 15, "International force and political reconstruction: Cambodia, East Timor, and Afghanistan", William Maley shows that one size definitely does not fit all when it comes to external peace support operations. He argues that, in the cases of post-conflict Cambodia, East Timor, and Afghanistan, mistakes were made based on the assumption that a common approach to security sector reform would yield equally positive results. He argues that "the wider character of the state, the nature of the conflict which led to international action, and the character of local actors will need to be taken into account in designing assistance measures". He identifies commitment to sustainable peacebuilding as the single most important factor that separates potential for success from potential for failure in post-conflict peace operations. In the final chapter of this volume, "Post-conflict societies and the military: Recommendations for security sector reform", Hans-Georg Ehrhart and Albrecht Schnabel take stock of the analyses presented in the book's case-study chapters and offer a series of recommendations to improve the effectiveness of security sector reform in post-conflict societies.

While lessons across various case studies are particularly useful to regional and international actors which are involved in numerous post-conflict theatres simultaneously, local, regional, and national actors are better served with case-specific experiences and advice. This book attempts to satisfy both of those needs, and thus focuses on general, thematic, and cross-regional challenges as well as case-specific experiences. The editors hope that readers will find value in each individual chapter, as well as in the volume as a whole, for their own analysis and practical work.

Notes

1. Newman, Edward and Albrecht Schnabel. 2002. "Introduction: Recovering from civil conflict", in Edward Newman and Albrecht Schnabel (eds) *Recovering from Civil Conflict: Reconciliation, Peace and Development*. London: Frank Cass, pp. 1–6.

2. Throughout the volume the terms "security sector reform" and "security sector transformation" are occasionally used interchangeably. In line with Rocky Williams's definition in his chapter, "security sector reform" is the more widely used and recognizable term, yet in some parts of the world the word "reform" depicts a top-down approach. In contrast, the word "transformation" signifies a more holistic approach that more appropriately defines reform efforts in the security sector as those that are driven and implemented by both government and society (a simultaneous top-down and bottom-up approach).

3. Boutros-Ghali, Boutros. 1992. *An Agenda for Peace: Preventive Diplomacy, Peacemaking and Peace-keeping*, A/47/277–S/24111. New York: United Nations.

4. *Ibid.*, para. 21. For Boutros-Ghali's more detailed description of post-conflict peacebuilding tasks, see paras 55–59.

5. United Nations. 1998. *The Causes of Conflict and the Promotion of Durable Peace and Sustainable Development in Africa*, Report of the UN Secretary-General, A/52/871–S/1998/318. New York: United Nations, para. 63.

6. *Ibid.*, para. 64.

7. *Ibid.*

8. International Commission on Intervention and State Sovereignty. 2001. *The Responsibility to Protect*. Ottawa: International Development Research Centre, para. 5.31.

9. See, for instance, Tschirgi, Neclâ. 2004. "Post-conflict peacebuilding revisited: Achievements, limitations, challenges", background paper for the WSP International/IPA Peacebuilding Forum Conference, 7 October, New York, p. 9.

10. Ehrhart, Hans-Georg. 2002. "Militärische Macht als außenpolitisches Instrument im 21. Jahrhundert," *Österreichische Militärische Zeitschrift*, No. 6, pp. 683–690.

11. United Nations. 2000. *Report of the Panel on United Nations Peace Operations*, A/55/305–S/2000/809. New York: General Assembly/Security Council, 21 August. See also Blagescu, Monica and Albrecht Schnabel (eds). 2002. *Reforming UN Peace Operations: New Challenges for Peacekeeping Training*, Proceedings of the 2001 Annual Meeting of the International Association of Peacekeeping Training Centres. Tokyo: United Nations University.

12. Guéhenno, Jean-Marie. 2002. "On the challenges and achievements of reforming UN peace operations", *International Peacekeeping*, Vol. 9, No. 2, pp. 69–80.

13. See the presentations at the panel entitled "Combating Terrorism and its Implications for Security Sector Reform", Seventh Annual Conference of the Partnership for Peace (PfP) Consortium of Defense Academies and Security Studies Institutes, Bucharest, 15 June 2004. A selection of these presentations is forthcoming in the consortium's quarterly journal *Connections*, Vol. IV, 2005.

14. Ehrhart, Hans-Georg and Albrecht Schnabel. 2004. "Changing international relations and the role of the military in post-conflict peacebuilding operations", *S+F: Sicherheit und Frieden/Security and Peace*, Vol. 22, No. 1, pp. 7–12; Jeong, Ho-Won. 2004. "Expanding peacekeeping functions for peace operations, *S+F: Sicherheit und Frieden/Security and Peace*, Vol. 22, No. 1, pp. 19–24; Thakur, Ramesh and Albrecht Schnabel (eds). 2001. *United Nations Peacekeeping Operations: Ad Hoc Missions, Permanent Engagement*. Tokyo: United Nations University Press.

15. Slocombe, Walter B. 2003. "Terrorism/counter-terrorism: Their impact on security sector reform and basic democratice values", in Alan Bryden and Philipp Fluri (eds) *Security Sector Reform: Institutions, Society and Good Governance*. Baden-Baden: Nomos, pp. 291–301.

16. For a comprehensive analysis and recent studies on the challenges of security sector reform, see Bryden, Alan and Philipp Fluri (eds). 2003. *Security Sector Reform: Institu-

tions, Society and Good Governance. Baden-Baden: Nomos; McCartney, Clem, Martina Fischer, and Oliver Wills (eds). 2004. *Security Sector Reform: Potentials and Challenges for Conflict Transformation*, Berghof Handbook Dialogue Series No. 2. Berlin: Berghof Research Center for Constructive Conflict Management.

17. Chalmers, Malcolm. 2000. *Security Sector Reform in Developing Countries: An EU Perspective*. London/Ebenhausen: Saferworld and Conflict Prevention Network, January, p. 6, available at www.saferworld.co.uk/publications/Secform.html.

18. *Ibid.*

19. OECD. 2004. *Security System Reform and Governance: Policy and Good Practice*, A DAC Reference Document. Paris: OECD, p. 16.

20. *Ibid.*, pp. 16–17.

21. The following lists draw on, and are an expansion of, the description of security sector reform activities by the EU, examined in *ibid.*, pp. 3–4, 8–16. For further recent analyses of security sector reform challenges, as well as pointers to further literature, see Wulf, Herbert (ed.). 2000. *Security Sector Reform*, Brief 15, June. Bonn: Bonn International Center for Conversion; GTZ. 2000. *Security Sector Reform in Developing Countries: An Analysis of the International Debate and Potentials for Implementing Reforms with Recommendations for Technical Cooperation*. Eschborn: Deutsche Gesellschaft für Technische Zusammenarbeit (GTZ).

22. Wulf, Herbert. 2004. "Security sector reform in developing and transitional countries", in Clem McCartney, Martina Fischer, and Oliver Wills (eds) *Security Sector Reform: Potentials and Challenges for Conflict Transformation*, Berghof Handbook Dialogue Series No. 2. Berlin: Berghof Research Center for Constructive Conflict Management, pp. 16–17.

23. Anderson, Mary. 1999. *Do No Harm: How Aid Can Support Peace – Or War*. Boulder, CO: Lynne Rienner Publishers.

Part I

The challenges of post-conflict peacebuilding and security sector reform

2

Security sector reform and donor policies

Dylan Hendrickson and Andrzej Karkoszka

The end of the Cold War gave new impetus to pressures for political and economic liberalization around the globe. States aspiring to democratic governance and strong economies require capable administrative and political structures. A key element is a well-governed security sector, which comprises the civil, political, and security institutions responsible for protecting the state and the communities within it. Reform or transformation of the security sector is now seen as an integral part of the transition from one-party to pluralist political systems, from centrally planned to market economies, and from armed conflict to peace. It is therefore a growing focus of international assistance.[1]

International interventions under the auspices of the United Nations, the North Atlantic Treaty Organization (NATO), or powerful individual states carried out since the early 1990s to resolve violent conflicts and assist these transitions have shown immense limitations. External forces have often supplanted the local security apparatus or, as in the recent case of Iraq, explicitly sought to dismantle it where it was considered to be a part of the security problem. However, without adequate efforts to restore a viable national capacity in the security domain, external interventions offer at best temporary solutions to security problems and may, in some cases, aggravate the situation.

Security sector reform aims to help states enhance the security of their citizens. The shift from state- and military-centric notions of security to a greater emphasis on human security has underscored the importance of governance issues and civilian input into policy-making. The kinds of se-

19

curity policies that governments adopt, the instruments used to implement these policies, and the interests served by these policies are critical factors.

The security sector reform agenda therefore encompasses – but is far broader than – the traditional civil-military relations approach to addressing security problems. Security sector reform has potentially wide-ranging implications for how state security establishments are organized and, by extension, for how international security and development assistance is delivered. These implications are only just starting to be understood and translated into policy, and they are eliciting mixed reactions from both the international actors which provide security assistance and the recipients of aid.

Developing countries have been cautious about embracing security sector reform. They are wary of the conditions attached to external assistance and the promotion of "one-size-fits-all" solutions to their problems, such as the structural adjustment programmes of the 1980s. Past security assistance programmes were often ill-conceived and poorly implemented, and resulted in outcomes that were not supportive of either citizen security or development goals.[2] The states of Central and Eastern Europe (CEE)[3] in particular have responded favourably to the reform agenda, which is seen as complementing the wider economic and political reforms in which many of them are engaged. Crucially, the prospect of integration into NATO and "the West" has provided a powerful additional incentive for CEE states to reform their security sectors.

Despite the fact that security sector reform is moving up on the international agenda, it remains a new area of activity. There is still no consensus on how to define the concept of security sector reform or on what the objectives and the priorities for international assistance should be.[4] Most actors are just starting to grapple with the political sensitivities of security sector work, and few have developed the policy instruments required to work in an integrated way with their partners.[5] As a consequence, there are different levels of acceptance among international actors, many of which remain wary of how security sector reform will impinge on traditional institutional mandates or foreign policy objectives.

While the general principles that underpin security sector reform have relevance for all countries, this chapter is principally concerned with how the agenda has been conceptualized and implemented by international actors in the context of developing countries and the CEE states. The chapter outlines the background to this policy agenda and some of its key features. It then examines the relevance of security sector reform to international security, particularly in light of the new "war on terrorism". Drawing on recent lessons, the chapter concludes by highlighting a number of key challenges for external assistance.

The policy agenda

The end of the Cold War set in motion a profound rethinking of the notion of security and of strategies for international assistance in this domain. The militarized notions of security that emerged during the Cold War gave rise to a narrow stress on territorial integrity and security through armaments which has been difficult to change.[6]

Before 1989, aid to the third world – including development, humanitarian, and security assistance – was closely linked to the dynamics of the Cold War. Security became synonymous with the stability of the international system and regime stability – the protection of client regimes from external and internal threats. Assistance programmes paid little attention to democratic civil-military relations, to effective legislative and executive oversight over the various security branches, or to the creation of a professional ethos within security services that was consistent with the dictates of a modern democracy. No real attempt was made to include important civilian sectors (e.g. the foreign policy and finance sectors) in the formulation of security policy.

In many developing countries and CEE states the provision of basic services such as security, employment, and social welfare has sharply eroded since the end of the Cold War. These problems have focused critical attention on how state security establishments shape and condition the processes of economic and political change.

In this environment, organizations involved in development assistance have been cautious about entering the arena of security sector reform, yet they have gradually realized that they cannot avoid it. International financial institutions (IFIs)[7] play a key role in setting the economic framework in which the major donors engage in developing countries and CEE countries. The IFIs have a clear impact on the outcome of security sector reforms by virtue of their involvement in macroeconomic adjustment and stabilization programmes, although their direct involvement has to date been limited to a concern with the issue of military expenditure.[8] Both the International Monetary Fund (IMF) and the World Bank have traditionally been cautious about becoming involved in security-related matters because of the differing views of their board members on this issue, as well as the ingrained conservatism of these institutions. Nevertheless, there is growing recognition that security sector reform should be a concern.[9]

The World Bank, in particular, is increasingly recognizing the need to set its support for demobilization programmes and the strengthening of public expenditure management systems within a broader framework of security sector reform. This is forcing the organization to reconsider the role of the traditional instruments of economic conditionality that it has often wielded, together with the IMF, in an attempt to obtain the adherence of the borrowing countries to military expenditure limits.

For similar reasons, recognition of the need for a broader approach to security has emerged from the debates on civil-military relations, particularly in relation to the CEE states where Western defence establishments have been active.[10] In Africa, Asia, and Latin America a parallel process of rethinking security concepts has also been under way and has influenced the security sector reform agenda.[11] Many countries were engaged in security sector reform activities long before this concept gained international prominence.[12]

The new security thinking is set apart from past approaches because it recognizes that ensuring the safety of citizens should rank alongside national defence as the primary goal of state security policy; greater emphasis needs to be placed on the role of civilian actors in both formulating and managing security policy (the critical role of governance was largely overlooked by Cold War security assistance programmes, and development actors avoided for the most part engagement in activities related to the security sector); and different means of achieving security objectives must be acknowledged. The traditional reliance on primarily military instruments of force should be complemented more effectively with diplomatic, economic, legal, political, and social mechanisms, and greater preventive action.

The need for a broad approach to security is underscored by the experiences of developing countries and the CEE states, where political and state-building processes are now seen as the foundation for efforts to enhance the security of states and their citizens.[13] In these contexts, state and regime legitimacy are constantly being challenged, and demands for economic redistribution and political participation are creating major overloads on weak administrative and political systems. Unmet social and political needs run the risk of provoking popular unrest and opposition to governments, ultimately making them more vulnerable to internal and external threats.

Defining the security sector

Because the actors involved in delivering security services and the relationships between them vary from country to country, there is not a universally applicable definition of the security sector. A narrow focus on the conventional Western security actors, such as armed forces, police, and intelligence services, for instance, does not capture the diversity of security actors in other countries. In Africa formations such as presidential guards and militia forces are common, while a whole range of "private" security actors are emerging because of the collapse of state security structures.[14] Similarly, in the CEE states there are a wide range of internal security forces, often linked to interior ministries, which rival the military in terms of numbers and influence.

In addition, it is also clear that the management of security policy in all countries, including the industrialized states, is influenced by a range of informal norms and practices that are closely shaped by national political, cultural, and social circumstances. Knowledge of these circumstances is the starting point for understanding the complex array of institutions and interactions that affect the relationship between the organizations authorized by states to use force and those mandated to regulate these organizations and formulate security policy.

The security sector is generally seen to consist of the following elements.

- *Forces authorized to use force*: armed forces; police; paramilitary forces; presidential guards; intelligence services (including both military and civilian agencies); secret services; coastguards; border guards; customs authorities; and reserve and local security units (civil defence forces, national guards, militias, etc.).
- *Security management and oversight bodies*: presidential and prime ministerial offices; national security advisory bodies; legislature and legislative select committees; ministries of defence, internal affairs, and foreign affairs; customary and traditional authorities; financial management bodies (finance ministries, budget offices, and financial audit and planning units); and civil society organizations (civilian review boards, public complaints commissions, etc.).
- *Justice and law enforcement institutions*: judiciary; justice ministries; prisons; criminal investigation and prosecution services; human rights commissions and ombudsmen; correctional services; and customary and traditional justice systems.[15]
- *Non-statutory security forces*: liberation armies; guerrilla armies; private bodyguard units; private security companies; and political party militias.

Strictly speaking, the security sector can be seen to comprise the first three categories, which are part of the state machinery for providing security. However, non-statutory security forces can have a significant influence on economic and political governance and need to be taken into account. In countries emerging from war, for instance, liberation or guerrilla armies will often need to be demobilized or integrated into a new national army as part of peace settlements. Similarly, private security companies and bodyguard units may also have important roles to play where state capacity in the security domain is weak. They need to be appropriately regulated.

The level of involvement by civil society and private sector actors in security sector governance differs widely from country to country. Their direct role is usually limited, although there is increased acceptance that these actors can be important agents for change when they apply political pressure and inform reform agendas. Relevant civil society actors include professional groups (lawyers and accountants), advocacy groups (human rights bodies), research and policy think-tanks, religious groups, and the media. Non-state groups have a particularly important role to play in conflict-torn societies, where statutory security sector capacity is usually weak.

While the concept of the security sector provides a framework for targeting international assistance, the challenges of the transformation of this sector cannot be understood in isolation from the wider institutional, societal, and political context. The security sector cannot function effectively if the administrative and legal framework is fundamentally weak or corrupt. The security sector is also crucial to political power, both in the "macro" sense of regime stability and in the "micro" sense of exercising day-to-day political control and generating revenue. Security sector reform is therefore closely tied to domestic processes of political and social change.

Defining security sector reform

There is an increased recognition that the security sector, like any other part of the public sector, must be subject to the principles of civil oversight, accountability, and transparency. How these principles are implemented, and the specific ways in which the security sector is organized, will depend on the circumstances.

Strengthening the institutional framework for managing the security sector involves three broad challenges: to ensure the proper location of security activities within a constitutional framework defined by law, and to develop security policies and instruments to implement them; to build the capacity of policy-makers to assess the nature of security threats effectively and to design strategic responses supportive of wider development goals; and to strengthen mechanisms for ensuring security sector accountability by enabling the state and non-state actors responsible for monitoring security policy and enforcing the law to fulfil their functions effectively.

Within this broad framework more specific, short-term objectives may include improving the management of security expenditure, negotiating the withdrawal of the military from a formal political role, dissociating the military from an internal security role, strengthening the effectiveness of the security forces, and demobilizing and reintegrating surplus security personnel. The wide range of governance objectives to which international actors are giving priority can be grouped in the following seven categories.[16]

- *Professional security forces.* Professionalization encompasses doctrinal and skill development, technical modernization, and an understanding of the importance of accountability and the rule of law.
- *Capable and responsible civil authorities.* The relevant civil authorities in the executive and legislative branches of government need to have the capacity to develop security policy and to manage and oversee the security sector.
- *High priority on human rights protection.* Respect for human rights must exist among civilians as well as members of the security forces.
- *Capable and responsible civil society.* Civil society should have the capacity to monitor the security sector, promote change, and provide input to government on security matters.
- *Transparency.* Although some security matters require confidentiality, basic information about security policies, planning, and resourcing should be accessible both to the civil authorities and to members of the public.
- *Conformity with international and internal law.* The security sector should operate in accordance with international law and domestic constitutional law.
- *Regional approaches.* Many security problems are shared by countries within a region, and the security of individual countries and individuals within those countries will benefit from regional approaches.

While the donor policy agenda has tended to approach security sector reform as essentially a governance issue, there is growing recognition that the agenda must accommodate an operational perspective if it is to be meaningful to countries affected by conflict and insecurity – thus ensuring that security forces can fulfil their legitimate functions in a manner that is both effective and accountable. In addition to civil management bodies, a specific focus on the security forces is therefore essential in order to build the human capacity and institutional instruments that they require to fulfil their legitimate functions.[17] Security forces are in a powerful position *vis-à-vis* other branches of government and citizens to influence governance processes. While central to preserving state sovereignty and authority, the armed forces in particular are one of the few institutions able to endanger states from the inside.[18] This makes it essential for appropriate incentives to be designed to win their support for reforms. Some reforms may focus on improving technical proficiency, but there is an increasing emphasis on organizational restructuring within the security sector in order to ensure adequate provision for civil oversight and direction of the security forces.

Approaches to security sector reform

There are different philosophies on how best to achieve reform objectives. Security sector reform is underpinned by a number of normative assumptions about the desirability of democratization, civilian control of the armed forces, a clear division between internal and external security functions, the independence of the judiciary, and a strong civil society role.[19] These are "ideal-type" situations that no country has fully succeeded in implementing. In practice, such institutional arrangements are difficult to achieve and not always consistent with the immediate needs or priorities of reforming countries. Instead, these are now seen as goals that countries can work towards from their different starting points.

Only a limited number of countries in which international actors are engaged today are able to undertake fundamental institutional reforms. In the past, international security assistance programmes relied excessively on external templates for reform, with little regard for the social, political, and institutional context in which they were being applied. This has resulted in unrealistic assumptions about how states and their security sectors function, as well as undue sensitivity to issues of national ownership. A key concern of governments is that reforms will undermine their power base and compromise their own efforts to address security problems. There is now increased recognition that the greatest potential for security sector reform exists where it is supported from outside but driven by strong internal dynamics. In the most successful examples, there will be a clear national vision for reform and political will at the highest levels of government.

In countries where these conditions do not exist, particularly in conflict-torn societies, the first priority is generally to restore political stability and basic capacity in the security sector before fundamental institutional problems can be tackled. Political support for reform has to be built up. The bureaucracy and the economy are generally weak. Key security sector institutions, including civilian bodies and the various branches of the security forces, tend to lack clearly defined roles and adequate skills. Consequently, it is not possible to develop a clear national vision for reform.

In these conditions, attempting to promote security sector reform may simply mobilize opposition to change. A broader focus on building basic capacity first may itself not go beyond developing skills and confidence building among security sector personnel. The fact that security sector reform is expensive means that progress will be closely tied to improvements in the economy and living conditions. This makes security sector reform a long-term endeavour.

Relevance to international security

The fragile security structures in developing countries and the CEE states have diverse historical roots that can be traced to the nature of state building as well as to more recent international development policies. Efforts to develop properly accountable security forces were hampered during the 1980s and 1990s by the immense pressures placed on countries to reduce public spending as a consequence of external pressures for economic liberalization. With the security forces often seen as a barrier to economic and political development, attempts were made to reduce their size and influence, and insufficient attention was paid to how the security void would be filled.

Security sector reform aims to improve governance, thereby reducing the risk of state weakness or state failure. It is often in weak or failed states that conflicts arise. Such states have contributed to a range of destabilizing transnational security problems such as population movements and trafficking in drugs, people, and arms, as well as stimulating the widespread incidence of violence and disorder, including groups that carry out terrorist acts. The majority of these problems have important regional dimensions because of weakened state capacity to police borders and regulate economic activity. Insurgent groups which have traditionally relied on neighbouring countries for support and shelter are increasingly exploiting commercial opportunities linked to the expansion of the global economy to sustain their activities.

At a time when weak states facing endemic insecurity and violence have become increasingly unable to rely on the international community for assistance, their internal problems are having greater spillover effects at both the regional and the global level. The sheer scale of the crises afflicting many parts of the developing world and the CEE states has meant that there has simply not been enough international capacity to address all the problems. There has also been reluctance on the part of Western governments to intervene in countries no longer deemed to be of strategic interest.

Consequently, the international community has a strong self-interest in integrating security sector reform into wider conflict prevention and state-building strategies that combine developmental, legal, military, and political instruments. These strategies may include the peaceful resolution of non-violent disputes, peacekeeping, post-conflict peacebuilding and reconstruction, political participation, reforming the criminal justice system, and strengthening governance across the public sector, specifically in the security sector.

Instruments of security sector reform

Any list of the instruments for promoting and implementing security sector reform can inevitably only be selective. Nevertheless, this section summarizes some of the main actors involved in this process.

Donor countries

The main sponsors of security sector reform have been the aid donor countries, including Canada, Germany, the Netherlands, Norway, Sweden, Switzerland, the UK, and the USA. Each of these countries is at a different stage in developing its policies and operationalizing programmes of assistance, and there tends to be great variation in approaches from country to country.

The British Department for International Development (DFID) has taken the lead, in cooperation with other British government departments, in developing a comprehensive security sector reform policy.[20] DFID, the Foreign and Commonwealth Office, the Home Office, and the Ministry of Defence have developed joint programmes of assistance for security sector reform in a number of countries in Africa and Asia. The Ministry of Defence's cooperation programmes in the CEE states, known as Defence Diplomacy, have been broadened to make them more supportive of security sector reform objectives. The UK has also actively pushed the security sector reform agenda at the multilateral level by seeking to encourage the further engagement of UN agencies and IFIs in this area.

In the USA security assistance is delivered by a number of government departments that focus separately on the military, the police, and civilian security sector actors, with a limited coordination of activities.[21] Security sector reform, understood in the sense of a comprehensive approach to security assistance consistent with the principles outlined above, has still not been officially adopted.

Donor countries have also become increasingly reliant on a wide range of non-state actors, including non-governmental organizations (NGOs), academic institutions, and private security companies, to address the gaps in their expertise and capacity. These actors are playing an increasingly important role in the delivery of security assistance, although the growing number of players has also made it more difficult to achieve policy coherence and ensure accountability.

Multilateral development actors

UN work on security sector reform is spread over its specialized agencies and missions, which are engaged in a range of relevant activities, including police and justice reform, regulation of small-arms transfers, and the demobilization and reintegration of ex-combatants. The UN Development Programme (UNDP) has gone furthest in defining a comprehensive framework for its involvement in security sector reform, but is still developing the capacity to operationalize it. Both the Department of Political Affairs (DPA), which is the focal point within the UN for conflict prevention and peacebuilding activities, and the Department of Peacekeeping Operations (DPKO), responsible for peacekeeping operations, have a clear interest and comparative advantage in other aspects of this agenda.[22]

The European Union's (EU) external assistance programmes have two dimensions that are relevant to security sector reform. One is EU assistance provided to the African, Caribbean, and Pacific countries under the framework of the Cotonou Agreement of June 2000, which emphasizes the importance of good governance and entails periodic performance assessments to measure progress towards implementing political and institutional reform.[23] The other consists of EU Common Foreign and Security Policy (CFSP) programmes, which do not mention security sector reform specifically but do require that all applicant states introduce democratic oversight of the military.[24]

Addressing security sector reform is a priority of the Organization for Economic Cooperation and Development's (OECD) Development Assistance Committee (DAC), whose Network on Conflict, Peace, and Development Cooperation carries out a range of research and policy-related activities designed to harmonize the work of its members in the conflict and security domain.[25] In April 2004 the OECD development ministers endorsed a new security sector reform policy statement and supporting paper, which underscores the need for OECD countries to adopt "government-wide" approaches to this issue.[26]

Regional security organizations

NATO adopted the Partnership for Peace (PfP) programme in 1994.[27] PfP programmes have elaborated norms and guidelines for the oversight of military institutions and the internal state security apparatus as well as the specific civil-military relations characteristic of a stable democracy.

This comprehensive framework for reforming the management of the armed forces is available to nearly all of the post-communist and post-Soviet CEE states. The Membership Action Plan[28] and the 1995 NATO study on enlargement[29] made it clear that the application of a set of basic principles of "democratic control over the military" is a precondition for NATO to consider any application for membership.

The role of the Organization for Security and Cooperation in Europe (OSCE) in security sector reform consists mainly of setting models and norms for the individual member states and the region as a whole. In 1994 the principles guiding the role of armed forces in democratic societies were further elaborated and "operationalized" in the OSCE Code of Conduct on Politico-Military Aspects of Security (sections VII and VIII).[30] The implementation of "democratic oversight over the military" became a political obligation for all members of this organization, thus mandating its implementation in internal legal norms, regulations, and procedures.

Compliance with these guidelines is assessed at periodic review conferences of the OSCE states. Equally important is the experience of the OSCE in confidence- and security-building measures, which has led to an improvement in interstate relations on the European continent since the mid-1970s. Among these measures are several which relate to building regional transparency in such areas as weapons procurement, budgets, and restructuring of armed forces. These transparency measures, however, remain focused on interstate relations rather than on the objective of full transparency within the security sectors of the countries concerned. Subregional arrangements in Europe include the Process of Good Neighbourliness, Stability, Security, and Cooperation of the Countries of South-Eastern Europe (South-East European Cooperation Process, SEECP), which provides a kind of subregional code of conduct for relations in the region.[31] The SEECP defence ministries have worked on cooperative security reform since 1997.

Outside Europe, regional and subregional organizations, including the Association of South-East Asian Nations (ASEAN), the Organization of American States (OAS), the Organization of African Unity (OAU),[32] the Economic Community of West African States (ECOWAS), and the Southern African Development Community (SADC), have initiated various programmes linked to the transformation or better management of the security sector in their member states. However, regional and subregional mechanisms are not always well coordinated and their objectives may differ, even within the same state. In Africa, for instance, there are a number of conflict prevention mechanisms, including the Conference on Stability, Security, Development, and Cooperation in Africa (CSSDCA) adopted by OAU leaders in 1989 and the New Partnership for Africa's

Development (NEPAD) adopted in 2001, which have not yet been harmonized.[33]

The implications of 11 September 2001

The 11 September 2001 attacks on the World Trade Center and the Pentagon, engineered and carried out by the Al Qaeda network, have underscored the link between state failure and international security.

While the "war on terrorism" led by the USA is being fought on many fronts, a central element of the strategy is to strengthen transnational intelligence and law enforcement cooperation and military action. The less developed states which have joined the "coalition against terrorism", and which are seen to harbour political elements that may be a threat to the USA and its allies, will probably receive increased support to bolster their intelligence and internal security capacity. These reforms may not be consistent with meaningful security sector reform, since significant trade-offs can be expected between the initial primary focus on strengthening effectiveness and the longer-term goal of improving transparency and accountability in the security sector.[34]

Some of the regimes that will be in the front line in the anti-terrorism campaign are authoritarian and have security institutions which operate in a manner that is far from open and accountable. These security services enjoy substantial political influence and institutional autonomy, making them resistant to change. Moreover, it is their appreciable counterterrorism capabilities, including powers of arrest and surveillance authority, which reform would curtail.[35] It is highly likely that, despite the potential costs to human rights and civil liberties, encouraging serious reforms will be given less priority than persuading political leaders that it is in their interest to use their intelligence and law enforcement capacities to help the USA and its allies.[36]

From the perspective of developing and transitional countries that are being strongly encouraged to support the US-led campaign, there is a clear conflict between security sector reform objectives and means. Many of these countries are aid-dependent and face significant external constraints on how they budget and manage resources, particularly in the security sector. Even as they come under persistent pressure from their key donors to reduce security spending, they are being urged to bolster their internal security and intelligence capacities. A number of leaders have also cynically used the pretext of the war against terrorism to clamp down on internal opposition figures who are deemed a threat to national security interests.

These developments raise the spectre of a return to Cold War security thinking, which revolved around regime security. A growing number of states are finding it necessary to curtail individual rights, including the right to privacy in the areas of communications and personal data. Cross-border traffic has become more tightly controlled, with new restrictions pending in a number of countries. Even as international cooperation in intelligence gathering and joint action against terrorist cells are increasing, there are corresponding demands for less scrutiny by elected officials over the plans, budgets, and operations of states' security organs. Increasingly "centralized" and strengthened security sectors cannot help but exert commensurably greater influence on states' security policy and budgetary decisions.

The problems are already apparent not only in a number of developing countries but also in the USA itself. In the wake of 11 September, the US government has tried to evade congressional oversight on defence spending related to the war on terrorism. Requests made for $10 billion to cover unspecified Department of Defense "anti-terrorism efforts", as part of a $48 billion overall increase in the defence budget, effectively mean the loss of some of Congress' "power of the purse".[37]

Challenges to security sector reform

The lack of a shared definition of security sector reform makes it difficult to give a clear overall statement on current progress and remaining challenges. International support for security sector reform, in the comprehensive sense of the term, has to date been relatively limited and of an ad hoc nature.[38] Apart from the CEE states, where the focus has been predominantly on issues relating to military reform and border security, the most notable programmes have been in developing countries emerging from war. At this more specific programme level there is only a cursory understanding of what international assistance has achieved. In part, this is because international actors have been slow to develop tools for assessing the effectiveness of their policies.

Nevertheless, it is increasingly apparent that the receptivity of different societies to the security sector reform agenda varies greatly depending on their internal circumstances and the external incentives for reform. In cases in which the domestic constituencies, institutional capacity, and incentives for reform are weak, a sharp reduction of the impact of external assistance should be expected. This underscores the limits of current international efforts to support security sector reform, which have to date focused primarily on spreading Western norms and practices to inform how the security sector of aid recipients should operate.

Substantive progress in building consensus around standards of security sector governance across the CEE states is apparent, although the extent to which these goals have been institutionalized in the working of the security sector has been variable.[39] At one level, "first-generation" institutional issues such as the creation of constitutional frameworks and mechanisms for civil oversight have been successful. However, a "second generation" of issues that relate to the acquisition of shared norms and values by civilians and the military has not yet made a significant impact.

The African, Asian, and Latin American experiences are much less clear cut. For the most part, the conditions for reform have not been as favourable as in the CEE states, owing to the institutional fragility of states, political instability, resource constraints, and the limited nature of external incentives on offer. The lack of strategic significance to the Western countries of those countries most in need has also played a considerable role. The larger cultural gap between these societies and the West has also underscored the need for international actors to reflect more carefully on what aspects of their national experiences have relevance to developing countries and on how to facilitate more effectively the development of a national vision and domestic constituencies to sustain reform processes.

Operationalizing concepts

International actors have been slow to develop a holistic and long-term approach to providing international assistance. Efforts to ensure that different national and international programmes fit together effectively on the ground have not been successful. This has led to a tendency on the part of many actors to rebrand long-standing activities as security sector reform without evaluating the needs of aid recipients or adapting policies to make them relevant to new circumstances.[40] Thus there continues to be a narrow focus, in many cases, on direct military and police training and on efforts to address the proliferation of light weapons, to demobilize and reintegrate ex-combatants, or to provide human rights training to members of the security forces. While all of these are important aspects of security sector reform, they will be of limited long-term utility unless they are carried out in such a way as to support the wider agenda of strengthening the institutional framework for managing the security sector.

The question of the sequencing of international assistance has also come to the fore as members of the development and security communities have begun to work together more closely in the context of multifunctional international assistance programmes. While the broad objective of strengthening management and oversight of the security sector is generally shared, within this framework international actors in the development and security communities often prioritize different goals that may not be compatible. For example, military assistance provided to foreign armies to increase their effectiveness may undermine efforts by other external actors to limit the political influence of the military and strengthen civilian capacities.

There are differences in national approaches to security sector reform. While there is an increased recognition that reforms cannot and should not be imposed from the outside, international actors have been constrained from helping to build local ownership by short programming cycles, poor understanding of the countries in which they work, and the sensitivities of engaging with governments which are not seen as committed to reform. The prescriptive approach of the US Department of Defense contrasts with the greater British emphasis on facilitating reform – although there is evidence that the USA is changing its approach in some contexts.[41]

Unfavourable environments

Implementing security sector reform in conflict-torn societies presents the greatest challenges. The lack in most cases of a strong national vision and capacity coupled with the urgency of reform results in an overwhelming emphasis on an external timetable and model. This is despite the fact that international actors rarely have a clear understanding of the situation on the ground, of what preceded a war, or of how the new power dynamics are arranged. Persisting tensions, along with the enhanced role of security forces in political matters, constitute major barriers to reform.

The value placed on institutional and political stability by post-war governments is often not fully appreciated by international actors. Government reluctance to embark on a reform process tends to be confused with a weak commitment to a peace process or to democratization rather than with a lack of the instruments, resources, and support needed to push through difficult changes. Civilian oversight mechanisms such as legislative select committees and financial auditing bodies, if they exist at all, are difficult to reactivate because of the centralization of security policy-making by the executive branches of government.

Overcoming these barriers poses significant challenges for external actors seeking to support reforms. In most cases there is a huge gap between the stated objectives of reform processes and the starting point, which is very hard to bridge because of the inadequacy of local and external resources. In these contexts, critical issues such as national ownership, civilian capacity building, and strategic planning in the security sector are given lower priority than other aspects of post-war reconstruction in the social and economic domains. For external actors concerned with the restoration of a national capacity in the security domain, this has required rethinking strategies of engagement.

The top priority in most conflict-torn societies is to prepare the political terrain for more fundamental institutional reforms. Greater priority should be given to small strategic interventions designed to build relationships and trust, and to setting out policy options for countries undertaking national strategic reforms in order to facilitate these efforts. This will often require international actors to become engaged in helping to create a "comfort zone" in which disparate groups which have never spoken with each other before can begin to shape a mutually acceptable reform vision.

Building a national vision for reform is also a priority in the CEE states, although, with the exception of post-war Bosnia and Herzegovina and Kosovo (Federal Republic of Yugoslavia, now Serbia and Montenegro), a relatively strong institutional framework for debate and policy planning is already in place. This is not the case in countries such as Sierra Leone and Uganda, which require more "root-and-branch" reforms and where the international community has helped to organize seminars which have served to stimulate dialogue between the military, the police, politicians, members of parliament, civilian policy sectors, and civil society groups. This move away from a narrow reliance on technical assistance is positive, although it has also brought international actors into a sensitive domestic arena which has traditionally, both in their own countries and in aid recipients, been out of bounds to foreigners.

Conflicting objectives

As international actors from diverse policy communities have become involved in joint assistance programmes, it has become readily apparent that security sector reforms involve conflicting objectives. Even where public investments in the security sector absorb the lion's share of state resources, they may be insufficient to meet national security needs. A number of countries, including Rwanda and Uganda, have come under intense pressure from aid donors to reduce military spending at a time when they face significant external threats to national peace and stability.

Unsustainably high levels of military spending are a legitimate cause for concern in view of the impact on macroeconomic stability and poverty reduction objectives. However, the failure of international actors to anchor efforts to manage military expenditure within a broader reform programme designed to enhance the security of states and their citizens can result in a number of unintended consequences.

Two specific problems have become apparent where donors and the IFIs have relied on economic conditionality to encourage countries to reduce military spending rapidly without reference to the quality of governance in the security sector.[42] First, this strategy avoids addressing the underlying political conflicts and institutional and human-resource weaknesses, of which high levels of military spending are only one manifestation. Second, it creates a perverse incentive for governments to resort to creative accounting in order to conceal portions of their expenditure.

While the off-budget problem is difficult to detect, there are good reasons to suspect that it is relatively common where security sector governance is weak. Addressing the problem involves creating incentives for both militaries and governments to keep military spending on budget as well as to strengthen fiscal management and the management of the defence sector. The binding constraints are often political in nature and require fundamental changes in civil-military relations that cannot be achieved fully until the civilian sectors, including defence and finance ministries and parliaments, can fulfil their mandatory oversight roles effectively.

Security sector reforms can also have other unintended consequences. The relationship between security sector downsizing and the enhancement of political stability or public investments in the social and economic sectors is far from straightforward. Recent examples of military restructuring in the CEE states, for instance, illustrate how reforms can increase instability. The attempts made by some countries to demilitarize their economies quickly and diminish the burden of defence budgets by drastic reductions in the size of their security forces have produced a number of undesirable outcomes. These include large numbers of untrained security personnel entering the labour market, adding to already high unemployment levels; visible disenchantment among demobilized personnel, especially in the officer corps, which has created anti-reform sentiments; and serious wastage of resources as ill-conceived reforms have had to be revoked. The decline of morale within the armed forces has also undermined combat readiness and military discipline, resulting in the illegal transfer of weapons into the hands of criminals.

Recent experiences also suggest that reductions in the size of the armed forces will not automatically lead to increased spending in other public sectors. African cases have clearly demonstrated that the processes of downsizing and restructuring military forces themselves require ample resources and will not save money in the short run because released personnel must be re-educated and assimilated into the economy or pensioned off.[43] Furthermore, the reallocation of public spending from the security sector to the social sectors will only come about if there is a change in spending priorities, which usually requires tackling vested political and military interests.

However, there is increased recognition that defence cooperation arrangements which bind many developing countries and CEE states with the industrialized countries can also impede other reform processes. In the case of a number of the CEE states, including the Czech Republic, Hungary, and Poland, the resources gained from military reductions and restructuring, which these countries had to commit themselves to undertake in order to prepare themselves for membership of NATO, have been channelled into modernization programmes for the armed forces. This has meant that the long-awaited "peace dividend", which a reduction in the size of the armed forces might bring about, can only be achieved after a longer period of sustained reforms which increase efficiency in the armed forces, usually concomitant with an overall transformation of the economy.

Integrated programmes

In practice, few countries will undertake to reform the security sector as a whole, even though there is recognition of the need for a holistic view of the process. The first test case for a comprehensive international programme to rebuild and reform the security sector was Sierra Leone. This initiative, led by the British government from early 1999, involved inputs from ministries responsible for defence, development, foreign relations, and home affairs. Initial activities supported by the UK were designed to strengthen and civilianize the defence ministry, produce a new national security policy, reform the police, and train and equip 2,500 soldiers for a new national army.

The resumption of hostilities between the Sierra Leonean government and the rebel Revolutionary United Front in mid-2000 led to a pronounced shift in the focus of the British programme, from strengthening the civilian components of the security sector responsible for oversight and management to winning the war. Military training provided to the national army, including the support of the UN peacekeeping mission, paid immense dividends in terms of restoring security and government control over the national territory. However, the longer-term governance agenda, including the strengthening of key regulatory mechanisms such as the finance ministry, took a back seat during this period.

The early experiences of security sector reform in Sierra Leone underscored the immense challenges facing external assistance in a context in which the security sector has been weakened by years of mismanagement, while at the same time there is a need to approach security sector reform as a part of a wider reconstruction programme.[44] In the urgency to rehabilitate the national army, the task of integrating the defence budget into the wider public expenditure management framework was given a back seat. Such a framework is essential if security spending is to be subject to the standard fiscal controls of the finance ministry and the appropriate legislative scrutiny, neither of which has seen their capacity to fulfil this role strengthened.

International actors have tended to overlook the development of the capacities required to make a sector-wide assessment of needs, including a clear understanding of the security threats a country faces and the options available to the state to meet these threats.[45]

There has been a tendency to underplay the extent to which security sector problems are exacerbated by external factors, including regional conflicts, interstate rivalry, and global economic forces.[46] The easy availability of arms on international markets and the emergence of lucrative "war economies" with regional and international dimensions have received the most attention from the international community.

Assistance has not been separated from the economic agendas of specific donors.[47] There has been a tendency for donor countries to concentrate on geographical areas or states where they have historical connections or strategic interests.

Different perspectives and voices also need to be integrated into the reform process. In many of the countries that are most in need of security sector reform, non-state actors offer a strategic entry point for international actors. In Africa, donors such as Denmark, Norway, and the UK have actively supported networks of NGOs working on security issues. The development of non-governmental networks, in which the atmosphere is more informal and sensitive political issues can be put aside, is particularly valuable in terms of promoting security sector reform.

Recent round-table discussions on security sector reform have begun to build linkages between states (e.g. within subregions of Africa and on an Africa-wide basis) as well as establish cross-regional linkages (for example, through participation by representatives from Asia and Latin America in African meetings).

Conclusions

Security sector reform is part of an attempt by donors to develop a more coherent response to the security problems posed by state weakness or state failure. Efforts to strengthen the norms, laws, and institutions by which the security sector is governed represent an important element of the overall effort to improve governance and prevent conflicts. But to have an impact, security sector reform must be effectively integrated into wider conflict prevention and state-building strategies and be sensitive to the unique and complex security challenges facing developing and post-communist societies, particularly those emerging from war.

Most conflict-affected states face a new array of security challenges of both a military and a non-military nature. These security problems, which can be explained in terms of the frailties and vulnerabilities of these societies, cannot be managed by traditional military responses alone. As a consequence, states are today being confronted with the need to develop more innovative and integrated policy responses to their security problems, which address underlying causes. This is a long-term structural reform agenda that may require fundamentally reconceptualizing security, changing the orientation of state security policy, and building new human capacities.

This process of transforming security cultures is furthermore severely hampered by the harmful legacies of war, including the militarization of social and political life, persisting instability, and resource constraints. Over and above the political declaration of new principles and guidelines, developing institutional frameworks that enable states to handle development and security policy as integrated areas of public action is therefore a highly complex challenge. Security reform efforts driven by external actors have as a consequence remained concentrated on security agencies devoted to traditional matters: defence, intelligence, and law and order. In the absence of effective institutional machinery for decision-making (the "soft" side of state security capabilities), however, it is extremely difficult to translate these "hard" capabilities into adequate security for states and populations.

While the security sector reform concept provides a useful framework for thinking about how to address these issues, to date donor policy efforts have focused on defining the broad goals of security sector reform and a set of policy prescriptions that largely reflect the Western experience. Priority has been placed on building accountable security forces, understood largely in financial terms. Less emphasis has been placed on understanding how security institutions in developing and transition states *actually* function, or the wider political and economic conditions that might facilitate state efforts to provide security. Better understanding of these issues will provide a stronger empirical basis for donor policy development efforts in the area of security sector reform.[48]

Development of the policy agenda is still at an early stage. Although the security sector reform terminology is quickly becoming established within the international security and development policy communities, there is still not a shared understanding of how to define the underlying concept or translate it into policy. Many donors have simply renamed existing security work as "security sector reform" without paying due attention to the key governance promotion element that distinguishes security sector reform thinking from past (and many current) security assistance strategies. These factors have constrained debate and policy development efforts. Another significant challenge stems from the fact that "buy-in" to the security sector reform agenda by developing countries is still limited. Sustainable reform depends on full ownership of the process, and participation by stakeholders in the countries concerned in the conception and implementation of reforms. While in some regions and countries reforms have been initiated in response to pressure from local or domestic actors, in other cases external forces – either states or international organizations – have actively pressed the case for reform, often relying on external models of security sector governance that do not meet local priorities or circumstances. The donor emphasis on governance, human rights, and "human security" is not always consistent with the overwhelming immediate need felt by populations in some countries for "security" in its narrower physical sense.

The incentives for security sector reform differ significantly within and across the regions where donors are promoting this policy agenda. While the prospect of participation in European integration has provided a significant positive incentive for reform among Central European states and in certain East European states, this cannot be matched by regional and subregional organizations in Africa, Asia, or Latin America. In these regions the primary incentive for reform has been based largely on persuasion and the use of (limited) economic assistance by donors to encourage countries to undertake reform. Experience suggests that there have been few cases of sustained externally driven reforms in African states in the past.[49] The response of states to the 11 September 2001 terrorist attacks on the USA presents perhaps the greatest challenge to development of the security sector reform policy agenda. Increased importance is being placed on developing cooperation with the armed forces, intelligence services, and law enforcement services of other states to identify and eliminate groups and individuals engaged in terrorist acts. There is a risk that security sector reform will become subordinate to anti-terrorism activities in countries where the development of this cooperation is seen as particularly important. This in turn may have an impact on the way in which "security" is conceived, by shifting the emphasis back from "soft" (or "human") security concerns to more traditional ("hard") security.

Acknowledgements

This chapter draws extensively on a larger study conducted for and published in the 2002 *SIPRI Yearbook*. The authors are grateful to SIPRI for giving permission to republish portions of this study as part of this chapter.

Notes

1. The terms "reform" and "transformation" are used interchangeably in this chapter, although "reform" is the term of choice because it is most commonly used by those working in the field. "Transformation" implies a more fundamental change than reform, and is emerging as the preferred term in some circles involved in security sector work. For arguments in favour of the use of the term "transformation" see Williams, Rocky. 2001. "African armed forces and the challenges of security sector transformation", *Strategic Review for Southern Africa*, Vol. 23, No. 2, pp. 1–34, as well as his chapter in this volume.

2. Washington Office on Latin America (WOLA). 1995. *Demilitarizing Public Order: The International Community, Police Reform and Human Rights in Central America and Haiti*, available at www.wola.org/pubs.html.

3. These states are Albania, Bosnia and Herzegovina, Bulgaria, Croatia, the Czech Republic, Estonia, Hungary, Latvia, Lithuania, the Former Yugoslav Republic of Macedonia, Poland, Romania, Slovakia, Slovenia, and Serbia and Montenegro.

4. Hendrickson, Dylan. 1999. *A Review of Security-Sector Reform*, Working Paper No. 1. London: Conflict, Security, and Development Group, Centre for Defence Studies, King's College London.

5. OECD Development Assistance Committee (DAC). 2001. "Security issues and development cooperation: A conceptual framework for enhancing policy coherence", *DAC Journal*, Vol. 2, No. 3, section II, pp. 31–71.

6. Baldwin, D. A. 1995. "Security studies and the end of the Cold War", *World Politics*, Vol. 18, October, pp. 117–141.

7. See e.g. www.wellesley.edu/Economics/IFI.

8. Ball, Nicole. 2001. "Transforming security sectors: The IMF and World Bank approaches", *Conflict, Security and Development*, Vol. 1, No. 1, pp. 45–66.

9. World Bank. 1999. *Security, Poverty Reduction and Sustainable Development: Challenges for the New Millennium*. Washington, DC: World Bank.

10. Edmunds, Timothy. 2001. "Defining security sector reform", *Civil-Military Relations in Central and Eastern Europe Network Newsletter*, No. 3, October, pp. 3–6, available at http://civil-military.dsd.kcl.ac.uk.

11. Cawthra, Gavin. 1997. *Securing South Africa's Democracy: Defence, Development and Security in Transition*. London: Macmillan, pp. 7–26.

12. Ball, Nicole, J. 'Kayode Fayemi, 'Funmi Olonisakin, Martin Rupiya, and Rocklyn Williams. 2003. "Governance in the security sector", in Nicolas Van de Walle, Nicole Ball, and Vijava Ramachandran (eds) *Beyond Structural Adjustment: The Institutional Context of African Developmentt*. Basingstoke: Palgrave Macmillan, pp. 263–304.

13. Ayoob, Mohammed. 1995. *The Third World Security Predicament: State Making, Regional Conflict, and the International System*. London: Lynne Rienner Publishers.

14. Williams, Rocklyn. 2000. "Africa and the challenges of security sector reform", in Jackie Cilliers and Anita Hilding-Norberg (eds) *Building Stability in Africa: Challenges for the New Millennium*, Monograph 46. Pretoria: Institute for Security Studies, available at www.iss.co.za/Pubs/Monographs/No46/Contents.html.

15. Unwritten, informal norms, stemming out of the local, tribal, and clan traditions, culture, and beliefs, are often more powerful or obligatory than the written, formal rules and norms established by central state authorities.

16. See e.g. Ball, Nicole. 2002. "Democratic governance in the security sector", paper presented at the UNDP Workshop on Learning from Experience for Afghanistan, New York, 5 February, available at www.undp.org/eo/afghanistan/index.html.

17. Williams, Rocklyn. 2002. "Development agencies and security sector restructuring", *Conflict, Security and Development*, Vol. 2, No. 1, pp. 145–149.
18. This is borne out by the frequency of military *coups d'état* in many parts of Africa, Asia, and Latin America. See e.g. Hanneman, Robert A. and Robin L. Steinback. 1990. "Military involvement and political instability: An event history analysis 1940–1980", *Journal of Political and Military Sociology*, Vol. 18, Summer, pp. 1–23.
19. Chalmers, Malcolm. 2001. "Structural impediments to security-sector reform", paper presented at the International Institute for Strategic Studies Centre for the Democratic Control of Armed Forces (IISS–DCAF) Conference on Security Sector Reform, Geneva, 23 April.
20. This policy is broken down into two components, administered by different departments. The security sector reform policy focuses on the defence sector and cross-cutting governance issues. The policy on safety, security, and access to justice covers personal security and justice systems.
21. Welch, Claude and Johanna M. Forman. 1998. *Civil-Military Relations: USAID's Role*, Technical Publication Series. Washington, DC: Center for Democracy and Governance, US Agency for International Development.
22. For a discussion of UN conflict prevention activities see Cockell, John G. 2003. "Early warning analysis and policy planning in UN preventive action", in David Carment and Albrecht Schnabel (eds) *Conflict Prevention: Path to Peace or Grand Illusion?*. Tokyo: United Nations University Press, pp. 182–206.
23. The text of the Cotonou Agreement is available at http://europa.eu.int/comm/development/cotonou/index_en.htm.
24. For a discussion of EU conflict prevention activities see Duke, Simon. 2003. "Regional organizations and conflict prevention: CFSP and ESDI in Europe", in David Carment and Albrecht Schnabel (eds) *Conflict Prevention: Path to Peace or Grand Illusion?*. Tokyo: United Nations University Press, pp. 91–111; Ehrhart, Hans-Georg. 2002. *What Model for CFSP?*, Chaillot Papers No. 55. Paris: Institute for Security Studies.
25. OECD DAC, note 5 above.
26. OECD Development Assistance Committee (DAC). 2004. *Security System Reform and Governance: Policy and Good Practice*, policy statement and background paper endorsed at the High Level Meeting of DAC Ministers, 15–16 April, Paris, available at www.oecd.org/dataoecd/8/39/31785288.pdf.
27. An account of the PfP initiative is given in Rotfeld, Adam D. 1995. "Europe: The multilateral security process", *SIPRI Yearbook 1995: Armaments, Disarmament and International Security*. Oxford: Oxford University Press, pp. 275–281.
28. See www.nato.int/docu/facts/2000/nato-map.htm.
29. NATO. 1995. *Study on NATO Enlargement*. Brussels: NATO.
30. See www.vbs.admin.ch/internet/GST/KVR/e/e-Codeofconduct.htm. See also OSCE. 1994. "Towards a genuine partnership in a new era", Budapest Document, available at www1.umn.edu/humanrts/osce/new/budapest-summit-declaration.html; *SIPRI Yearbook* 1995, note 27 above, pp. 309–313. According to the guidelines, the armed forces should be placed under, and used by, state institutions which enjoy democratic legitimacy and abide by legal norms, democratic values, neutrality in national political life, and human and civil rights, as well as by a rule of individuals' responsibility for possible orders and deeds inconsistent with the norms of domestic and international law.
31. Information on this process is available at www.seecp.gov.mk/general_info.htm.
32. The OAU member states adopted the Constitutive Act of the African Union on 11 July 2000; it entered into force on 26 May 2001, formally establishing the African Union (AU), with headquarters in Addis Ababa.

33. Fayemi, Kayode and Dylan Hendrickson. 2002. "NEPAD: The security dimension", *Journal of West African Affairs*, Vol. 3, No. 1, p. 85.

34. Stevenson, Jonathan. 2001. "Counter-terrorism and the role of the international financial institutions", *Conflict, Security and Development*, Vol. 1, No. 3, pp. 153–159.

35. *Ibid.*

36. This is a particular issue of concern in Afghanistan, where the desire to limit the exposure of international forces to combat with Taliban forces has resulted in the hasty training and arming of factional forces by the USA and its allies. However, limited attention has thus far been devoted to the question of how to integrate these forces into a national army with appropriate management and oversight structures. See e.g. Graham, Bradley and Vernon Loeb. 2002. "US special forces to train recruits for Afghan army", *Washington Post*, 26 March.

37. Laurenz, R. 2002. "Top legislator wary of contingency fund", *Defense Week*, 11 February, p. 1, available at http://ebird.dtic.mil/Feb2002/e20020211top.htm.

38. For a detailed global survey of the state of security sector reform, see the report by the OECD DAC which covers 110 countries across Africa, Asia, Latin America and the Caribbean, the Baltic states, the Commonwealth of Independent States, and south-east Europe: "A survey of security system reform and donor policy: Views from non-OECD countries", in OECD DAC, note 26 above.

39. Forster, Anthony. 2000. "Civil-military relations and security sector reform: West looking East", paper presented at the Fourth International Security Forum Conference on Civil-Military Relations and Democratic Control of Armed Forces, Geneva, 15–17 November, available at www.dcaf.ch/publications/papers/ISF_WS_III-4_Forster.pdf.

40. *Ibid.*

41. The US Africa Center for Strategic Studies (ACSS) provides senior African military and civilian leaders with academic training in civil-military relations, national security strategy, and defence economics. When it was launched in 1998 the initial emphasis of the ACSS programme was on the wholesale transfer of the US model of civil-military relations into the African socio-cultural context. The initial opposition to this approach from African participants at the first regional seminars hosted by the ACSS has resulted in a greater effort to engage Africans in shaping the programme. See www. africacenter.org.

42. Hendrickson, Dylan and Nicole Ball. 2002. *Off-Budget Military Spending and Revenue: Issues and Policy Perspectives for Donors*, Occasional Paper No. 1. London: Conflict, Security, and Development Group, King's College London.

43. Marley, Anthony D. 1997. "Military downsizing in the developing world: Process, problems, and possibilities", *Parameters*, Vol. 27, No. 4, pp. 137–144.

44. Ero, Comfort. 2000. *Sierra Leone's Security Complex*, Working Paper No. 3. London: Conflict, Security, and Development Group, Centre for Defence Studies, King's College London.

45. As the case of Cambodia has demonstrated, this has made it difficult to develop a logical and sustainable reform plan, to assess effectively what level of security spending is affordable in relation to other public sectors, or to buy in the support of government and the security forces themselves for reform. See Hendrickson, Dylan. 2001. "Cambodia's security sector reforms: Limits of a down-sizing strategy", *Conflict, Security and Development*, Vol. 1, No. 1, pp. 67–82.

46. OECD DAC, note 5 above; Cooper, Neil and Michael Pugh. 2002. *Security-Sector Transformation in Post-Conflict Societies*, Working Paper No. 5. London: Conflict, Security, and Development Group, Centre for Defence Studies, King's College London.

47. E.g. the British government approved the sale of a radar system to Tanzania in spite of opposition from a cross-section of groups in Tanzania and the international community.

This is important to note in view of the leading role that the UK is playing in setting the security sector reform agenda, and given the fact that Tanzania is dependent on aid for nearly 50 per cent of its annual budget. See World Bank. 2001. "World Bank could bar $40 million Tanzania air traffic deal", *World Bank Development News*, 21 December, available at www.worldbank.org/developmentnews.

48. For a detailed examination of the complexity of security sector reform see Cawthra, Gavin and Robin Luckham (eds). 2003. *Governing Insecurity: Democratic Control of Military and Security Establishments in Transitional Societies*. London and New York: Zed Books.

49. For a detailed assessment of security sector reform in Africa, see the Africa chapter in note 38 above.

3

African armed forces and the challenges of security sector transformation

Rocky Williams

A major shift within the thinking of bilateral donor organizations, international financial institutions, and development agencies is beginning to occur around the issue of what is commonly referred to as "security sector reform". This is a significant development which carries with it both opportunities and nascent risks for the donor community. Traditionally, donor bodies have tended to treat security sector issues in one of two ways. Firstly, they have tended to see security sector restructuring and assistance as being the preserve of either their foreign ministries or, more appropriately, their respective defence establishments. Secondly, when considering issues of a security nature they have tended to adopt a zero-sum approach to military expenditure. This rather simplistic line of logic (best exemplified in the structural adjustment programme interventions of the World Bank over the past two decades) maintains that a reduction in military expenditure (milex) is both a "good thing" in itself and, once effected, releases valuable resources required for the ongoing development of the country concerned.

The reality is, of course, infinitely more nuanced than such mechanistic equations would have us believe. There is no necessary correlation between reductions in force levels, their budgets, and their respective armouries and the ongoing development of a country. Admittedly such reductions have, on many occasions, been accompanied by an increase in political stability and a redirection of military expenditure towards tangible developmental goals (for instance in South Africa, Zimbabwe, or Namibia during their post-election scenarios). Yet there are compelling examples of countries where an ill-considered security sector restructuring programme has actually bedevilled political stability and, in some cases, worsened civil-military relations.[1] The relation between security sector downsizing on the one hand, and the attainment of political stability and development on the other, is at best a contingent relationship conditioned by a host of political, economic, social, and institutional factors that are utterly unique to the country concerned. It is only on the basis of a scientific and empathetic reading of these highly diverse contexts that appropriate interventions in the security sector can be made.

This chapter seeks to examine some of the key issues that need to be explored if "security sector" programmes (as being presently articulated within the donor community), or various attempts by African governments to democratize their security sectors in general and their armed forces in particular, are to be successful. Indeed, the concept of "security sector reform" in Africa, far from being novel, constitutes part of a long intellectual and strategic history going back to the pan-Africanist movements of the 1950s (the role of the armed forces as being one of the primary vehicles for nation building, for instance). Strategies determining the involvement of African and non-African actors in the restructuring of their security establishments have undergone many variations over the past 50 years, and presently incline in a direction that increasingly prioritizes democracy, development, and governance as the key cornerstones of the transformation of the security sector.

This chapter argues that the formulation of strategies designed to engage African security establishments in security sector reform processes needs to be predicated on a series of interrelated concepts, principles, and strategies to ensure their optimal efficacy. Critical to all these processes is for African security practitioners, policy analysts, and intellectuals to disenthral themselves of many of the concepts which they previously have adhered to so religiously. Unless security sector reform (herein referred to as security sector transformation) initiatives are thoroughly indigenized and imbued with practical, local content, then African civil-military relations will be no more than a mere reflection of "imported" non-African systems. This chapter accordingly seeks to "unpack" some of the much-used (and often abused) concepts within both the security sector transformation and the civil-military relations literature. It outlines some of the key principles upon which robust civil-military relations can be predicated, and it suggests some broad issues which need to be considered when African countries and their governments consider the restructuring of the security sector in general and their armed forces in particular.

Operationalizing security sector reform: Conceptual and terminological considerations

Indigenizing the concept of security sector reform: From security sector reform to security sector transformation

The concept of security sector reform, despite its laudable intentions and notwithstanding the fact that it is predicated on noble normative principles, is currently largely Eurocentric in origin. This should not, at a philosophical level, disqualify it from being introduced into the political discourses of the developing world. Indeed, its normative content, emanating largely from the centre-left discourses of the Nordic countries, the European social democracies, the Democratic administration in the USA, the Canadian government, and the New Labour government in Britain, is remarkably similar to the vision of an African renaissance being articulated by Presidents Mbeki, Obisanjo, and others on the African continent.

A rigorous and strategic indigenization of the concept is going to be required on the African continent if any semblance of local ownership is to be achieved and any potential discrediting of the concept, most notably from certain opportunistic and predictable political quarters, is to be avoided. Practically, this will require a series of strategies to determine how security sector reform (SSR) will be internalized within the political and institutional discourses of the developing world in such a manner that it is both consistent with the indigenous traditions of the African continent and supportive of the ongoing attempts by Africans to take control over the political processes of which they are, inseparably, a part. This begs a series of partnerships with legitimate actors within the recipient countries to ensure that SSR succeeds.

An initial step towards such an indigenization process is to refer to the restructuring of the security sector as a "security sector transformation" process. The term "reform" has many pejorative connotations within the African environment. Politically it is often associated with the implementation of policy decisions from "above" without any attempt to secure the broader participation and consultation of non-state or legislative actors. Many of the "reform" strategies adopted by diverse African countries have had as their objective the legitimization of unpopular regimes, and have failed to alter meaningfully the existing balance of power within both state and society. Transformation, for its part, is a wide-ranging concept that encompasses a variety of interrelated fields. Transformation processes, if thoroughly pursued, have an effect on virtually all aspects of an organization's existence, and as such require astute management if the success of such processes is to be ensured. For transformation processes to be successful it is essential that three mission success factors be acknowledged during the management of the process:

- the importance of providing decisive and strategic leadership over the process
- the importance of ensuring that high levels of legitimacy ("buy-in") accrue to the process
- the importance of determining the scope of the transformation process – organizational culture, traditions, leadership style, racial and gender composition etc.

In essence four major transformation "clusters" can be determined within the management of any transformation process. *Cultural transformation* entails the transformation of the culture of the institution in question, the leadership, management, and administrative ethos of the institution, and the traditions upon which the institution is predicated. It also entails the transformation of the value system upon which the institution is based. *Human transformation* entails the transformation of the composition of the institution with regard to its racial, ethnic, regional, and gender composition and its human resource practices. *Political transformation* strives to ensure that the conduct and character of the institution in question conform to the political features of the democracy within which it is located – acknowledgement of the principle of civil supremacy, the institution of appropriate mechanisms of oversight and control, adherence to the principles and practices of accountability and transparency, etc. *Organizational transformation* constitutes a more technocratic process within which the organization in question is right-sized, its management practices and its diverse organizational processes made more cost-effective, and its ability to provide services rendered more efficient.

Wide-ranging transformation processes of the type referred to above are immensely difficult to accomplish in their entirety, as the transformation of the Lesotho, Sierra Leone, and, partially, the South African security sectors has demonstrated. Shifting priorities, resource limitations, skills deficits, weak leadership, and the sheer novelty of the transformational terrain may bedevil such initiatives. The restructuring of the security sector of many African countries, particularly those which have emerged from either an authoritarian or a violent past, demands, however, a visionary and integrated transformational strategy capable of ensuring that the country's security institutions do not regress into previous behavioural patterns.

During the process of managing transformation processes it is critical to ensure that the terminology utilized is both conceptually and practically accurate. The four concepts that often tend to confuse African defence transformation processes are the terms "civilian control" as a multiple concept; the term "control" as a singular concept; the concept of the "apolitical soldier"; and the tendency to erect models of civil control that overemphasize the role of mechanisms rather than the role of partnerships in creating robust civil-military relations. Unless adequately explained and conceptualized, and unless freed from their potential misapplication, these terms tend to create divisions and antagonisms between the civil and the security sectors. The terms are discussed below.

Civil versus civilian control

Much of the debate regarding the subordination of the armed forces to democratic control has focused on the centrality of ensuring appropriate "civilian control" over these institutions. This is a problematic, flawed, and potentially divisive concept and needs to be critiqued from two angles – conceptual and historical – if any justice to the civil-military relations debate in Africa is to be done.

The term "civilian control", popular if somewhat misapplied, confuses the *civilian* content of many democratic institutions (legislatures and governments, for example) with the political principle of *civil* oversight over the armed forces. Civilian institutions and personnel do not inherently make for more effective and accountable management and oversight of the activities of the armed forces. Africa provides a compelling example of how civilian leaders and civilian institutions can, in various forms, mismanage the armed forces towards their own partisan and often brutal political ends. Innumerable examples substantiate this assertion, as the experiences of Mobutu Sese Seko, Idi Amin, Sani Abacha, Charles Taylor, and others demonstrate.

For instance, virtually no successful military *coup d'état* in Africa has been achieved without the support of significant sectors of political society, government, business, and, on occasions, elements within civil society. The rise in prominence of the armed forces in South Africa during the P. W. Botha period (1978–1989), for example, was the result of Botha (himself a civilian leader) and his civilian administration's decision to "invite" the armed forces into the executive reaches of state power. The success of the repeated military interventions in Nigeria were due, to no small extent, to the support the military received from a complex web of primarily Northern business interests, sectors of political society, and certain civil society groupings (such as religious groupings and rural chiefs).

The following quote by Brigadier-General S. O. Ogbemudia on the origins of the first Nigerian coup in 1965 provides a chilling example of how civilians often create the environment within which intervention can succeed:

In 1965, I was an instructor at the Nigerian Military Training College, Kaduna. The late Chukwuma Kaduna Nzeogwu was also there. We were majors on a salary of 125 pounds per month. One of the subjects I taught was current affairs. Civilians were regular visitors to our college. Some of these civilians asked us leading questions as to what we were doing under a corrupt civilian government. We consistently replied that our duty was to support civil power. One such concerned visitor was a prominent chief from the east who was a parliamentary secretary and who felt very disturbed about the state of affairs in the country at that time. He asked Major Nzeogwu whether he and his colleagues were going to allow the trend to continue. The chief gave us six books on Nasser's coup in Egypt. With hindsight, I can recall that Major Nzeogwu started caving in when he complained that with a paltry salary of 125 pounds, there was no way he and his colleagues could do what the chief was suggesting. The rest is now history.[2]

The principle of "civil control" (derived from the Latin word *civitas*, meaning "the state") refers to those processes whereby the people ensure that their representatives govern on their behalf within a democracy. This process and the principles that underpin it are not particularly unique, and are generic to the study of any democratic political system. The electorate elect their representatives, who serve in the legislature. The powers conferred on this body are those of legislation, approval of resources, and oversight over the activities of the mandated government which governs on their behalf. At least in theory, in fulfilling this mandate it is the state which controls the activities of all government departments, including the armed forces, on behalf of the elected representatives of the people.

This is a relatively uncontentious concept in a democracy, but its conceptual origins are sometimes blurred by the tendency of many analysts and practitioners to juxtapose artificially the civilian and the military sectors in the management of a country's defence sector. Although in most stable democracies the legislative and executive reaches of government are overwhelmingly civilian in composition, this is more the product of historical circumstance and cultural peculiarity than a generic norm. The legislatures of such countries as Mozambique, South Africa, Namibia, and Uganda, to name but a few, consist of parliamentarians who mostly have a military background of one form or the other. This does not detract from their ability to perform their duties as overseers of the armed forces, but rather refers to their ability to differentiate their current roles from their previous military identities.

It is a somewhat self-evident observation that civil control over the armed forces can also be achieved in situations where no semblance of democratic tradition exists. The ability of authoritarian systems (one-party administrations and autocratic systems) to control their armed forces – whether via party political penetration of the institutions or the creation of parallel mechanisms of command and control – is well chronicled. The key aspect of civil control that needs to be stressed is its ability to manage and oversee the activities of the armed forces in a democratic context.

Control in the positive sense versus control in the pejorative sense

Control in the positive sense refers to two potential terrains: the terrain of political oversight and the terrain of effective management. Political control over the armed forces is necessary and desirable not simply for reactive reasons (for example, attempts to remedy the aberrant behaviour of subordinate institutions) but for proactive reasons – attempts to provide the security sector with clear and unambiguous political leadership and a coherent and intelligible policy framework, for instance.

In managerial terms "control" refers to the ability of the management echelons, in this case the appropriate political and executive authorities, to manage an institution so as to ensure its optimal utilization in support of defined objectives and its cost-effective management with regard to its resource allocation and expenditure. The management and control of the armed forces by non-military actors also provides for insights and alternative perspectives that otherwise would not have been considered by the armed forces in the course of their strategic and planning processes.

Control in the pejorative sense refers to either the misuse of the armed forces for partisan purposes or the inability or incompetence of either the political or civil authorities to manage the security forces in a professional and responsible manner. Explicit political mismanagement of the armed forces was referred to above and has occurred in innumerable African countries – often with devastating consequences. Unintended mismanagement of the armed forces through a lack of requisite policy or management expertise tends to be a more common phenomenon in the African civil-military relations discourse. Attaining a situation within which the security sectors and the armed forces of African countries can be controlled in a positive sense requires a series of interventions, which are referred to in more detail below.

From "apolitical" armed forces to non-partisan armed forces

The concept of the "apolitical" soldier (popular, if somewhat misapplied, in the discourses of many third world armed forces) needs to be critically re-examined in the course of defence transformation processes. Even in democracies and countries with little experience of the intrusion of the armed forces into the political realm, the armed forces are invariably involved in politics in varying degrees. This involvement (be it of a benign or more assertive nature) inevitably results in the penetration of political themes and concepts into the discourse and, ultimately, the very construction of the corporate identity of the armed forces. This is exemplified by identities as diverse as those of the revolutionary soldier, the Western professional soldier of the USA and the UK, or the "citizen-in-uniform" of the Bundeswehr. While the influence of the "political" may be manifest in an asymmetrical and differentiated manner within the practices of different armed forces, depending on the peculiarities of the country concerned, it is always present at the heart of their activities. This may be reflected in the constitutional obligations to which the armed forces are expected to adhere, the involvement of the armed forces in the parliamentary, policy, and state budgeting process, the access that the armed forces enjoy to the president as commander-in-chief, or, simply, the different political persuasions of the different members of the armed forces.

It is not only inevitable that the armed forces will be "political", but it is also perhaps desirable that they are so inclined. It is imperative that the armed forces of developing countries, and particularly those which are involved in the delicate task of consolidating democracy, are fully conversant with the democratic features of the system which they serve (hence the need for a robust civic education programme amongst its members), understand and are integrated into the government's key policy initiatives (especially when these relate to the encouragement of domestic development and stability), and are able, on a discursive and interactive basis, to interact with the elected civil authorities around a range of issues critical to their national mandate. What is critical about this "political" role, however, is the fact that it does not include the terrain of the party political (and armed forces as such must always be non-partisan in orientation), that their partnership with the civil authorities is not an equal partnership, and that their involvement in the terrain of national policy (politics with a small "p" as opposed to politics with a big "P") is clearly circumscribed and mutually acknowledged. It will be on this basis that a more fruitful debate on civil-military relations in developing countries, a debate less ascriptive than many of the present largely Western theoretical assumptions, will be generated.

Civil-military relations as a process and civil-military relations as mechanisms

The influence of Western civil-military relations concepts over the discourses of armed forces in Africa is extensive. The establishment of robust and enduring civil-military relations systems in Africa, however, will require a judicious combination of traditional forms of civil control as they have operated on the continent with the more recent, and primarily Northern, civil-military relations "models".

In a number of recent critiques some civil-military relations theorists have referred to the pervasive influence of the USA's experience of civil-military relations over Western military sociology, and have illustrated how this tradition has become universalized and absolutized within both the theory of civil-military relations and its practice. Much of this tradition can be traced back to the earlier writings of Samuel Huntington, who emphasized the subordination of the armed forces to a diversity of more "traditional" Western-styled checks and balances emanating from regulations, military procedures, military command and control patterns, and legislative oversight, for instance.[3] However, recent critics, including Rebecca Schiff, have challenged this tradition.

A major conclusion of current civil-military relations theory is that militaries should remain physically and ideologically separated from the political institutions. By contrast, the alternative theory ... argues that three partners – the military, the political élites, and the citizenry – should aim for a cooperative relationship that may or may not involve separation but does not require it.[4]

Schiff's theory of concordance has direct relevance for both the study of civil-military relations and their practical application in the developing world. She argues that:

Concordance theory considers the importance of context in studying the military and society. Some of the indicators, such as military style and the inclusion of the citizenry as a partner, deal with the norms, customs, and values of particular nations. Concordance theory explains which major aspects of a nation should be in agreement in order to prevent domestic military intervention. How a particular society achieves such an agreement is largely dependent upon the nature of that society, its institutions, and its culture. That is what makes concordance theory unique: it causally predicts conditions for domestic military intervention without superimposing a particular historical or cultural context upon a nation.[5]

Schiff has argued, quite cogently, that the effective subordination of the armed forces to civil control is not a necessary outcome of the institutional separation of the armed forces from the civil authorities. Effective civil-military relations are achieved, in her opinion, via the extent to which political, military, and civil actors find agreement, and accommodate one another, in the definition of the values and objectives of the armed forces. Within this equation disruptions to stable civil-military relations are, more often than not, caused not by the failure of formal institutional mechanisms but by a breakdown in trust and its attendant consequences.

In light of Schiff's critique and from an appraisal of the current Western literature on civil-military relations, three key characteristics of the institutional separation model can be discerned.

- The key feature of this tradition is its emphasis on the institutional dimension of civil-military relations – the assertion that militaries should remain physically and ideologically separated from political institutions.

- This approach emphasizes the importance of formal institutional mechanisms in ensuring the subordination of the armed forces to civil control. It downplays the roles that non-institutional forms of civil control and civil society and culture can play in determining the parameters of a country's civil-military relations (what is referred to in this chapter as the collaborative-partnership model of civil-military relations).

- The corporate identity of the armed forces in this tradition is defined as being that of the professional, apolitical soldier, loyal to the government of the day and possessing its own value framework. The armed forces eschew politics and concentrate their energies on developing and applying their functional military expertise.

Not all writing on civil-military relations by Western scholars has confirmed the current dominant institutional-separation paradigm. A number of influential Western civil-military relations scholars, such as Finer and Janowitz, have written extensively on the role that societal factors and non-institutional factors play in ensuring the armed forces' adherence to the principle of civil supremacy. Notwithstanding these arguments, however, Western civil-military relations theory has been dominated in the second half of the twentieth century by a focus on the institutional (and hence formal, legal, and constitutional) dimension underpinning civil-military relations and the importance of securing the ideological and political separation of the armed forces from the body politic.

Whilst it is important not to dismiss elements of the Western tradition, it is equally important to avoid reifying one aspect of this tradition to the detriment of other traditions and to reclaim and reintroduce into the contemporary African debate on civil-military relations those elements of the *collaborative-partnership* approach that argue for the introduction of a creative range of additional measures whereby the subordination of the military to civil control can be ensured. For this reason it is important to differentiate between objective and subjective forms of control over the armed forces. Some suggested strategies as to how this could be accomplished are outlined in more detail below.

Restructuring African armed forces: Critical assumptions, criteria, and principles

The restructuring of African armed forces will be inextricably determined by the specific context within which such initiatives occur. It is therefore difficult to advocate a general strategy that can be adopted by different African governments in the restructuring of their civil-military relations. It is possible, however, to provide a generic set of principles, criteria, and methodological assumptions which will be applicable to all transformation processes regardless of historical, political, and cultural peculiarities.

Principles underpinning the process of security sector transformation

Notwithstanding the diversity of political systems that one encounters in Africa and the changing parameters of civil-military relations in all the subregions of the continent, any attempt to engage in a process of security sector transformation (SST) should explicitly outline those principles upon which SST will be based. The following broad principles are proposed as foundations in this regard and should, ideally, find reflection in the appropriate constitutional provisions, legislative frameworks, standard operating procedures, and institutional culture of the armed forces themselves.

- The principle of civil supremacy entails four key principles, which should be respected by both the civil authorities and the armed forces in the execution of their respective responsibilities; namely the principles of the separation of powers, legality, accountability, and transparency.
- The determination of the roles, responsibilities, tasks, organizational features, and personnel requirements of the security forces should be done in a manner that is appropriate to a developing country engaged in a difficult and complex transition.
- The determination of the roles, responsibilities, tasks, organizational features, resource requirements, and personnel requirements of the security forces should be done in a manner that is affordable to the country concerned, particularly in light of a limited resource base and the pressing demands on the budget from all sectors of society.
- The roles and responsibilities of the security sector should be enshrined in the constitution. The constitution should ensure that the security sector will respect human rights as reflected in the constitution and domestic and international law, and will understand and operate within the framework of the democratic process in the country concerned.

- The security forces will be non-partisan in their political behaviour and will not further the interests of and/or involve themselves in party political activities.
- The conduct of security policy and the management of security matters shall be undertaken in a consultative and transparent manner and shall encourage as high a level of parliamentary and public participation as is possible without endangering the lives of personnel and without prejudicing the ability of the security forces to conduct legal and legitimate operations.
- National security shall be sought primarily through efforts to meet the political, economic, social, and cultural rights of a country's people, and the activities of the security sector shall be subordinate to and supportive of these efforts.
- Both the political authorities and the leadership of the armed forces shall strive to build and maintain high levels of dialogue and partnership in all their dealings with one another. Such a dialogue should be predicated on regular and continuous interaction between the two arenas and will occur within the hierarchy of authority and oversight as established in the country concerned.[6]

Whilst the aforementioned principles should be reflected in appropriate constitutional and legal provisions, it is important to stress that they should become, over time, inscribed into the very culture and practice of civil-military relations themselves. Africa is littered with well-intentioned constitutions and capable legislatures whose efforts to ensure robust civil oversight over the security forces were rendered ineffective in the face of praetorian armed forces.

Criteria governing the transformation of the security sector

Security sector transformation is never mounted for its own sake but is always an inseparable part of broader political and developmental objectives. This requires that a broad set of criteria govern the process of SST to ensure the optimal development of the institution in question. Some suggestions for the transformation of African armed forces include the following.

Both civilian and military personnel should be involved in the process of defence management. Apart from the political benefits of such a strategy (for example, increased legitimacy and more extensive civil-military dialogue), it also provides for a richer defence product, harnessing, as it does, the competencies of a range of non-military and non-technocratic actors.

Transformation should, somewhat self-evidently, provide for the cost-effective management of the security sector. This is often difficult to accomplish given the tension between budgetary constraints on the one hand and an increased demand for services from the security sector on the other. No instant formula exists whereby this tension can be remedied, but creative approaches can be adopted. These may include the adoption of cheaper, and often militarily more effective, defence strategies such as civilian-based defence, doctrines of irregular warfare, and an emphasis on lighter and more mobile, rather than heavier and more technologically sophisticated, armed forces.

Transformation can also include a greater degree of centralization of the country's military and paramilitary forces and the elimination of both organizational duplication and overlap of roles and responsibilities. Transformation will also benefit from the adoption of a flexible systems-based approach to organizational restructuring. This will ensure that organizations are created not on the basis of an ad hoc response to security crises or vested institutional and bureaucratic interests. Rather it will ensure that the structures of the armed forces logically reflect their ability to provide the services for which they are constitutionally entrusted.

Transformation should not adversely affect the operational readiness and the institutional capabilities of the armed forces. Whilst some initial dissonance will ripple out into the organization (an inevitable consequence of the uncertainty inherent in any transformation process and the shift in the balance of power that will occur within the institution in question), the success of the transformation process will be measured by the extent to which it maximizes the ability of the institution to deliver its services.

Restructuring should provide for the optimal development of human resources during the transformation process. The successful management of the long-term consequences of an SST process is critically dependent on the policy coherence, competencies, management abilities, and transformational leadership qualities within the institution. These are qualities that remain underdeveloped in African governments in general and, to a lesser extent, within the armed forces in particular, and require prioritization for transformation to be successful.

Most developing countries continue to face threats and challenges to their national interests, sovereignty, and internal stability that will continue to require the maintenance, preparation, and deployment of security forces in a variety of roles in the medium to long term. Typically these tasks, based on a preliminary assessment of the country's strategic environment, will require the maintenance of the capabilities to execute a wide variety of secondary and "non-traditional" tasks (peace missions, internal law and order responsibilities, and, in some cases, reconstruction and development tasks).

Critical assumptions underpinning the restructuring of the security sector

The management of the African security sector in general, and the armed forces in particular, has remained a policy arena that has largely been closed to broader public and parliamentary scrutiny since independence. It is imperative that strategies designed to transform African armed forces take stock of the very real obstacles which they may encounter in the initiation and management of SST processes. Three critical assumptions, all present in most African countries in varying degrees, are outlined below.

Firstly, the establishment of effective processes and mechanisms of civil oversight over the security sector will take time to accomplish in all those countries where such a tradition is absent. The establishment of such mechanisms cannot occur in isolation, and is critically dependent on the broader relationship between the executive and the legislature. An emasculated legislature and timid parliamentary committees will serve no more than to "rubber stamp" key policy and budgetary initiatives emerging from the executive.

The oversight role played by most legislatures over the security sector on the African continent is generally weak. This is partially the product of the Anglophone and Francophone tradition from which these states have been crafted (strong executives versus relatively weak legislatures) and the central role which the state has played in directing the post-independence development of most African countries. In those countries where the oversight role is more robust (South Africa, Mozambique, and Mali), this is more often than not the result of the mass-based tradition from which new governments were created and the prominence afforded to civil society in the national governance equation.

Building capacity within the legislative nodes of oversight will require the reconfiguration of the relationship between the legislature and the executive, the building of capacity amongst parliamentarians responsible for security sector oversight, and the deliberate facilitation of an ongoing dialogue between the executive echelons of the armed forces, parliamentarians, and civilian members of the executive.

The prospects for building capacity amongst the executive nodes of oversight remains favourable within most African governments, given the fact that both *de jure* and *de facto* political power tends to reside in the executive branch of most functioning African governments. Most African armed forces reside under the political authority of a ministry of defence or, in the case of countries such as Swaziland, the Seychelles, Botswana, and Lesotho, an institutional equivalent (normally the president's office or the office of the monarch). In most of these ministries the legal and administrative frameworks exist for activating a more robust ministry of defence than that which exists presently. The involvement of non-military personnel in the management of defence matters is not a new phenomenon in post-colonial Africa. Virtually all ministries of defence possess the position of permanent secretary for defence (also known variously as the secretary for defence, the general secretary, and the principal secretary), who is invariably the department of defence's chief accounting officer and the administrative head of the department itself. Even in countries such as Nigeria, which has endured successive military administrations, the tradition of strong civilian ministries has persisted throughout these abnormal periods.

The oversight role played by ministries of defence can be greatly strengthened by the addition of new roles and responsibilities to the present ministry of defence. In addition to retaining responsibility for oversight of budgetary expenditure within the armed forces, ministries of defence can also assume responsibility for the management of national defence policy processes and the management of the defence procurement cycle – both of these being inherently political processes that would benefit from the involvement of civilians.

Secondly, the "opening up" of the civil-military relations discourse will see civil society increasingly demanding a higher level of involvement in and consultation on national defence issues than has hitherto been the case. The involvement of civil society in the management of national security sector processes is complex for a variety of reasons. On the one hand civil society can play an immensely constructive role in both the legitimization of security sector discourses and the enriching of the final product emerging from national security sector policy processes. This is particularly the case in those countries where the institutional capacity of the state is either discredited and/or weakened. Yet, on the other hand, the involvement of civil society in SST processes can remain problematic. Civil society in Africa, as with civil societies elsewhere in the world, reflects a contradictory amalgam of interests – some progressive, some benign, some manifestly partisan. In involving civil society in security sector transformation initiatives one should be cognizant of the motives, capabilities, and representative character of these diverse groupings. Urban-based groupings often tend to be more urbane, sophisticated, and familiar with broader governance issues. Many NGOs (both rural and urban) that tend to have a more direct interest in defence and related decisions (trade unions, women's organizations, veterans' organizations, etc.) are often marginalized from defence and security discourses through a lack of capacity and unavailability of resources.

The proactive involvement of civil society groupings in security and defence discourses requires a realistic assessment of the capacity of civil society to influence the national defence debate (mostly limited in the African context), the willingness of civil society to engage with the defence sector (mostly lacking, with a few exceptions such as South Africa, Mali, Lesotho, and Sierra Leone), and the extent to which the fragmented articulation of interests within civil society can be either beneficial or destructive to the consolidation of democratic civil-military relations.

However, the incorporation of civil society into national defence planning and the national defence debate should not occur at the expense of the legislative institutions. It is parliament that has the mandate to represent the electorate and it is parliament that should, ideally, be the guarantor of the will of the majority. Whilst civil society's capacity needs to be strengthened, it is the legislature that needs to benefit from capacity-building programmes – particularly via the development of analytical and policy-interrogative skills and defence parliamentarians' understanding of the defence policy, planning, budgeting, and programming cycle.

The third critical assumption, linked to the critical assumptions outlined above, is that building a culture of consultation and openness on defence issues will take time to accomplish. The mere institution of mechanisms and processes will, by itself, be insufficient in creating the necessary climate of trust and tolerance within which an open-ended debate can survive. Creating this culture will require considerable maturity from the major institutional actors involved in the civil-military relations equation (executive, legislature, armed forces, and civil society), the astute management of the civil-military relations interface (both formal and informal) over the medium to long term, and the development of skills that are commensurate with the task at hand (such as empathy, situationally cogent judgement, and facilitation skills).

The content of security sector transformation processes

The conceptual and strategic content of SST initiatives will need to be determined in each country depending on overall transformational challenges. There is a tendency for much of the "traditional" donor assistance to focus on those issues that have traditionally occupied the defence ministries of donor countries – tactical training, doctrinal development, officer and non-commissioned officer development, equipment and weapons systems familiarization, or organizational restructuring. Security sector transformation, however, has as much to do with broader strategic and normative issues as with the "nuts and bolts" of organizational transformation.

As such SST initiatives need to focus on meta-level processes such as the national decision-making process, the role of the government, parliament, and the armed forces within this process, and the inculcation of the normative principles of civil-military relations within the officer corps of African armed forces. Indeed, failure to determine the depth and breadth of this conceptual content could lead to the underutilization of opportunities that are redolent with strategic potential (it could also lead, more practically, to considerable interagency infighting within the donor community and interdepartmental friction within the national government of the donor country itself over what it is that SST denotes and requires).

As stated on repeated occasions above, SST should, ideally, be a holistic process that not only integrates diverse actors into the national and even subregional defence process, but also attempts to integrate and synthesize the different levels of the SST process itself. Most African armed forces do not have the luxury or the latitude of dealing with their various transformational processes in a sequential manner. African armed forces are compelled, therefore, to deal with a range of transformational issues simultaneously, to the best of their ability, and with often limited strategic and financial resources. To ensure the creation of healthy civil-military relations it is essential that the following issues be addressed during the process of security sector transformation.

First is the clear and unambiguous elucidation of the key constitutional principles upon which the management of the armed forces will be predicated. Such principles should outline the chain of political command, the chain of military command, the roles and tasks envisaged for the armed forces, and the broad democratic principles to which the armed forces should, in their conduct as professionals, adhere.

Next is the clear and unambiguous elucidation of the key responsibilities which the government has towards the armed forces of the country. These principles should be outlined in the constitution, but can also be further clarified in subordinate legislation. Such principles should include the provision of adequate resources for the armed forces to accomplish their constitutionally designated missions, the provision of clear political leadership to the armed forces, and the prevention of political interference in the chain of command by the political leadership.

Another issue is the provision of a clear policy framework within which the transformation of the armed forces will be managed. This generally tends to assume the form of white papers, strategic defence reviews, concept documents, and transformational strategies. The advantage of the provision of such a policy framework for both the armed forces and government is threefold. Firstly, it provides both armed forces and government with a clear understanding of those activities upon which the resource allocation to the armed forces should be based. Secondly, the management of such processes can provide the opportunity for governments to ensure that as wide a range of non-military actors is included in the policy formulation process as possible – thereby removing defence decision-making from the hands of a small group of technocratically inclined individuals. Thirdly, if correctly managed such processes can bestow considerable levels of legitimacy on both armed forces and government in the management of the nation's civil-military relations and can significantly defuse the often adversarial relationship that exists between the civil and the military sectors.

A further issue is the identification of the key strategic areas that require immediate attention during the process of managing national defence transformation. Given the immensity of many major transformational initiatives, the issues which transformation is called upon to address, and the limited institutional capacity to deal with these issues, it is imperative that realistic, and sustainable, interventions are made. From a consideration of defence transformation initiatives that have been completed (Namibia, Zimbabwe, Uganda), those that are currently nearing completion (South Africa and Mozambique), and those that are in the process of being initiated (Nigeria, Sierra Leone, Lesotho, the Democratic Republic of the Congo, and, possibly, Burundi) it is apparent that a generic set of issues present themselves for immediate consideration in the management of such processes. These include capacity building amongst parliamentary oversight committees; the requirement for a clear policy framework within which the country's civil-military relations can be both articulated and managed; the successful management of the human resource issues confronting the armed forces (demobilization, institution of equity programmes in the recruitment and promotional policies of the armed forces, and transformation of the leadership, command, and management culture of the armed forces); reprofessionalization of the armed forces; and preparation of the armed forces for new roles and tasks (such as peace missions and military aid to the civil community). Prioritization of these issues should not be at the expense of other pertinent transformational issues (such as involvement of the armed forces in truth and reconciliation processes, or transformation of the education and training institutions), but should rather strive to create an enabling environment within which the longer-term transformation of the institution can proceed.

Any transformation process that ignores the balance of power within the armed forces, regardless of the intentions, policy products, and consultative nature of this process, will fail to transform the armed forces of a democratizing country in any depth. It is imperative that the political leadership of the country, once it has initiated a security sector transformation process, understands both the *de facto* and the *de jure* balance of power within the armed forces. Many African armed forces have been notoriously fictionalized during the period of their post-colonial existence – a phenomenon attested to by the innumerable coups and counter-coups that pervade praetorian societies (such as Nigeria, Ghana, Sierra Leone, Zaire, and Lesotho). Many of these factions are, however, not necessarily anti-democratic, and even those countries which have emerged from decades of praetorian rule possess officers within the command echelons who are constitutionally inclined and supportive of the non-partisan and professional role of the modern military (such as Nigeria, Ghana, South Africa, and Lesotho).

The transformation of the armed forces needs to ensure that progressive and constitutionally inclined officers are deployed in those key nodal points within the command and staff hierarchy of the armed forces that are essential for long-term transformation of the institution. Typically these positions will include, particularly in the short term, such posts as the chief of the defence force, the chief of the most influential arm of service within the country concerned (in most African countries this tends to be the army), the chief of the military intelligence function, the key operational commanders (particularly at divisional and brigade level), and the defence strategy and planning staff.

In the medium to long term it is important to ensure that the key socializing institutions within the armed forces are placed in the hands of the constitutional and professional officers referred to above. Such institutions will include the planning, personnel, education, and training components of the armed forces. The transformation of the armed forces should also ensure that the institutional capacity of the civilian component of the defence head office is strengthened, and that supportive military personnel are seconded to the ministry of defence to assist civilian managers with the formulation of realistic policy, planning, and budgetary forecasts.

Specific interventions in the transformation of the African security sector

It is impossible to predict exactly what type of interventions should be made in the transformation of the diverse security sectors in contemporary Africa. These interventions will be conditioned by a continually changing range of political, economic, and security factors. It is possible to suggest certain generic approaches to the restructuring of the security sector – approaches sufficiently broad to be applicable to most SST scenarios. These process considerations are outlined below, and include the design of appropriate civil-military partnerships, the design of appropriate methodological principles whereby the restructuring of the defence sector can be effected, and the consideration of alternative doctrinal approaches to the design of African armed forces.

Creating civil-military partnerships: Cooperation is better than conflict

As stated above, current Western civil-military relations theory places great store on the importance of external guarantees – a range of institutional checks and balances – to ensure healthy civil-military relations. It maintains that it is via formal mechanisms of control (parliamentary oversight, or civilian control over the defence budgeting process) that military activities can be constrained and their involvement in the political process pre-empted. This system works to great effect in the industrialized democracies of Western Europe, and is a model that is "exported" from Western countries to African countries via the military academies and defence colleges of the West, as well as via the various mobile training teams on civil-military relations who work regularly throughout Africa (for instance, the International Military Education and Training Programme of the USA and the British military assistance training teams).

Yet the arguments privileging the role of formal institutional mechanisms of control are problematic for a variety of interrelated reasons. First, this concept possesses limited utility in explaining the diverse forms of civil control that can be instituted over the armed forces which are not formal-legalistic in nature and which involve other social actors, processes, and interfaces beyond those located in both the legislature and the executive. Second, there are inherent limitations of formal mechanisms of control "in themselves". The institutional-separation model presumes the efficacy of formal mechanisms standing separate from and "above" the armed forces they seek to control, yet the efficacy of the mechanisms depends on three critical variables (variables that are often absent in specific situations).

- Formal-legalistic measures tend to operate retroactively and only address a small area of organizational behaviour. They are designed more to prevent an abuse of power than to contain the security forces within a legitimate and mutually agreed sphere of activity.
- Formal-legalistic measures are largely externally focused and do not address the behavioural patterns of military officers themselves, the way they view their mission and responsibilities, and the way their seniors view their role orientation towards the political leaders of the day.
- To be effective, political control mechanisms require significant political will to make them work. Given the lack of familiarity displayed by

many political leaders with the world of the military, and the fact that political leaders often depend on the support of sectors of the armed forces for their political ambitions (particularly with regard to their organizational and intelligence capabilities), there is often a reluctance to utilize these formal mechanisms of control fully. This also explains the ability of the (South African?) armed forces to intervene in African countries where such mechanisms have already existed – Zambia (1997), Nigeria (throughout the 1970s and 1980s), and Lesotho (1985).

Given Africa's history it is not surprising that the contours of civil-military relations practice have tended to mirror those of its former colonial masters. The influence of Western intellectual and political traditions over both the political and the intellectual traditions of the developing countries of the periphery has been well chronicled by a range of scholars and political analysts alike. For instance, the economic dependence of African countries on their former colonial masters was skilfully replicated in the introduction of various political, educational, and intellectual systems that were markedly similar in both form and content to those of the departing Western colonizers.

Both the armed forces of African countries and the patterns of civil-military relations that began to emerge during the post-colonial period mirrored this close ascriptive relationship between the colonizer and the colonized. Although the ethnic and racial composition of the armed forces of the newly independent countries changed significantly in the first decade following independence, their culture, their traditions, and their corporate identity remained strongly influenced by the discourses and ideological themes of the Western armed forces.

The emerging patterns of post-independence civil-military relations were also marked, at the level of institutions and mechanisms, by a strong similarity between the formal mechanisms and institutions of civil control found in the former colonial country (the UK, France, the Netherlands, etc.) and those introduced in the newly independent countries. Virtually all African countries possess, on paper at least, the battery of formal mechanisms via which, it is claimed, civil control over the armed forces is ensured (although the form of these mechanisms may vary depending on the country concerned and the politico-juridical system which it has inherited and subsequently adapted). Countries possessing a stronger legislative tradition tend to emphasize the role of those legislative mechanisms entrusted with the task of civil oversight – such as parliamentary committees, ombudsman systems, and approval of the military budget. Other countries with a stronger executive culture may rely more extensively on the regulatory role of civil servants, finance ministries, and presidential control to ensure the subordination of the armed forces to civil control.

Virtually all African security institutions in general, and armed forces in particular, are near mirror reflections of their former colonial security institutions. The rank structure is the same with very few exceptions (one of them being the largely unsuccessful attempts by the National Party in South Africa in the 1950s to create a rank structure based on those of the original Boer commandos), the doctrine has admitted to few indigenous revisions (notwithstanding the fact that many of the new defence forces were constituted out of indigenous African guerrilla armies with their own, non-Western, traditions and doctrines), their institutional culture imitates that of either the British, the French, or the American value system, and, alas, the ideological themes that pervade their discourse are manifestly European in origin.

An analysis of the political institutions of most African countries also reveals a range of formal mechanisms designed to ensure the maintenance of stable civil-military relations that are uncannily Eurocentric in origin. Typically these include constitutional provisions regulating the functions of the armed forces, parliamentary defence committees, public accounts committees, audit and exchequer acts, internal audits, and service regulations. In some countries fully fledged ministries of defence and military ombudsman systems exist, whilst in others creative and varied forms of both civil and civilian oversight over the armed forces have been instituted.

Yet, notwithstanding this range of formal mechanisms, the salient reality underpinning African civil-military relations (and indeed the civil-military relations of most developing countries) is the fact that in most countries the subordination of the armed forces to civil control, when this has occurred, has been achieved by a complex system of processes and interfaces of a non-institutional nature. In virtually all those countries where the armed forces remain subordinate to the civil authorities (regardless of whether the latter are democratically elected or not), real control over the armed forces is wielded via a range of subjective interfaces and partnerships of which the formal mechanisms are either a component or, alternatively, merely the formal expression of these power relations.

If African countries are to indigenize their civil-military relations tradition, and avoid this "doctrinal mannerism" referred to here, then it is imperative that some of the key assumptions underpinning current Western civil-military relations theory are revisited. A conceptual geography of civil-military relations needs to be developed that is more consistent with the realities of civil-military relations in general. The reification of one tradition and theoretical system to the detriment of other discourses can stifle and impede constructive intellectual debate as well as producing unintended political consequences if literally applied. A number of suggestions can be made regarding the proposed re-examination of the theoretical assumptions underpinning the study of civil-military relations in African countries, as outlined below.

Firstly, the adoption of a more flexible and less absolute approach to the current Western civil-military relations tradition should not be construed as constituting a negative attack on the positive principles of traditional civil-military theory. The limited utility of certain formal mechanisms in developing countries, or their inapplicability, does not detract from the principles upon which these mechanisms are predicated (such as the principle of civil supremacy and the importance of precisely defining the roles and tasks of the armed forces). The limitation of current civil-military relations discourse lies with its ontological pretensions and not the formal, epistemological status of its central concepts. The latter can be redeemed and key categories of civil-military relations can be reconstructed via a critique of their ontological status – the manner in which they are constructed in relation to a plurality of contexts and realities. A key area of research in the future should be to investigate how these mechanisms can be made more effective and, significantly, how objective mechanisms can interface with subjective mechanisms to improve the overall levels of oversight over the armed forces.

Secondly, the exploration of the hitherto neglected realm of partnerships (the subjective component) in civil-military relations does not imply an abrogation of the utility of objective mechanisms in "traditional" civil-military relations theory. The primacy of the political and the importance of ensuring the subordination of the armed forces to elected civilian government continue within this expanded scope of civil-military relations. It is via a combination of both objective and subjective mechanisms, each developed in relation to the political and cultural peculiarities of the country concerned, that effective and context-specific civil-military relations can be developed.

At a practical level, a range of measures can be instituted to build capacity and mutual trust between the political and civilian élite and the command echelons of the armed forces. Active involvement of parliamentary representatives and non-military civilian experts in the defence policy process can contribute immensely to their understanding of both the nuances of the defence decision-making process and the peculiarities of military culture. Similarly, the exposure of the senior officer corps to the parliamentary process, the party political process, and the civilian budgeting process will sensitize them to the exigencies of political and civilian rule. Joint seminars, team-building exercises, active involvement by political and civilian representatives in the reservist formations of the armed forces, and joint visits to military installations are some of the mechanisms that can be instituted in this regard. It is important to stress that such partnerships are not equal partnerships, however, and take place within the hierarchy of authority provided for by either a democratic dispensation or, where a "traditional" liberal democratic system does not prevail, a situation in which the inviolable authority of the elected civilian authority is respected (as for instance in Uganda).

Thirdly, the scope of civil-military relations needs to be expanded to incorporate non-institutional actors and mechanisms into its orbit as well as a consideration of the role which police agencies, intelligence services, and, in some cases, private security companies may play in either ensuring or undermining civil-military relations. In the case of the former, the South African defence transition illustrates the critical role that can be played by organs of civil society in contributing to the shaping of the mission of the armed forces and ensuring their subordination to civil control. In the case of the latter it is instructive to note that the downsizing of armed forces in many developing countries (a product of both budgetary constraints and interlined donor agency/IMF injunctions) has led to a corresponding increase in the size and power of the police force and civilian intelligence agencies. Notwithstanding the emphasis on their civilianization, and although not equipped with the organizational and logistical ability to influence civil-military relations at a national level, they do possess the capacity to influence civil-military relations at a regional and, more particularly, a local level.

Fourthly, whilst it may not be possible to erect a integrated and overarching theoretical system or an axiomatic foundational basis which proves capable of explaining all civil-military relations scenarios, it will be possible to elucidate the central values of such a project. The normative dimension of civil-military relations theory needs to be stressed and bolstered, and this should provide a lodestar for all interventions in the civil-military debate in developing countries. The basis of this normative framework emphasizes the importance of democratic civil-military relations and stresses those universal moral values of transparency, accountability, and the primacy of elected government within this equation.

Fifthly, a new methodology is required which proves capable of both providing a radical critique of the assumptions of much of contemporary civil-military relations theory and constituting the basis for an ongoing and active intervention in the civil-military relations debate within the developing world. It is proposed here that theoretical revision can only be effected on the basis on an interdisciplinary approach that incorporates into its orbit both African and Western intellectual traditions as evident in such disciplines as sociology, political science, international relations, state theory, and the critical-reflective traditions developed in such schools of thought as the Frankfurt school, postmodernism, and elsewhere.

From threats to national interests: The roles of armed forces of the developing world

Almost all modern armed forces of the developed world, particularly during the post-Second World War period, have maintained that the primary role of a defence force is to protect the territorial integrity and sovereignty of the nation. This remains its central *raison d'être*, its right to existence. Yet is this an accurate reflection of what armed forces have been used for in the past, and the roles in which they are likely to be deployed in the future? It is not an accurate reflection of what modern armies, with few exceptions, have busied themselves with in the twentieth century, nor of the roles that the African armed forces have been expected to execute since their establishment.

Notwithstanding the crucial responsibility of the state to guarantee the security of its citizens, much of the justification for the retention of armed forces for utilization in their primary role concentrates on a narrow definition of the role which "threat" plays in modern interstate relations (such threats always being seen as that of a conventional external aggressor). What is rather required is a "paradigm shift" that allows for the creation of new concepts and theories which are capable of explaining the role and functions of armed forces in an increasingly complex and postmodern world. Thus, it has been precisely in the "non-traditional" military arenas, the secondary functions, that African armed forces have historically been deployed and are currently being deployed (such as in peace support operations, developmental tasks, police support, or regional security).

Two observations can be made in light of the above if one contrasts the actual use of African armed forces, both historically and presently, and the manner in which current African defence doctrine justifies the retention and design of our armed forces. The first is the extent to which the notion of a classic modernist defence force, configured to protect the country against an external conventional threat, continues to enjoy a disproportionate influence in the minds of the defence force planners and strategists. This appears to be the twin product of the dominance of certain concepts and categories in the minds of African defence strategists, and the historical influence of Western (largely twentieth-century) concepts on defence thinking (an influence that was also noted in the civil-military relations debate). Secondly, the preceding examples illustrate the extent to which African armed forces have been involved, both historically and currently, in the execution of a variety of secondary functions on a continuous and regular basis. What are the implications of this for the theoreticization of a more appropriate African defence architecture?

The answer to the strategic and intellectual challenges outlined above lie not in a reformulation of answers, but in a reconstruction of the questions that underpin much of the logic and methodology of defence thinking. Rather than positing an external threat (invariably the conventionally armed aggressor) as being the justification (and answer) for the question "what are armed forces used against?", it would be more appropriate to rephrase the question to read "what are armed forces for?". The answer to this question is less complex than it seems. It would be more appropriate to define armed forces as those policy instruments (be they landward, maritime, or airborne) which are placed at the disposal of the state to manage those crises of sufficient magnitude which other state departments, either collectively or individually, are not equipped to manage. They do this because of their unique features – their ability to project force, their superior organizational abilities, and their ability, if required, to manage judiciously the instruments of state violence. The nature of those tasks that the state may expect the armed forces to execute will be determined by the short- to medium-term environment within which a country is placed, based on continually changing political, developmental, and budgetary realities.

Notwithstanding the belief of most defence planners in the aphorism that "we design and budget for the primary function and we execute the secondary functions with the collateral utility derived from our primary force design", a real tension does appear to be developing between this perspective and the emerging realities of the secondary-function arena. This tension is reflected at two levels. Firstly, it is partially reflected in growing political and public pressure calling for the increased deployment of armed forces in their secondary roles – particularly when it concerns political and financial motivations for maintaining defence expenditure at its present levels. Secondly, African armed forces cannot, and with growing pressure to participate in the secondary-function arena will be less likely to, execute secondary functions on the basis of collateral utility. Most African armed forces have neither the budget, the equipment (in terms of inventory size and capabilities), nor the personnel to do so. A much more realistic assessment of the role which the secondary function plays in determining force design, equipment purchase, and training requirements needs to be made. This is already a process with which many modern armed forces struggle. The influence of Canada's and Denmark's participation in peace support operations on their respective force designs and the role of the UK's foreign policy requirements in determining the size and capabilities of British armed forces are examples.

Some suggestions with regard to a more precise "balancing" of primary and secondary functions in African force planning are as follows.

First, although forces will be maintained for preservation of territorial integrity and sovereignty, these will probably tend towards cheaper, lighter, and less technology-intensive forces with a strong emphasis on re-servist and part-time components. Certainly a more detailed appreciation needs to be made of the extent to which underexplored doctrines such as civilian-based defence and guerilla tactics could be utilized in national defence strategy (particularly in those post-independence countries that have emerged from a liberation struggle tradition).

Second, greater recognition needs to be afforded to the secondary functions within the context of defence policy and planning. Two important factors need to be considered in this regard.

- Involvement in secondary functions does not entail an abrogation of the responsibility of the state to provide for the preservation of territorial integrity and the protection of sovereignty. It simply entails executing this in as cost-effective a manner as possible and in such a way that the state does not lose the ability to execute the other tasks which the armed forces will be called on to perform in the short, medium, and long term.

- It is crucial to prioritize those secondary functions for which it will be necessary to budget and design. While for financial and practical reasons it is clearly impossible to consider all of them, it is clear that some secondary functions will have a direct impact on defence budgeting and force design configuration. These will include such activities as peace support operations, border security, support to the police service in the maintenance of law and order, and maritime protection.

Certain "task clusters" should either be avoided or only executed if the armed forces have the short-term capacity to do so. These include "task clusters" such as support to reconstruction and development programmes (as in the case of South Africa), specific foreign policy initiatives, disaster relief, and humanitarian assistance. Allowing a developing country, and a country oriented towards the judicious use of its scarce resources, to design its armed forces solely for their primary function appears to be a luxury that few developing countries can afford.

Lessons learned from African SST processes for countries in both the developed and the developing world

Although Africa is undergoing profound security transformation processes – a phenomenon underscored by the recent inauguration of the African Union and the institution of the New Partnership for Africa's Development – virtually all countries, either developed or developing, are facing unique SST challenges. Some of the key lessons learned from these processes include the following.

- The scope of the security sector in the twenty-first century is far broader than many people tend to assume. In addition to the existence of "traditional" security organs of state – defence forces, police, and intelligence agencies – it also includes paramilitary organizations, custodial services, presidential guards, and coastguards. Equally importantly, and this is something that cannot be factored out of the equation, many of these security organizations are often of a non-statutory nature (i.e. they possess no legal or constitutional basis). Typical examples in this regard include liberation armies (as was the case in Southern and East Africa), rebel groupings as disparate as Sierra Leone's Revolutionary United Front and Uganda's Lord's Resistance Army, organized people's militias (the *Kamajors* in Sierra Leone, for example), and the "Green Bombers" of Zimbabwe which function as President Mugabe's party political militia. During the process of SST all these entities need to be included in both the restructuring and the demobilization process.
- SST initiatives must be "home grown" and must reflect the peculiarities of the country concerned, its national and military cultural traditions, its force requirements, and its financial resources. Attempts to impose non-indigenous "models" on post-conflict societies (such as the current attempts by the USA to do so in both Iraq and Afghanistan) will create institutions lacking in legitimacy, culturally isolated from the governments they are supposed to serve, and limited in their ability to execute their mandates.
- SST is inseparable from the broader governance equation. Effective security sector governance must occur within the context of a scenario within which all government departments are appropriate to the country's needs, affordable in terms of the national budget, accountable to the duly elected authorities, and adequate in terms of their requirements.
- SST processes require dynamic, visionary, and charismatic leadership fully and firmly supported by government and the relevant political authorities. SST mounted for the sake of appeasing donors will result in a partial and unsatisfactory approach, and will invariably lead to the "ghettoization" of the process within the state itself.

Conclusion

The security sector reform debate is still in its embryonic stages. Considerable political, practical, conceptual, and strategic work still needs to be done on SST before a fully fleshed and sufficiently flexible SST approach can be developed – one that will be easily applicable to most situations. SST represents an ideal opportunity for both donors and recipient countries to begin with the serious task of reconstructing the battered security sector within many parts of the developing world – an architecture that has been used and abused by both colonizers and post-independence governments alike.[8]

Notes

1. Ogbemudia, S. O. 1997. "The coup syndrome: Plague of African governance?", in *Militaries, Democracies and Security in Sub-Saharan Africa*. Sub-Saharan Africa Security Project, Nigeria.
2. *Ibid*.
3. See Schiff, Rebecca L. 1995. "Civil-military relations reconsidered: A theory of concordance", *Armed Forces and Society*, Vol. 22, No. 1, p. 17.
4. *Ibid*.
5. See *ibid.*, p. 19.
6. These principles draw heavily on the principles that were used to guide the South African defence transformation process, especially its integration process, its white paper, and its defence review.
7. President Lincoln's message to the US Congress, 1 December 1862.
8. Along with a number of previously published articles, an earlier version of this chapter, with the title "African armed forces and the challenges of security sector reform", was published by the online *Journal of Security Sector Management*, Rocky Williams' Tribute Issue, Vol. 3, No. 2, March 2005, pp. 1–35. See www.jofssm.org/index.cfm.

4

Military forces' training for post-conflict peacebuilding operations

Fernando Isturiz

This chapter examines the particular training requirements posed by post-conflict peacebuilding scenarios for military forces operating under the auspices of international peace and security organizations.

The first part of the chapter illustrates how peacebuilding operations entail challenges and tasks that are only partially addressed by conventional warfare doctrine and training. While some skills are applicable in both cases, this study aims to identify others that are unique in peacebuilding scenarios and thus need specific training. The chapter finally summarizes the main training issues that post-conflict peacebuilding operations demand.

Post-conflict peacebuilding

A common understanding of the meaning of "post-conflict peacebuilding" is necessary in order to identify the role of the military in such operations. Role definition will state the specific tasks to be performed and the knowledge and skills to be acquired through education and training processes.

Both "post-conflict" and "peacebuilding" concepts, if ill defined, can be misleading in regard to the subsequent role of the military in the field. One can assume a "post-conflict" scenario implies that hostilities among former warring factions have come to an end, a cease-fire or peace agreement is in place and resumption of hostilities is unlikely, and major

74

armed warring factions have been disbanded or can be trusted in regard to their commitment to fulfil achieved cease-fire or peace agreements. "Peacebuilding" embraces all forms of international assistance to societies devastated by armed conflict, and the overall tasks to be carried out focus on political, social, and economic reconstruction efforts. These are embedded in the mandates of international or regional organizations, geared at the prevention of a relapse to conflict.

According to the *Report of the Panel on UN Peace Operations* (the Brahimi Report):

Peacebuilding is a term of more recent origin that, as used in the present report, defines activities undertaken on the far side of conflict to reassemble the foundations of peace and provide the tools for building on those foundations something that is more than just the absence of war. Thus, peacebuilding includes but is not limited to reintegrating former combatants into civilian society; strengthening the rule of law (for example through training and restructuring of local police, and judicial and penal reform); improving respect for human rights through the monitoring, education and investigation of past and existing abuses; providing technical assistance for democratic development (including electoral assistance and support for free media); and promoting conflict resolution and reconciliation techniques.[1]

Post-conflict situations, however, do not necessarily imply a completely peaceful atmosphere, since remnant non-demobilized or non-disarmed factions of wartime can still pose risks to external military forces. Moreover, peacebuilding undertakings may very well overlap with peacekeeping operations still in place, since the peacebuilding activities may start at very early stages of the peace process, making the dividing line between peacekeeping and peacebuilding scenarios not easy to draw. In Haiti, for instance, the UN mission (UNMIH) was mainly a military and police integrated mission, and its mandate included typical peacekeeping tasks such as the maintenance of a secure and stable environment, along with peacebuilding tasks such as assisting in the modernization of the local armed forces.[2] Moreover, various national contingents under the UN banner implemented projects to install and rebuild infrastructure along with their peacekeeping duties.[3]

The case of the second UN operation in Somalia (UNOSOM II) is even more interesting in regard with the overlapping of peacekeeping and peacebuilding tasks at the strategic level. While the main task of the UN military contingents was to take appropriate action to establish a secure environment for humanitarian assistance throughout Somalia, they also got involved in institution-building efforts, such as the establishment of the Somali police. This was tied into the military concept of UNOSOM II operations.[4]

The peacebuilding *atmosphere*, therefore, can be characterized as non-violent and cooperative. Although not completely free from risks, full-scale engagement of military forces should not be expected. Substantial variances in this atmosphere will certainly change the nature of the military involvement and tasks, and will be reflected in the military component's organization, equipment, and training.

The role of the military

In peace support operations other than peace enforcement, the main task of the military component is to assure a stable atmosphere in which substantial agreements and long-standing peace can be reached or maintained through diplomatic efforts and political processes. Within this framework, the military component's role will vary according to the overall security situation. As the *Guide to Peace Support Operations* notes:

Incipient cease-fire or peace agreements, uncontrolled former combatants' factions, defiant populations, severe humanitarian suffering, fragile governance and flimsy rule of law, may indicate that priority should be given to security issues. On the contrary, in a secure and stable scenario, military forces may shift their priorities to other tasks more related to political, social and economic developments.[5]

Troops (observers) may be armed or unarmed and their strength will be tailored according to the deterrence effect to be obtained. However, it is not through their firepower that the peace forces will deter eventual opposition, but through their status as representatives of the international community, provided the local factions and population acknowledge this status. But specifically, in a peacebuilding operation other tasks may come into the military field of action. According to the British armed forces' *Army Field Manual*, a post-conflict peacebuilding response group will mainly address political, social, and economic reconstruction issues, including *demobilization operations* (such as the controlled withdrawal, demobilization, and rehabilitation of belligerents), *military assistance* (such as supervising a transfer of power, reforming security forces, and developing or supporting civil infrastructure facilities), and *humanitarian relief operations* (such as relief for residents, refugees, or displaced persons).[6]

Employment of armed forces in political development, institution building, and economic rehabilitation, however, implies a sub-utilization of military resources. Armed forces are organized, equipped, and trained for combat. Troop-contributing countries to peacebuilding operations, therefore, may reasonably be inclined to support other organizations rather than the military to perform these tasks. But at the same time the military capabilities for self-sustained operations in remote environments, their logistical support means, and their readiness standards allow them to perform ancillary roles that will increase the peacebuilding response group capabilities. As the *Army Field Manual* also notes:

a crisis that is precipitated by several distinctive factors will require a response group that has a corresponding span of diverse capabilities, but for a multinational response group operating in a post-war zone, military awareness is essential. Acting individually or as a group, the response elements – the military component included – may have to address a broad spectrum of tasks, such as provide immediate humanitarian relief, resettle displaced populations, rehabilitate demobilized militias, restore essential services, establish an internal government, establish rule of law, restore the economy, rebuild the civilian infrastructure, reconcile opposed parties, investigate human rights issues, and organize elections.[7]

Accordingly, in post-conflict peacebuilding operations:
- besides security maintenance, all other post-conflict peacebuilding tasks do not fall into the nature of military operations
- the nature of the military role will vary substantially according to the overall security status
- the military involvement will become less relevant in direct proportion to the success of the peacebuilding process
- the military will not be the lead component in peacebuilding undertakings (although its role will be essential for the peace process)
- the military will have to adjust to perform tasks that may be characterized as subsidiary, secondary, and ancillary to their *raison d'être*.

The case of the UN mission in El Salvador (ONUSAL) is enlightening in this regard. From its establishment as a peacekeeping operation in July 1991, ONUSAL's strength was of 15 military observers. Once the peace agreement was signed in 1992, the military component grew to 380, with the main task of monitoring the peace agreement provisions. However, it also engaged in typical peacebuilding activities such as mine clearance. Following the culmination of the cease-fire process in December 1992, the military contingent was reduced. It was further reduced after May 1993 and again in December 1994, given the advance of the peace process. At that point the operation shifted from a peacekeeping to a peacebuilding concept, focusing on electoral and human rights issues. The main tasks of ONUSAL fell into the Human Rights Division and the Electoral Division, whose strength increased to 900 during the elections period. Although a downsized military contingent remained on the spot, it no longer had the relevance it had had in ONUSAL's initial stages, when the security status was the major concern and a *sine qua non* condition for the political, economic, and social reconstruction.

Training

National defence planning is essentially a matter of interest assessment and threat perceptions. Interests and threats induce defence policies and practical strategies and guide the armed forces' (along with other national resources) structure and training to implement them. Since not all perceived interests and threats can be addressed simultaneously with equal effectiveness, priorities are to be determined. Major interests and imminent threats will demand prior attention, and the structures and training to address them will receive prior financial allocation, deeper doctrine development, and more intensive training.

Although for most countries the role of external defence will remain as the main role of national armed forces, the changing nature of modern conflict has to be acknowledged. The challenges posed by civil wars and all types of intrastate conflict have to be addressed by armed forces as an additional role if defence policy-makers intend to prepare their military forces for current and future challenges. As Clausewitz observed, "every age has had its own kind of war, its own limiting conditions, and its own peculiar preconditions".[8] However, while militaries throughout the world will continue to reflect the societies they defend, the armed forces' traditional role of external defence seems no longer enough to address the modern conflict involvement needs, and additional roles – such as participation in the whole spectrum of peace support operations (PSO) – have to be incorporated into armed forces' doctrine, organization, and training.

It could be argued that there is no need for PSO training as long as the forces involved have high training standards for conventional warfare, since PSO are supposedly much easier to deal with than high-intensity combat. Troops appropriately trained to face worst-case scenarios in conventional warfare would be naturally endowed to deal with the easier case. Any military force organized, equipped, and trained for high-intensity combat should be able to enter a PSO scenario, even at very short notice, and adequately fulfil the mission requirements. Also, without specific training, troops entering peace operations scenarios would be ready to enforce, if needed, a Security Council mandate (robust means and conventional warfare skills). Should enforcement not be necessary, they could timely de-escalate and shift to less complicated tasks. Lieutenant-General Kinzer, former UNMIH force commander, argues:

My experience in Haiti reaffirmed my belief that combat trained soldiers, given a focused objective, time and resources to prepare, and led by adaptive and mentally agile leaders at all levels, will perform superbly as peacekeepers. The mission in Haiti clearly demonstrated that if the right conditions are created and sustained by the military component – and the military component is able to synchronize its actions with the international, diplomatic, economic, informational and humanitarian components – success is achievable. Our experience in Haiti has reinforced my belief that preparing for war must be the priority for any Army. The key is to understand the complexities of the peace operation environment you are facing and then adapt your war fighting skills to meet them.[9]

Unfortunately, the Brahimi Report does not address this issue. It rather focuses on the opposite situation in which UN military contingents are not robust enough to perform the mandate's duties. As the report argues:

Once deployed, United Nations peacekeepers must be able to carry out their mandates professionally and successfully and be capable of defending themselves, other mission components and the mission's mandate, with robust rules of engagement, against those who renege on their commitments to a peace accord or otherwise seek to undermine it by violence.[10]

It is difficult to disagree with this idea. Modern warfare demands high training standards and deep technological knowledge. Peace support operations, on the other hand, mainly demand common sense, reasonable organization and discipline standards, and low technological knowledge. Appropriate training, however, will provide troops with a full understanding of the PSO concept, will enhance awareness regarding the particular characteristics, challenges, and risks of PSO, and will allow commanders and junior ranks at all levels to have a more confident approach. A perhaps more realistic assessment is presented by Sam Tangredi, who argues that:

Future conflicts – particularly those within failed states – will present little opportunity for firepower-intensive warfare. There will be no fronts or rear areas, and in some cases no clearly identifiable enemy force. Rather, there will be an overall atmosphere of chaos in which the primary mission of military forces will be to establish order and quell violence in the most humane way possible. Often referred to as a police function, establishment of order in a chaotic situation without a functioning government or court system is more similar to anti-guerrilla operations or wartime occupation duty than policing. But obviously the rules of engagement and the military skills required are different than those of force-on-force combat.[11]

Conventional warfare military training is the basis for PSO training. However, PSO pose particular conduct difficulties and demand unique performance skills. The basic PSO concepts of consent of the parties, impartiality, and limited use of force do not exist in the conventional warfare training syllabus. Accordingly, they require a particular conceptual approach and imply a different training process. These difficulties have been often underestimated and therefore not always appropriately addressed by training. Training for post-conflict peacebuilding should thus focus on both the approach and the skills of the military for this particular kind of operations. In this context, training should address the following issues, unique to the PSO context: troop attitude; use of force; "enemy" perception; exit strategies; the role of civilians; key decision-making; command and control; media scrutiny; and the role of technology. All these will be discussed in more detail in the sections below.

Attitude

Troops' attitude in peace operations spells restraint. The involvement of international or regional organizations in intrastate conflicts – even at stages of advanced peace processes – entails that, to a certain degree, the host/target state relinquishes its sovereignty. If that involvement includes military forces (carrying weapons, wearing foreign uniforms and symbols, raising a distinctive flag, restraining local population movements through roadblocks and checkpoints) the infringement on sovereignty is even more significant. An aggressive, irritating, or narrow-minded attitude only destabilizes the operational environment. However, the dividing line between restraint and cowardice, energy and arrogance, will be always very difficult to draw, particularly among the lower ranks. While high-intensity combat training promotes aggressiveness, an attitude of restraint demands a de-escalation training process based on a comprehensive understanding of the PSO concept and mechanisms, and broad-minded decision-making aimed at demonstrating resolve without being unnecessarily provocative. According to the US Army's *Joint Task Force Commander's Handbook for Peace Operations*, "it is important to remember that well-intended actions can be especially dangerous in peace operations, where they can threaten impartiality as well as undermine long-term programs. In many cases, inaction will be better than action."[12] This represents a meaningful difference to the conventional warfare attitude, according to which there is no such thing as "well-intended actions". Actions are doctrinally and tactically assessed and, at junior levels of command, undertaken in disregard of their intention.

Use of force

While conventional war-fighting forces are trained to destroy targets as they appear, in PSO the use of force is regulated by rules of engagement

(ROE). ROE describe, sometimes very restrictively, the circumstances that allow force to be used and the progression with which it can be used. Simply put, they specify "when, where, against whom, and how force can be used". However, nothing is as alien to military forces' conventional warfare employment as the concept of rules of engagement. Restrictions in the use of force distort the very nature of any armed force. In conventional warfare maximum use of the available force leads to more rapid achievement of operational objectives. It is a fundamental component of operational initiative, increases cost-effectiveness and force protection, and reduces the probability of casualties. Thus, use of force principles in PSO requires specific training in ROE at both the conceptual and the practical level. As Liu notes:

> The nonviolent nature of these [UN peacekeeping] operations is at the same time their most important and least understood characteristic. It is the characteristic that makes peacekeeping forces acceptable both to the governments and parties engaged in conflict, and to the governments that contribute the troops. The principle of nonviolence sets peacekeeping forces above the conflict they are dealing with. Violation of the principle almost invariably leads to the peacekeepers becoming part of the conflict and therefore part of the problem. When force may be used is perhaps the most difficult decision that peacekeepers on the spot can be faced with. Although use of force requires most careful consideration, the urgency of the situation demands immediate decisions.[13]

Enemy

The absence of a clear enemy in PSO affects the direction of efforts and measurement of success. The enemy's capabilities and vulnerabilities are essential to military planning procedures, and lack of an enemy will make it difficult to concentrate efforts in a defined direction. Success – of utmost importance for morale of field-deployed military forces – is often measured through damage inflicted on the enemy. Peacebuilding troop contingents should be trained to expect measurement of success to be elusive, blurred, and appearing in political rather than in military achievements.

Information gathering and intelligence, although essential for planning and force protection, will be severely prejudiced by political constraints in a host country. The concept of intelligence is linked to conventional warfare operations, and it will raise understandable sensitivity and distrust in a PSO environment. Collecting information will be an intellectual or practical, not aggressive, activity when the information emanates from individuals, publications, photographs, films, media, or any other source of a public nature available not only for military purposes. This type of information-collecting activity will not need to overcome local resistance or bend an adverse will to protect concealed data from being discovered. But it will only partially meet the PSO force's intelligence requirements. There will be other intelligence needs that imply collecting information usually unavailable to the public; data that the parties to a conflict deliberately conceal and protect. In this context, security and counterintelligence systems will have to be introduced.

The Brahimi Report underlined the need to have more effective collection and assessment of information at UN headquarters, and the sensitivities that information-gathering initiatives by the Secretary-General might raise. Although referred to the UN headquarters strategic level, these considerations are also applicable in the field.[14]

Since PSO entail the consensual deployment of military contingents within the sovereign territory of the parties concerned, information gathering and intelligence production will face particular challenges. While commanders in the field are not allowed to carry out information gathering beyond a given mandate's provisions, very few will refrain from doing so if their soldiers' lives depend on it, opting for the risk of facing an embarrassing political problem rather than having their soldiers killed or contemptuously taken as hostages by rebel factions.

The frequently used euphemism of *information* does not mitigate the real need for timely intelligence. Training for PSO should provide commanders at all levels with appropriate awareness of the difficulties of this most sensitive issue, as well as recommendations to overcome them.

End state

The end state in post-conflict peacebuilding will be ambiguous by default and will need continuous refinement throughout the operation. The very strong sense of achievement that is common to conventional warfare will be absent in these operations. Objectives will be defined in broad political terms that are difficult to grasp from a military perspective. The end-state setting is determinant both for long-term operational planning and for troop morale, since personnel rotations and sustained logistical support cannot be improvised. Only a very few developed countries and NATO – as an international security organization – have a rapid-deployment capability of military forces. For most UN troop-contributing developing countries the organization and deployment of national contingents in peace operations demand a huge effort, and for their logistical support they have to rely on the United Nations or on leading countries' capabilities. Even organizations such as the Standby High Readiness Brigade (SHIRBRIG), mainly composed by developed countries, face serious unresolved problems in their field logistical support. A contingent rotation implies a long administrative domestic process that will include

– among other provisions – a unit's appointment for a UN mission, its reorganization or reinforcement (for instance with staff officers and senior NCOs with proficiency in the mission's working language), and the unit's assembly, training in PKO, and deployment, often overseas and for at least a four-month tour. Also, the political decision-making process and budgeting issues require long-term anticipation. Commanders at all levels may have to develop their own criteria to define mission success and will have to be prepared, at the same time, both to exercise patience and to take action to overcome "mission-creep" feelings.

The mission's senior military officer will work on intimate cooperation with – and subordination to – the SRSG, ensuring that the SRSG's political goals are translated correctly into military operational objectives. This political-military interface should initially be developed by the UNDPKO, but on a day-by-day basis the reformulation of these objectives will fall into the senior military officer's area of assessment and responsibility.

Civilians

Civilian populations often represent an obstacle to conventional warfare operations. Refugees and displaced persons may saturate or block roads, prejudicing troop movements. Built-up areas should be avoided unless they have clear military interest, and humanitarian relief is provided by specialized organizations. In post-conflict peacebuilding, on the other hand, the civilian population operations are the focal point of the mission and their welfare is the ultimate operational target. All military tasks, including security issues, are to be addressed through this lens. The military component will have to be prepared to relinquish its own resources, equipment, and supplies if required by severe humanitarian needs. As Kenneth F. McKenzie Jr argues:

if innocent civilians are starving, left exposed to the elements, or attacked in any one of a number of ways available to a modern state, their condition will become of intense interest to commanders in the field. Commanders will have to take their well-being into account in their operational plans and be prepared to allocate scarce assets to care for them. Anyone who asserts that this will not become a competing priority with ongoing military operations is unfamiliar with the power and political sophistication of non-governmental organizations and the pressures exerted by the CNN effect.[15]

Protracted internal conflicts may create a vacuum of leadership, institutional weakness, and an absence of law and order. Further, as *A Guide to Peace Support Operations* notes:

In a host state divided by inter-communal conflict, the civilian population may have been victims of every kind of misfortune including dislocation, starvation, and the physical dangers of existing in a war zone. Very often this trauma will cause profound social changes that challenge long-established hierarchies and alter ethnic distribution, power structures, and clan values. In these turbulent circumstances, populations may be manipulated, very often in a ruthless manner by warlords or even the host government, armed forces, and officials.[16]

Societies emerging from anarchy to post-conflict scenarios will naturally turn to the first external organization that seems capable of restoring a sense of guidance, institutional guarantees, and law enforcement capabilities. A military presence under international auspices should be able to meet these expectations and generate strong public confidence and respect. On the other hand, the military component of a peacebuilding force will have to adjust its operations to a strict code of conduct, since moral or discipline offences will have a negative impact directly proportionate to the high public expectations that its presence may have generated. Again, the peacebuilding force's moral behaviour and discipline are important assets for success. Moreover, training in human rights is indispensable, not only for monitoring and repressing local violations, but also to assure the peacebuilding force's own compliance with human rights principles.

This also raises the question of the military involvement in policing responsibilities. While many states routinely use their military forces as gendarmerie or a national police force, many other states have been historically reluctant to involve the military in maintaining domestic order. Anyhow, police and law enforcement duties do not fall within the nature of military operations. Armed forces are not organized, equipped, or trained – nor predisposed – to perform law enforcement duties. However, UN PSO lessons-learned studies show that the deployment of civilian police forces normally takes much longer than the deployment of military contingents.[17] The question of how to address police issues in early stages of PSO, when military forces but not police forces are already in the mission, remains unanswered.

Key decisions

In conventional warfare key decisions are adopted at the highest possible level of command. Planning and orders are issued so as to leave to subordinate levels of command as little assessment trouble as possible. The lower the level of a given command, the less time and information it receives. PSO, however, imply deployment of scarce troops in large territories. This will lead to "atomization" – junior leaders will perform their duties far from the guidance and supervision of their senior leaders. Decisions made by junior leaders – whose correct assessment and common sense cannot be taken for granted – may at a very local level have disproportionate strategic and political consequences. As US Army General Wesley Clark, former NATO commander in Bosnia, experienced:

> The way I saw it, each action and decision involved four elements: the political, the strategic, the operational, and the tactical. Actions that were relatively small could have potentially large political impact, and therefore affect the course of an entire campaign. Lower-level units had to pay close attention to the political overtones of seemingly insignificant actions.[18]

Also, compared to conventional warfare, decisions in PSO at all levels will be strongly influenced by more complex legal considerations. Agreements between international organizations and troop-contributing countries, host country's legislation, and international law will all have to be taken into account. Thus, besides providing junior leaders and soldiers with awareness of the eventual tactical and legal consequences of their decisions, training has to equip commanders at all levels, in addition to the corresponding staff legal advice, with a broad span of legal troubleshooting tools.

Command and control

The military contingents of peacebuilding operations will most likely be multinational. Multinational command and control poses particular challenges to military leadership at all levels, as each troop-contributing country will have different interests for joining the coalition and perhaps different military doctrinal approaches for their forces' employment and operations. They may have subtly different agendas, although completely rational for their own purposes. The cement of keeping national contingents assembled will be clear common goals for the multinational force. National command links will need to be carefully managed so as not to inhibit operational effectiveness. Cultural differences will also have to be taken into account, and national contingent commanders will have to commit themselves to striving towards common objectives. Otherwise, cohesion may be compromised by hazy objectives and undefined success. Decentralized command and control will also demand assuming the risks inherent in delegating initiatives.

Operations under the auspices of international organizations, such as the United Nations, pose an additional particularity to command and control relations. The United Nations exercises the Secretary-General's (UNSG) political executive authority and guidance in the field through officials appointed by the Security Council, normally in the person of a special representative of the Secretary-General (SRSG). Invested with indisputable and legitimate representation, any given SRSG will exercise a direct and close overall supervision of military operations in fulfilment of the Security Council's mandate and the intent of the Secretary-General. It will not be uncommon for political decisions to take precedence over military requirements. The SRSG will also administer (or advise the UNSG in the administration of) the operational resources' allocation (as established by the General Assembly) through the UN financial system both in the field and in UNHQ. This implies a very different approach to command and control issues than could be expected in a strictly national chain of command with clear national interests at stake, common identified goals to be achieved, and a culturally identified civil-military leadership. The military leadership of multinational forces will have to be aware of the UN's financial constraints, logistical support mechanisms, procurement processes, and expenditure management, all of them comprehensively described in the Brahimi Report.[19] The UN international leadership and staff may not be experienced regarding military operational needs and may be pressed to balance budget provisions in two (not always coincidental) directions by the UN's own financial bureaucratic system and the field necessities – the military operational needs among others. The military, on the other side, should not expect their demands to be satisfied as quickly as in a conventional warfare scenario in which political success – and consequently the resource allocation to achieve it – is much more closely linked to the military operations' successful development. The presence of the political authority – the SRSG – on the spot will also pose a substantive difference in the process of military decisions compared to the relative autonomy that may be exercised in the command and control of operations abroad, far from the direct surveillance of national political leadership. Mission success, accordingly, will be closely linked to the military leadership's ability to harmonize interests and accommodate different perceptions in a manner that helps unity of efforts.

Media scrutiny

In conventional warfare operations freedom of movement of media representatives may be restricted due to security constraints and an operation's secrecy needs. In PSO the media will not only be allowed free movement, but media coverage is also necessary for the domestic constituency's support of peacebuilding operations in troop-contributing countries. The main concern regarding the media is that it may blow minor tactical events out of proportion to strategic and political exposure.

While in PSO censorship is unthinkable, the media's free access gives the news an immediacy that even anticipates the flow of information up and down the chain of command. Training will have to be provided in order to inculcate awareness of the political and strategic consequences of troop actions under close media scrutiny.[20]

Technology

PSO use low-sophistication technology. The US Army Training and Leader Development Panel notes that:

Stability operations may explode into firefights without warning, requiring Army forces to interact with local populations and displaced persons whilst in the midst of decisive operations. The dominance of Army forces in high-intensity, open maneuver compels adversaries to attack asymmetrically, exploiting physical and mental vulnerabilities. At the same time, Army forces must retain the ability to close with and destroy the well-equipped and motivated enemy who refuses to yield vital terrain and facilities, with each operation being conducted under the close scrutiny of the media. Technology will not provide convenient solutions to these challenges.[21]

Accordingly, reliance on technological means will yield to intensive use of manpower, and high exposure of personnel will be normal. All military personnel will have to be trained to rely on their common sense, organization, and discipline, rather than on high-technology weaponry.

Concluding remarks

As former UN Secretary-General Dag Hammarskjøld once noted, "Peacekeeping is not a job for soldiers but only soldiers can do it." Peacebuilding is not a job for soldiers either. Moreover, there are many international organizations and agencies (the OCHA, UNHCR, UNICEF, FAO, WFP, WHO, and UNDP on the UN side), NGOs (the ICRC, CARE, Save the Children, Médecins Sans Frontières), and even private companies that are much better qualified than the military to undertake peacebuilding tasks. This may lead to:
- nations' reluctance to provide troops for peacebuilding operations
- a sense, within the deployed forces, of performing unwanted tasks
- a tendency to underestimate the difficulties of PSO and, consequently, to assign low priority, if any, to PSO training.

Another matter of concern for many armed forces may be the fear that PSO engagement will degrade high-intensity combat training standards. In fact, the particular pace of PSO activities may prejudice certain combat skills acquired through constant, intensive, and costly training, and will demand upgrading upon repatriation of PSO forces. On the other hand, PSO experience will provide unique opportunities for developing other skills applicable to conventional warfare. Post-conflict peacebuilding situations are not fictitious. They pose real problems involving real people. They provide a scenario in which military leadership will be tested, since decisions will sometimes be made under strong pressure, uncertainty, blurred military objectives, media scrutiny, and conditional cohesion among coalition partners.

Many developing countries' armed forces are used to undertake humanitarian relief tasks, playing a support role to civil authorities and providing resources that may not be readily available in the civil sector. In cases of natural disasters and complex domestic emergencies many national administrations call on the military for humanitarian aid, and the military is ready to demonstrate an institutional commitment to take care of people. On the other hand, developed societies have the necessary civilian agencies to deal with these issues. The military is exclusively seen as the country's main defence resource and as a "back-up" for the nation's foreign policy. Paradoxically, these armed forces might need more training for post-conflict peacebuilding than those of developing countries already used to undertaking emergency relief tasks due to their own domestic needs.

While some PSO troop-contributing countries have realized these challenges a very long time ago – and accordingly have given PSO training high standing and priority – other countries (the USA for instance) seem to be reluctant to adopt the training process that the new strategic environment demands. According to US Army research reports:

Today's operational environment is not new. It has evolved since 1989 with the fall of the Iron Curtain and breakup of the Warsaw Pact. The Army has recognized for a decade the need to change to remain relevant in the strategic environment. Left to its own devices, the Army has been slow to adapt. Today, it continues to fall behind in adapting training and leader development programs. The operational environment has changed faster than the Army has adapted its training and leader development programs. Consequently, these programs must change quickly to become relevant.[22]

These US Army considerations are applicable to any peacebuilding troop-contributing nation. Some nations have acknowledged this need to change a long time ago, and have therefore implemented the necessary training programmes.

No armed force desires to turn into a professional PSO force, and nations' peace operations troop contribution sometimes seems to be more an issue of international exposure and domestic political interest than serious military business. However, those populations involved in protracted internal conflicts, enduring overwhelming humanitarian suffering, and facing a hopeless future for themselves and their offspring deserve much more than amateur peacekeepers. Balanced training for post-conflict peacebuilding can and should meet both goals.

Notes

1. United Nations. 2000. *Report of the Panel on United Nations Peace Operations*, H/55/305–S/2000/809, 21 August. New York: United Nations, para. 13.
2. See UNMIH at www.un.org/Dpts/dpko/dpko/co-mission/unmih.htm.
3. See Kumar, Chetan. 2001. "Peacebuilding in Haiti", in Elizabeth M. Cousens, Chetan Kumar, and Karin Wermester (eds) *Peacebuilding as Politics: Cultivating Peace in Fragile Societies*. Boulder, CO: Lynne Rienner Publishers, p. 21.
4. See Jan, Ameen. 2001. "Somalia: Building sovereignty or restoring peace?", in Elizabeth M. Cousens, Chetan Kumar, and Karin Wermester (eds) *Peacebuilding as Politics: Cultivating Peace in Fragile Societies*. Boulder, CO: Lynne Rienner Publishers, p. 68.
5. Watson, Thomas J. Jr. 1996. *A Guide to Peace Support Operations*. Providence, RI: Institute for International Studies, Brown University.
6. British Army. 1994. *Wider Peacekeeping*, Army Field Manual Vol. 5, Operations Other Than War, Part 2, Army Code 71359(A). United Kingdom.
7. *Ibid.*, pp. 15–17.
8. Von Clausewitz, Carl. 1976. *On War*, edited and translated by Michael Howard and Peter Paret. Princeton, NJ: Princeton University Press, p. 593.
9. Kinzer, Lieutenant-General J. W. 1997. *Joint Task Force Commander's Handbook for Peace Operations*. Fort Monroe, VA: Joint Warfighting Center, p. i. The author's own understanding is based on four years' experience as director of the Argentine PKO Training Center (CAECOPAZ). The author not only repeatedly had the opportunity of discussing this issue with senior military officers of the central powers (who shared Lieutenant-General Kinzer's approach), but also personally observed the UK armed forces' training for PKO (Armed Forces Combined Training Centre, Warminster, UK), carried out as conventional warfare training with slight PKO training in issues such as rules of engagement, use of interpreters, etc.
10. See the summary of key recommendations on peacekeeping doctrine and strategy in *Report of the Panel on United Nations Peace Operations*, note 1 above, Chapter II, para. 55.
11. Tangredi, Sam J. 2000. "All Possible Wars? Toward a Consensus View of the Future Security Environment", McNair Paper 63. Washington, DC: Institute for National Strategic Studies, National Defense University.
12. Kinzer, note 9 above, pp. 1–7.
13. Liu, F. T. 1992. "United Nations Peacekeeping and the Use of Force", International Peace Academy Occasional Paper Series. New York: International Peace Academy, p. 7.
14. *Report of the Panel on United Nations Peace Operations*, note 1 above, Chapter I, para. 6 and Chapter II, para. 32.
15. McKenzie, Kenneth F. Jr. 2001. "The Revenge of the Melians: Asymmetric Threats and the Next QDR", McNair Paper 62. Washington, DC: Institute for National Strategic Studies, National Defense University, p. 40.

16. Watson, note 5 above, p. 18.

17. Ong, Kelvin. 2000. "Policing the peace: Towards a workable paradigm", paper presented at a conference of the International Peace Academy in partnership with Jane's Conferences, New York, 2–3 November. See www.ipacademy.org/reports.

18. Clark, General Wesley. 2001. *Waging Modern War*. New York: Public Affairs Publications, p. 82.

19. *Report of the Panel on United Nations Peace Operations*, note 1 above, Chapter III, paras 151–168.

20. This refers to the consequences, effects, or results of having very little space in which mistakes will remain unnoticed, the political top-down, media-driven focus, and the constraints of having the whole world as a live battlefield spectator.

21. Army Training and Leader Development Panel. 2001. *Officer Study, Report to the Army*. US Army, available at www.army.mil/features/ATLD/report.pdf, sections OS-6 and OS-13.

22. *Ibid.*

Part II

Experiences from Europe: Macedonia, Bosnia, Russia, Georgia, and Northern Ireland

5

Ethnic-military relations in Macedonia*

Biljana Vankovska

The paradigm of civil-military relations, and particularly democratic control of the armed forces, has been one of the focal points of the democratization agenda in many post-totalitarian and post-communist countries. Still, there is an obvious void in building a consistent theory of civil-military relations in transitional societies. The Western theories are being rapidly challenged by global developments, and they are not always useful for countries in transition to democratic governance. The starting premise of this chapter is that the paradigm of military-society relations provides a wider framework for an analysis of the interplay between politics, security structures, and society. In transitional societies the democratization process is often pushed aside by grave identity problems, intrastate conflicts, and state- and nation-building processes. Hence the need arises to determine very carefully the priorities in donor community policies of promoting good governance in the security sector.

The chapter spells out the dilemma of what matters more in a transitional society: civil-military relations or ethnic-military relations. The former are concerned with the relationship between the military and politics, and the latter with ethnically tailored and balanced relationships between ethnic groups within security sector structures. How does one reconcile the requirements for professionalism and merit with ethnically defined criteria when shaping security forces? This only mirrors the challenges of building liberal democracies in divided societies.

The Macedonian case study, the focus of this chapter, elucidates the aforementioned problems as it combines the problems of historical lega-

---

* *The author uses the term "Macedonia" throughout this text. The term "Former Yugoslav Republic of Macedonia" has been adopted by the United Nations.*

cies, hardships of transition under trauma and conflict, and also the challenges of post-conflict peacebuilding and security sector reform (SSR). Having being born out of an ethnically mixed and conflictual parent society, today's Macedonia exists somewhere between its past (the former Yugoslav experience) and the future. Not genuine democracy building, but healing the wounds of the 2001 armed conflict is prioritized; and, clearly, ethnic-military relations weigh heavier than the civil-military relations.

Theory of civil-military relations in transitional societies: If any?

Civil-military relations are a never-ending story and an enduring subject of interest for the theory and practice of democracy. Throughout history numerous philosophers, intellectuals, and policy-makers have been concerned with the crucial question of "who guards the guards?" – a question that was raised centuries ago by Juvenal.[1] The simplest answer, which has become an intrinsic democratic principle, is that democratically elected civilian politicians have supreme decision-making power, while the military obey and execute orders. Understandably, this "basket" is usually loaded with various models, mostly dependent on issues such as a country's historical traditions, political constellation, economic capabilities, security perceptions, or societal configuration.

Interestingly, the age-old problem of civil-military relations has been given a theoretical framework as late as in the aftermath of the Second World War. At least in the Western developed democracies, since then the theoretical deliberations and practical solutions have been more or less wavering between two "poles" of objective and subjective control of the armed forces formulated by Huntington and Janowitz.[2] Soon the focus of research moved to the civil-military developments in the developing (i.e. third world) countries, and recently to so-called post-communist countries. However, the recipes and suggested solutions have never gone beyond the "classical" theories of objective and subjective control. Moreover, the situation in the well-established democracies was neglected and out of the scope of any deeper theoretical examinations until the end of the Cold War: the major questions were seen as resolved and the practice as more or less satisfactory. Thus the research focus has been limited to details related to some professional and sociological aspects of the military's internal "life". This rather disdainful attitude neglects the fact that civil-military relations are a never-ending story, and the contours continue to change even in developed democracies.

The end of the Cold War urged reconsideration of civil-military "philosophy" in the light of the new international security environment and, accordingly, of the new military missions. Again, the theoretical mainstream comes from the West and is self-centred, i.e. takes into consideration mainly the challenges for political-military relationships in the countries belonging to the Western security community. It seems that the major concern is the expected shift of classical military missions – from combat and deterrence towards so-called military humanitarianism, peace support operations, and the war against terrorism.

However, in regard to the examination of these major developments in the sphere of civil-military relations in the Western hemisphere, there is understandable reluctance among Western scholars and policy-makers. The last decade of the twentieth century brought to the fore two allegedly opposite tendencies in the military/security realm, i.e. internationalization and privatization of security.

The former is related to the emergence of supranational international organizations (such as NATO) with armed forces at their disposal. These organizations are often granted new roles, and are expected to act as conflict managers and accordingly define the concrete military missions and operations in which they deploy – to the degree that they decide on the use of force in international relations.[3] At the same time, the internationalization of armed forces is not accompanied by internationalization of democracy. There are no internationally elected democratic bodies that would establish efficient oversight and management of such multilateral forces. Thus the democratic mechanisms and principles valid for nationally focused civil-military relationships are not applicable to this new phenomenon. The EU could possibly serve such a role through its democratically elected parliament. Yet it has not been granted the necessary competencies by its member states, which are reluctant to share their sovereign powers with international institutions. NATO is even less representative, as members of its political bodies are not directly elected but appointed by member governments. This seems to be a challenge that has not yet been addressed by the classical (democratic) theory of civil-military relations.

The second problem is related to the post-Cold War phenomenon of outsourcing military expertise. As a consequence of the process of force reductions of Cold War armies, a market of redundant military expertise and weaponry appeared on the international arena. Usually, retired or dismissed military professionals offer their services to their own and other governments. The privatization of security and the role of the international private security actors (such as MPRI, Executive Outcomes, or Sandline International)[4] have opened a range of problems related to their missions, democratic accountability, and transparency. This is the second major challenge for the academic and political debates in the Western democracies, which appear to be the countries of origin of such private firms.

Having ignored the problems in their own backyards, it seems that advocacy and promotion of democratic control of armed forces, or better SSR, has become a priority task of some circles within the Western security community. However, after a decade-long constant process of transforming the democratic control of armed forces into a universal international norm, there is an obvious lack of both theoretical accomplishments and practical achievements. The roots of the problem are to be found in the fact that the question concerning the role of the military in the democratization process has never been appropriately addressed. On the one hand, the governments of the countries in transition, which are merely obsessed by joining the "NATO club", have been ready to play double-cross games – one for the domestic public, and another for the "international community". At the same time, the West has been delighted by the opportunity to develop its "democratization business" in recently closed societies, and especially in the domain previously covered by much secrecy.

A further paradox marks the Western policy in these countries: there have been numerous examples of contradicting and even conflicting endeavours undertaken by the same governments or international organizations. What has been done in terms of conflict management endeavours has provoked opposite effects to the efforts to promote democratic principles and good governance.[5] In other words, "peace business" has not been in accordance with "democratization business". Analysis of the international assistance programmes in the countries of south-eastern Europe (i.e. the focal point of all these efforts in the last 10 years) easily shows that civil-military relations were never put in a holistic perspective and have never been defined as equally important for both peacebuilding and democracy-building processes.

From the perspective of those countries that are the subjects of these transformations, it seems they are more concerned with their identity problems and how to catch up with the developed part of the world than with building self-awareness of the real difficulties and searching for solutions to existing security sector problems. On the other hand, there is also a lack of expertise due to the communist legacy of closeness and conspiracy over everything concerning national security. Even when there is some expertise on security matters, prevailing self-censorship prevents any critical thinking. Thus on the surface it seems as if there is a common agreement on what exactly civil-military relations in democracy (or better, in democratizing countries) should look like – but Western scholars seem to lack new ideas, while their "Eastern" colleagues find it easier to adopt Huntington's idea of increased professionalization of the armed forces than to criticize the state of affairs in their countries.

Interestingly, exactly the ruling political and military élites prefer "Huntingtonianism" – i.e. his idea of "objective control" that implies more space for professionalism of the military. The problem is not so much in the concept but rather in the various ways of its understanding and interpretation. Under the disguise of "professionalization" the military usually claim and receive a privileged position *vis-à-vis* the society's scarce resources. On the other hand, authoritative political élites pursue a policy of politicization in an alleged process of promoting the most capable cadres. In societies driven by intrastate conflicts the policy of politicization is *de facto* an ethnic policy that promotes only members of the (usually major) ethnic group. Such policies have nothing to do with instilling democratic control over armed forces. In sum, there is still no consistent theory of civil-military relations applicable to the post-communist countries. In an endeavour that one could characterize as "going back to the future", the majority of the countries in transition have been looking back to the historically already proven and workable recipes and solutions originating in the Western democracies. These endeavours have been overwhelmingly supported by Western politicians and practitioners.

In addition to certain progress achieved during the 10 years of post-Cold War transition, there are still many glitches and problems. By selling out typically Western models to countries with hidden or overt intrastate conflict potentials, a crucial contradiction was exported to politically immature and socially explosive societies: Western models of civil-military relations only provoked many dilemmas in ethnic-centred states that are fraught with deep identity problems and are in the midst of nation-building processes.

The role of ethnicity and military in the process of state building in the Yugoslav successor states

The interplay between ethnicity and the military in Yugoslavia's dissolution, as well as in the Yugoslav successor states, represents an illustrative example of one of the most neglected aspects of the theory and practice of civil-military relations. The basic premise is that the question of civil-military reforms has not (only) been a problem of the post-communist transition, but rather a matter of peace and/or war in each of these countries and in the region as a whole.

With an extremely complex ethnic mix in a relatively small territory, in many respects former Yugoslavia was a unique case in Europe. For many years it was also seen as an example *par excellence* in terms of its policy and experience of multi-ethnic representation in the Yugoslav People's Army (YPA). It looked as if the Yugoslav leadership had been aware of the significance of ethnic-military relations. The measures undertaken in order to provide balanced ethnic representation and equality included several endeavours, such as an equal language policy within the armed forces at least at declaratory level, and a quota system ("national key"), especially among the top brass. The final stage of Yugoslavia's dissolution manifested a clear failure of the tailor-made policy of the ethnic composition of the YPA. On the contrary, the opposite attitude was *de facto* stimulated among young military cadres: while educated in the spirit of "Yugoslavness", it was easier for many of them to be promoted due to their ethnic origin than due to professionalism and merits.

Many external observers were astonished to see the bloody outcome of the state's dissolution, in which the YPA took an active part. The focal issue, however, was whether ethnic conflict shaped civil-military relations in the collapsing Yugoslavia (and consequently in the emerging successor states) or *vice versa*? One of the lessons learnt can be drawn in the following (although not very original) way: due to the conflict potential of the country, unavoidably the military had to become a part of the conflict structure. All rhetoric and symbolism surrounding the YPA, particularly the claim that it was a supranational and all-Yugoslav institution, could not have dismantled the conflict potential whose roots had been deeply embedded in the society.

The transition towards democracy on the territory of former Yugoslavia has been dramatic and turbulent since its onset. Furthermore, the basic democratic principles and rhetoric were misused by the hard-liners in all national camps in order to promote the new nation-states (or better, ethnically exclusionist "democracies"). In the nationalist agendas the military was, as a rule, given a priority role, assuming that the military is an indispensable institution for the new states as well as the personification of patriotism – or better, ethno-nationalism. The federal military that should have been the only legitimate one had already lost its credibility and reliability. The YPA leadership not only did not dare to "save" the country from collapse with a military coup, but it also failed in the role of a peacekeeper in the zones of tension. Finally, the unavoidable breakdown of the state coincided with a military split along ethnic lines.

Civil-military reforms in all transitional societies have been dependent on many internal and external factors, which differed from country to country. In the case of the Yugoslav successor states the major factor of the transitional civil-military relations has been war/conflict. The problem is even subtler due to the common perception of the Yugoslav conflicts as merely ethnic ones, a very significant parameter of the interplay of civil-military and ethnic-military relations in the context of the conflict cycle. In other words, one should pose the hypothetical question that, had there been democratic control of the YPA, could the bloody collapse have been avoided? Was the crucial problem of the military's legitimacy its undemocratically designed relationship with the political (party) leadership, or the fact that some of the ethnic groups did not perceive the state and the military as their legitimate representatives? According to some analysts, Yugoslavia's existence was possible only in an undemocratic fashion, while the military was the only pan-Yugoslav core institution.[6] If that is true, then the principal problem of the democratic constitution cannot be found in the way civil-military relations are shaped. Whatever strategy is applied to the security forces in terms of their representation of the ethnic make-up of the population, particularly if there are deep rifts between various groups, results will be insufficient. The ethnic profile of the security forces can be shaped (to a certain degree), while the constellation of interethnic relations is more difficult to manage. In case these two tracks (i.e. institutional and societal) do not coincide, it is more likely that the societal dimension will prevail and exert greater pressure than the institutional one.

In the Yugoslav case there is also solid ground to explain the roots of the conflict through different – historical, social, economic, political, and even cultural – arguments. That approach sheds a different light on to the question of ethnicity and the military/police, and also gives more manoeuvring space for policy interventions and political manipulations. However, the dilemma rises from the fact that ethnicity has become a political currency and that ethnic affinity is often subject to political manipulation due to its endless resources and various forms of use.[7] Since the most dramatic expression of ethnic mobilization has been the claim to independent statehood, the military becomes a particularly interesting "battlefield" for this struggle. Being a symbol of national unity and state sovereignty, the military has "natural" (i.e. structural) impotence to resist what it sees as an attack from hostile societal groups, and the only appropriate way to respond would be to let the political leadership settle the problem.

The process of post-conflict reconstruction in some of the Yugoslav successor states also proves that the core problem is not the classical question of the relationship between the political (democracy) and military spheres, but predominantly the way the military mission is defined in regard to internal security and the ethnic profile of the military forces.

It does not mean that ethnic-military relations prevail over civil-military relations. On the contrary, the democratic deficit allows ethnicity to grow to be the most important aspect of civil-military relations. The Yugoslav case indicates that, given the military's very significant role in the process of nation building and state building, it is intentionally involved in political and interethnic quarrels, which further affects the (lack of) democratic potential of the political system. The very fact that none of the Yugoslav successor states (with exception of Slovenia, which has always been an ethnically homogeneous society) has resolved the question of ethnic-military relations in a satisfactory way proves how difficult it is to break this vicious circle. Interestingly, this is still a highly underexplored issue in the scholarly literature.

The military in a divided society: Macedonia's challenges

For more than a decade the Macedonian case seemed to be an exception to the bloody pattern of state building that dominated all over the region. While violent conflict had been the crucial determinant of all major developments in the other former Yugoslav republics, on the surface and for a while it looked as if Macedonia was a normal country in transition. While the other newly independent states as well as their militaries were born in an atmosphere of ethno-nationalism and violent conflict, in Macedonia political and military reforms seemed to take place in a peaceful environment. The key question is whether Macedonia was really relieved from war threats and succeeded in taking advantage of peace to pursue its democratization process.

Despite the peaceful divorce from the federation, the threat of intrastate conflict had always been pertinent for Macedonia's security prospects. For years only a few were ready to face this fact. What represents today's Republic of Macedonia was historically considered a "powder keg" due to traditional rivalries of the neighbouring peoples and countries over the territory and the population, as well as an internally explosive ethnic mix. According to the Census held in 1994 the population is comprised of 66.5 per cent Macedonians, 22.9 per cent Albanians, 4.79 per cent Turks, 2.73 per cent Roma, and 2.17 per cent Serbs and others. The figures were first contested by the Albanians, and later on they most probably ceased to reflect the real situation, given the refugee influx in 1999 and 2001. The question of ethnic composition is still a highly politicized issue, and due to the grave security situation it is not surprising that the results of the latest Census of November 2002 (which were not made public until late 2003) are also disputed by at least one of the major ethnic groups.[8]

While the relationship of the military to the state is seen as the very essence of civil-military relations,[9] it is rarely acknowledged that the relationship of society to the military (as a state symbol and institution) is of high importance. An analysis of the features of the Macedonian state (which includes the idea of the state, its institutional dimension, and the physical base)[10] and the military illustrates the complexity and interdependence of civil-military and society-military relations. Today's Macedonian state can be singled out on the European political map as a country where a large number of citizens harbour simultaneous feelings of affiliation and repulsion against its reality and historical-political aims. Having gained independence in 1991, Macedonia found itself in what it perceived as a historically hostile regional context. The old historical refrain ("To whom do Macedonians belong?") on a contesting Macedonian national identity has been raised again among the neighbouring Balkan states. As Buzan stresses, "unless the idea of the state is firmly planted in the minds of the population, the state as a whole has no secure foundation. Equally, unless the idea of the state is firmly planted in the 'minds' of other states, the state has no secure environment."[11]

State institutions materialize the idea of the state. The Macedonian challenge was as follows: which idea of a state should be implemented within the institutional settings – a nation-state or a so-called multi-ethnic democracy, neither of them, or something in between? The institutional answer to this state paradigm appeared to be of crucial importance, especially during the crisis of 2001. Obviously, the concept of the state affects the nature of institutional solutions, and in this very case even the military's posture in regard to the country's intrastate problems. When the state idea is weak and not embedded within the conscience of the population, state institutions, especially those with repressive functions, are likely to be given a very substantial role within the political system, and consequently within the national security system. The lack of legitimacy is often "compensated" by threat or actual use of repression. The feeling of insecurity emphasized the need to strengthen the repressive state institutions, which is exactly one of the characteristics of so-called "weak states".[12] It did not necessarily mean that the state put more emphasis on the security structures, but rather on methods of governance that imposed state unity and domination principles (be it domination by a political or an ethnic élite). In Holsti's words, state strength is not measured in military terms: "It is, rather, in the capacity of the state to command loyalty – the right to rule – to extract the resources necessary to rule and provide services, to maintain that essential element of sovereignty, a monopoly over the legitimate use of force within defined territorial limits, and to operate within the context of a consensus based political community."[13]

However, in Macedonia state institutions were primarily expressions of the narrow interest of a dominant political élite or ethnic group; at least, that is the perception held by a significant part of the population. The resulting legitimacy gap forced the state to build more unity within society, construct national identity, and create legitimacy in an artificial way. Particular importance was given to measures that unite society as well as to security institutions. Yet this made the state weaker rather than stronger. The misbalance in the distribution of resources and power between different ethnic and societal groups and inadequate ethnic representation in public administration – particularly in the security forces – further deepened the legitimacy gap. The lack of capacity and resources to accomplish state unity and to create a solid ground for the state's legitimacy additionally worsened the vicious circle: "Everything it does to become a strong state actually perpetuates its weakness."[14]

An analysis of the way in which the security structures (the military and police) were configured indicated a concept of national security in which internal security concerns prevailed over external ones. For years the police enjoyed a better social, material, and political status than the army. A functional rivalry existed on the ground over competing financial demands from both sides. The 2001 conflict brought to the fore the latent institutional clash in its full intensity. Since the very beginning of the Macedonian state's independence in 1991, the Army of the Republic of Macedonia (ARM) represented more a symbol of (and decoration for) statehood than a military that could live up to its ascribed military mission. It was supposed to support Macedonia's fragile state-building efforts and contested identity in the international community (including the country's name, borders, and membership in international organizations). Legally, the army was defined as an "armed force of all citizens of the Republic of Macedonia" (1992 Law on Defence), which should have been accompanied by a number of actions that would have promoted the integrative social role of the military.

In reality the implementation of this policy faced great difficulties. In the first few years young Albanian conscripts boycotted compulsory military service. The government and the judicial system deliberately ignored this phenomenon in order to avoid worsening of interethnic relations, while in the public it was a taboo. The situation was partly inherited from former Yugoslavia, in which Albanians had always been highly underrepresented in the professional officer corps. Unofficially, the Macedonian leadership considered the traditional remedy of national quotas as the best solution, at least in the case of high-ranking officers. Although this principle might sometimes be the simplest way to achieve ethnic balance, the opposite standpoint argued that this criterion for recruitment was in direct opposition to the ethos, or at least the myth, of the military as an institution based on professionalism. For years, calls for the professionalization of the ARM had been an alibi for ethnically tailor-made institutions. The factual situation was very "favourable" – there were many more Macedonian than Albanian military professionals. Even 10 years later improvements were far from being satisfactory, as Albanians, who comprised around 23 per cent of the population, made up only little more than 4 per cent of the army staff.[15] Indeed, the military is, or should be, an institution where the principles of professionalism and merit primarily determine the policy of promotion in military ranks. This, however, does not release the civilian and military authorities from taking measures aimed at stimulating interest in the military profession among members of ethnic groups that are poorly represented in the military hierarchy. Data from the first five generations of cadets enrolled in Macedonia's military academy indicated an alarming situation, as very few cadets of Albanian origin seemed to have shown interest in a military profession. However, the problem was never spelled out publicly, and thus no efforts to increase interest among young Albanians were undertaken.

There had been many worrisome indications since 1991 concerning the Albanians' attitude towards the Macedonian state; at least, they were seen as such by the overwhelming majority of Macedonians. These include events such as the Albanian community's boycott of the referendum on independence in 1991, and of the Census; the Albanian parliamentary group's boycott of the adoption of the 1991 constitution; the declaration of the so-called autonomous "Republic Illiryda" in the western (predominantly Albanian-populated) part of the Republic; and the 1993 issue of an Albanian paramilitary, involving some high-ranking MOD officials. In addition, the Macedonian side persistently insisted on a "civic concept of the state", declining even some reasonable demands of the Albanians.

The societal atmosphere of distrust heavily affected ethnic-military relations. The so-called Trojan horse dilemma or question of loyalty[16] had been hanging over Macedonian society even before the dramatic events of 1999, and later in 2001. During the NATO military intervention in neighbouring Yugoslavia, the population of Macedonia held an informal plebiscite which unearthed deep divisions over perceptions of security threats (and security providers). Young Albanians from Macedonia[17] rushed to join UCK (Kosovo Liberation Army) fighters in Kosovo, while their ethnic leaders stated that the Albanians would decline an eventual call for mobilization in case of a state of emergency or war declared by the Macedonian authorities. On the contrary, the majority of Macedonians perceived the bombing campaign as unjust and dangerous for the state's stability. Having seen Albanians as a common enemy (or secessionists both in Kosovo and in western Macedonia), they deeply empathized with the Serbian population, while the Albanians perceived NATO and the USA as mighty allies.[18]

Apart from this worrisome reality, a legal approach offers a more favourable perspective on the problem. Constitutionally, the external dimension of the military mission is clearly defined, which should be seen as an assurance that they will refrain from involvement in the internal political scene. Although never officially recognized, the threat of intrastate conflict made some lawyers (including one of the founding fathers of the 1991 and 2001 constitutions and then Minister of Defence, Vlado Popovski) give more flexible interpretations of the constitutional provisions determining the armed force's military mission. However, when the conflict broke out, the military force was used in a strange situation, as neither a state of war nor a state of emergency was ever proclaimed. The bizarre justification of the decision to employ military units was that the country had been attacked from outside (i.e. Kosovo), which created a problem of how to explain that the enemy was not invading from another state but from a territory under international (UN) protection. It is believed that at least 20 per cent of the NLA (National Liberation Army) fighters in Macedonia came from Kosovo.[19] The entire situation was strange and unconstitutional (in terms of use of the military force), but, even more interestingly, nobody (neither Macedonians nor Albanians) seemed interested in the legality of the issue.

In this conflict, with a clear interethnic dimension, the military (and the police) achieved the highest ratings for public confidence among ethnic Macedonians since 1991. Regardless of their obvious lack of success (even clumsiness), not to mention the lack of coordination between the military and police efforts, a majority of ethnic Macedonians clearly defined the security structures of their state as capable, trustworthy, and patriotic. As for the Albanian part of the population, one can only guess their attitude, as no public surveys have been conducted on this issue. Nevertheless, the (Macedonian) public reacted harshly to an indication that military officers of Albanian descent demanded swift promotion or threatened to quit the army collectively.[20]

From the perspective of the post-conflict situation in Macedonia there is a need to estimate the "weight" of civil-military versus ethnic-military relations and redefine their respective importance. For more than a decade Macedonia was living in a type of virtual reality, pretending to be a normal state in transition and even an "oasis of peace" amidst a turbulent region. The focus of SSR was on democratization of civil-military relations, especially in terms of strengthening democratic control of the armed forces. Since the state-building and nation-building processes were pursued within an ethnically divided society, the focus should have been on a different agenda that should have responded better to the existing conflict potential in the country. The question of how to manage the military's multi-ethnic composition was never properly addressed or, worse, not tackled at all. Instead of dealing with the issue as an integral part of a conflict prevention strategy, the opportunity was missed and has now reappeared in the context of post-conflict reconstruction endeavours.

Post-conflict reconstruction of the security sector in Macedonia: Facing reality

In early 2001 Macedonia was at a turning point, while the security challenges were growing rapidly. Internal peace and the state's existence were at stake, while the ethnic-military relationship overshadowed the civil-military relations paradigm.

The task of implementing SSR and performing democratic management of national security was far from accomplished when the Macedonian state started sliding into general erosion and degradation. SSR took place in an intermezzo between the two tendencies of privatization[21] and internationalization of security. When violent conflict occurred in Macedonia, the issue of democratic control of the military transformed into an issue of control over all armed forces operating on legitimate and illegitimate bases, sometimes with the blessing of some parts of the state establishment and even certain political parties, various paramilitary and parapolice forces, *mujahedin*, and desperado and mercenary groups. While in some other Balkan countries the security sector was built up during an armed conflict (Croatia, for example)[22] by reorganization of various (more or less) private security actors, the developments in Macedonia happened the other way around – i.e. state security actors slowly transformed into a form of private security actors.

On the other hand, after a decade of being an "oasis of peace", Macedonia became dependent for its security on the presence of various international peace support missions. In sum, the state drastically lost its ability to provide security for all citizens, or at least the situation was perceived as such by a significant part of the population. The current problem in post-conflict Macedonia is the existence of too many security sector players with contested legitimacy and conflicting goals. The divided society has a divided security sector, while the international community tries to fill the gap and provide a common ground. In-theatre coordination of domestic and international forces is ill performed, and more security providers have in fact translated into less security for the citizens.

The local security actors have provided security on an exclusionist basis, sometimes even against their original intention (for example, the ARM has never claimed to defend only ethnic Macedonians against Albanians). Because of the deep distrust (sometimes with good reason, and sometimes groundless), members of the two ethnic groups tend to view everyone who is not of the same ethnic stock as unreliable and even hostile.[23] A time of crisis may be very tempting for restructuring power relationships between and within the political and security structures on both sides of the interethnic division. The issue of equitable ethnic representation of Albanians in all state structures had been on the agenda of political negotiations for years, while the newly emerged NLA structures and their leaders achieved what looked like a quick "victory" only when violence occurred. The "heroes" of armed conflict easily overshadowed the heroes of political negotiations among both Macedonians and Albanians. The Framework Agreement of 13 August 2001 (which should have been a peace agreement)[24] mediated by the international community included provisions on equitable ethnic representation in police units and other security structures as well as in the whole public administration. The Macedonians saw it as an imposition, favouring Albanian demands, while for the Albanian side in the negotiations it was an indication that their armed fight was just and their demands justifiable.

In the context of the current state of affairs, however, the issue of equitable ethnic representation within the security structures is of minor importance despite its visibility on the surface of the political and peace process. From an "oasis of peace", Macedonia has transformed into a completely militarized society.[25] This situation has not changed much even with the change of the government in September 2002. The new coalition government, which includes the political parties of the former combatants, hesitated for a long time before starting the disarmament process. According to the Small Arms Survey, between 110,000 and 170,000 people in Macedonia illegally possess guns, some of them more than one piece.[26] It took a violent conflict for the Macedonian government and society to become aware of the need for disarmament and demilitarization of the country. Yet perceptions along ethnic and political divides differed greatly, especially in regard to who was more or better armed (Macedonians or Albanians), and who was to be disarmed: paramilitary groups and UCK renegades and ex-combatants, or privatized and politicized special forces ("Lions"), or volunteers and illegally armed police reservists. The so-called "weapons amnesty"[27] programme took place in November/December 2003. It allowed full anonymity and impunity for arms-holders who surrendered their weapons, as well as the possibility to ask for their legalization. Overall, 7,571 items (6,400 of which were guns), over 100,000 pieces of ammunition, and 165 kilograms of explosives were collected. This result was officially declared a success.[28]

Even if the security reforms are close to achieving equitable ethnic representation (which was defined as an absolute priority in the post-Ohrid period), the problem of violence remains unresolved. The cease-fire agreement may have reduced the level of direct violence, but restructuring the political system and security apparatus may still preserve the elements of structural violence. In their political battles, the conflict parties in Macedonia widely rely on the "successes" of the armed forces under their control. The citizens from both communities are pushed to believe that everything is about justice and human and/or collective rights – or statehood, patriotism, and survival. Thus the solution is seen in the security structures (i.e. the repressive institutions in the political system), and people tend to believe that they will be more secure if only the members of the security institutions are of the same ethnic stock as they are. Understandably, the ethnically coloured interpretation of the conflict easily becomes embedded in the collective memory and has a potential to strengthen the cultural violence in this society. In sum, the overall situation diminishes possibilities for implementation of democratic oversight of the security sector in the long run.

However, the most serious issue to be resolved in the coming years is how to balance the question of loyalty and the question of mutual trust among members of the various ethnic groups in Macedonia, as the country's ethnic mix includes not only ethnic Macedonians and Albanians, but also Turks, Serbs, Romas, Vlachs, etc. The painful process of reconciliation and dealing with the past should take place in this society. In that sense Toqueville's warning that it is not within the army that one is likely to find the remedy against the vices of that army, but within society as a whole, still rings accurately.[29] The Macedonian case clearly shows that the missed opportunities in building ethnic policy create tremendous problems later on. There is ground for the presumption that it will not be the Macedonian security sector's task to come up with solutions, but it will at least partly be the task of international facilitators and mediators, and most of all of Macedonian society itself.

The international-local alliance is of crucial importance for the endeavour to be successful, but the experience drawn from the Yugoslav conflict(s) proves the tendency to take ownership of the conflict instead of building up the ability of the respective societies themselves to find appropriate solutions. When external interventionists rush for fast results and quick fixes, they usually forget that SSR depends heavily on acceptance by local stakeholders. Conditionality of international assistance may also become an obstacle in the reform process, especially if one of the parties perceives it as unjust blackmail. For example, for the majority of ethnic Macedonians the accomplishment of the Ohrid Agreement, which requires equitable representation of Albanians in state and security structures, appears as an unjust proposition. Emotions grew high when former NLA combatants, i.e. those who took up arms against the state, were to be integrated in the security forces. This problem is exacerbated by the fact that the security forces need to be downsized (according to NATO standards) and their composition adjusted to reflect the country's ethnic diversity. As the dismissed officers will thus mainly be of Macedonian origin, in the general perception this appears as if international assistance only improves Albanians' rights. Moreover, there is a lack of financed projects to retrain dismissed officers and police personnel of Macedonian origin. As tailoring the security structures' composition has proved to be a long and sensitive process for national actors, the same applies to external actors as well. The rush into direct and overt interventions that are seen as favouring only one side may have detrimental effects in the long run. Finally, investments in SSR only are doomed to failure if not followed by overall post-conflict rehabilitation and reconstruction of society.

Conclusion

The aftermath of violent clashes creates numerous challenges, and the post-conflict peacebuilding experience in Macedonia confirms that. The abilities of armed structures (state, para-state, local, and international) to build true, sustainable peace are quite limited as long as they are not supported by other non-military efforts. Many case studies in this volume attest to this conclusion. The main difficulty concerns the necessity to conduct two divergent processes: to keep the regular (state) security forces on board and to transform them (i.e. make them an object of SSR), and to disband the private security forces through their integration into the existing security structures. The former task is important for state security reasons, while the latter concerns attempts to disarm and demilitarize (a part of) the society. These are complex tasks, mainly for two reasons. First, the state structures do not meet all institutional and legal criteria applicable to such types of forces (given the process of privatization of security and the erosion of state power). Second, the non-state security actors are a result of spontaneous social dissatisfaction and self-organization. Two ambiguous processes are taking place, in which the state structures slowly slide towards para-state structures while the para-structures behave as would-be state actors.

Macedonia's main problem is self-awareness of the real dimension of its conflict. This includes the fiction of its decade-long characterization as an "oasis of peace", and the real nature of the 2001 conflict. In order to avoid any discussion on reconciliation and war crimes, many people in the country prefer to believe that there has not been a conflict at all; others stick to the uncompromising position that it is impossible for both communities ever to live together in peace. While the question of ethnic-military relations is a problem of great importance, it is not a core problem. It rather reflects and manifests other difficulties in society-state relationships, including society's identity, institutions, and sustainability.

In a rational distribution of scarce resources in a post-conflict society, it is important to invest in demilitarization of society through disarmament, demobilization, and reintegration of former combatants (known as DDR programmes). The same applies to the rational utilization of international assistance. DDR programmes will only work once conflict parties end their violence and commit themselves to a peaceful dialogue to further the process of conflict resolution/transformation. The Macedonian case seems to be fitting for DDR programmes. Since the NATO-led Essential Harvest mission, NLA guerrillas have been transformed into a political party and have taken part in the governing coalition.[30] At first glance one might conclude that this has been a miraculous success.

However, a reality check shows that none of these reforms has reached a satisfactory level yet. Macedonia still suffers from too many weapons, disobedient guerrilla-police officers, and pushy demands for "reintegration" by former combatants who are now found in the highest posts in the state administration. There is also a misperception of the complexity of DDR programmes, as if one could select one or two dimensions of them while neglecting the rest. The immediate reaction of the majority ethnic Macedonian population is that DDR applies only to Albanians. In addition, preference is given to the disarmament and demobilization dimensions, while there is reluctance (and distrust) when it comes to reintegration of former combatants. The Albanians, however, believe that they fulfilled their part of the deal by yielding 3,000 pieces of weapons during Essential Harvest and disbanding NLA units. Now they expect the "reward" in the form of reintegration of the former guerrillas as well as equitable ethnic representation in the state administration.

On the other hand, members of the state security forces who also fought in the conflict should also be disarmed and demobilized. Downsizing of army and police forces is rarely a painless process, thus reintegration and resocialization into civilian life is a *sine qua non*. It is a particularly delicate matter to dismiss people of one ethnicity in order to hire those of another ethnicity. It appears that post-conflict reconstruction is a costly endeavour.[31] There is no precise estimation of how much the implementation of the Ohrid Agreement will cost in financial terms. Only recently, the government estimated that this will not only absorb all financial means provided by the donor conference, but that in addition it will call for more money from the state budget.

As the Macedonian case indicates, the strife for democratic control of the security sector strengthens in the light of post-conflict recovery and peacebuilding. Advocacy of "democratic control" may be misleading in a post-conflict society. Democratic control (or better, oversight) presupposes functioning democratic institutions and a total abolition of the use of violence. Conflict-driven societies only have the capacity to imitate, or even misuse, democratic principles. Traumatized and belligerent societies do not have the critical mass required for democratic oversight of the political decision-making process. On the contrary, all too often they easily and wholeheartedly support militant politics.

Despite these grave constraints, the process of recovery and peacebuilding must start somewhere. Both local and international actors should carefully analyse the points at which it is possible to intervene in the short, medium, and long run. For instance, if it is impossible to facilitate democratic transition, it may be more feasible to facilitate legal and societal reforms.

Financial assistance is of crucial importance. The donor community should invest in the post-conflict SSR and bolster the development process. However, while doing so, the priorities of SSR should be carefully balanced, as they may appear contradictory. For instance, promoting development and peacebuilding may not go hand in hand with professionalization and integration into NATO. External interventions into a sensitive and delicate matter like SSR may incite suspicion and inhibit reforms. It is therefore all the more important that SSR integrates local stakeholders. Indirect interventions in the security sector may be preferable compared to direct ones, and reform efforts should not exclusively focus on security forces but also on political institutions and civil society, which are entrusted with democratic monitoring functions.

Promotion of an open and democratic security culture among all ethnic groups takes time. The first step towards this goal is to initiate an overall reconciliation process as the basis for restructuring the security forces as legitimate and democratically directed institutions. The existence of the Trojan horse dilemma is often deeply embedded in the societal groups' beliefs and perceptions. Increasing public awareness about its existence is a necessary step. Open dialogue on mutual interethnic distrust, particularly when it comes to diverse groups' equal participation in the security structures, may reveal and help to overcome many stereotypes and misunderstandings and thus lead to overall societal reconciliation.

Notes

1. Juvenal, "Sed quis custodies ipsos custodies?", *Omnia Romae*, VI, 347.
2. Huntington, Samuel. 1957. *The Soldier and the State: The Theory and Politics of Civil-Military Relations*. New York: Random House; Janowitz, Morris. 1960. *The Professional Soldier: A Social and Political Portrait*. New York: Free Press.
3. For example, the NATO Washington Summit in April 1999 *de facto* gave *carte blanche* for the alliance's "out-of-area" operations in a way that may bypass the prior authorization of the UN Security Council.
4. See Lilly, Damian and Michael von Tangen Page (eds). 2002. *Security Sector Reform: The Challenges and Opportunities of the Privatisation of Security*. London: International Alert.
5. An illustrative example is the Dayton Agreement for Bosnia, where the peace accord brought an effective cease-fire but has failed to build a sustainable democratic system. Democracy building had to be postponed in order to preserve a negative peace, and the role of the High Representative has matched that agenda. Moreover, the dubious "Train and Equip" programme (run by the US-based Military Professionals Resources Inc.) creates imbalances in military power (and fear) between the entities, rather than supporting peacebuilding and democracy building in the war-torn society.
6. Hadzic, Miroslav. 2002. *The Yugoslav People's Agony: The Role of the Yugoslav People's Army*. Aldershot: Ashgate; Vankovska, Biljana and Hakan Wiberg. 2003. *Between Past and Future: Civil-Military Relations in Post-communist Balkan Countries*. London and New York: I. B. Tauris.
7. Goulbourne, Harry. 1997. "Ethnic mobilization and changing concepts of nationalism", paper presented at the Seventeenth IPSA World Congress, Seoul, Korea, 17–21 August.
8. According to the 2002 Census, the ethnic composition of the Republic of Macedonia looks as follows: Macedonians 64.18 per cent, Albanians 25.17 per cent, Turks 3.85 per cent, Romas 2.66 per cent, Serbs 1.78 per cent. It took one year for the State Statistical Office to release these results, through a process that was highly tense and controversial. However, it was the strong influence of the representatives of the international community that gave legitimacy to the official results.
9. Bracken, Paul. 1995. "Reconsidering civil-military relations", in Don M. Snider and Miranda A. Carlton-Carew (eds) *US Civil-Military Relations in Crisis and Transition*. Washington, DC: Center for Strategic and International Studies, pp. 145–165.
10. Buzan, Barry. 1991. *People, States and Fear: An Agenda for International Security Studies in the Post-Cold War Era*. Boulder, CO: Lynne Rienner Publishers.
11. *Ibid.*, p. 78.
12. For further information about the structural characteristics of a "weak state" see *ibid.*, pp. 96–112; Holsti, Kalevi J. 1996. *War, State and the State of War*. Cambridge: Cambridge University Press, pp. 104–108.
13. Holsti, *ibid.*, p. 82.
14. *Ibid.*, p. 117.
15. Due to contradictory data from different (official and half-official) sources, it is very difficult to give an exact picture of the ethnic make-up of the ARM and other security structures. See Musliu, Sefer. 2002. "Albanians drop boycott of Macedonian army", *IWPR'S Balkan Crisis Report*, No. 382, 14 November.
16. The Trojan horse dilemma refers to the question of loyalty (or better, questioned loyalty) of the members of some ethnic groups to the state as such, and particularly to the national security interests. Societal distrust between various ethnic groups is often used as a pretext for shaping the ethnic outlook of the militaries, referring to the claim that members of ethnic minorities may serve as Trojan horses and act against their fellow

military men and women in times of emergency or war. Peled, Alon. 1998. *A Question of Loyalty: Military Manpower Policy in Multiethnic States*. Ithaca and London: Cornell University Press.

17. The exact figures are still a matter of speculations and dispute as the action was illegal, and thus secretive. The Albanians from Kosovo and Macedonia have always had tight kin bonds. For example, one of the main Albanian political leaders in Macedonia (Arben Xhaferi) is of Kosovar descent. That explains why such a degree of mutual solidarity was shown both in the Kosovo fights in 1999 and in Macedonia in 2001.

18. For further analysis see Vankovska, Biljana. 1999. "Macedonia after the Kosovo war: The way away from the 'powder keg' to the 'oasis of peace' – And back again". Transnational Foundation for Peace and Future Research meeting point, available at www.transnational.org/forum/meet/Macedoniaafterwar.html.

19. This information was given by a serving KFOR general at a conference held under Chatham House rules in Berlin in December 2001. See Dragsdahl, Joergen. 2001. "The internationals in the Balkans: Lessons for Macedonia", in *BITS Conference Report 01.2*. Berlin: Heinrich-Böll Foundation, available at www.bits.de/public/conferencereport/cr01-2.htm.

20. See "Oficeri-Albanci ke si odat od ARM ako ne gi unapredi Buckovski!?" (Albanian officers are going to leave the ARM if not promoted by Buckovski!?), *Dnevnik*, 15 November 2001; "Oficerite-Albanci sakaat da izvlecat korist od krizata" (Albanian officers want to profit out of the crisis), *Dnevnik*, 16 November 2001.

21. A bizarre detail about the privatization of security in Macedonia comes from the fact that it was the ruling party (the VMRO) which transformed state structures into parastate ones – or better, into party militias. On the other hand, the MPRI was infamous as an example of a private military company. It was allegedly involved in military conflict on both sides, i.e. formally giving advice to the government and informally to the Albanian forces. See Vankovska, Biljana. 2002. "The privatisation of security and security sector reform in Croatia", in Damian Lilly and Michael von Tangen Page (eds) *Security Sector Reform: The Challenges and Opportunities of the Privatisation of Security*. London: International Alert.

22. *Ibid.*

23. In June 2001 a public opinion survey was conducted by the Skopje-based Centre for Ethnic Relations at the Institute for Sociological, Political, and Juridical Research, with a random sample of 1,200 ethnic Macedonians. The results showed that the army and police are considered to be most successful state institutions (with 94 per cent and 87 per cent support, respectively); in addition, only 5 per cent of the respondents answered affirmatively to the question as to whether they consider the Albanians to be loyal citizens. See "Background paper" presented at the Conference on Intra-Macedonian Dialogue, Interlaken, Switzerland, 25–26 November 2001.

24. For an in-depth analysis see Vankovska, Biljana. 2003. "Current perspectives on Macedonia: The struggle for peace, democracy and security", Heinrich Böll Stiftung Article Series, 20 February, available at www.boell.de/en/05_world/1733.html. The Ohrid Framework Agreement can be found at www.president.gov.mk/eng/info/dogovor.htm.

25. According to some expert estimates, both ethnic groups are well armed. It is difficult to estimate the exact number of pieces of weapons in free circulation, but figures range between 250,000 to 400,000 pieces of small-arms and weapons.

26. Grillot, Suzette R., Wolf-Christian Paes, Hans Risser, and Shelly O. Stoneman. 2004. *A Fragile Peace: Guns and Security in Post-conflict Macedonia*, Small Arms Survey Special Report No. 4, June, endnote 79.

27. The name was meant to convey a symbolic meaning, referring to the wide amnesty given to ex-combatants as part of the peace process.

28. However, there were no clearly defined criteria for failure or success. Yet, in comparison to NATO's disarmament efforts in Kosovo, much had been achieved. See Geshakovska, Julia. 2004. "Macedonia: Weapons amnesty a success, but many stick to their guns", RFE/RL Feature Articles, 17 December, available at www.rferl.org/features/2003/12/17122003170425.asp.
29. de Toqueville, Alexis. 1961. *La démocratie en Amérique*, abridged edition. London: Macmillan, p. 277.
30. One of the most recent surprises happened during the (early) presidential elections (April 2004) when the ex-chief of staff of the NLA, G'zim Ostreni, ran for the presidency.
31. For more detail see ICG. 2003. *Macedonia: No Room for Complacency*. London: International Crisis Group.

6

Democratization in Bosnia:
A more effective role for SFOR

Allison Ritscher

In the post-Cold War world peacekeeping has evolved from missions involving little more than monitoring a cease-fire to ones that seek to help former combatants develop the conditions necessary for a sustainable peace. This requires a fresh approach – particularly on the part of the American military – to defining the role of the military in post-conflict peacebuilding and democratization.[1]

Until the end of the Cold War, international involvement in peacekeeping missions was motivated in large part by a desire to preserve the *status quo* and prevent a widening of the conflict that might eventually draw both superpowers into a direct confrontation with each other.[2] The UN mission in Cyprus, which has so successfully preserved the *status quo* there since 1964 despite concerted efforts over the past years by negotiators from both the United Nations and the European Union, is one such example. Recent operations, however, ranging from Haiti to Bosnia, Somalia, and East Timor, reflect, with differing degrees of success, the ways in which short-term peacekeeping missions have evolved into long-term peacebuilding interventions. The goal of these missions, far from being merely the preservation of the *status quo*, is the development of a sustainable peace. As a result, their long-term objectives extend well beyond the traditional tasks of separating the combatants and monitoring a cease-fire, to the more complex problems of conflict resolution and security sector reform – and, more often than not, democratization. This new type of mission – peacebuilding coupled with democratization – requires an enhancement of the role of peacekeeping troops.[3]

The purpose of this chapter is to examine the international military intervention in Bosnia and suggest specific ways in which the Stabilization Force (SFOR) could be a more effective partner in post-conflict peacebuilding in that country. It is intended to provide a concrete, context-specific picture of what an "enhanced" role for the military could look like in a post-Cold War, long-term peacebuilding intervention.

Peacekeeping: A good start

In practice and in theory, the American military has typically viewed its role in peacekeeping as limited to monitoring or enforcing a negative peace. In their report to the Carnegie Commission on Preventing Deadly Conflict, *Civilian-Military Cooperation in the Prevention of Deadly Conflict*, retired general George A. Joulwan and Christopher C. Shoemaker write that "the daunting challenges of building the kinds of institutions and processes that are at the heart of conflict prevention are far beyond the capabilities of any military. The military can bring about an absence of war; the military cannot bring about an enduring peace."[4] It may be true that the military alone cannot bring about an enduring peace; but, acting in conjunction with the civilian organizations of the international community, military forces do have a much greater capability to play a direct, constructive role in promoting democratization and building a positive peace.

In Bosnia specifically, the many thousands of soldiers from mostly democratic countries who make up SFOR could make substantial and unique contributions to strengthening respect for the rule of law, enhancing the commitment to democracy among both élites and the masses, and increasing the legitimacy of the Bosnian government in the eyes of its citizens through military reform.[5] All three of these elements – respect for the rule of law, commitment to democracy, and government legitimacy – are critical pillars of the ultimate policy objective in Bosnia, which Ivo Daalder describes as the "construction of a multi-ethnic, democratic and prosperous state".[6]

The contributions of both the Intervention Force (IFOR) and SFOR to date have been both immense and indispensable. It is thanks to IFOR's deployment and successful execution of its mission that the civil war in Bosnia came to an end at all. That mission was defined in the military sections of the Dayton Accords, and included separating the warring parties, ensuring freedom of movement (FOM), and controlling the movement of military traffic over key ground routes in Bosnia. These tasks were accomplished largely without incident, and within a mere eight months after IFOR first deployed on 20 December 1995.[7] Rear Admiral Charles W. Moore Jr, briefing the US Senate Armed Services Committee on 1 August 1996, noted that "today is the 225th day of our deployment, and ... our military missions are, for all intents and purposes, complete".[8]

In addition to outlining IFOR's tasks, the Dayton Accords (General Framework Agreement for Peace – GFAP) gave IFOR the authority but not the obligation to "help create secure conditions for the conduct by others of non-military tasks".[9] This clause provided the basis for IFOR's secondary responsibilities. The US Under Secretary of Defense for Policy at the time, Walter B. Slocombe, explained the policy that was guiding IFOR's approach to complementing and assisting the civilian implementation effort: "IFOR will, subject to its responsibility for all military tasks of Dayton and within its capabilities and force protection tasks, provide material and resource support to civilian agencies. This assistance, including intellectual, staff, and coordination support, will be proactively pursued by IFOR."[10] For example, Admiral Moore told the US Senate Armed Services Committee that IFOR had begun to increase its patrols in support of FOM, because FOM is critical to free and fair elections.[11] IFOR also dismantled checkpoints and worked out procedures for refugee return with the Office of the UN High Commissioner for Refugees (UNHCR) and the International Police Task Force (IPTF) to promote peaceful movements of refugees and internally displaced persons (IDPs).[12] Additionally, the improvements IFOR made to civilian infrastructure, such as roads, bridges, and railways, enhanced both IFOR's primary mission and civilian FOM.

In support of the September 1996 elections, IFOR increased its presence near polling stations to minimize the chances of disruption or intimidation, provided the Organization for Security and Cooperation in Europe (OSCE) with personnel and logistics support, and assisted in printing and distributing voter lists and information materials.[13] To the International Criminal Tribunal for the former Yugoslavia (ICTY), IFOR "provided area security, threat assessments, communications support, accommodations, storage of ICTY-owned heavy digging equipment, and emergency assistance for Tribunal teams investigating war crimes in and around Srebrenica, Brcko, and other areas of Bosnia".[14]

At the same time, civilian organizations ranging from the United Nations and the European Union to the OSCE, the World Bank, and hundreds of non-governmental organizations (NGOs) contributed their resources and expertise to meet the challenge of bringing peace to Bosnia. The total aid package, in fact, ended up being proportionately many times larger than the Marshall Plan to rebuild Europe in the aftermath of the Second World War, according to Carl Bildt, a former High Representative in Bosnia and Herzegovina. But despite this outpouring of assistance, success in the form of an enduring democratic peace continues to elude the Bosnians and the international community. In fact, in 2001 Bildt argued that "if troops were withdrawn today ... a new war would break out tomorrow. Self-sustaining regional stability remains a good distance away."[15]

Four years later, the picture is unarguably rosier. Now, the challenge for both the Bosnians as well as the military and civilian members of the international community is primarily one of economic, governmental, and security sector reform at an institutional level. In his March 2004 report to the Secretary-General, High Representative Paddy Ashdown wrote: "My priorities continue to center on consolidating the rule of law and advancing economic reform – justice and jobs – while further improving the functioning and effectiveness of BiH's key governing institutions."[16] Perhaps the most compelling evidence of change, however, is the fact that by June 2004 NATO expected to have only 7,000 troops stationed in Bosnia, down from a high of 64,000 in 1995.[17]

Nevertheless, as demonstrated by the sudden and rapid deterioration of security in Kosovo in mid-March 2004, regional stability is far from certain. Furthermore, the troop reduction and restructuring in Bosnia were driven as much by internal developments as by external events. The USA and NATO needed to free up resources and troops for employment in Afghanistan and the broader war on terrorism.[18] Moreover, events such as the deployment of multinational troops to Liberia in 2003, the recent return of international forces to Haiti, and the likelihood of a sustained foreign presence in Iraq make it clear that the need for international peacekeepers to do more with less is becoming more, not less, urgent.

However, this need not be as insurmountable a dilemma as it seems. By becoming more effective partners in security sector reform and democratization, peacekeepers can make their presence count for more. As Anderson explains, intervention forces operating in a contingency role are typically underutilized, and this pattern has held true in Bosnia as well.[19] No matter what the troop level, SFOR brings to the table a range of existing military capabilities that could be better employed to meet some of Bosnia's continued shortcomings, particularly in the previously mentioned areas of rule of law, commitment to democracy, and government legitimacy.

Peacebuilding: Developing rule of law

Rule of law is commonly viewed as one of the most fundamental elements of a democracy.[20] In fact, looking back on the record of international intervention in Bosnia, High Representative Paddy Ashdown mused: "In hindsight, we should have put the establishment of rule of law first, for everything else depends on it: a functioning economy, a free and fair political system, the development of civil society, public confidence in police and the courts."[21]

In its report entitled *SFOR Lessons Learned in Creating a Secure Environment with Respect for the Rule of Law*, SFOR defines the rule of law as a "process by which conflicting interests are aired, mediated, regulated, and resolved in a *non-violent* fashion *through governmental institutions* ... that are *accountable to the public*".[22] But respect for the rule of law also goes beyond institutions and legislation to govern relationships between individuals and between individuals and institutions in accordance with norms and values that must be internalized in a society.[23]

Examples ranging from the inability or unwillingness of local police to control vandals and provocateurs, discriminatory hiring practices, rampant corruption, and the widespread non-payment of taxes suggest that respect for the rule of law has not yet been internalized in Bosnian society.[24] However, in pursuit of this end SFOR can take a number of concrete steps. First, consistent with a traditional military role, it can continue to deter the use of force or intimidation by maintaining a high profile around the country. Second, it can vigorously pursue and arrest indicted war criminals. Third, it can provide civilian organizations, particularly the Office of the High Representative, with intelligence on criminal activity and corruption.

The first step is the straightforward one, and although the specific tasks have changed as the security situation has evolved, IFOR/SFOR's role in deterring violence has been central to its mission since the GFAP was signed. Today, according to the SFOR website, "Normal Framework Operations are the core of SFOR's day-to-day activities. They consist of patrolling, random searches, control of training and movement activities of the Entity Armed Forces (EAF), weapon and ammunition storage site inspections and monitoring mine-clearing activities."[25] Although freedom from violence and intimidation is essential for peacebuilding, it is by no means sufficient, and SFOR must expand its efforts in the other two areas.

The second step, arresting indicted war criminals, is absolutely critical. Commentators ranging from diplomats like Richard Holbrooke to policy experts like Ivo Daalder, as well as members of the military community with experience in Bosnia, as evidenced by the authors of *SFOR Lessons Learned*, cite the continued presence of war criminals, particularly Radovan Karadzic, as one of the most serious obstacles to implementation of the GFAP.[26] Ideally, because of the benefits to an intervening military force of being perceived as neutral and apolitical, some other organization would pursue war criminals, such as (previously) the IPTF, the ICTY itself, or eventually even the local police. Neither is it necessarily desirable to set an example of military involvement in judicial affairs in a fledgling democracy. But in Bosnia the local police will not arrest their own leaders, the ICTY does not have the ability, and the IPTF mandate was limited to training and advising, leaving a tremendous gap in the international community's enforcement capability.[27]

SFOR, by contrast, has always had both the legal authority and the ability to arrest indicted war criminals. Annex 1A of the Dayton Peace Accords very specifically directs SFOR to "help create secure conditions for tasks associated with the peace settlement", which includes establishing an environment conducive to the rule of law. It also explicitly gives SFOR the right to "fulfill its supporting tasks", to accept further directives from the North Atlantic Council, and to do "all that the Commander judges necessary" in the execution of its mission; it makes the Commander the final authority on military aspects of implementation.[28] Therefore, although SFOR is far from the ideal choice, it is in this case the only force on the ground capable of carrying out this mission-essential task.

Although the NATO-led forces have the authority to arrest war criminals, they were initially reluctant to use it. To its credit, IFOR did take steps – short of arresting war criminals – to curtail the political activities of prominent ultra-nationalists such as Karadzic. Slocombe told the US Senate Committee on Armed Services that:

We have made a conscious decision, "we" being IFOR, to step up the pace of patrolling in the areas around Pale, which is where Karadzic's operation has been run out of. This is not with any realistic expectation that we, IFOR, will catch him as a result of this ... The patrolling is more to make it more difficult for him to take an active role in public life.[29]

Nevertheless, during IFOR's deployment and the first few SFOR rotations, American troops, at least, were told to avoid persons indicted for war crimes (PIFWCs). Ben Higginbotham, a US Army captain who commanded a company from March to October 1997, said that "we were actually given explicit instruction to avoid certain situations where we might be put into the position of having to detain a PIFWC".[30] Later SFOR did adopt a more aggressive approach. The first instance of NATO troops attempting to arrest war criminals was on 10 July 1997, when British soldiers arrested one Bosnian Serb and shot another in self-defence. The two Bosnian Serbs had been secretly indicted for complicity with commitment of genocide.[31] But given the number and notoriety of the indicted war criminals yet to be arrested, more progress is needed on this front.

The pressure to take a harder line is not coming solely from people outside the military. The authors of *SFOR Lessons Learned* also stress the importance of arresting war criminals. They argue that the failure to arrest well-known PIFWCs has eroded the credibility of SFOR in the eyes of both the public and members of organized crime and corrupt political elements, which together wield a considerable amount of influence in Bosnian politics. Leaders in civilian implementation have also pointed out that their ability to negotiate and leverage reform is tied to SFOR's credibility, and that their authority is suffering too. Furthermore, despite the increased posture against PIFWCs, there are many indications that such people continue to exercise significant political influence and control behind the scenes. Therefore, the authors of *SFOR Lessons Learned* conclude, "we could more easily dismantle the old anti-Dayton power structures, empower the new democratic institutions, and build a more sustainable peace if the most notorious PIFWCs were to be apprehended".[32] The solution is not necessarily immediately to embark on a manhunt reminiscent of the operations against Mohamed Farah Aideed in Somalia. But neither is the answer to be found at the other extreme, represented by Admiral Leighton Smith's announcement on Pale Television early in IFOR's deployment that he would not be pursuing war criminals.[33] As the security situation evolves, the ground can be prepared for taking aggressive action against PIFWCs by marginalizing them within their communities. As Captain Higginbotham argues: "Once you've cut that link between the individuals in question and their support base – admittedly not an easy task – then you can operate against them with greater confidence, impunity, and greater likelihood of success."[34]

Peacebuilding: Targeting crime and corruption

In addition to arresting people accused of war crimes, the military can also make a substantial contribution to breaking the connection between organized crime, corrupt nationalist politicians, and the secret police, paramilitaries, and intelligence services – an alliance which the authors of *SFOR Lessons Learned* refer to as the "iron triangle".[35] This alliance possesses significant power in Bosnian politics and, among other things, actively prevents the establishment of institutions supporting the rule of law. It is able to do this because, at present, corrupt nationalist politicians, who get funding in part from organized crime, control the salaries and appointments of parliamentarians, judges, police, and prosecutors. These leaders have also been guilty of threatening those who would enforce the law against their interests.[36]

SFOR can do several things to minimize such problems. It can continue to threaten to act in support of civilian organizations like the IPTF, which are also involved in combating crime and corruption. It also ought to maintain – or even increase – its presence in places like courtrooms, polling stations, exhumations, IDP and refugee returns, and evictions of illegal residents.[37] But the most important additional contribution SFOR can make in this regard is to use its unique intelligence-gathering and analysing capabilities to support efforts to target organized crime. The prime example of this is Operation WESTAR, a series of operations that attacked illicit intelligence and criminal activity in Stolac, a town in the Croat-controlled portion of Bosnia.[38] The operations were conducted over the course of several months, ending in October 1999. They were closely coordinated with civilian organizations such as the IPTF, entity police forces, and the Office of the High Representative, which passed laws strengthening the prosecutor's office and established a new court to take the fullest advantage of SFOR's assistance. The operations targeted the Renner Transportation Company, known to be a cover for transnational criminal activity and a source of violent resistance to Muslim resettlements in Stolac. A subsequent operation also targeted illicit Croat intelligence activity in west Mostar, and uncovered evidence of covert intelligence operations against the international community.[39]

Operations like this must of course be conducted judiciously, or the military intelligence community's sources and methods may be put at risk. But once again, the local police are not going to target the organized crime and corruption that may be providing them with their income, or at any rate are providing their bosses with income. Nor can the IPTF, in its advisory role, effectively target these problems, because it has neither the mandate nor the resources. Once again, SFOR is the only organization that has the authority, the means, and the will, and it has clearly already had some success in doing so. But it must do more.

Not only would an expansion of these activities in conjunction with civilian authorities help establish respect for the rule of law, particularly among Bosnia's political élite, but it could also have a secondary advantage of reducing the risks of taking a harder line against war criminals. One commonly voiced objection to using SFOR to arrest PIFWCs is that apprehending popular leaders could create a hostile environment for the soldiers to work in. Publicizing information about criminal activities these leaders were engaged in, such as misappropriating international funds earmarked for reconstruction, for example, could help to mitigate any popular backlash.[40] Patrick Roberson, a US Army captain who deployed to Bosnia for two six-month tours as a joint commission observer (JCO), recalled that the local reaction had been very positive in one instance where an indicted war criminal had been arrested by

SFOR. "They were like, good; he was a psycho; I'm glad you caught him."[41] The case was unusual, because the individual involved had a very negative reputation in his own community, but it nevertheless suggests a solution to the problem of increased force protection risks caused by arresting war criminals.

Peacebuilding: Strengthening democratic values

Although these measures would go a long way to providing a stronger motivation for Bosnia's élites to commit themselves to governing democratically and in accordance with the rule of law, they have so far been negative incentives. SFOR can help strengthen the commitment of the Bosnian public to democracy as well, and in more positive ways, by supplying opportunities for and examples of democratic citizenship. A major source of public faith in the legitimacy of democracy is personal experience with democracy, which makes a participatory ethic and a vibrant civil society extremely important.[42] According to Larry Diamond: "There is no better way of developing the values, skills, and commitments of democratic citizenship than through direct experience with democracy, no matter how imperfect it may be."[43] There are at least two avenues open to SFOR whereby the military could support this. One is more formal, and entails the conscious use of civil affairs and civic action programmes to provide opportunities for democratic action. The second involves recognizing that the thousands of democratic citizens serving in SFOR right now can play a valuable role in teaching "intangible lessons" of democratic citizenship simply through interacting with the local populace.[44]

SFOR already possesses a considerable capacity for reconstructing and repairing infrastructure, and although a nation-building role was explicitly rejected in Bosnia, both IFOR and SFOR did rebuild roads, transportation systems, and public utilities that have benefited not only the military but also international civilian organizations and the local people. The military often coordinated these projects, with civilian organizations participating in the implementation effort. However, now that most mission-essential infrastructure needs of the military and civilian organizations have been met, SFOR engineers and civil affairs personnel could continue doing similar projects, but this time in conjunction with local governments as part of a consistent overall strategy designed to enhance democratization. The benefits of such a programme would be considerable. First, civic action of this sort would strengthen local governments and enhance their legitimacy by giving them an opportunity to prove their usefulness. Second, if a community could apply for assistance based on prioritized needs arrived at in a public forum, this would encourage a town or village to establish and utilize mechanisms for democratic governance, such as town meetings. Forums designed to elicit citizen input would, in turn, reinforce in the minds of the citizens the norms of democratic conduct built around compromise and consensus. Such projects could potentially also have a positive impact on reconciliation by offering opportunities for reintegrating society.

Landrum Bolling, senior adviser to Mercy Corps International, recommended to NGOs that they include locals in some sort of advisory committee to consult on projects for similar reasons. These committees would have very practical benefits, such as providing ideas and feedback, warning of potential problems or repercussions, and serving as a communications link to the community. Also, the existence of such a committee in and of itself could have a positive influence on the community. According to Steven Riskin: "Working together in that kind of relationship can be a far more effective lesson in democracy and civil society responsibility than many lectures and seminars."[45]

Opportunities for SFOR to promote democracy also exist through less formal structures. One way would be by allowing troops serving in Bosnia to become involved in community service. Such activities could range from short-term projects, such as repainting a school or planning a day when the community and the military got together to clean up litter along a river bank, to long-term investments in the local community, such as running an intramural sports programme for area high-school students or teaching English at an adult night school. These are all types of services the military encourage their members to perform in their own communities, and, by continuing that tradition of volunteerism in Bosnian communities, soldiers would be exemplifying participatory citizenship, democratic leadership, and a functioning civil society.[46] The interaction does not even need to be this organized to be effective. A Special Forces colonel who once served as the defence attaché officer (DAO) at the US Embassy in Sarajevo suggested that by "lifting the siege" and allowing off-duty troops to go into town for food, relaxation, and shopping, they could very well play a positive role in transmitting democratic values (in addition to providing troops with some relief from the boredom of being stuck on a military installation for six months). Bosnia is not a primitive culture which cannot understand modern concepts about governance and democracy. But they must be articulated by someone other than "the suits from the International Community who are seen as having a vested interest in the process. Who better to represent the benefits of democracy and market economy than the young men and women in the US military?"[47]

The combination of these two approaches, encouraging troops to volunteer in the communities and allowing them to interact informally with locals, could also have a positive impact on the problem of widespread emigration among Bosnian youths. This exodus is troubling for several reasons. First, it signals a lack of confidence in the government to provide a better future. Second, it is indicative of a lack of confidence on the part of individuals in their own ability to make a difference. Finally, the large-scale emigration of educated young people bodes poorly for the ability of Bosnia to recruit qualified individuals for work in government and businesses in their home country. Goran Tinjic, a Bosnian analyst at the World Bank, commented that reaching out to local youth should be a top priority for the international community: "The IC should also systematically seek for partnerships with local intellectuals and young people and contribute to making a better and more positive climate which would result in less young people leaving the country. This trend has been totally discouraging over the last couple of years."[48] SFOR, being composed primarily of young people, may be particularly well positioned to do this.

Peacebuilding: Enhancing government legitimacy

The lack of confidence in the ability of the government to provide a better future is indicative of a lack of legitimacy in the government as a whole. In a democracy, this legitimacy is derived in large part from the ability of a government to put democratic principles into practice. As Diamond argues, "Regime performance is assessed in terms not only of economic growth and social reform but also several crucial political dimensions: the capacity to maintain order, to govern transparently, to maintain a rule of law [particularly with regard to human rights], and to otherwise respect and preserve the democratic rules of the game."[49] In this arena, police performance is typically among the most critical, because the police are the representatives of government authority whom citizens are most likely to encounter on a regular basis.[50] In Bosnia, however, the relationship between the Bosnian people and their armed forces may be as important as the relationship between the people and the police, for two reasons. First, Bosnia is in the middle of a transition from a communist system, under which the Yugoslav National Army, like the Interior Police (MUP) and the local police, was oriented towards regime survival. The armed forces, therefore, were never viewed as a positive force in the country; they were always seen as an instrument of oppression. Second, and even more importantly, Bosnia is dealing with the aftermath of a very brutal civil war. The people need to have confidence that peace will continue even without the presence of SFOR.

Unfortunately this is not the case at the moment, because far from being a source of stability, the Entity Armed Forces continue to be a cause for concern. According to a US Institute of Peace special report on Bosnia:

The security environment in Bosnia today is artificially stable, because of the international military presence ... Each of the three ethnic groups in Bosnia continues to maintain an army, which creates risks of renewed war as well as obstacles to self-sustaining peace. These armies remain postured against one another. All three forces maintain active intelligence gathering and order-of-battle doctrines to fight against one another.[51]

To be fair, the Law on Defence and the amendments to the entity constitutions that were enacted in November 2003 by the parliamentary assembly and the legislatures of the federation and the RS (Republika Srpska), which established state-level joint command and control of the entity armed forces and made a number of other reforms that have put Bosnia on track for membership in the Partnership for Peace and eventually perhaps even in NATO, represent a tremendous achievement.[52] But in this realm as well, more could be done. Before SFOR's mission can be called complete, "the citizens of Bosnia and Herzegovina must be able to have confidence in the personal integrity, constitutional loyalty and military competence of EAF officers in general and specifically, the General Officer Corps".[53]

SFOR has been heavily involved in this aspect of security sector reform right from the start, at both the institutional and the individual level. For example, the establishment of the Office of the Inspector General (OIG) and the Standing Committee on Military Matters (SCMM), and SFOR's involvement in issues of EAF (Entity Armed Forces) restructuring, are all ways in which SFOR has encouraged structural changes in order to promote the development of a professional, democratic military in Bosnia.

It is in its efforts to professionalize the EAF at an individual level that SFOR needs to reconsider its focus. Thus far, much of SFOR's work has targeted senior officers, who, like their counterparts in the civilian world, frequently have the least incentive to embrace reform. Brigadier-General Eldon Bargewell, former SFOR assistant chief of staff for operations, suggested that focusing on mid-grade officers who are willing to change in order to join the EU would be more effective.[54] The general's comments were echoed by Captain Higginbotham, who observed that "sending 30 captains from each faction to the Infantry and Armor Officer Advanced Courses in the US will have a much greater long-term impact than selective schooling of senior officers".[55] On a broader scale, training conducted in-country by SFOR troops could help the EAF build the capacity for humanitarian and emergency relief missions, and reorient them from defending one ethnic group against the others to being a "force for good" in Bosnian society as a whole. Engaging them in civic action projects would improve their legitimacy in the eyes of the public, especially if SFOR could encourage them to cross ethnic boundary lines to do so. For example, an Oregon National Guard colonel told a story of one of the Multi-National Division North (MND(N)) Joint Military Commission chiefs who arranged to have some sandbags, donated by SFOR, transported by a Bosniac corps commander to a Croat division commander in a region that was threatened by flooding.[56] This is precisely the type of engagement that will help change attitudes in the long run, but it has to be part of a coordinated effort across the board to be most effective.

The plans for Joint Task Force Haiti, which – until a peaceful transfer of power was negotiated – had the similar objective of creating an army "respected for its ability to serve and protect Haitian society instead of one feared for its ability to terrorize that society at gunpoint" out of the Forces Armées d'Haiti (FAD'H), offer an example of how a coordinated campaign to professionalize the Bosnian EAF at every level might have been carried out.[57] The training for the FAD'H would have included an intensive programme in areas like coastal and frontier security, disaster relief, and search-and-rescue operations. It would have focused on areas like physical fitness, military appearance and deportment, and the role of a soldier in a democracy. Acting with Special Forces A teams, the FAD'H also would have "coordinated and executed small-scale humanitarian and civic-action projects".[58] The logic behind the mission was that, by convincing the FAD'H they would benefit from professionalizing, the FAD'H itself would become committed to professionalizing. Working and training side by side with professional role models of discipline, integrity, competence, toughness, and dedication to duty, the Haitian soldiers could have learned to take pride in these virtues and build their self-respect and public image upon them. Once the FAD'H had become interested in professionalizing itself, follow-on military training missions could have completed the task.[59]

In the long term, using military advisers may be one of the best ways to instil lasting, meaningful reform at all levels of service. According to retired Army Special Forces colonel Joe Andrade, who was a military adviser from 1990 to 1991 in El Salvador, as long as the US government is willing to take a long-term approach to solving the problem, military advisers can be a very effective catalyst for change.

Frequently, the goal of military advising includes helping the host nation's armed forces to internalize the principles of democratic, professional military service. Colonel Andrade described this as a four-part process involving setting the example; explaining why one chooses to do things that way; explaining how this will benefit the host nation's military as an institution; and, finally, making sure that the same message is being transmitted at every level. He noted that "Whatever values are reinforced at the top are the ones that remain when you leave."[60] Being in a position to influence things like the behaviour of troops on a daily basis, and the understanding of how that behaviour affects the legitimacy of the government and military, is a unique ability properly trained military advisers bring to the table. Andrade argued that "When you're on the ground living with the people you look at all aspects of a particular operation or challenge ... since we're living there we'll look at the economic, social, political and cultural aspects of doing something."[61]

To be effective, however, any programme of democratization and professionalization must be geared towards both the federation and the Bosnian Serb Republic. Eventually, the international community hopes to create a single state of two entities and three peoples in Bosnia and Herzegovina. Currently, however, because the Bosnian Serb Republic is not cooperating fully with the Hague Tribunal, the Bosnian Serb Republic is not being as fully engaged nor receiving as much aid as the federation. But when it comes to professionalizing the armed forces and initiating military projects to strengthen civil society and communicate democratic values, there is nothing to be gained by not also working with the Bosnian Serb Republic. This means that if SFOR expands training and education opportunities for the federation's armed forces and becomes involved in community projects, it should invite the Bosnian Serbs to participate as well. As Riskin notes: "The only way for Bosnia to achieve peaceful unification is to encourage each entity's simultaneous development."[62]

Training and education programmes that target junior as well as senior officers, civic action, and military advising will go a long way towards helping the Bosnian armed forces become the type of military that deserve the trust and confidence of the people they serve. This, in turn, would greatly enhance the legitimacy of the government and the military in the eyes of a population that currently has more reason to fear its soldiers, and provide an example to the government and bureaucracy of an institution that is acting to serve the common good. These programmes also all build on existing military capabilities and traditional forms of military engagement to foster positive change in a sphere that is clearly the military's domain.

Conclusion

There is much that SFOR and its successor organization could have done and could still do better in Bosnia to effect change and support the peace-building process.[63] By pursuing war criminals, targeting criminal activity, and maintaining its security presence, all of which are also operations that draw on typical military capabilities, SFOR would be putting some muscle behind the international community's plea that Bosnia's politicians support democratization because it is the right thing to do. And, simultaneously, SFOR would also be encouraging the development of greater respect for the rule of law, a critical element of a functioning democracy and sustainable peace.

There are also a number of less-traditional military capabilities that SFOR could take advantage of in support of security sector reform and democratization if it were to look for innovative ways to support the entire peacebuilding process. Becoming engaged with the Bosnian community through civil affairs, civic action programmes, volunteer work, and plain person-to-person interactions would contribute significantly to the reconstruction and reconciliation effort, while providing an example of democratic citizenship in action. This would demonstrate to the people of Bosnia how a citizen can actively participate in democracy and what can be gained by doing so.

The challenge for the military, and in particular the American military, in a world where post-conflict peacebuilding is no longer a charitable act but a strategic necessity is to become a more effective partner in supporting the development of a self-sustaining, democratic peace. This means that intervening military forces can no longer solely define their role in terms of "conflict suppression", and limit themselves merely to standing guard over a negative peace. It was to IFOR's credit that its military missions were completed a short 225 days after its arrival, but the job of an intervening military force is not actually complete until it can go home.

An intervening military force must also ask itself what it can do to support – directly and indirectly – the international community's goal of building a positive peace. This will not mean doing the same thing in every case. For example, SFOR is not in theory the best candidate for pursuing war criminals. This activity does pose a force protection risk, and it also sets an example for military involvement in judicial affairs that is quite contrary to the lessons one would want the EAF to absorb. However, in the case of Bosnia, because of the "enforcement gaps" in the GFAP, SFOR is the only organization that can perform this critical task. Yet redefining the military's role in helping to build a positive peace does mean actively looking for ways to support all aspects of post-conflict peacebuilding, ranging from the traditional requirements of monitoring a cease-fire to non-traditional applications of military capabilities to meet a specific need (for example, to arrest PIFWCs) and finding creative ways to support the development of other pillars of democratic peace, such as reinforcing the values of democratic citizenship.

The US Army captain who railed against being told to stay away from PIFWCs said that when he first went to Bosnia he bought into Joulwan and Shoemaker's minimalist interpretation of the role of the military. Now, however, he believes that there is much more the military can and should be doing:

It is naïve to think that our plans and self-imposed constraints developed at the outset of a mission like Bosnia will survive first initial contact, much less that they will be enough to get us in and out successfully ... Therefore, we have a responsibility to step up to the plate when necessary and occasionally perform non-standard tasks, especially when that is the only way that the mission – in this case, long-term peace – will ultimately be accomplished.[64]

The military cannot and should not replace civilian organizations in post-conflict peacebuilding. But neither can the world community afford to keep thousands of underemployed soldiers in Bosnia for generations. Particularly now, in light of the potentially long-term, costly international involvement in countries ranging from Afghanistan to Iraq, the lesson for foreign military intervention forces to take away from Bosnia is that there is in fact an "enhanced" role for them to play in peacebuilding.

Notes

1. The term peacekeeping is used to describe a military intervention in a conflict by a third party (or parties) that has as its primary goal the monitoring or enforcing of a cessation of hostilities, or negative peace. The term peacebuilding is used to refer to an intervention in a conflict that operates across the spectrum of military, political, social, and economic affairs etc., and that has as its goal the development of a sustainable, or positive, peace between the parties involved in the conflict.
2. See Jeong, Ho-Won. 2004. "Expanding peacekeeping functions for peace operations", *S+F: Sicherheit und Frieden/Security and Peace*, Vol. 22, No. 1, pp. 19–24.
3. See Anderson, Anthony W. 2004. "Enhancing the role of military peacekeepers in post-conflict peacebuilding: Revisiting the center of gravity", *S+F: Sicherheit und Frieden/Security and Peace*, Vol. 22, No. 1, pp. 1–7.
4. Joulwan, George A. and Christopher C. Shoemaker. 1998. *Civilian-Military Cooperation in the Prevention of Deadly Conflict*, report to the Carnegie Commission on the Prevention of Deadly Conflict. New York: Carnegie Corporation of New York, pp. 12–13.
5. When IFOR first entered Bosnia in 1995 it had 64,000 soldiers. SFOR had 32,000 soldiers initially, was down to 19,000 in 2002, then further reduced to about 13,000 by January 2003, and was expected to include no more than 7,000 troops by June 2004.

6. Daalder, Ivo H. 2000. *Getting to Dayton: The Making of America's Bosnia Policy.* Washington, DC: Brookings Institution Press, pp. 144–145.

7. "The Role of IFOR in the Peace Process", available at www.state.gov/www/regions/eur/bosnia/iforrole.html, 26 October 2000, p. 1.

8. Senate Hearing 104–855. 1997. Hearing Before the Committee on Armed Services United States Senate One Hundred Fifth Congress Second Session 1 August, 2–3 October 1996, "US Participation in Bosnia". Washington, DC: US Government Printing Office, p. 5.

9. "The Role of IFOR in the Peace Process", note 7 above, p. 1. The text of the General Framework Agreement for Peace is available at www.state.gov/www/regions/eur/bosnia/bosnia-hp.html.

10. Senate Hearing 104-855, note 8 above, p. 17.

11. *Ibid.*, pp. 5, 9.

12. *Ibid.*, p. 55.

13. Stewart, George and Frederick D. Thompson. 1998. *IFOR's Experience in Bosnia: Three Case Studies*, CRM 98-113/September 1998 Research Memorandum. Alexandria, VA: Center for Naval Analyses, p. 99.

14. Senate Hearing 104-855, note 8 above, p. 54.

15. Bildt, Carl. 2001. "The Balkans' second chance", *Foreign Affairs*, Vol. 80, No. 1, pp. 149, 152.

16. Ashdown, Paddy. 2004. "25th Report by the High Representative for the Implementation of the Peace Agreement to the Secretary-General of the United Nations", available at www.ohr.int/other-doc/hr-reports/default.asp?content_id=32024, 2 May, p. 1.

17. "SFOR Fact Sheet: SFOR Restructuring", available at www.nato.int/sfor/factsheet/restruct/t040121a.htm, 2 May 2004, p. 1.

18. Piatt, Gregory. 2001. "Allies to look at cuts in Balkans", *Stars and Stripes*, Vol. 60, No. 256, 30 December, p. 8.

19. Anderson, note 3 above.

20. Carothers, Thomas. 1999. *Aiding Democracy Abroad: The Learning Curve.* Washington, DC: Carnegie Endowment for International Peace, p. 164.

21. Ashdown, Paddy. 2003. "Bosnia is the Model for Resolving Conflicts", available at www.iht.com/articles/75809.html, 16 February, p. 1.

22. *SFOR Lessons Learned in Creating a Secure Environment with Respect for the Rule of Law*, final draft sent to General Meigs, 14 March 2000, p. x. Emphasis in the original.

23. Carothers, note 20 above, p. 165.

24. Dziedzic, Michael J. and Andrew Bair. 1998. "Bosnia and the International Police Task Force", in Robert Oakley, Michael J. Dziedzic, and Elliot M. Goldberg (eds) *Policing the New World Disorder: Peace Operations and Public Security*. Washington DC: National Defense University Press, pp. 283–285; Daalder, Ivo H. and Michael B. G. Froman. 1999. "Dayton's incomplete peace", *Foreign Affairs*, Vol. 78, No. 6, p. 110.

25. "SFOR Fact Sheet", note 17 above, p. 1.

26. *SFOR Lessons Learned*, note 22 above.

27. The establishment of a domestic War Crimes Tribunal in Bosnia, which Paddy Ashdown, note 16 above, highlights as a significant accomplishment, represents a marked change in the willingness of Bosnians to prosecute war criminals on their own.

28. *SFOR Lessons Learned*, note 22 above, p. 4.

29. Senate Hearing 104-855, note 8 above, p. 40.

30. Captain Ben Higginbotham, US Army, e-mail correspondence with the author, 19 November 2001.

31. US General Accounting Office. 1997. Testimony Before the Subcommittee on European Affairs, Committee on Foreign Relations, US Senate, "Bosnia Peace Operation:

Progress Toward the Dayton Agreement's Ultimate Goals – An Update", statement of Harold J. Johnson, Associate Director, International Relations and Trade Issues, National Security and International Affairs Division. Washington, DC: General Accounting Office, p. 4.

32. *SFOR Lessons Learned*, note 22 above, p. 27.

33. Holbrooke, Richard. 1999. *To End a War*, New York: Modern Library, p. 222. In response to a question about whether IFOR was going to arrest Serbs in the Serb suburbs of Sarajevo, the admiral replied, "Absolutely not, I don't have the authority to arrest anybody."

34. Higginbotham, note 30 above.

35. *SFOR Lessons Learned*, note 22 above, p. x.

36. *Ibid.*, p. 5.

37. *Ibid.*, pp. 7, 35.

38. *Ibid.*, p. 31.

39. *Ibid.*, p. 32.

40. *Ibid.*, p. 19.

41. Captain Patrick Roberson, US Naval Postgraduate School, interview by the author, 23 October 2000.

42. Diamond, Larry. 1999. *Developing Democracy: Toward Consolidation*. Baltimore: Johns Hopkins University Press, p. 170.

43. *Ibid.*, p. 162.

44. Colonel Steve Bucci, then US defence attaché officer, Sarajevo, during a meeting on 9 January 2001 at the American Embassy in Sarajevo with Colonel Robert Tomasovic, which the author attended.

45. Riskin, Steven M. (ed.). 1999. "Three dimensions of peacebuilding in Bosnia: Findings from USIP-sponsored research and field projects", *Peaceworks 32*. Washington, DC: US Institute of Peace, pp. 33–34.

46. This chapter draws heavily on the experience of the US military in SFOR, and does not reflect the varying approaches of other nations. Because of the considerable influence of the USA in planning peacekeeping missions, the author believes this experience is highly relevant. Such community-building activities have been tried at different times by different militaries (including some US units) in different locations throughout Bosnia. However, these programmes are not part of a comprehensive, SFOR-wide plan to promote democratization and peacebuilding, which is needed.

47. Bucci, note 44 above, e-mail correspondence with the author, 3 February 2001. Clearly soldiers from all developed democracies can perform this function as well.

48. Goran Tinjic, e-mail correspondence with the author, February 2001.

49. Diamond, note 42 above, pp. 170–171.

50. *Ibid.*, p. 94.

51. Western, John W. and Daniel Serwer. 2000. *Bosnia's Next Five Years and Beyond*, US Institute of Peace Special Report. Washington, DC: US Institute of Peace, p. 7.

52. Ashdown, note 16 above, p. 1.

53. Tomasovic, Colonel Robert, United States Army National Guard. 2000. "Entity Armed Forces in a Democratic Society: Ethics, Development and Cooperation", Change 18/1 to the Instructions to the Parties, Chapter 14, Version 15, August.

54. Tomasovic, Colonel Robert, "Trip Report to Bosnia 6 Jan–12 Jan 01", for the Center for Civil-Military Relations, and comments made by Brigadier General Eldon Bargewell, SFOR assistant chief of staff for operations, during an 8 January 2001 meeting between the general and Colonel Tomasovic, which the author attended.

55. Higginbotham, note 30 above.

56. Tomasovic, Colonel Robert, interview with the author, 20 February 2001.

57. Epstein, Stephen M., Robert S. Cronin, and James G. Pulley. 1994. "JTF Haiti: A United Nations foreign internal defense mission", *Special Warfare*, Vol. 7, No. 3, p. 4.
58. *Ibid.*, p. 3.
59. *Ibid.*, p. 4.
60. Colonel Joe Andrade, US Naval Postgraduate School, interview by the author, 25 January 2001.
61. *Ibid.*
62. Riskin, note 45 above, p. 21.
63. The European Union, which assumed responsibility for Mission Amber Fox and the International Police Task Force (through the EU Police Mission), also declared its willingness to take over responsibility for SFOR in 2004.
64. Higginbotham, note 30 above.

7

The use of Russia's security structures in the post-conflict environment

Ekaterina A. Stepanova

Before turning to Russia's recent experience of using its security structures[1] in post-conflict operations, it has to be noted that many of the problems faced by Russia in this field are, indeed, specific to the Russian model, as compared to those of most Western states. For that reason, more general problems of the use of the armed forces in a post-conflict environment should first be briefly addressed. That will serve as a general background, against which the performance of those of Russia's multiple security structures that seem to be best tailored for operations in a post-conflict environment – the Ministry of Interior and the Ministry for Civil Defence, Emergencies, and Elimination of Consequences of Natural Disasters (EMERCOM) – will be assessed.

In the past decade, the level of military participation in post-conflict stabilization, reconstruction, and rehabilitation activities has been steadily growing.[2] The armed forces' increased involvement in these activities can be explained by several factors:

- the search by governments and armed forces for a new global role for the military with the passing of the Cold War (an imperative so strong that it was able to overcome the traditionally sceptical attitude of the professional armed forces towards "non-military" activities)
- the availability of significant military assets at the time when civilian organizations were overwhelmed with humanitarian relief and post-conflict reconstruction and development tasks
- the lack of alternatives for most Western states to deploying their

armed forces to perform essentially non-military tasks in post-conflict environments.

While in a post-conflict environment the division between security and non-security elements of peacebuilding and stabilization efforts is often relative, for the sake of clarity it makes sense to follow the basic division between security tasks, performed by the security or military component of an international peacebuilding effort or of a national "stabilization" campaign; and humanitarian, political, economic reconstruction and development, civil-society-related, and other peacebuilding tasks that have long-term implications for solidifying the achievements made by the military (security) component of the mission. The armed forces face a number of problems in dealing with these two main groups of tasks in post-conflict settings.

Addressing security issues in a post-conflict environment requires one to distinguish between various security needs. The regular troops have proved to be most effective in demilitarization (especially controlling the withdrawal of heavy arms) and provision of a basic security environment, with the emphasis still on force protection. At the same time, the functional division between traditional military and "normal" civil police duties has become increasingly blurred in the post-conflict environment, creating a "grey area" between cessation of hostilities and lasting peace. It is into this "grey area" of militarized police or other special duties that most of the security tasks in the post-conflict environments fall (patrolling refugees camps; escorting humanitarian convoys, refugees, and internally displaced persons (IDPs); providing protection to them upon their return, as well as to international civil personnel and local population; controlling riots and mob violence; dealing with war criminals; fighting terrorism, etc.).

The civilian sector has to rely on the "security component" of the mission to perform these tasks. As demonstrated by the extensive experience of the past decade, however, the armed forces normally lack special training and, fearing "mission creep" and its unforeseen implications, are often reluctant to perform "grey area" duties in post-conflict settings. At the same time, civil police (even if armed, as the UN police in Kosovo) cannot effectively carry out post-conflict police functions that, in contrast to "normal" police duties, are performed in an environment which could easily escalate into an armed conflict and thus requires more robust, militarized police capacities.[3]

The international community is thus in need of forces and mechanisms for maintaining order in the post-conflict environment – during the critical period after mission deployment, but before the rule of law is fully established or restored (so that control can be handed over to a local police force). Ideally, the forces to forge this "missing link" in conflict management should have the discipline, cohesion, and war-fighting skills of the military, plus the special equipment and training of the police, with an emphasis on anti-terrorist and special capacities and more robust policing efforts as opposed to "normal" police duties. Apparently, most functions required from the security component of the mission in a post-conflict environment are very close to those performed by internal security forces (or national police forces with military status) in countries that have such forces. With a few notable exceptions, such as the French gendarmerie and Italian carabinieri (law enforcement units responsive to their respective ministries of defence, financed from military budgets, and forming the core of NATO multinational specialized units in the Balkans), in most NATO states, including the USA, "intermediate" militarized police capacities are either lacking or insufficient. Thus, most of these states have no tenable alternative to deploying their regular troops in post-conflict environments and letting them drift towards police functions.

The growing involvement of the armed forces in post-conflict environments for non-security purposes can be even more controversial. While resort to the use of military assets and personnel is often inevitable, especially at the critical "emergency" stage of crisis, it also has the potential of weakening or undermining the comparative advantages of the civilian sector, such as technical expertise, knowledge of the region, ties to local communities, and especially longer-term commitment to reconstruction and development. As demonstrated by the experience of the past decade, the generic comparative advantages of the military (long-haul lift, logistics, communications, intelligence, and demining) tend to decrease gradually when the situation becomes less critical and moves from a state of conflict to a post-conflict stage, and as the military's tasks shift to activities more directly related to civilian (humanitarian, reconstruction, and development) work. The unprecedented level of militarization of non-security tasks, such as that seen in NATO operations in and around Kosovo, is, however, rather an exception than the rule: it usually results from direct international military involvement in the conflict on behalf of one of the parties, and is unlikely to be seen in most post-conflict environments that are less politically and strategically important to the West.[4]

In contrast to the West, Russia's post-Cold War involvement in post-conflict settings has been commonly related either to conflicts on its own soil (Chechnya) or to cross-border disturbances and conflicts in neighbouring or CIS states (Georgia/Abkhazia, Moldova/Transdniestria, Tajikistan). While some operations in more distant regions (for instance, in the Balkans) are possible, they are increasingly becoming exceptions rather than the rule. So for Russia the problems of countering sub-conventional violence in a state between conflict and peace, restoring law and order, and recovery and reconstruction in post-conflict areas are a matter of more direct political, economic, and security concern. Also, in most cases in which Russia is involved, the boundary between the conflict and post-conflict environments, which is generally not always easy to define, is particularly blurred, as the situation in Chechnya has vividly demonstrated.

MVD (Ministry of Internal Affairs): Coping with "grey area" security tasks

The emphasis on security structures' activities rather than just on the armed forces' performance in the post-conflict environment, as mentioned in the title of this chapter, reflects one of the most evident characteristics of the Russian model of post-conflict security building. While most Western states lack forces other than the military to perform "grey area" security tasks, for many countries that have not yet developed solid democratic traditions or face constant internal disturbances, most of these duties are very similar to "internal security" tasks. So are they for the Russian Federation, where the number of internal troops of the Ministry of Interior (up to 300,000 gendarmerie-type soldier-police) may soon be almost comparable to the country's land armed forces, which are subject to dramatic cuts. Internal troops are composed of formations that are in many respects similar to light infantry, and of special detachment units (*spetsnaz*), with the difference that they are trained to deal as much with civilians as with enemy troops. Internal troops are armed with light arms, light and heavy mortars, and armoured troop-carriers. However, unlike the armed forces, they cannot use heavy arms (artillery, tanks, and rocket-launchers) and ammunition, or assault aircraft, combat helicopters, and cassette rocket-launchers in public security operations.[5]

Internal troops have become the key force component to be deployed to post-conflict areas within the country, as they are made directly responsible by the Russian federal legislation for "grey area" security tasks at the transitional stage between the suspension of full-scale hostilities and the re-establishment of functioning state structures. According to the law, internal troops' tasks include, among others:

- sealing off areas declared under the state of emergency and zones of armed conflicts; prevention of hostilities and separation of the conflicting parties; confiscation of weapons from the population; disarmament of illegal armed groups or, in case of armed resistance, their elimination (in cooperation with other MVD structures)

- reinforcement of public order and security in areas adjacent to the "emergency" or conflict zones
- prevention of mass public disorders in settlements.[6]

Both regular internal troops and special units (special rapid reaction units – SOBR – and militia units of special detachment – OMON) are actively used in domestic operations other than war. These formations are better prepared to conduct specific "grey area" security tasks than regular armed forces. It should be noted, however, that this is only true for operations that do not involve combat: in combat-type missions on Russian territory (in conflict zones or at early stages of post-conflict stabilization) there is no alternative to the use of the armed forces, as demonstrated by the situation in and around Chechnya. While it was the internal troops and other MVD units who were the first to stand against the August 1999 invasion of armed Chechen groups into neighbouring Dagestan, they had to be replaced with regular armed forces as soon as that was possible. At the military stage of the second campaign in Chechnya, internal troops played support functions (rear and flank cover, cordon-off operations, etc.). Normally, after the army units neutralized the rebels' artillery in a certain area, internal troops and MVD special units arrived to conduct cordon-off (mopping-up) actions, population screening (passport regime control), and other operations.

By mid-2000 the focus of full-scale armed confrontation moved to the south of Chechnya. The rest of the republic's territory, especially the central region, remained subject to operations other than war, designed to prevent and counter occasional guerrilla attacks, skirmishes, ambushes, or terrorist acts. In these regions it was the internal troops, supported by regular police personnel (delegated by regional criminal police departments from all over Russia), who assumed the primary responsibility for restoring public order and security, in contrast to their military support functions at the military stage of the campaign. The internal troop units replaced the military at block-posts on the roads to settlements, took part in special operations, guarded objects of critical importance, and provided protection to humanitarian convoys. As compared to the first campaign in Chechnya (1994–1996), more attention was paid to building relations with the local population, especially in relatively "loyal" regions (while in Dagestan these relations were very cooperative, in many parts of Chechnya they remained highly problematic).

In addition to internal troops, in Chechnya's administrative districts the MVD formed interim departments of internal affairs, working in close cooperation with local military commandants' offices. A decision was taken to assign Russian regions (*oblast'*) and provinces to take responsibility for public security tasks in Chechnya's administrative districts by delegating part of the MVD's regular regional department personnel, such as the criminal police. For instance, an interim internal affairs department from Volgograd *oblast'* was deployed to Chechnya's Shelkovskoi district; and public security tasks in Chechnya's Naurski and Nadterechnyi districts were assigned to Krasnodar and Rostov regional MVD structures, respectively. MVD interim departments, supported if necessary by internal troops, also checked the identity of IDPs leaving Chechnya and took over passport control in general. The neighbouring Republic of Ingushetia's MVD structures and the North Caucasus regional unit on combating organized crime (RUBOP) evacuated civilian populations from particularly insecure regions (for instance, they organized the evacuation of elderly people from Grozny). As the federal campaign's main focus gradually shifted towards non-military security tasks, the MVD structures had to take up additional responsibilities. In August 2000, for instance, the task of ensuring public security and order in view of the Federal State Duma's deputy election campaign assumed primary importance for the MVD in Chechnya.

MVD structures also played a key role in providing security to humanitarian personnel in the North Caucasus. According to UN assessments, "the main threat to the humanitarian personnel is posed by organized criminal groups that have created a complex network of kidnapping (both foreign and Russian citizens) for financial gain".[7] Moreover, as the risk of hostilities in many regions of Chechnya decreased, the risk of hostage-taking activities and other forms of criminal violence increased. With the UN's growing humanitarian presence in the region, the problem of providing protection for international and local humanitarian personnel working in the field became more pressing. In practice, these security functions were mainly performed by the MVD's regional structures, particularly by North Caucasus RUBOP units. For instance, the UN office in Vladikavkaz was guarded by the North Ossetia RUBOP, while the Ingushetia RUBOP escorted UN humanitarian convoys to Chechnya.

As the security situation in some of the regions slowly normalized, other problems started to emerge, such as the problem of avoiding duplication of functions between federal police deployed in the republic and local police units which were being formed, as well as the gradual, slow transfer of police functions from the former to the latter. One of the criteria of assessing the effectiveness of the MVD structures' performance in Chechnya is precisely the extent to which their functions are being transferred to local Chechen police, answering to the MVD of the Chechen Republic. By 2002 there were three Chechen MVD departments working in a relatively stable northern Chechnya (to the north of the River Terek), and 42,000 federal MVD personnel still deployed in the republic (the Internal Troops 46th Brigade is deployed in Chechnya on a permanent basis). Under a decree signed by President Putin in late June

2003,[8] it was the MVD that took over the regional operational staff for the North Caucasus, i.e. the overall control of all of Russia's security operations in the region, including those of the Federal Group of Forces (OGV) and the Federal Security Service, with the more remote goal of ultimately transferring law and order responsibilities to the Chechen republican MVD.

While the participation of MVD internal troops, special units, and regular police has been critical for the implementation of "grey area" tasks in post-conflict settings on Russian territory, it also raised a number of wider issues. One of them is how the involvement of MVD units in security tasks in the North Caucasus affects their regular performance throughout the country. While this problem is less relevant for internal troops in general (operations in conflict-type or post-conflict environments are part of their primary functions), it is more pressing for regular police units (such as criminal police), and especially for special units, such as OMONs. The latter are in strong demand throughout the country as a robust militarized rapid-reaction capacity to fight organized crime and be used in counterterrorist, counternarcotics, and other operations. An urgent need for these formations in non-conflict areas has been one of the reasons for their frequent rotation in Chechnya and in the North Caucasus in general. Yet it is widely recognized within the MVD itself that frequent rotation undermines MVD units' advantages in implementing post-conflict security tasks. In order to make MVD operations in Chechnya more effective, a decision was taken by the MVD's new head, Vladimir Gryzlov, to extend the period of their deployment in the region from an average of three months to an average of six months, and even up to one year.[9]

The first "administrative" MVD reform efforts (stronger centralization of the criminal police, coupled with greater decentralization of public security police structures) were reactivated during President Putin's first term in office by a group of his loyalists in the ministry's leadership, guided primarily by domestic law enforcement priorities rather than by post-conflict security-building requirements. Of particular relevance to security operations in the post-conflict environment was the preservation of the RUBOP structures, which proved to be effective in protecting humanitarian convoys and humanitarian personnel. At the same time, the special rapid-reaction units (SOBRs) were separated from RUBOPs and faced further reorganization to become MVD special forces. Developments in federal police training included the organization of regular special courses in international humanitarian law for internal troops officers – as a result of both the MVD's active interaction with the United Nations and other international humanitarian organizations in the North Caucasus, and increasing involvement in UN peace support missions (although, as compared to the MVD's involvement in domestic operations, the latter remained very limited).[10]

During Putin's second term, general domestic political, economic, and security priorities, such as the need to improve general law and order conditions on the territory of the Russian Federation, have stimulated further attempts to streamline the huge and complex structure of the Ministry of the Interior and make it more efficient both operationally and financially. Apparently, this time Russia's experience in the North Caucasus has had a greater impact on the reform efforts. On 19 April 2004 Putin declared the launch of the "administrative" security sector reform and reorganization "in the spirit of the ongoing reform of the state administration" that had already affected most governmental "civilian" bodies.[11] Less radical than the reorganization of civil ministries, the "security sector reform" was aimed at reducing the number of top officials, as well as of intraministerial structural bodies, departments, services, and agencies in the ministries of the security bloc, and at delegating most specialized functions to federal agencies subordinate to, but structurally autonomous from, the "umbrella" ministries.

Unsurprisingly, the reform's central focus has been on the Ministry of Interior. According to the commander-in-chief of the internal troops, General Vyacheslav Tihomirov, the reform of the internal troops is both dictated by the overall economic reform agenda that calls for greater effectiveness of the entire MVD system, and based on practical experience in managing interethnic and other conflicts and post-conflict situations and countering political extremism and terrorism.[12] So far, the reform has involved measures aimed at greater mobility and gradual professionalization (by the end of 2004 the Internal Troops 46th Brigade, deployed in Chechnya on a permanent basis, was to be formed entirely on a professional contract basis); slow and selective downsizing (in 2004 alone, internal troops have been cut by 7,000 soldiers, and by 2005 this number should reach 33,900, or slightly more than 10 per cent of all personnel); modernization of arms and equipment, with a new emphasis on non-lethal weapons; and better financing (while at the start of the second federal campaign in Chechnya in 1999 only 29 per cent of the internal troops' financial needs were met by the government, in 2004 these forces have received 84 per cent of their requested financing).[13]

Proposals for a more radical structural reform of the MVD are also under discussion. Such a reform would be directed towards further specialization and division of the MVD's main functions – to the point of delegating them to several new bodies, such as the Federal Police (responsible for all regular law enforcement duties, except for criminal investigation), the Federal Service for Investigations, and the Municipal Militia (an entirely new body that would respond to local self-government bodies and be financed from local municipal budgets). In this context, of critical importance to post-conflict peacebuilding and restoration of law and order would be the formation, on the basis of the current internal troops, of a separate security structure that may be renamed the "National Guard" – the "state militarized organization tasked with the protection of the public order and security under extraordinary/ emergency conditions, guarding functions for the objects of high importance, and the fight against illegal armed groups". This scenario would underscore the importance of the ex-internal troops and secure a higher profile for them by making the "National Guard" directly responding to the president.[14]

EMERCOM: Emergency aid, basic recovery, and reconstruction

The pattern described above does not only apply to security-related tasks, but extends to include humanitarian relief and some of the most urgent reconstruction functions performed by Russia's EMERCOM, a militarized civil defence and disaster relief agency.

While previously mainly limited to natural disaster mitigation, since the early 1990s the deployment of national civil defence or emergency relief agencies in man-made humanitarian crises and post-conflict environments has been growing steadily on a worldwide scale. However, no state or international organization has used the potential of civil defence and emergency agencies for humanitarian, recovery, and reconstruction purposes in post-conflict settings as widely as the Russian Federation. In the first 10 years after its creation in 1990, the Russian Civil Defence and Emergencies Agency conducted more than 150,000 rescue, humanitarian, and other operations in 47 countries, physically saved 57,000 people, and evacuated more than 1.5 million people from conflict zones.[15] This makes it one of the 10 most effective emergency services in the world. The agency was later elevated to a cabinet level and renamed the Ministry for Civil Defence, Emergencies, and Elimination of Consequences of Natural Disasters, or EMERCOM for short.

EMERCOM is not a civilian agency, unlike most civil emergency/ emergency agencies in Western countries. Apart from EMERCOM's military-type organizational hierarchy, 40 per cent of its 70,000 employees are in fact arms-carrying service personnel. Forty per cent of those serve on a contract basis. EMERCOM has a countrywide structure of regional departments, working in cooperation with local governments. Local EMERCOM branches are especially active in remote regions (such as in some parts of Siberia, the far east, and the north), where they are often the only well-maintained and conspicuous authority. Beyond that, EMERCOM has taken over some executive supervision and police functions to ensure that federal funds allocated for coping with crises and natural disasters are efficiently used and not stolen by local bureaucracies. EMERCOM enjoys high public respect, and its political neutrality and strong political profile guarantee a strong level of funding. This is helped along by the fact that natural and technological disaster mitigation is one of the most conspicuous ways for the central government to demonstrate its effectiveness, while failure to respond may lead to serious political consequences. Apart from regularly paid salaries to its employees, EMERCOM is known for its utilization of high-tech equipment. In fact, the agency seems to be one of the most technically advanced state security structures, equipped with speedboats, helicopters, and long-haul air-lift capacities. In sum, domestically, EMERCOM proves to be one of the very few successful experiments in post-Soviet state institution building.[16]

Apart from its disaster mitigation functions, throughout the 1990s EMERCOM became increasingly involved in conflict zones and post-conflict settings both inside and outside Russia. Since 1992, when EMERCOM was first tasked with helping and accommodating refugees from South Ossetia, its specialists have worked in Transdniestria, North Ossetia, Ingushetia, Abkhazia, Tajikistan, former Yugoslavia, and Chechnya.

Particularly in the North Caucasus, EMERCOM seemed to be the best-organized federal force, especially during and in the aftermath of the second Chechen campaign. EMERCOM's militarized organization allowed the agency to start working in Chechnya proper at the earliest stage of the military campaign. The first to be deployed were officers of EMERCOM's Centre for High-Risk Rescue Operations, whose specific responsibility was to provide security to the agency's personnel as they were deployed into the region. In February 2000 EMERCOM's Central Air-Mobile Rescue Unit was deployed; by the summer of 2000 a combined mobile unit, formed by several EMERCOM regional divisions, was fully operational; and in July 2000 an EMERCOM branch in the Chechen Republic was formed.

EMERCOM's activities in and around Chechnya were not limited to traditional search-and-rescue functions, such as evacuation of the population from highly insecure areas. Rather, they embraced a range of functions that could be described as complex humanitarian emergency operations. In 1999–2000 EMERCOM's priorities in the North Caucasus were as described below (in July 2000, many of these tasks were transferred to the republican EMERCOM).

• In the first days of the crisis EMERCOM started to construct temporary camps in Ingushetia for IDPs from Chechnya (whose number reached 250,000 at the peak of the crisis). By the end of September 1999 four tent camps had been built by the EMERCOM of Ingushetia, with a capacity to host from 360 to 3,000 people; by June 2000, 12 camps were operational. EMERCOM's operational efficiency in camp construction and the quality of the camps were highly appraised by UN representatives, acknowledging that the professionalism of EMERCOM specialists sometimes even exceeded their own.[17]

- EMERCOM organized nutrition for IDPs both outside and inside Chechnya, as well as for the most needy (women, children, elderly people) throughout Chechnya. Overall, food aid was regularly provided to more than 240,000 individuals.

- Humanitarian aid, from food and living essentials to field kitchens, diesel power stations, and oil heaters, provided by the central government and particularly by Russia's regions, was collected and delivered to the region by air and trucks. Also, EMERCOM was responsible for ensuring customs clearance for and delivery of international humanitarian aid to the region and, at earlier stages of the campaign, its distribution among the beneficiaries. Later on, EMERCOM mostly escorted convoys into Chechnya, while local NGOs, under contract with the UNHCR, distributed the emergency supplies among needy families and individuals.

- EMERCOM medical teams provided medical aid to more than 60,000 people. Also, EMERCOM deployed two field hospitals to Chechnya, reconstructed 23 medical facilities, and served as an ambulance service by providing most urgent medical assistance on the spot and delivering the sick or injured to a nearby hospital.

- Water supply was organized by reconstructing or repairing water pumping stations, purification and distribution of potable water, and well cleaning.

- Along with the army's engineering force responsible for mine clearance and deactivation, EMERCOM actively participated in "humanitarian demining". Despite the high professionalism of EMERCOM demining teams and the impressive quantities of detected and removed unexploded ordnance, demining activities in Chechnya proved to be one of the least effective functions, as most of the demined areas were soon discovered to be mined again.[18]

Apart from these functions, EMERCOM has also performed a variety of other tasks, from burying bodies and setting up communications systems (first of all radio communication) to assistance for IDPs to register with the civilian Federal Migration Agency and reclaim their social status.

The humanitarian crisis in the North Caucasus has vividly demonstrated that EMERCOM has emerged as Russia's leading humanitarian agency. Compared to both civilian humanitarian organizations and the armed forces, EMERCOM's advantages in the field of humanitarian emergency response are mobility, flexibility, intensive specialized professional training, and a militarized organization, the latter being critical for operating effectively in an insecure post-conflict environment. For instance, a typical mobile group of the EMERCOM Central Air-Mobile Rescue Unit, operating in every district of the city of Grozny and formed exclusively on a voluntary basis, included professional guards in addition to a driver, a physician, rescue workers, and other "functional specialists". In cases of minor attacks or hooligan acts, EMERCOM units had the right to use light arms. At the same time, in order not to stand out among the city's residents (should that be required for security reasons), the Central Air-Mobile Rescue Unit did not require its personnel to operate in official uniforms. EMERCOM tactics, to be "invisible for illegal armed groups, but open to the federal services, inaccessible to the media, but carefully explaining its activities to the local population",[19] proved to be effective in Chechnya.

In addition to emergency response skills, EMERCOM's high level of specialization and professional training allowed its personnel to accommodate specific humanitarian demands. For instance, EMERCOM units tried their best to observe the principle of humanitarian neutrality by not publicly siding with the federal authorities (!) when communicating with the local population, and by always stressing that their agency is "above politics". To facilitate interaction with the local population, a tactic of "local connections transfer" in the process of personnel rotation was particularly effective. In line with humanitarian standards, for security reasons EMERCOM insisted on IDP camp locations at some distance from an administrative border with Chechnya. At the same time, EMERCOM experts opposed camp construction outside of the North Caucasian region, as that would have made it very difficult for many IDPs to return to Chechnya.

In sum, EMERCOM proved to be effective and efficient in performing humanitarian emergency response tasks, especially as compared with the chronically underfinanced civilian agencies. As demonstrated by operations in the North Caucasus, in humanitarian emergencies in Russia there is no alternative to EMERCOM, which manages to reconcile a seemingly irreconcilable militarized organization with a high humanitarian profile.

Apart from EMERCOM's domestic functions, its advanced technical equipment (in line with most international standards), considerable airlift capacity, and operational flexibility, mobility, and efficiency, as well as its militarized personnel and organization, make the agency similar to a rapid-reaction force, ready to be deployed anywhere in the world. Unlike the MVD, as a humanitarian/disaster relief agency EMERCOM is not bound by many legal restrictions for deployment outside Russia. EMERCOM involvement might be particularly welcome in cases when Russia's military or peacekeeping involvement is unwelcome, or politically undesirable for Russia itself, as already effectively demonstrated by EMERCOM operations in Afghanistan.

Among other things, EMERCOM's humanitarian mission to Afghanistan, labelled by its participants "a peaceful version of the Kosovo raid",[20] has vividly demonstrated the shift in Russia's foreign policy to more pragmatic and rational behaviour. EMERCOM activities in Afghanistan included:

- delivery of humanitarian supplies to the population of Afghanistan (food aid, non-food items, medicines, medical equipment, vehicles, and construction materials) by railroad to Dushanbe and then by trucks to Afghanistan, via the Osh-Faizabad route
- medical assistance to the local population in Kabul (in line with local customs, men and women were examined on different days in an EMERCOM-operated field hospital; Russian-speaking Afghan doctors were actively recruited and EMERCOM medical brigades were set up to work in towns and settlements outside Kabul)
- reconstruction works (at the Salang tunnel, which connects the north with the rest of the country, and elsewhere)
- additionally, EMERCOM has expressed its readiness to organize emergency relief training for Afghans and assist in the formation of a local professional rescue team etc.[21]

Security for EMERCOM personnel operating in Afghanistan was provided by Russian special services in cooperation with the new Afghan Ministry of Defence, as well as by EMERCOM's own guards (who were mistaken for the Russian military by the Western media).[22] In its humanitarian and reconstruction operations in Afghanistan, EMERCOM closely cooperated with individual states (Germany, France, and the UK) and international organizations (such as the World Food Programme), not to mention the local Afghan agencies, particularly the Ministry of Refugees and Repatriates.

Overall, as demonstrated by EMERCOM's experience in performing humanitarian and basic reconstruction tasks both inside and outside Russia, this militarized humanitarian agency is highly effective in the post-conflict environment. At the same time, it must be stressed that EMERCOM is ideally suited for operational emergency response only, and cannot provide humanitarian assistance on a long-term basis[23] nor deal with all of the consequences of a humanitarian disaster, nor with the entire post-conflict range of reconstruction and recovery tasks. These tasks have to be implemented by governmental, non-governmental, and international civilian organizations.

Implications for the military and for civil-military relations

The availability of several state-run militarized organizations, legally entitled to perform security and some non-security tasks in the post-conflict environment, means that there is no need for Russia to overburden its armed forces with non-combat post-conflict missions, most of which are likely to be domestic or have an important domestic aspect (such as cross-border missions). With EMERCOM effectively performing emergency humanitarian and basic relief, reconstruction, and recovery functions, there is no major need to involve the military in humanitarian assistance operations. While the military's occasional involvement in some humanitarian actions in the North Caucasus, especially at the earlier stage of the second campaign in Chechnya, was more active than in the 1994–1996 campaign (by delivering food, medicines, and fuel to residents of Dagestan and the northern and central regions of Chechnya), these activities were still limited, dictated primarily by political considerations, and only sometimes driven by technical necessity (such as the occasional use of military cargo planes for humanitarian aid delivery).

In the security field, the armed forces' involvement in non-combat activities, particularly in areas that could be described as post-conflict environments (most of the northern and some of the central regions of Chechnya), was mostly limited to:

- attempts to create "humanitarian corridors" from Grozny and some other cities and towns
- providing protection to two IDP camps near Znamenskaya in northern Chechnya (a task that was transferred to MVD forces as soon as that was possible)
- participation, alongside EMERCOM demining teams, in humanitarian demining (as well as in demining for military purposes).

In addition, there were also several bizarre cases of military involvement in apparently non-military activities, such as an attempt by the Joint Group of Federal Forces to impose restrictions on crossing the Chechen-Ingush border in both directions by all men aged from 10 to 60 – a decision so heavily criticized both inside and outside Russia that it had to be revoked three days after it was made.[24]

An important implication for civil-military relations is that several militarized security structures play a role of a buffer between the professional military and the civilian sector, reducing potential for civil-military tensions. The UN agencies operating in the North Caucasus, for instance, had few problems with the Russian armed forces for the simple reason that they had little interaction with these forces: most of their security problems were dealt with by the MVD or, in critical cases, by special services. Most transport, communication, and other logistical as well as coordination problems were settled in cooperation with EMERCOM. Even keeping in mind the internal character of Russia's involvement in the North Caucasus, as opposed to NATO's out-of-area mission in the Balkans, the contrast between the two patterns is clear. For instance, if a NATO officer at the peak of the humanitarian emergency in the Balkans in the spring and early summer of 1999 happened to be unaware of the difference between the Office of the UN High Commissioner on Refugees (UNHCR) and the UN Office for Coordination of Humanitarian Affairs (OCHA), it would have been problematic for the mission as he would have probably found himself in a position of dealing directly with these agencies. The same unawareness on the part of a Russian officer in the North Caucasus, however, was not a problem at all, as it was EMERCOM that was fully responsible for dealing with these UN agencies.

This does not mean that there have been no problems in the field between the civilian sector and Russia's security structures other than the armed forces. In the North Caucasus, the general record for these Russian-style paramilitary-civilian relations has been rather mixed. Of all force structures it was undoubtedly EMERCOM as a humanitarian, although militarized, agency that demonstrated the highest propensity to cooperate with international and domestic civilian personnel, as well as with the local population. For such a large, complex, and multilevel structure as the MVD, cooperation patterns varied from extremely negative to extremely positive. On the negative side, there have been serious tensions with the local population over so-called *zachistka* operations.[25] One of the reasons for the highly problematic nature of these operations was that, instead of being used only in critical situations as a selective measure of last resort, and only when based on solid operational intelligence, they have not just become a routine, but often served as a substitute for most other security-related activities, such as regular patrolling. On a positive side, in contrast to the humanitarian situation in and around Kosovo, there have been no major problems in arranging for protection of UNHCR convoys to Chechnya – this task was regularly and effectively performed by the regional MVD anti-organized-crime units from neighbouring Ingushetia.

If the record of paramilitary-civilian relations has been rather mixed, it is nevertheless much better compared to that of the military-paramilitary relations within the "security bloc". One of the most critical adverse effects of the Russian model, a lack of both "separation of tasks" and sufficient coordination, particularly between the armed forces and the MVD, was most evident during the first campaign in Chechnya. It has not been fully overcome in the course of the second campaign, although some lessons have been learnt. Interestingly, tensions between the armed forces and the MVD were at their highest during the military stage of the second campaign. However, as soon as the focus shifted towards non-military tasks, where the advantages of the MVD were obvious, the tensions substantially decreased.

A further disadvantage of the Russian system is an apparent lack of multi-agency civilian presence in the field. It tends to be replaced by militarized security and emergency response structures, and can be only partly compensated by an international humanitarian presence. With the civilian (and particularly NGO) sector still underrepresented in Russian post-conflict operations, an excessive "militarization" of these activities is inevitable. As a result, civil-military relations in the field remain underdeveloped, and therefore paramilitary-military instead of civil-military relations have so far been more important. The option of demilitarizing many post-conflict tasks and increasing civilian participation in the field, which would theoretically be more suitable to long-term post-conflict requirements, is not workable for present-day Russia for a number of objective and subjective reasons. The main objective factors include financial constraints, ineffective state management (excessive bureaucratization and corruption), and general underdevelopment of civil society institutions and the non-governmental sector, which is unlikely to be overcome in the foreseeable future.

Throughout the first post-Cold War decade, the Russian government seemed to take little notice of the special character and structural advantages of militarized security forces, other than the military. However, several developments in the late 1990s to early 2000s indicate that the situation has begun to change. Among the most controversial of these developments has been the abolishment of the civilian Ministry for Federal Affairs, National and Migration Policy, which used to be responsible for registering and assisting IDPs in Ingushetia, Chechnya, and Dagestan – a move seen by some observers as the ultimate blow against a civilian presence in the field.[26] However, this chronically underfinanced and periodically reformed ministry was one of the most ineffective in the Russian government. As the leading state civilian agency involved in humanitarian operations in the North Caucasus in 1999–2000, the Federal Migration Service (FMS)[27] failed to perform even its direct task of registering IDPs, particularly at the peak of the crisis on the Chechen-Ingush border (September–October 1999). It was in fact the FMS's inability to set up IDP registration procedures effectively which contributed to the humanitarian crisis at the border crossing, when thousands of people were unable to cross the border. At the same time, the FMS was involved in humanitarian aid delivery to IDPs from Chechnya, a task that it was poorly prepared to implement and which, strictly speaking, was not a priority for this civilian agency. As a result of the FMS's poor performance in the North Caucasus, and because of political concerns over the potential "floods" of refugees from Central Asian states, most of its functions related to refugees and IDPs were transferred from civilian structures (the Ministry for Federal Affairs, National and Migration Policy) to the MVD. While few migration experts have been enthusiastic about this move, there has been general recognition that it was dictated by pragmatic concerns.[28]

At the same time, the most hopeful sign in years has been the official assignment of the Ministry of Economic Development as one of the main state bodies responsible for post-conflict reconstruction – the first-ever attempt in Russia to link post-conflict stabilization institutionally with economic development. Several potential improvements for coordination have also long been under discussion, such as the creation of an interagency group on humanitarian and post-conflict reconstruction issues which could serve as a prototype for an interagency humanitarian agency.

Counterterrorism at the stage of post-conflict peacebuilding

Although counterterrorist tasks, operations, forces, and priorities are not the central subjects of this chapter, they cannot be ignored in an overview of the performance of the security structures at the stage of post-conflict peacebuilding. While this subject deserves a separate and detailed analysis,[29] some general observations are appropriate, particularly as, in the Russian case, by and large they confirm the pattern described in previous sections of the chapter, i.e. the need for and the primacy of skills, structures, and security forces other than the military (with selective support by the military) in performing counterterrorist tasks effectively at the stage of post-conflict peacebuilding.

The role of the armed forces in combating terrorism, particularly in low-intensity conflict areas and post-conflict environments, is a highly contentious issue. On the one hand, the approach conflating counterterrorism with the "war on terrorism", which relies primarily on the use of military force and tends to be event-driven, reactive, and short term in nature, is neither specifically tailored to counterterrorist needs nor particularly effective in meeting them, and has neither worked well for the US-led global war on terrorism nor helped curb the terrorist violence generated by local conflicts, such as those in Chechnya, Kashmir, or the Middle East. On the other hand, conflict-related terrorism[30] has become a standard mode of operation of militant resistance groups, and a military defeat can affect their performance in more ways than one (while, in some cases, it can provoke militant groups to resort increasingly to terrorist activities, in other cases an organization can suffer such a decisive military blow that its ability to mount both guerrilla-type and terrorist attacks is drastically curtailed, forcing it to invest significant time to re-establish its operational capability). In sum, the armed forces, and special operations forces in particular, can certainly play a useful role in support of counterterrorism, but military tools and structures are not best tailored for specific counterterrorist tasks and should not assume the primary role.

While the role of the military in counterterrorist operations is by definition limited (otherwise an operation would probably not even qualify as a counterterrorist one), the critical challenge is how to achieve an optimal division of functions and establish working cooperation between the two key sectors that bear primary operational responsibility for counterterrorist activities – the law enforcement and the intelligence/counterintelligence communities. It has been more or less recognized internationally that counterterrorism requires extensive collaboration between these two branches. In this context, however, it must be stressed once again that terrorism is always a form of political violence, which, while it can and should be "criminalized" to the greatest extent possible, can never be reduced to plain crime. Its political, religious, or ideological motivation, its psychological effects on society, and its diffuse financial, logistics, and operational links need to be countered by highly specialized capacities which need to develop solid intelligence on the perpetrators of violence and their networks on a permanent basis. Given the centrality of pre-emption, disruption, and prevention in counterterrorism, it becomes extremely important to obtain timely information about the planning and preparation of terrorist attacks by means of heightened use of human intelligence and undercover methods in order to penetrate groups involved in terrorist activities from within. In Russia, the law enforcement sector may have some of these capacities, but most of them are more directly associated with the intelligence community (the Federal Security Service and the Foreign Intelligence Service, as well as military intelligence).

In the end, however, the problem of performing counterterrorist tasks at the peacebuilding stage goes much deeper than just the need for better demarcation and coordination of security tasks and proper division of responsibilities. The key issue here is whether and to what extent counterterrorism in a post-conflict area can be viewed and undertaken as an enforcement-type activity. In fact, what distinguishes counterterrorism in the narrow sense from other security tasks is that its central goals are always the *prevention and pre-emptive disruption* of terrorist activities and networks, rather than post hoc *punishment, coercion, or retaliation*. While coercive measures can be used selectively in support of counterterrorism (for instance, to prevent a specific act of terrorism), they are not what counterterrorism is primarily about. The most proactive and effective counterterrorist policy is never the one that is the most offensive and re-taliatory. In conflict or post-conflict areas in particular, operations whose impact goes far beyond the individual terrorist suspects themselves – such as "collective impact" or "collective punishment" measures, from curfews to large-scale mopping-up operations – can hardly serve counter-terrorist needs unless they are applied for a pre-defined period of time, cover a limited area, are based on very solid intelligence, and are selec-tively implemented for specific operational purposes. (Such a purpose would, for instance, be to detain a group of persons suspected of mount-ing a specific terrorist action while they are based in, operating from, or trespassing in a certain location.) When undertaken primarily for pu-nitive and essentially "counterinsurgency" purposes, collective impact measures, such as the Russian-style *zachistka* operations, tend to create greater problems than those they are meant to solve, because they cause serious tensions with and grievances among the local population. In sum, although collective impact measures have become almost standard coun-terinsurgency instruments for a number of states, including Russia, they have not been particularly effective as specific counterterrorist tools and are often counterproductive from the broader and longer-term peace-building perspective.

Conclusions and recommendations

The most pragmatic way to improve the effectiveness of Russia's opera-tions in the post-conflict environment would be to build on, and make better use of, the few structural advantages of the present system. For in-stance, while most Western countries lack forces other than the military (especially militarized police capacities) who could perform "grey area" security tasks in the post-conflict environment, in Russia these security components (especially the Ministry of Interior's troops and special units, and EMERCOM) are well-established, financed separately from the de-fence budget, readily available, and legally entitled to operate in post-conflict environments. This means that, structurally, there is no need for Russia to overburden its armed forces with non-combat post-conflict mis-sions, especially within the country. Given Russia's financial constraints, it makes sense to improve and develop further the existing organizational pattern by limiting the armed forces' responsibilities to tasks that might involve combat, while charging other security components with all "grey area" security tasks and selected non-security tasks, including humanitar-ian relief and basic reconstruction functions.

From the post-conflict stabilization and peacebuilding perspective, the emphasis of security sector reform on modernization, professionalization, improved coordination, separation of tasks (specialization), downsizing, and greater civilian control over the militarized agencies and forces (such as the internal troops) is particularly important. In the future, further separation of tasks and improved coordination within the security bloc, especially between the armed forces and the Ministry of Interior, and further specialization of MVD troops and special units in "grey area" post-conflict security tasks, as opposed to military support or regular police functions, should be pursued. The modernization of equipment, arms, training, and logistics remains an absolute priority, while downsizing should not be viewed as a goal in itself (although important, this is less important for the MVD and other militarized force structures than for the armed forces).

As far as the tasks of combating terrorism are concerned, in addition to heavy reliance on the specialized capabilities of the intelligence/counter-intelligence sector, the specific conditions, constraints, and demands of an unstable post-conflict environment will still require the MVD to play a larger role in support of counterterrorist tasks. The effectiveness of counterterrorist operations will be more dependent on the ability of the law enforcement sector to provide basic law and order than it is in relatively stable or peaceful areas. More broadly, any further operational or structural reforms concerning Russia's ability to combat terrorism in a conflict or a post-conflict environment should stem from the highly specific nature of counterterrorism which distinguishes it from other types of security-related activities – in particular its essentially preventive, preemptive, disruptive, and highly selective character, and its complete dependence on solid, accurate, and constantly re-evaluated intelligence.

While MVD structures should bear primary responsibility for all "grey area" security tasks, except counterterrorism, in Russia's domestic post-conflict theatres, Russia's humanitarian relief agency EMERCOM, the best organized of all state forces (and, as such, the least affected by "administrative reorganization") could and should be used abroad more widely. This is the case especially when Russia's military or peacekeeping involvement is unwelcome, politically problematic, and undesirable for Russia itself. This approach has already worked well during the deployment of EMERCOM units in Afghanistan. While Russia's military involvement in post-conflict operations in regions outside of the CIS has become almost exceptional, EMERCOM's militarized organization, huge air-lifting capacity, modern technical equipment, and humanitarian relief focus make it the most appropriate rapid-reaction-type force to be deployed in post-conflict settings abroad.

This brief analysis suggests that Russian operations in the post-conflict environment are quite different from Western approaches. This does not mean that there is no place for external actors in the reform or modernization of Russia's security sector in general. But as far as Russia's security structures' performance in domestic post-conflict situations is concerned, at the present stage the main priority should be given to practical cooperation in the field. The latter is politically less controversial, could be very instructive in logistical terms (through modernization of management, equipment, and communications capacities), and might have wider institutional implications. More generally, as compared to other international organizations (such as NATO and the OSCE) and individual Western states, UN structures could take up a more active role in encouraging security sector reform in general, and improved effectiveness of the Russian security structures in the post-conflict environment in particular. This proactive approach may well come as a logical progression of the UN's large-scale humanitarian involvement within Russia, particularly in the North Caucasus, its effective cooperation with Russian security/emergency structures both within and outside the country, and the uncontroversial political status and high professional profile of UN agencies in the eyes of the Russian government and society.

Notes

1. Security structures – a synonym for the state security sector that includes armed forces, law enforcement agencies, intelligence services, and other militarized formations. In the Russian case, security structures, other than the armed forces, are Ministry of Interior troops, special units, and regular police structures, Ministry of Emergencies forces, border guards, railroad troops, Ministry of Justice forces, special services, etc. The focus of this chapter is on the Ministry of Interior and the Ministry for Civil Defence, Emergencies, and Elimination of Consequences of Natural Disasters, as the ones most closely involved in post-conflict settings.

2. The changing role of the military and its increased involvement in non-military operations in crisis areas were reflected in national military doctrinal documents of that period. See, for instance, *Peace Operations*, FM 100–23, Draft 6, 30 December 1994. Washington, DC: US Department of the Army; National Defense Panel. 1997. *Transforming Defense, National Security in the 21st Century*, Report of the National Defense Panel. Washington, DC: Department of Defense; MoD. 1995. *Wider Peacekeeping, Army Field Manual*. London: Ministry of Defence; MoD. 1998. *Strategic Defence Review*, white paper presented to Parliament by the Secretary of State for Defence, CM 3999. London: Stationery Office; *Livre Blanc sur la Defense 1994*. Paris: Documentation Francaise; Etat-Majors des Armées. 1999. *Doctrine Interarmees d'Emploi des Forces en Operation*. Paris: Etat-Majors des Armées, Division Emploi. See also the documents of various international and regional organizations, such as UNDHA. 1994. *Guidelines on the Use of Military and Civil Defence Assets in Disaster Relief*, Project Dpr 213/3 MCDA. Geneva: UN Department of Humanitarian Affairs; NATO. 1994. *NATO Doctrine for Peace Support Operations*, draft, 28 February. Mons: Peacekeeping Section, Supreme Headquarters Allied Powers in Europe (SHAPE). See also Findlay, Trevor (ed.). 1996. *Challenges for the New Peacekeepers*. Oxford: Oxford University Press; Foster, E. 1995. *NATO's Military in the Age of Crisis Management*. London: RUSI; Mackinlay, J. and J. A. Chopra. 1993. *A Draft Concept of Second Generation Multina-*

tional Operations. Providence, RI: Thomas J. Watson Institute for International Studies; Minear, L. and P. Guillot. 1996. *Soldiers to the Rescue.* Paris: OECD; O'Hanlon, M. 1997. *Saving Lives With Force: Military Criteria for Humanitarian Intervention.* Washington, DC: Brookings Institution; Record, J. 1998. *The Creeping Irrelevance of US Force Planning.* Carlisle Barracks: Strategic Studies Institute, US Army War College; Leicht, R. C. 1992. *The New World Order and Army Doctrine. The Doctrinal Renaissance of Operations Short of War.* Santa Monica: Rand.

3. On the role of police forces in post-conflict situations, see for instance Chauveau, G. M. and G. Migone. 2000. *CIMIC and Police: Forging The "Missing Links" in Crisis Management,* Subcommittee on Civilian Security and Cooperation, Civilian Affairs Committee, 23 March. Brussels: NATO Parliamentary Assembly; Oakley, Robert B., Michael J. Dziedzic, and Eliot M. Goldberg (eds). 1998. *Policing the New World Disorder: Peace Operations and Public Security.* Washington, DC: NDU Press; Dwan, R. (ed.). 2002. *Executive Policing: Enforcing the Law in Peace Operations.* New York: Oxford University Press.

4. For more on this, see for instance Minear, L., T. Van Baarda, and M. Sommers. 2000. *NATO and Humanitarian Action in the Kosovo Crisis.* Providence, RI: Thomas J. Watson Institute; Suhrke, Astri, Michael Barutciski, Peta Sandison, and Rick Garlock. 2000. *The Kosovo Refugee Crisis: An Independent Evaluation of UNHCR's Emergency Preparedness and Response,* Evaluation and Policy Analysis Unit, EPAU/2000/001. Geneva: UNHCR, available at www.unhcr.ch/cgi-bin/texis/vtx/research/opendoc.pdf? tbl=RESEARCH&id=3ba0bbeb4; Stepanova, E. 2001. *Voyenno-grazhdanskiye otnosheniya v operatsiyah nevoyennogo tipa (Civil-Military Relations in Operations Other Than War).* Moscow: Human Rights Publications, pp. 110–134.

5. For general information and literature on the MVD, see for instance (in Russian) Kikot', V. (ed.). 2000. *Bibliograficheskii ukazatel' trudov o deiatel'nosti MVD Rossii (1802–2000 gg.): MVD 200 let.* Moscow: MVD Research Institute; Kozhevnikova, G. and P. Gazukin. 1999. *Silovye Struktury Rossii.* Moscow: Panorama.

6. Federal Law "On Internal Troops of the Ministry of Internal Affairs of the Russian Federation", *Sobraniye Zakonodatel'stva Rossiiskoi Federatsii (Code of Laws of the Russian Federation)*, No. 6, 27 February 1997, Art. 711.

7. UN Consolidated Inter-agency Humanitarian Appeal for the North Caucasus (Russian version), December 1999–December 2000, p. 14.

8. Ukaz No. 715 "O dopolnitel'nykh merakh po bor'be s terrorizmom na territorii Severokavkazskogo regiona Rossiiskoi Federatsii", 30 June 2003, in *Sobraniye zakonodatel'stva Rossiiskoi Federatsii*, No. 31, 4 August 2003, Part II, Art. 2889.

9. Minister of Interior Boris Gryzlov, cited by Rosbusinessconsulting News Agency, 25 December 2001.

10. The largest deployment in a UN mission has been that of more than 200 police officers as part of the UN mission in Kosovo. Roughly half of them served in CIVPOL, and others as special police units. Russian police personnel in Bosnia continued their work as part of the EU Police Mission in Bosnia and Herzegovina (EUPM) that replaced the UN International Police Task Force on 1 January 2003. There are also legal restrictions on the use of MVD forces outside Russia (similar to other countries), and every such deployment has to be decided on a case-by-case basis and approved by the parliament.

11. Press Service of the President of the Russian Federation, 19 April 2004.

12. Interview with the commander-in-chief of interior troops of the Russian Federation, General Vyacheslav Tihomirov, in *Nezavisimaya Gazeta*, 20 April 2004.

13. *Ibid.*

14. For more detail on this scenario, which has been under discussion for some time, see for instance *Nezavisimaya Gazeta*, 4 and 27 November 2002, 21 April 2004; *Kommersant*, 20 April 2004.

15. See Shoigu, Sergei. 2001. "Vazhnyi etap stanovleniya MChS" (An important stage of the EMERCOM formation), *Grazhdanskaya zaschita (Civil Defence)*, January, pp. 6–7.
16. Of the very few references available on EMERCOM in English, see Thomas, T. L. 1995. "EMERCOM: Russia's emergency response team", *Low Intensity Conflict and Law Enforcement*, Vol. 4, No. 2, pp. 227–236; on EMERCOM's humanitarian and emergency role in the North Caucasus, see Stepanova, note 4 above, pp. 210–216. Of EMERCOM's own publications, see for instance Legoshin, A. D. and M. I. Faleev. 2001. *Mezhdunarodnie spasatelnie operazii* (International Rescue Operations). Moscow: Ayaks Press; Vorobyov, Yuri L. (ed.). 2002. *Gumanitarnie operatsii mMChS Rossii (Humanitarian Operations of Russia's EMERCOM)*. Moscow: Kruk Press.
17. Author's interviews with UN representatives in Moscow, July and August 2000.
18. See for instance *Ob okazanii kompleksnogo sodeistviya vnutrenne peremeschennym litsam i zhitelyam severo-kavkazskogo regiona po linii mchs rf (On complex humanitarian assistance to internally displaced persons and residents of the North Caucasian region by the EMERCOM of Russia)*, EMERCOM Fact Sheet 24, June 2000; *"O rabote territorial'nogo upravleniya mchs rossii v chechenskoi respublike" (On activities of EMER-COM's territorial department in Chechnya), Grazhdanskaya zaschita (Civil Defence), May 2000.*
19. For more detail, see "Gumanitarnaya missiya Tsentrospasa" (The Central Rescue Unit's humanitarian mission), *Grazhdanskaya zaschita (Civil Defence)*, February 2001, pp. 16–20.
20. Quoted in *Nezavisimaya Gazeta*, 5 December 2001. On 12 June 1999 Russian peacekeepers from Bosnia were transferred to Kosovo through Serbian territory and set up camp at the Prishtina airport before NATO troops entered the province.
21. See, for instance, "On Russia's humanitarian projects to aid Afghanistan", *Daily News Bulletin of the Ministry of Foreign Affairs of the Russian Federation*, 9 January 2003.
22. See, for instance, "US OK with Russians in Kabul for now", *Newsmax.com wires*, UPI, 29 November 2001; Franchetti, Mark. 2001. "Russians in Kabul on spying mission", *The Sunday Times*, 2 December.
23. For instance, citing financial debts, EMERCOM reportedly had to cut off hot meal and bread distribution in most camps in Ingushetia from June through to mid-August of 2000.
24. See, for instance, "Conflicting reports about border ban on Chechen males", *CNN*, 14 January 2000; "Chairman slams Russian policy in Chechnya as 'Hippocratic Oath in reverse'", US Helsinki Committee press release, 13 January 2000.
25. *Zachistka* is an intense cordon and search/population screening operation by special police units in a certain populated area after it has been sealed off by the military or Ministry of Interior troops, or both.
26. See, for instance, interview with Ramazan Abdulativ, Radio Mayak, 18 November 2001; "Changes in the government: Russia becoming more militarized?", *SMI.ru*, 17 November 2001.
27. The FMS was later merged with the Ministry of Federation and Nationalities.
28. See, for instance, "MVD's new role makes reform vital", *The Moscow Times*, 6 November 2001, p. 10; *Nezavisimaya Gazeta*, 16 November 2001.
29. On the problems of integrating anti-terrorism into the broader and more fundamental peacebuilding framework in a cross-regional context, see Stepanova, Ekaterina. 2003. *Anti-terrorism and Peace-building During and After Conflict*. Stockholm: SIPRI, available at http://editors.sipri.se/pubs/Stepanova.pdf.
30. The deliberate and politically motivated use of, or threat to use, violence against civilians or civilian targets by a weaker side in an asymmetrical armed conflict.

8

Civil-military relations and security sector reform in a newly independent transitional state: The Georgian case

David Darchiashvili

Civil-military relations are crucially important for stable statehood and a successful security sector reform process, which, in itself, can be regarded as an important element of a country's transition to democracy. They require efficient, capable, and legitimate institutions (and a clear procedural basis) that are responsible for and guide the definition and implementation of security and defence policy. At the same time, civil-military relations affect the effectiveness of the state and the population's political loyalty to the state. If military and paramilitary structures in charge of the country's security and political authorities of the state are out of balance, and if there is no mutual trust between the society and the security apparatus, the entire political system may be eroded. If the quality of government and national morale are important characteristics of a country's strength,[1] the interrelationship between politicians, military/paramilitary, and ordinary citizens reflects the might and security of the nation-state.

This chapter describes the Georgian model of civil-military relations and its role and place in security sector reform. It illustrates that little progress can be achieved in the security sector and the context of security policy without regulating these relations and resolving fundamental long-standing problems of the national security system. The chapter analyses the national security discourse, the context and peculiarities of the development of respective draft concepts, and the level and quality of civil control over the armed forces. Paramilitary agencies are also examined, as until recently there was no clear distinction between the country's military and paramilitary/police structures. In fact, the changing nature of current risk factors, security policy, and institutions obscures even more the difference between the military and paramilitary roles. Although the chapter focuses mostly on the period until the November 2003 revolution, which resulted in the ousting of President Shevardnadze, some directions of the emerging post-revolutionary security policy are also briefly outlined.

The development of a national security strategy of Georgia

Like other weak states, Georgia is currently facing such dangers as organized crime, terrorism, and weapons and drugs trafficking. The security of thousands of ordinary citizens is at risk, and until very recently law enforcement bodies were barely in compliance with principles of human rights and the rule of law. If a new, post-revolutionary government is determined to tackle inherent state weaknesses and curb corruption, so characteristic of former President Shevardnadze's rule, then among other things a number of security issues must be urgently addressed: reforms of law enforcement agencies; maintenance of law and order in conflict zones and involvement of military/paramilitary structures in post-conflict rehabilitation programmes; social rehabilitation of combatants; and efforts to curb illegal proliferation of arms. In order to accomplish all this, increasing attention should be paid to the development of a national security strategy and civil democratic control over security/military institutions, and the relationship between the army and society on a nationwide scale.

Georgia has not become a full-fledged state[2] yet and, therefore, it needs to tackle seriously traditional problems of state and security building. By their very nature, these fall under the broad traditional realm of civil-military relations. The following analysis addresses these fundamental aspects of security building. It does not attempt to downplay the importance of other issues, such as – important in the Georgian context – police reform. Given the Georgian situation, the role of the police in the country's political life until today could be easily compared to the role of the military in a praetorian state, and thus may be included into a traditional discourse of civil-military relations. However, to humanize[3] the Georgian security sector, one must either first resolve previously unsolved fundamental dilemmas of national security policy, or carry out these and other more concrete tasks simultaneously.[4] Particular issues of security sector reform, such as the existence of private, poorly controlled military agencies and arms proliferation, are only part of a more common problem. This assumption may be illustrated by the fact that, without the creation of a democratic model of government providing for an optimal role of law enforcement agencies in the state system, and without developing a strategy of national development and political will for its implementation, these issues will never be fully resolved. The problems of private paramilitary units and arms trafficking, for instance, both seemed to have faded away by 1995, but they recurred in 2001.

Themes of the strategic discourse

Civil-military relations encompass the process of developing a strategic discourse and, as a result, formulating national interests and strategy. It lies in the nature of democracy that, the more multidimensional and participatory this framework, the greater are the chances for making well-considered and legitimate decisions. On the surface, Georgia does not lack public debate on strategic issues. Hundreds of relevant NGOs and independent think-tanks, as well as independent media outlets, have emerged after the collapse of the USSR. The country's leadership has repeatedly announced fundamental reforms that aimed to establish these principles in everyday life and build a society based on the rule of law. As a result, in 1999 Georgia was admitted to the Council of Europe. In this context, both the society and the ruling élite were considering the country's military-strategic choices, security sector reform, and the development of modern civil-military relations.

Active cooperation with NATO in the framework of the Euro-Atlantic Partnership Council (EAPC) and Partnership for Peace programmes has been facilitating the process of building a contemporary security discourse that has been developed and tested in democratic societies. Bilateral cooperation with NATO members, especially the USA, is also very important in this respect. At the same time, while the security discourse was developing under strong Western influence, it remained of course also affected by local views. In the perception of Georgian society, until now many social, economic, or cultural problems tended to be seen for their conflict potential. Every more or less significant political move arouses fears that the national statehood may be at stake. The seemingly permanent weakness of the evolving Georgian state accounts for this paranoia. State survival has become a cornerstone of the Georgian security discourse.

Over the last decade the Georgian political élite and large parts of society have viewed Russia as the main challenge to the national sovereignty of Georgia.[5] Russian imperial circles were accused of provoking local ethnic conflicts and providing support to any secessionist group or force interested in destabilizing Georgia.[6] However subjective these views may seem, even some Russian official strategic documents and statements of Russian politicians indicate Russia's destabilizing "hidden hand".

The 2000 version of the Russian national security concept unequivocally stated that NATO expansion and the lack of progress in CIS integration threatened Russian national security. Russia insists that its national security interests require the transformation of the CIS into a common economic zone, and the creation of a collective border defence system. However, this approach contradicts frequent statements of the Georgian political élite in favour of the country's pro-NATO orientation. The Russian national security document also offers ground to believe that Russia views Georgia's withdrawal from the CIS's collective security treaty in 1999 as a threat to its national security. In February–March 2002, Russian media and politicians became enraged at the news that US army commando units were to arrive in Georgia to assist local forces. Such US-Georgia military cooperation came after American and Georgian officials admitted that Al Qaeda terrorists might be hiding among criminal groups which found shelter in the Pankisi Gorge on the Georgian-Chechen border.[7]

Against this background, in a live interview with Georgian TV on 5 March 2002, Dmitri Rogozin, the chairman of the Russian parliamentary committee for foreign relations, claimed that, as one-third of the population of the breakaway regions of Abkhazia and South Ossetia had already acquired Russian citizenship, Russia should defend them for the sake of its national security. Earlier, the Russian foreign minister warned that deployment of US troops in Georgia might complicate the already unstable situation in the country. Although the Russian president's public comments on the issue were very diplomatic, these events illustrated that the Russian political establishment still tended to meddle in Georgia's domestic affairs. On the other hand, some press publications and statements by intellectuals claimed that the West was endangering Georgia's cultural identity and Georgia would turn into a Western satellite, a "banana republic". There were proposals for protectionism, cutbacks in cooperation with international financial institutions, and, by the end of Shevardnadze's regime, foreign investors were already encountering enormous problems in Georgia.[8]

The process of formulating a national security policy goes through the following stages. At the initial stage, the so-called security actor – the government or any of its members, a politician, or a leader – tries to prove that a particular event must be viewed as an existential threat to the country's national security, a move towards "securitization of the issue". If the audience – the nation – shares this view, the securitization can be considered complete. Securitization of the issue can open the door to extraordinary solutions or create an opportunity to alter the usual peaceful political process. After a particular issue is "securitized", the political actor claims the right to handle it by imposing bans and limitations of rights.[9] At the next stage statements are followed by real actions – security policy. However, radical "securitization" of the problems of national economy, culture, and ethnic identity is not in line with liberal democracy, and may be a sign of economic nationalism and paranoia.[10]

On the eve of the November 2003 revolution, Georgia had not yet entered the final phase of radical "securitization" of economic and cultural issues. Democratic and pro-Western rhetoric was still dominant. To some extent imperatives of democracy and human rights were also reflected in the national legislation. However, until recently, for fear of Russia and a frail international environment, the official national security policy of Georgia had been fragile. The pragmatism-based pro-Western stance lacked ideological determination, adherence to respective values, and political will and courage. For these reasons Shevardnadze's Georgia found it difficult to develop a modern security policy and system.

Towards a national security concept

It is very alarming that despite numerous efforts, with the active involvement of foreign missions and NGOs, no strategic documents have so far been made official in Georgia, although these documents are needed to regulate the implementation of a security policy and the planning and programming of respective agencies, and they must gain broad public support. As early as 1996 President Shevardnadze decreed the setting up of an ad hoc state commission for the development of a national security concept. In 1998 the Georgian government began to cooperate with the International Security Advisory Board (ISAB). The ISAB was expected to generate recommendations on the strategy of security reforms – it was an initiative of Revaz Adamia, then chairman of the parliamentary defence and security committee and famous for his pro-Western and democratic stance. In 1999 the ISAB completed its draft, entitled "Georgia and the World: Future Vision".[11]

After a long pause, the Georgian Foreign Ministry presented the document at an international conference in autumn 2000. According to the draft, cooperation with the European Union was the top priority of Georgia's foreign policy, while cooperation with NATO was a necessary precondition for the country's long-term goal of joining NATO. The document required the withdrawal of all Russian military bases from Georgia, and it took a critical approach towards the CIS, a regional alliance initiated and controlled by Russia. However, the status and validity of this strategic document remained vague: many relevant government agencies did not have an opportunity to examine the draft before it was published; the publication itself was not widely promoted in Georgia; and it was not signed by the president or another high-ranking official. At the same time, the government refrained from defining this document as a national security concept, assuring that such a comprehensive strategic document was under development in the National Security Council, the president's consultative body.

Until the November 2003 revolution, the concerned public had not heard of any progress in the development of the concept, although there were several draft national security concepts prepared by Georgian experts and governmental officials. These drafts offered useful insights into the Georgian security discourse. They highlighted such problems as internal separatism; interference of external forces into domestic affairs; corruption; growing social tension; conflict potential of the regions; military backwardness in comparison with neighbouring states; and technological and environmental threats. Several drafts specifically emphasized that people tended to identify themselves by ethnicity rather than common citizenship, that law enforcement bodies were unpopular, and that law enforcement authorities ignored human rights. The drafts underscored the importance of political pluralism and self-government, and the need to improve the human rights situation in the country, subject power structures to democratic control, and resolve ongoing conflicts by peaceful means.[12]

However, almost all of these draft concept papers were incoherent and eclectic, and tended to bypass specific issues. For instance, a state commission, founded by a presidential decree in 1996, prepared one such draft. On the one hand, its initial version prioritized consolidation of civil society, protection of human rights, and cultural integration with the world community, while denouncing ethnic thinking; on the other hand it argued that globalization might jeopardize ethnic identity, while individualism without social obligations could undermine the country's territorial integrity. Other drafts included such phrases as "the danger of weakening ethnic immunity", which hardly contributed positively to the development of a democratic national security system based on respect for human rights. Most of the drafts placed problems of education and culture in the security discourse. At the same time, almost all drafts of these Georgian authors either left out the Russian threat, a dominant theme of the social-political debate, or addressed it only very superficially.

By summer 1999 the state commission prepared another revised version of its draft, which was more advanced in comparison with its predecessor. Firstly, it was shorter and more integrated. The foreign policy priorities were defined more clearly. A new clause was added to the paragraph on cooperation with all democratic countries and international institutions – it set a goal for the country to integrate with main Euro-Atlantic structures. It was also underlined that the education system must popularize values relevant to the country's pro-Western orientation. However, this version, too, included some obscure or excessively academic notions, such as the need for "a social organization and political system relevant to cultural self-sufficiency", and the need to defend "the country's strategy" from "such impacts that did not result from the society's thoughtful decisions". The draft again addressed such issues as cultural identity, spiritual environment, public healthcare, and various social problems. It also left out the theme of foreign military presence in the country. The draft highlighted the need to define potential military threats, but fell short of defining any. It was not structured as a traditional strategic document, i.e. there were no separate chapters on interests, risks, and ways to neutralize them.

However, the main problem was that neither this nor any other draft had ever been adopted. Although there was a significant boost in Georgian-US military cooperation in February 2002, and a large part of the Georgian army was supposed to receive American military training and equipment, the Georgian government still hesitated to offer clear directions in its security policy.

Inconsistencies of a practical security policy

The Russian threat is a serious factor for closer cooperation with NATO and the USA. At the same time, Georgian security policy has often displayed opposite tendencies, which could be described as "appeasement" policies, or efforts to appease the source of the threat. This is illustrated by Georgia's membership in the CIS's collective security system until 1999.

Not long ago, relations with Russia were characterized by a number of contradictions: President Shevardnadze proposed in October 2001 that the parliament should officially demand the withdrawal of Russian peacekeeping forces from the conflict zone in Abkhazia (Georgia). The parliament passed a relevant resolution, but soon afterwards the president declared it a mistake and in January 2002 he consented to an extension of the Russian peacekeeping mandate. Late in 2001 Shevardnadze "forgot" what various Georgian politicians and even the foreign minister had repeatedly stressed earlier – the need to withdraw Russian military bases from Georgia as soon as possible. Instead he adopted a new approach, claiming that the issue would be settled in the framework of a new Russian-Georgian treaty, which he reported to be under development.

On 30 January 2002, during talks with his Russian counterpart, Nugzar Sadjaia, then secretary of the National Security Council, assured that Georgia was ready for close cooperation with Russia to resolve the difficult situation in the Pankisi Gorge. The problem of this gorge, a north-eastern region uncontrolled by the Georgian law enforcement structures and an alleged safe haven for Chechen militants, was on the table. For years Georgian authorities denied the presence of Chechen rebels on Georgian soil, but in autumn 2001 Chechen guerrillas passed throughout the entire country, penetrated into the Georgian-Abkhazian conflict zone, and launched a military operation there. As a result, the Georgian government found itself in an awkward situation *vis-à-vis* Russia, its own people, and the international community. Moreover, Georgian officials were allegedly involved in the operation. In the words of political scientist Ghia Nodia, the stories of the Russian peacekeeping mandate and the Chechen raid on Abkhazia demonstrated that the Georgian government was "incapable and unprincipled" – its words, deeds, and covert intentions differed sharply from each other, which tainted the country's reputation and invoked Russia's aggression.[13]

The absence of a security strategy, revealing itself in the lack of a conceptual statement and in embarrassing situations like the one described above, was also an impeding factor for the development of stable civil-military relations and a stable security sector. The head of the coordination bureau of anti-corruption policy complained at a governmental meeting in September 2001 that security services failed to defend the country's economic security.[14] Yet it was hard to defend what was not clearly defined. During a 29 October 2001 hearing in the parliamentary defence and security committee, which focused on the Abkhaz crisis (the Chechen guerrillas' raid and ensuing clashes), the Defence Minister, David Tevzadze, admitted that he had no clear idea what he should do. According to Tevzadze, Georgia unfortunately lacked strategic documents of national security and, as a result, it was hard to define missions of the armed forces and the military doctrine. Apart from vague action policies, the Georgian government did not have a clear-cut approach to the frozen conflicts in Abkhazia and South Ossetia.

One further conclusion can be drawn from the contradictory development of the Georgian security strategy. The working procedure and coordination between various government agencies were poorly developed. At the same time, the process lacked transparency: participation of the parliament, mass media, NGOs, and academic circles in the process was at best occasional and informal. Georgia was yet to develop an "integrated" security community that would make strategic activities legitimate and press the government to step up the process. Alienation between the civilian and military segments of society was one of the most evident obstacles to developing a security community. At the above-mentioned sitting of the parliamentary defence and security committee, General Chkheidze, the commander of the border troops, claimed that the state budget did not reflect the country's priorities. In response, the finance minister replied that all priorities of the state were clearly defined and only the military did not agree with the ministry's priority list.[15] Naturally, one could not reach harmony in civil-military relations in a country with meagre budgets, in the absence of strategic visions and policies, and lacking dialogue between the various government agencies.[16]

The US war on terror created new conditions for serious reforms in the Georgian security policy and sector. The expansion of the American anti-terrorism campaign into the Southern Caucasus seemed to be boosting hopes for the improvement of Georgia's security and a renewed focus on the problems of civil-military relations. The USA began to provide training and equipment to four Georgian battalions – a considerable force for a small country such as Georgia. At the same time, a treaty to build a gas pipeline from Shah-Deniz (Azerbaijan) to Turkey through Georgian territory was signed in Tbilisi on 14 March 2002. The treaty was perceived to encourage Western, but first of all American, interests in Georgia's future national security. As a result, the Russian fear might have abated and Georgia's strategic choices would have become clearer.

However, all these changes were inspired by external factors and were not in line with the logic of previous actions of Georgia's political élite. Against the background of the changing international environment, Georgian politicians fell into euphoria. Many started suggesting that Georgia should have taken advantage of American military assistance to regain the breakaway regions. However, here one again confronted the consumerist attitude of the Georgian political élite, which still lacked clear vision, strategy, or agreement on concrete programmes and steps. Few had any clear idea what Georgia should do if American priorities suddenly changed. The president said late in 1999 that it was not very important whether the country had a Western or Northern orientation – first of all one should find out who is giving what for the country's interests.[17] However, Georgia should have also done something in return – it should have been ready to undertake long-term obligations and require certain guarantees in exchange for its loyalty. In addition, the society should have been aware that the interests of the entire country, not only its élite, were concerned. This could have been achieved by creating a security community, by implementing a democratic dialogue, and by developing and implementing a national security concept.[18] Such thinking was lacking; all the more as subsequent events showed that the USA and the entire international community were becoming increasingly uneasy in regard to their support of Shevardnadze's regime. They were irritated with its inability to handle internal, systemic problems of mismanagement and corruption. Those problems were revealing themselves in many spheres, including the security sector and civil-military relations. As a result, the

West abandoned Shevardnadze and new, reformist forces came into power through a peaceful revolution.

Shortcomings of civilian democratic control over the armed forces in Georgia

The absence of a national security concept and contradictory practical policies made it difficult for the armed forces to identify and implement their missions. The commanders of the military and paramilitary structures, and many professional officers, were well aware of this shortcoming. They did not understand the size of funds that the government was ready to allocate for defence and security, as the lack of strategy was accompanied by permanent budget cuts. Georgia had been in a deep budget crisis at least since 1998, and the state treasury was overburdened with multimillion GEL[19] arrears in military salary. Such a situation hampered implementation of the security sector reform.[20]

The power agencies were not the only state structures to suffer from disordered civil-military relations.[21] At the end of the day, security must serve the entire society, while power structures, as security providers, will always be tempted to act greedily if the society and the political élite fail to create clear-cut guidelines for their activities. The institutional interests of power agencies are especially dangerous for countries which lack the political culture and traditions of democracy and the rule of law. Georgia is one of them. As a result, inefficient spending of meagre budgets, corruption, and large-scale violations of human rights – no matter whether it meant hard service conditions for conscripts (in the army or interior troops) or unlawful treatment of businessmen and ordinary citizens (by the police and security service) – had become common in the military and paramilitary institutions. To curb such practices, one should have strengthened civil control over these security institutions.

There were many precedents for excessive politicization of the power agencies and illegitimate military operations in the modern history of Georgia. Unfortunately, although Georgia had gradually achieved some progress in the development of civilian supremacy over the military, building an efficient system of civil democratic control remained one of the most fundamental tasks in reforming Georgia's civil-military relations and security sector during the entire period of Shevardnadze's rule.

Military and paramilitary forces in Georgia

By the end of Shevardnadze's rule, the following troops were part of the national armed forces: several army brigades, rapid-reaction forces, the air force, the navy, and the National Guards – all subordinated to the Ministry of Defence (MOD). The interior troops and several special task units were subordinated to the Ministry of Internal Affairs (MIA). The Ministry of State Security (MSS) also had special units. In addition, there was the State Department for Border Defence and the Special State Guard Service. All these structures had more than 40,000 servicemen in total. In addition, the MIA also employed 35,000–40,000 police personnel. Although the latter were not part of the military forces, the experience of past years showed that the police had often been involved in armed conflicts.

On the whole, the MIA played an important role in the 2001 events in the Pankisi and Kodori Gorges, which ended in a joint Georgian-Chechen military raid on Abkhazia. At that time many experts and journalists argued that top officers of the MIA had planned the operation, which was officially labelled as uncontrolled guerrilla warfare. When the situation dramatically worsened in the conflict zone and news about the military operation spread across society, the interior minister announced that he ordered the police, interior troops, and special task forces to go on standby, emphasizing that he was also in charge of military affairs.[22] These events and statements indicate that the Georgian military and police structures and their roles somehow merged together. The special unit of the Ministry of Justice and the extraordinary legion of the Ministry of State Revenues augmented the military/paramilitary forces of the country.

In analysing the military and paramilitary structures of Georgia, one should not ignore various illegal or quasi-legal forces in different regions. They operated quite openly until 1995, after which point their activities became more covert. In reality, however, completely illegal or quasi-legal military units continued to operate in Ajaria and Javakheti, in conflict zones and adjacent territories, and in the Pankisi Gorge at the Georgian-Chechen border.[23] Apart from Georgian military structures, which must be controlled by the civilian government, one must also take into account the Russian military bases stationed in Georgia.[24] Russian troops and Russian peacekeeping forces in Abkhazia and South Ossetia totalled an alleged 6,000–8,000 service personnel.[25]

Legal and political framework of civilian control: Achievements and discrepancies

Controlling these diverse structures was a serious challenge for the newly independent state. However, Shevardnadze had achieved some progress. The laws on the National Security Council and on defence, adopted or revised in 1996–1997, substantially facilitated civil-political control over the armed forces. The law on state secrecy was passed during the same period. The law on the parliamentary Group of Confidence, which was adopted in March 1998, increased the parliament's role and weight in defence. The Group of Confidence strengthened parliamentary control over defence spending: a special three-member parliamentary group, one member of which represented the parliamentary minority, acquired the right to full access to classified state programmes. A new general administrative code was enacted in 2000, creating favourable grounds for transparent government and civil participation. The code did not address military issues directly. According to its Article 2, the code could not be applied to those activities of executive structures that had any connection with military decision-making or military discipline. At the same time, however, the code stipulated that this restriction had to be lifted when citizens' constitutional rights and freedoms were concerned. Article 28 of the code permitted the classification of information only if its disclosure would apparently damage military, intelligence, or diplomatic activities – either planned or under implementation – and the physical safety of their participants. Obviously, the authors of the code believed that most parts of the defence policy should remain unclassified. This extended the legislative base for democratic control over the armed forces.

With the adoption of the constitution in 1995 and two parliamentary and two presidential elections, Georgia made some progress in the process of independent democratic state building. However, the quality of the elections and legitimacy of their results, as well as some specific features of Georgian legislation and the constitution, appeared to undermine the consolidation of democracy and the rule of law. Most importantly, the necessary political will and civic culture still had to be developed – all these issues were directly linked to the shortcomings of civil control over the national security policy and military forces.

Analysing the history of American constitutionalism in the context of civil-military relations, Samuel Huntington emphasized that vague division of civil control functions between the two branches of government in various periods led to either usurpation of legislative rights by the president or distortion of the vertical chain of the military command by Congress.[26] The Georgian constitution followed the American example. Shevardnadze has always admired the coexistence of a strong parliament and a powerful president. As a result, the Georgian parliament could impeach the president only in theory, while the president was unable to dismiss the parliament. This constitutional model created ample grounds for conflicts, as the division of responsibilities in security policy was left unclear. In Georgia, a country with an embryonic legal and consensus-building culture and poor experience of transparency, such conflicts were often regulated by unlawful measures or the subjective will of one of the power branches.

Article 98 of the constitution was an impeding factor for the development of a clear-cut framework of civil supremacy: it entitled the president to define the structure of the military forces, while the size of the forces had to be approved by a majority vote of the parliament. As a result, the president and the parliament would have come to a standstill. It was unclear how the problem could be solved legally: how could the president maintain his preferred structure of the military forces when the parliament voted down their relevant size? The law on defence adopted in 1997 contradicted this constitutional provision, requiring that the law define the structure of the military forces. In some cases legislation regulating the security sector contradicted the constitution and did not comply with the democratic practice of civil control, such as the division between military and police. For instance, Article 78 of the constitution prohibited merging the military, police, and security forces in any way. At the same time, Article 8 of the 1997 law on defence specified the internal troops, which were subordinated to the MIA by another legislative act, the law on interior troops, as part of the military forces. The commander of the interior troops was entitled to coordinate district police units in emergency situations.[27]

Some provisions of the Georgian constitution hampered crisis management procedures. According to Article 3 of the constitution (as well as the law on defence), the military forces could not be put in action in emergency situations without preliminary parliamentary approval. This article could have become detrimental to national security under certain conditions – if, for example, the parliament failed to convene an extraordinary session or the president and the legislators did not find common ground during an attempted coup, when every minute counts. Naturally, such laws were very hard to observe: for instance, in October 1998 the president ordered the army to quell a rebellion of the Senaki Brigade without declaring an emergency law and gaining parliamentary approval. The list of counterproductive contradictions is long: competencies were not divided clearly among security and defence; respective laws remained on paper; and a relatively liberal law could be neutralized by another one inherited from the Soviet past.

Poor coordination was a further problem of the various military forces of Georgia. At a briefing in the MOD on 29 January 2002, the defence minister openly complained about weak coordination between force agencies, emphasizing that the agencies usually cooperate only in time of actual crisis, but this cooperation lacks preliminary planning, procedural guidelines, and clear division of competencies. Until recently, coordination between the institutions responsible for national security was done only at the presidential level. The president was the supreme commander-in-chief of the armed forces and chaired a consultative body, the National Security Council. He endorsed regulations of ministries and departments; awarded the military rank of general; and appointed deputy ministers, the chief of the general staff, and commanders of large structural units of the army. Many cases have proven, however, that defence management is rather inefficient if direct cooperation between various military and paramilitary forces is weak and thus requires the interference of the country's political leader, and if the president takes part in professional military decision-making.[28]

Although the constitution was supposed to guarantee the coexistence of a strong parliament and president, the Georgian president has enough leverage to reduce the parliament's role in civil control. The presidential control of military forces was part of civil supremacy over security policy, yet parliamentary control did not extend over the president's office and some significant executive structures. Details of the defence and security policy of Georgia were often clarified not by laws but by executive orders. Such a situation was more advantageous for the president than the parliament. A presidential decree was hierarchically higher than a parliamentary resolution, overshadowing the parliament's constitutional right to define the country's domestic and foreign policies. At the same time, only the president could correct the budget bill. In case of the president's request, the parliament had to change the sequence of the bills to be passed. Although the constitution and parliamentary regulations still used to ensure the defence minister's accountability to the parliament, the situation was completely different with regard to the State Border Defence Department, interior troops, and the Special State Protection Service. The constitution and the parliamentary regulations both stipulated that at the request of an MP any executive official appointed or approved by the parliament could be summoned to account to a parliamentary committee hearing or plenary session. However, although those officials appointed by the president were influential actors in the defence and security systems, none of them was appointed or approved by the parliament, and thus, legally, could not be summoned.

The already mentioned parliamentary Group of Confidence was entitled to control classified defence and security programmes. There was also a temporary investigation commission to probe into criminal activities of governmental officials. However, unlike in the American model, whose constitutional idea of checks and balances inspired the authors of the Georgian constitution, parliamentary investigations could yield results only if the procurator's office decided to launch legal proceedings, which was not always the case.[29]

The law on the National Security Council was adopted on 24 January 1996. It defined the National Security Council (NSC) as the president's consultative body. The same law granted the "consultative" institution the right to control and coordinate defence, security, and law enforcement agencies.[30] In emergency situations the powers of the NSC were to be further extended – under the emergency law only the NSC was responsible for crisis management. The NSC had the right to take legislative initiatives, including the constitutional right to introduce bills on force sizes. As a "consultative" body of the president, the NSC was not accountable to the parliament.

Not only strategic issues of "high politics", but also details on institutional arrangement needed to secure the support of the president. Even food suppliers to the army were often chosen from those lobbying at the presidential level. The positions of the president and the NSC on security sector reform were not always clear. As American experts concluded as early as in spring 2000, the NSC did not seem enthusiastic about consolidating the armed forces.[31]

Civilian control in practice: Problems of professionalism and political will

When examining positive and negative aspects of civil control, one should take into account that parliamentary control was sometimes weak not only due to legislative barriers, but also because MPs lacked experience or political will. The Georgian parliament could, but did not, protest against the above-mentioned contradictions between various laws or the fact that the NSC used to exceed its consultative functions. The parliament almost unanimously approved amendments to the law on defence in October 2002, which granted the general staff the right to control all of the country's military forces in emergency situations. After one MP remarked that the law should have elaborated on particular mechanisms of coordination, he was told that the matter was beyond the parliament's competence and the cooperation details would have to be developed by the military themselves. Interestingly, the parliament did not seem upset by such a reply.

Although the existence of widespread corruption in the Georgian government had become common knowledge both within the country and abroad, and although law enforcement officials defiantly missed parliamentary hearings, the parliament never launched impeachment proceedings. As a rule, the most detestable ministers either resigned voluntarily or were "advised" to do so by the president. Some of them would afterwards find shelter in the president's consultative bodies. For instance, Shota Kviraia, former security minister, later became a member of the NSC apparatus, despite the fact that the parliament suspected him of serious crimes in the 1990s. Parliamentary committees and subcommittees encountered numerous problems in their routine work. Some MPs complained that the agenda of parliamentary debates was often ill prepared, while hearings produced few, if any, results. On the other hand, according to the chairman of the parliamentary defence and security committee, MPs often missed committee hearings, which made it hard to achieve a quorum.[32]

At the end of 2001 MPs resolved to postpone parliamentary debates over the 2002 budget bill by one month because of the failure to agree on basic figures. This could have been a sign of the strengthening of parliamentary democratic control *vis-à-vis* not only the army but the whole executive branch of the government, since one of the reasons for the postponement was the failure of Defence and Finance Ministries to propose an integrated vision over defence spending and the failure or reluctance of the president to solve this problem. The parliament was pressing the government to come to an agreement and submit an integrated and detailed defence budget. The promising news was that, with assistance of American experts, the Defence Ministry subsequently worked out the first-ever programme defence budget. MPs had the opportunity to look into basic structural elements of the armed forces – and their size and share in the general defence spending. In addition, the draft budget complied with NATO standards – it divided all the expenses into three blocks: personnel, maintenance of combat efficiency, and investments.

However, the results of Georgian-American military cooperation in budgetary affairs did not enhance transparency in this field. During the extra month offered by the parliament, nothing changed. The Ministry of Finance refused to take into consideration the military's calculations, while the Defence Ministry refused to reconsider its programmes under the ceiling given by the Ministry of Finance.

Tired and failing in its intention to force the government to work more effectively and to enable MPs to understand the rationale behind the 2002 defence figures, the parliament approved the entire state budget, including the figures for the military, which were proposed by the Ministry of Finance. The Ministry of Defence stopped arguing, but nobody explained to MPs the interrelationship between the finally submitted defence funds, military programmes, and the size of the armed forces; the MPs were not told about a proposed schedule of personnel cuts in the Defence Ministry and expected financial effects. Besides, non-budgetary incomes of governmental agencies evaded parliamentary control. The 2002 budget was the first to specify their likely volumes, yet it clarified neither their sources nor spending regulations.[33]

The state minister's statement that there was no time to develop a better budget appeared acceptable to most MPs. The programme defence budget was of little use, as the parliament approved only GEL38 million for defence spending while the programmes required GEL71 million. It seemed that nobody cared about adapting the programmes to the new figures. At the end of the day few legislators remained interested in the issue. The president and the NSC ended up deciding how to allocate budgetary funds among various governmental structures. As to the parliament, it once again missed an opportunity to exercise civil democratic control in the parliamentary procedure to debate and approve the budget.

The lack of political will and courage largely accounted for the weakness of parliamentary control. Sometimes the problem was caused simply by unprofessionalism and indifference. The everyday life of Georgian service personnel had been regulated by Soviet-made regulations for years. The human rights situation in the army was extremely worrying. Meanwhile, the parliament took measures neither to solve the problem nor to bring legal action against responsible officials.

The government operation in the already mentioned armed conflict in Abkhazia in the autumn of 2001 was planned in secrecy: legislators knew nothing about it, and even after it began they received information mainly from journalists. The parliamentary Group of Confidence was also unaware of the operation. Some MPs, such as the chairman of the parliamentary defence and security committee and the speaker of the parliament, quite correctly regarded this fact as dangerous and irresponsible, an act of total neglect of the parliament on the part of executive officials, including the leadership of the force agencies. The situation further aggravated as the international community grew deeply concerned with the escalation of the conflict, while Russia accused Georgia of sheltering terrorists. However, the parliament again fell short of launching a parliamentary investigation. Organizers and participants of the operation, which ended as suddenly as it began, were never held accountable for their actions. The parliament had to (and did) put up with general explanations by the leadership of the force agencies, who claimed that the events unfolded spontaneously and the situation was too complicated to manage it better.

The civil-military implications of the revolution and the way ahead

In October–November 2001 a significant development affected the Georgian security sector. The interior minister, who had been repeatedly criticized (by journalists) for the Abkhazian affair and the failure of the police to control a criminal enclave in the Pankisi Gorge, threatened to shut down the independent Rustavi-2 TV company. He boasted that he was an "iron man" and nobody would ever be able to challenge him. Several days later the security service attempted to raid the company and check its financial files. The incident triggered what Georgia had not seen for years. Thousands of students and ordinary citizens blocked the capital's main street, demanding the resignation of the government. The protest of the people, a previously silent actor in Georgian civil-military relations, proved a decisive factor in these developments. For the first time in years the leadership of the parliament, which had long tolerated the actions of the ministers and president and the constant shortcomings of the security policy, and who did nothing to investigate the above-mentioned military operation in Abkhazia, took an uncompromising stance against the government's attempt to curb the freedom of speech.

The political crisis and the looming danger of chaos in the streets seemed to have frightened the president and his "iron" minister. The president dismissed the entire government. In short, Shevardnadze received a serious blow caused by various factors, among them the shortcomings and problems of the security sector and civil-military relations. Shevardnadze attempted to make some institutional changes, perhaps not so much to bring legitimacy to the regime when it was confronted by the first signs of the revolution, but more so due to increasing Western criticism about the Georgian state's impotence and corruption. In late 2001 the president issued Decree 499 to set up an ad hoc interdepartmental commission of the NSC to work out recommendations on institutional reforms in the security and law enforcement structures. However, his government continued to make only superficial steps, thus provoking further discontent among ordinary citizens and strengthening the opposition.

The revolution of November 2003 was caused by fraudulent parliamentary elections. By and large, it was democratic in nature. Exit polls and parallel counting showed the victory of the opposition, led by young democratic leaders who had formerly belonged to Shevardnadze's camp, but who separated in 2001. Shevardnadze did not accept defeat, and the state-controlled central election commission attempted to falsify the results in favour of pro-Shevardnadze forces. In return, tens of thousands of citizens from all over Georgia were rallied by the opposition, encircled governmental buildings, and finally occupied them. The ability of the opposition to raise mass support and force Shevardnadze to step down was based not only on general democratic slogans and promises to reduce poverty, but also on security-related rhetoric, perceptions, and objectives.

The opposition's first and foremost message was Shevardnadze's responsibility for the impotent and corrupt political system in Georgia. Corruption is regarded to be a security issue for many newly independent countries.[34] The opposition was also using national sentiments concerning the lost Abkhazian and South Ossetian autonomies, and Shevardnadze's inability to protect Georgia's sovereignty from Russian incursions. Last but not least, as extra-legal political action, the revolution itself, as a fight for vital rights and interests, is a security issue.

On the eve of and during the revolution, the opposition also emphasized its intent to strengthen the Georgian armed forces, blaming Shevardnadze for persistent neglect of soldiers' and officers' needs, and his reliance on corrupt police leadership. The opposition also established links with some NATO- and US-trained Georgian commanders, ensuring their support should Shevardnadze decide to use force. At one point, Shevardnadze's circle was in fact considering the option of a military attack against the opposition. However, neither the army nor other armed structures appeared to be willing or even able to protect the by then bankrupt regime. Only the top élite of the military and paramilitary establishment was benefiting from uncontrolled corruption, while at the officer level regime loyalty was eroding. As a result, Shevardnadze was left defenceless. Unresolved problems in the security sector therefore played their part in (the success of) the revolution. The subjective and authoritarian style of civil-military relations, nurtured by Shevardnadze, did not pass the test of mass discontent.

The country's new leadership, which received full legitimization through presidential elections on 3 January 2003 and parliamentary elections on 28 March 2004, seemed to learn some important lessons from the contemporary history of Georgia's security sector. Its statements as well as its deeds indicate that the security sector is a top priority on the governmental agenda. Through effective campaigning, demonstration of force, and covert work among adversaries, in late spring 2004 President Saakashvili's government achieved the ousting of the authoritative ruler of the Ajara autonomy, Aslan Abashidze, returning this region to the jurisdiction of central authorities in Tbilisi. Abashidze's armed units were either abolished or incorporated into the national armed forces and other power agencies. On 1 November 2004 the merger of army and interior troops was announced.[35] This came as a fulfilment of repeatedly suggested Western recommendations aimed at minimizing parallel structures of the Georgian armed forces. At the same time, the national armed forces and security and police agencies were subjected to drastic personnel changes, downsizing the force, as Western experts had long advocated. Some were dismissed for incompetence or corruption. Institutional changes within the security and defence agencies acquired new momentum. For instance, the intelligence department merged with the Security Ministry, while the Ministry of Defence developed a new bill on its structure and functions. The government also improved the financing of security and defence agencies. For example, the Ministry of Defence, which was not given the requested funds of GEL70–80 million under Shevardnadze's regime, was now promised GEL119 million for the year 2005.

The courage of and speed of reforms initiated by Saakashvili's government can best be illustrated by the abolishment of the traffic police –

which used to be one of the most corrupt bodies – and the introduction of a new patrol police, staffed by those who passed newly established training courses at the police academy. The academy itself was subjected to comprehensive reforms with the supervision and support of Western donors and advisers.

Saakashvili also began to address some urgent threats to Georgia's security sector, including curbing corruption at high levels of state structures and fighting organized crime. At the same time, he attempted to break the deadlock of Georgia's frozen ethnic conflicts and develop a new relationship with Moscow. In all instances, attempts were visible, although not always successful and consistent. For example, many NGOs and lawyers are warning of dangers that the anti-corruption campaign violates principles of human rights and rule of law. Clear procedures, transparency, and objectivity are lacking in this process. Some corrupt persons were left untouched while others were arrested. Detention of those charged with corruption was not followed by clear and transparent trials, and detainees were forced to pay large amounts to the state without clear justification of the legality of such demands. Later on the parliament adopted amendments to the criminal procedure code, which stipulate pre-trial bargaining between a prosecutor and detainees so as to reveal more facts about corruption and other crimes of high-ranking officials. However, the law is not always respected, either.[36] At the same time, the Liberty Institute conducted research on torture occurrences since the so-called "Rose Revolution". The results reveal numerous incidents of torture in police pre-detention facilities.[37]

In terms of the conflicts with the breakaway Abkhazia and South Ossetia, little progress has been made. This hampers improvement of Georgia's relations with Russia, which is still accused by the Georgian government of supporting the separatist Abkhazian and South Ossetian regimes. At the end of May and beginning of June 2004, Georgian authorities closed the Ergnety wholesale market in the Georgian-Ossetian conflict zone, in order to cut smuggling routes for Russian goods into Georgia. As compensation for the commercial losses of Ossetians, the Georgian government launched a so-called "humanitarian blitz" into South Ossetia, sending humanitarian aid into Ossetian villages without the consent of the *de facto* South Ossetian government. The Ossetians perceived this as an attempt to export the Rose Revolution. This resulted in a new wave of hostilities and several casualties. It seems that some high-ranking officials from the Georgian side hoped that the issue of Ossetian separatism was simply about criminal interests of smugglers, and thus could have been easily solved through the humanitarian blitz. Many local independent experts as well as political opposition groups argued that such assumptions were incorrect, expressing their concern that the new leadership was taking serious political decisions without thorough and clear procedures.

Among others, these shortcomings indicate that, while drastic security sector reforms were pursued, the government has so far paid less attention to the human dimension of security, as well as to classic themes of civil-military relations. As an institutional level of security policy,[38] civil-military relations in a democratic country are essentially about clear rules and inclusive processes of decision-making in the defence and security fields. The rule of law, transparency, and accountability are about the normalization of civil-military relations when national security is concerned.

Nevertheless, the subject of civil-military relations, particularly civil control over the armed forces, is not being completely ignored. On 6 February 2004 the new leadership amended the constitution. Among other issues, the "hardly performable clause", which prohibits the use of armed force in emergency situations by the president without prior consent of the parliament, was abolished. The rule that parliament should agree on such presidential decisions within 48 hours was left intact.[39] Paragraph 78, which prohibited any form of integration of the armed forces, police, and security services, contradicting the laws on defence and police, was not included in the new version of the constitution.[40]

At the same time, the constitutional changes maintained some previous clauses and created new ones that offer opportunities for duplication of responsibilities of civilian control at the highest governmental level; this might give rise to subjectivism and risky impacts of élite struggles in security and defence policy. For instance, paragraph 98 maintains that the structure of the armed forces should be defined by the president, and their size by the parliament. However, in case of a deadlock on this or any other matter, the constitutional changes allow the president to dissolve the parliament, which was not possible previously.

Other amendments have created the position of prime minister. Georgia has thus moved towards a mixed system of semi-presidentialism. This creates new problems regarding civil-military relations, particularly due to a vague division of responsibilities between the prime minister and the president in defence and security matters. According to the new constitutional amendments, the prime minister forms the cabinet with presidential consent. The prime minister also coordinates and controls the work of the government. According to the new law on structure, rights, and rules of the work of the government of Georgia, which derives from the new constitutional amendments, the government takes the necessary measures to ensure defence and state security. Thus, the prime minister becomes *de facto* responsible for defence and security policy. Nevertheless, the ultimate decision-maker in these fields is the president, who remains the supreme commander of the armed forces and, according to paragraph 73 of the constitution, can dismiss the ministers of interior, security, and defence without consent of the prime minister. According to paragraph 78, if exceptionally important issues (which are not defined) are concerned, the president can call and chair governmental sittings. Thus, on the one hand, a new design of civilian control and decision-making in defence and security is characterized by a still-unclear delineation of rights between parliament, prime minister, and president. On the other hand, such arrangements give advantage to the ultimate and subjective will of the president, since he can ignore the opinions of the prime minister and parliament by dissolving the cabinet or parliament.

As far as recent practice of decision-making is concerned, from time to time it is still characterized by a lack of transparency and legality, and newly emerged revolutionary chaos and instability. For instance, the very adoption of the new constitutional amendments has occurred in violation of constitutional provisions. The amendments were not subjected to a broad public debate. Moreover, they were passed by MPs whose constitutional term of service had already expired. In less then a year after the revolution, the minister of defence and the head of the general staff were changed twice. This was also accompanied by the redesign of the structure of the Defence Ministry, based on previous agreements with NATO experts and partners. One such expert notes, however, that so far one can only trace the structural changes in the Georgian Ministry of Defence, not the expected progress.[41] The new government also failed to launch and finalize a transparent and inclusive process in developing a national security strategy, thus making reform of the security sector ad hoc, incongruent, and sometimes contradictory. Is this a way towards presidential authoritarianism; is the violation of the rule of law and good governance principles intentional? Hopefully not. So far, one can clearly observe an unfinished revolutionary rush and the fear of the new élite that counter-revolutionary forces might take revenge unless decisions are quickly made, "enemies" are isolated, and power is consolidated at the central level.

So far, the democratic division of powers is rather formal. However, hopefully, if not with the help of local genuine democrats then at least due to the insistence of Western partner nations and organizations, deviations from the rule of law and democracy will be corrected. Regarding security sector reform and stable civil-military relations, one might think about IPAP as a tool for improvement.

In June 2004 the Georgian government submitted to NATO a proposal for the Individual Partnership Action Plan (IPAP), which was subsequently reviewed and endorsed by the North Atlantic Council. IPAP aims at bringing Georgian security, as well as the overall political system, closer to the standards of Western democracies. Developed by a joint team from the Defence, Security, and Foreign Affairs Ministries, IPAP is backed by repeated statements of the president that Georgia aims to join the Euro-Atlantic community and its military organization, NATO. It is hoped that such pronouncements, and Georgia's pledge to improve its adherence to the rule of law and its security sector and build genuine democracy, expressed through IPAP, will finally help overcome the current revolutionary radicalism and the corrupt legacy of the Shevardnadze period.

Lessons learned

First and foremost, the Georgian case of security sector reform indicates that unless the process of reform falls under the definition of good governance and rule of law, unless classical themes of civil-military relations are properly addressed, attempts at improving individual as well as national security, curbing new and old risks, remain ad hoc, partial, and contradictory. Without a properly developed and respected national security strategy, clear laws and rules of governance in the security and defence fields, and clear division of responsibilities of military, paramilitary, police, and civilian authorities, concrete plans of action will not be developed or will remain only on paper. The Georgian case indicates that neglect of these issues might contribute to internal struggles, the downfall of governments, and revolutions and/or coups. Micro-management, interference of biased political motives into security and military affairs, and, finally, encouragement of corruption in relevant agencies were some of the key factors that contributed to the end of Shevardnadze's rule. Interestingly, the first president of Georgia, Zviad Gamsakhurdia, also created serious problems in civil-military relations and was subsequently ousted by force.

However, to make even best rules work, a general national will for state building is required. This presupposes that the élite are coherent, genuinely devoted to democracy, and engage society in a constant dialogue on political and security matters. As in many developing countries, ethnic nationalism and patriarchal/feudal traditions that feed corruption are prevalent in Georgia. Adherence to the fatherland, native language, and faith competes with universal principles of democracy, human rights, and rule of law. The élite should be able to communicate to the society at large that these two sets of principles can coexist, transforming ethnic nationalism into a civic one. Without such ideological transformation, the country's mains security tasks – defeat of corruption and organized crime, and an end to ethnic conflicts – cannot be achieved.

If such a breakthrough on the ideological level is achieved, genuine security sector reform and strengthening of national security, in balance with human security considerations, can be realized. Otherwise, such intentions will remain intentions, or lip service to please and deceive international donors. Hopefully, IPAP is the expression of an honest move towards genuine modernization in Georgia.

Notes

1. Morgenthau, Hans J., revised by Kenneth W. Thompson. 1993. *Politics Among Nations: Struggle for Power and Peace*. New York: McGraw-Hill, pp. 149–154.

2. Despite the long history of the country, the modern Georgian state is only 12 years old. Until the "Rose Revolution" of November 2003, Georgia had no experience with peaceful transfer of power from one political group to another; the state bureaucracy was inefficient, believed to be totally corrupt, with little legitimacy in the eyes of the population; and the population still prioritized ethnic and religious allegiances over citizenship. At the same time, the Georgian government did not fully exercise control over the entire territory of the state and failed to exercise efficient control over its borders. Later in the chapter it will be explained how this might change after the end of Shevardnadze's rule.

3. In this context, the term "humanize" refers to the security sector's responsibility to protect citizens in their daily life and respect human rights, even at the expense of the short-term efficiency of security institutions.

4. "Fundamental dilemmas" refer to the very basics of state building, including development of a security strategy, building of efficient army, police, and governmental institutions and policy procedures for their management and control, and building a common understanding between the government and society. "Concrete tasks" refer to the responsibility to address particular issues, such as terrorism, ethnic disputes, arms proliferation, or drug trafficking.

5. For instance, Charles Fairbanks pointed to the deeply founded belief in the South Caucasus that Russia tried to impose its control over the region's energy resources and transit infrastructure by instigating local political conflicts. See Fairbanks, Charles H. 1995. "A tired anarchy", *The National Interest*, No. 39, Spring, pp. 15–25; Fairbanks, Charles H. and Elshan Alekberov. 1994. "Azerbaijan and the ominous rumbling over Russia's 'near abroad'", *Washington Times*, 1 November.

6. CIPDD. 1996. *Developing the National Security Concept for Georgia*. Tbilisi: Caucasus Institute for Peace, Democracy, and Development, p. 62.

7. See, for example, Cohen, Ariel. 2002. "Moscow, Washington and Tbilisi wrestle with instability in Pankisi Gorge", *Eurasianet*, 19 February, available at www.eurasianet. org.

8. For example, one of the largest foreign investors in Georgia, the American company AES, which owns the electric distribution network in Tbilisi, encounters constant problems of mass tax avoidance and assaults from populist politicians. The government has done little to protect the legitimate interests of this company. See *New Agency Caucasus Press*, 5 December 2002; *News Agency Prime-News*, 10 February 2003.

9. Buzan, Barry, Ole Waever, and Jaap de Wilde. 1997. *Security: A New Framework for Analysis*. London: Lynne Rienner Publishers, pp. 24–25.

10. *Ibid.*, pp. 105, 115, 223.

11. For information on the ISAB, the original draft report, and the ISAB Report 2005, see www.nipp.org/Adobe/ISAB%202005.pdf.
12. These draft reports have been presented and discussed at various seminars at the Caucasus Institute for Peace, Democracy, and Development, Tbilisi.
13. *Akhali Versia*, 7–13 January 2002.
14. *Sakartvelos Respublika*, 6 September 2001.
15. Hearings in the defence and security committee of the parliament of Georgia, 29 October 2001. The author attended those meetings as head of the parliamentary research service.
16. The Georgian power structures are not very familiar with the above-mentioned drafts of the security concept, as well as with the document "Georgia and the World: Future Vision", circulated by the Foreign Ministry in 2000.
17. *Evropa*, 25–31 December 1999.
18. The term "security community" refers to what is in the UK called the "defence village", a mixture of governmental and non-governmental organizations, academic people, and knowledgeable journalists who can provide a forum for thorough discussions on security/defence matters and thus, to a certain degree, guarantee that all pros and cons are duly assessed.
19. US$1 corresponds to 1.79 Georgian lari (GEL) (January 2005 rate).
20. Funds are needed even for downsizing the army: to fire staff one has to pay for retirement; to hire better staff, one has to offer increased salaries. Funds are also needed to conduct structural changes.
21. The term "power agencies" refers to heavily armed state institutions, i.e. army and law enforcement (or paramilitary) agencies.
22. TV channel Rustavi-2, news programme *Kurieri*, 12 September 2001.
23. After reportedly successful operations in 2002 of the Georgian MIA and the Security Ministry, headed by the newly appointed ministers Valeri Khaburdzania and Koba Narchemashvili, Pankisi Gorge was claimed to be free of Chechen guerillas.
24. Officially, there are two such military bases. However, the base in *de facto* separated Abkhazia, which had to be closed under the Istanbul Agreement in 1999, is still operating.
25. Armed forces of the *de facto* independent former autonomous republics of Soviet Georgia, Abkhazia, and South Ossetia are not included in the list, as the Georgian government has no formal leverage and does not claim the right to control them. These forces, as well as political entities under their protection, are not recognized by the Georgian state.
26. Huntington, Samuel P. 1995. *The Soldier and the State: The Theory of Politics of Civil-Military Relations*. Cambridge, MA: Harvard University Press, pp. 162–192.
27. The law on interior troops, 30 April 1998.
28. Brooks, Risa. 1998. *Political-Military Relations and the Stability of Arab Regimes*, Adelphi Paper 324. London: IISS, pp. 41–46.
29. Interview with the head of the law department of the parliament of Georgia, L. Bejashvili; interview with one of the authors of the Georgian constitution, MP V. Khmaladze, October 2001.
30. The law on the National Security Council, Article 3.
31. The report of a mission of the US European Command, spring 2000.
32. Statement of the chairman of the parliamentary defence and security committee at a parliamentary board sitting, 30 January 2002.
33. Statement of MP K. Kemularia at a meeting of the Board of the Parliament, 30 January 2002.
34. Donnelly, Chris. 2000. "Rethinking security", *NATO Review*, No. 3, Winter, p. 33.

35. Rustavi-2, news programme, 1 November 2004.
36. Interview with representatives of the Georgian Young Lawyers Association, Tbilisi, October 2004.
37. Interview with representatives of the Liberty Institute, Tbilisi, October 2004.
38. Huntington, note 26 above, p. 1.
39. Constitution of Georgia, paragraph 100, amended 6 February 2004.
40. However, in this case it might have been better to correct the relevant laws instead of the constitution, as amalgamation of armed institutions could pose a real risk for countries without long-standing experience with democratic rule.
41. Confidential interview, October 2004.

9

The politics of fear versus the politics of intimidation: Security sector reform in Northern Ireland

Stefan Wolff

With the conclusion of the Good Friday Agreement on 10 April 1998, a long-lasting peace process in Northern Ireland moved into a qualitatively new stage, which, in relation to other conflicts, is often described as post-conflict reconstruction.[1] In the case of Northern Ireland, this is a misleading term: the fundamental conflict between the proponents of two competing visions of national belonging is far from over, and (some of) the conflict parties have merely agreed on a new framework in which they want to pursue these distinct visions. From this perspective, it is more appropriate to speak of post-*agreement* reconstruction. That the conflict thus remains unresolved is an important factor in the post-agreement reconstruction process, and particularly in relation to security sector reform, which, as far as Northern Ireland is concerned, evolves primarily around the decommissioning of paramilitary weapons arsenals, police reform, and the demilitarization of security arrangements in the province.

Although several years have passed since the conclusion of the Good Friday Agreement in 1998, the situation in Northern Ireland is far from stable. In all three dimensions of post-agreement reconstruction – the building of political institutions, economic development, and social reconstruction – progress has been made, but this process has been slow and marred by often painful compromises, which on many occasions could only be achieved against the strong resistance of significant sections of the population and political élites in Northern Ireland.

In a society scarred by 30 years of violent conflict, persisting uncertainty about the future opens political spaces in which fear and intimidation become tools in the quest for power and often triumph over reason and the force of rational arguments. This impedes the process of post-agreement reconstruction in general, but has particularly important consequences for the possibilities of security sector reform. In order to examine and assess these dynamics in Northern Ireland, this chapter proceeds in four steps. Following a conceptual clarification of "post-agreement reconstruction" and of the role and place of security sector reform within it, the chapter offers a short background on the nature of the Northern Ireland conflict and its significance for security sector reform. It then looks at key developments in different areas of security sector reform and examines to what extent they have been influenced by past and present conditions in Northern Ireland and whether, and how much, they have contributed to achieving a degree of sustainability in the peace process. Finally, some conclusions are drawn as to whether the current efforts to carry out security sector reform will contribute to bringing a permanent and stable peace to Northern Ireland in the context of the wider post-agreement reconstruction process.

Post-agreement reconstruction: Conceptual clarification

Protracted ethno-national conflicts[2] shape the societies in which they take place in many different, yet almost always exclusively negative, ways, resulting in a lack of functioning or legitimate political institutions, weak economic performance, non-existing or polarized structures of civil society, and antagonized élites. Thus the setting in which post-agreement reconstruction is to begin is often unfavourable in the extreme for the task to be accomplished. However, without a comprehensive programme aimed at rebuilding a conflict-torn society, no settlement would be worth the paper on which it had been written.

Elements of post-agreement reconstruction

The essential aim of post-agreement reconstruction is to create a set of political, economic, and social structures in accordance with an agreed conflict settlement which allow the conduct of a non-violent, just, and democratic political process.

It is important to bear in mind the multidimensionality of post-agreement reconstruction and take a holistic and long-term view of transforming conflicts, as "rushed agreements aimed primarily at stopping conflict may not be the best base on which to try to build a viable democratic state".[3] The nature of post-agreement reconstruction also means that *re*construction is, in fact, a misleading term, as it really involves "the creation of new, sustainable, institutions which are more democratic, fair and responsive to the needs, concerns, and aspirations of an entire population".[4] That is, the aim is to establish institutions that are superior to those which existed before the violent escalation of the conflict in that they do not contain the same shortcomings as those which may have led to the conflict in the first place. In order to achieve this, post-agreement reconstruction needs to address three different areas – the building of (political) institutions, economic recovery, and establishing conditions conducive for the development of civil society.

Security sector reform as a component of post-agreement reconstruction

Security sector reform[5] is a vital element in any post-agreement (or post-conflict) reconstruction process, in particular if the society in question has experienced long-lasting civil war resulting in alienation not just between different communities, but also between them and the state (including its security forces, widely understood as military, police, and the criminal justice system).

Except for a few sporadic episodes, since 1969 Northern Ireland has never experienced a complete breakdown of security, nor has there been a state of lawlessness or actual state collapse. The total number of people killed (about 3,300) compares "favourably" to most other ethnic civil wars, as does the number of those injured as a result of the conflict (about 45,000), especially if one takes into account that these figures cover the entire period of the current stage of the conflict since 1969.

Security sector reform in Northern Ireland thus happens in a context where the task is essentially not one of building a new security sector, but of making existing institutions acceptable to, and beneficial for, society as a whole. At the same time, a process of decommissioning of paramilitary weapons has to occur, which has so far posed grave challenges to post-agreement reconstruction as a whole, but also to the "security thinking" of the involved groups. Old and new security dilemmas have to be resolved in a situation where much depends on the willingness of former antagonists to cooperate with each other in building viable political institutions, reinvigorating the economy, and establishing new structures for a more inclusive civil society.

Factors determining the dynamics and outcome of post-agreement reconstruction

Apart from the overall suitability of the agreed settlement for a conflict, the factors determining the dynamics and outcome of post-agreement reconstruction can be grouped in a number of relatively broad categories:

Table 9.1 Factors determining the dynamics and outcome of post-agreement reconstruction in Northern Ireland

Northern Ireland	UK/Republic of Ireland	International
General political factors • Power differential and its interpretation • Performance and legitimacy of government organs and their institutional set-up Intraethnic factors • Group identity, awareness, and solidarity • Party political homogeneity • Basis for and degree of mobilization • Policy agendas and policies of major intra-group actors and their mutual perception Interethnic factors • Ethnic stratification of society and its perception • Relationship between ethnic groups, their members, and their leaders • Influence of identity-related aspects on inter-group policies • Policy agendas and policies of the principal conflict parties and their mutual perception	• Policy aims of the two governments and the way in which they are perceived in Northern Ireland • Means by which aims are sought to be realized • Role and degree of involvement in the post-agreement reconstruction process • Approach *vis-à-vis* each other and the two communities in Northern Ireland • Domestic and international policy constraints	• Motivation of international actors for their involvement • Availability and commitment of resources • Skill and determination of intervention

interethnic and intraethnic relations in the actual conflict zone; in case of a regionally confined conflict within a state, the situation in this state in general; when ethnic groups in the conflict have a kin-relation with a neighbouring state, the situation in that state; and, almost as a matter of course, the broader international context and the actors within it. More precisely, the particular nature of the Northern Ireland conflict suggests that the factors displayed in Table 9.1 are those most likely to determine the dynamics and outcome of the post-agreement reconstruction process.

Indicators to measure the success of post-agreement reconstruction

Bush suggests grouping indicators for the success of post-agreement reconstruction into five categories – security, psychological, social, political, and judicial indicators.[6] Apart from the fact that a separate category of economic indicators would need to be added to this classification, in the context of Northern Ireland it seems more sensible to measure success in each of the three main dimensions of post-agreement reconstruction – institution building (political, security, and judicial indicators), economic recovery, and the rebuilding of civil society (social and psychological indicators). Table 9.2 specifies the relevant indicators in each of the three dimensions for Northern Ireland.

The nature and characteristics of the Northern Ireland conflict

In order to assess properly the nature and characteristics of the Northern Ireland conflict, and more importantly its impact on society during the process of post-agreement reconstruction, it is particularly significant to consider the conduct of the conflict itself: how long and how intense has it been, have there been any previous attempts to settle it, and if so, why have they failed? Finally, there is the question of the long-term impact of the conflict on society. No conflict simply erupts in a peaceful and harmonious society, but is normally preceded by more or less lengthy periods of latent conflict, political radicalization, and group antagonization. A prolonged period of violence, as Northern Ireland has seen for over 30 years, leaves its mark on society in many different ways that all affect post-agreement reconstruction, such as victimization of civilians, economic decline, and social segregation, to name just a few.

The intensity of the Northern Ireland conflict

As already mentioned, by global standards of death tolls in violent inter-ethnic conflicts, the conflict in Northern Ireland has not been very intense. Between 1969 and 1994, when, in the current peace process, the first cease-fires by the Irish Republican Army (IRA) and Loyalist paramilitary groups were announced, about 3,200 people were killed. Yet these statistics only tell half the story. Apart from killings, paramilitaries have committed many more acts of violence, ranging from beatings and kneecappings to intimidation, and these were directed at both the alleged enemy and members of their own communities. The conduct of British and Northern Irish security forces, too, has at times been questionable:

Table 9.2 Indicators to measure the success of post-agreement reconstruction in Northern Ireland

Institution building	Economic recovery	Rebuilding of civil society
Political indicators • Level and type of political participation (e.g. pro- or anti-agreement) • Vote share of political parties (moderates, cross-communal, radicals, parties linked to paramilitary organizations) • **Performance and legitimacy of government institutions** Security indicators • *Conflict-related killings and other forms of violence, including intra-ethnic "policing" and internal feuds* • *Conduct of security forces (arrests, detention, treatment)* • *Decommissioning* • *Demilitarization* • *Reform of the policing system* Judicial indicators • *Rule of law* • *Even-handed law enforcement* • *Prisoner release and prison conditions* • Human rights bill and commission • **Judicial inquiries in past**	• Growth rates • Level of inward investment • Level of FDI • Unemployment rates (total and community-specific) • Community participation in, and support for, regeneration and development	Social indicators • Level of residential segregation • Level of integrated education • Level of intermarriage • Number of intra- and cross-communal organizations • Number of cross-communal local print and electronic media Psychological indicators • **Perception of security situation (individual and collective)** • Perceptions of "others", including persistence of stereotypes and prejudice • Level of confidence in future • **Significance of "symbols" (flags, police name, uniforms, badges, oath, etc.)**

Key: *direct indicator* for security sector reform; **indirect indicator** for security sector reform

detention without trial, mistreatment and torture, shoot-to-kill raids and ambushes, and collusion with Loyalist paramilitaries have all attracted media headlines over the past 30-some years. These many forms of violence have had a significant impact on inter- and intra-community relations in Northern Ireland, as well as community-state relations. Their examination can provide a good understanding for the degree to which the conflict as a whole has affected society.

Violence, and its increasing acceptance as a means to achieve political objectives among some sections of both communities, has had an impact on community relations and vice versa at three levels – segregation, polarization, and alienation.[7] Violence may not be the primary cause, or result, of any of these three dimensions of community relations, yet there is a strong interrelation between them.

Although a long-term trend, segregation has increased as a result of inter-communal violence. This was the case especially in the late 1960s and early 1970s, and on a lower level it has continued in subsequent decades. While intimidation from the "other" community and fear of violence have contributed to increasing residential segregation, peer pressure from within one's own community has also played a role in establishing today's largely segregated structure of residence in Northern Ireland. Segregation has important consequences in societies affected by interethnic conflict because it makes it easier to develop and maintain stereotypes about the other community and its intentions towards one's own community. Because of this, there will be even less understanding of the position of the other community, which, in its rejection, increases homogeneity and solidarity within one's own community. On this basis, violence against this other community becomes more easily acceptable and justifications for its use are more readily available.

The degree to which both communities differ in their perceptions of the nature of the Northern Ireland conflict and its potential solutions is influenced by more or less informed judgements about the other community and its political agenda. Violence and the interpretation of violent acts are likely to reinforce the degree of polarization between the two communities. At the same time, the significant differences in views of what could be an acceptable and desirable future for Northern Ireland, and the inability to reach an agreement on this by peaceful means, increased the preparedness of some sections within each community to engage in violence either to achieve their goals or, at least, to prevent the other community from achieving theirs.[8]

The lack of political progress over almost 30 years of violent conflict and the inability of the security forces to provide protection from acts of terrorist violence have also contributed, although unequally, to an increasing alienation of both communities from the British state and its institutions. While this has always been characteristic for the Nationalist/Republican community, alienation has also affected the Unionist/Loyalist community, especially after the Anglo-Irish Agreement of 1985 and the recent Good Friday Agreement.[9] The sense of being left alone with unresolved problems has triggered processes in both communities in which paramilitary organizations have partly replaced organs of the state, including policing and the "administration of justice", as well as basic social services "supervised" by paramilitaries such as childcare, youth centres, and care of the elderly. This is more obvious and widespread within sections of the Republican community, where paramilitaries not only protect their community from sectarian attacks but also police it. Unionist and Loyalist alienation from Britain has its origins in the days of partition when national political parties withdrew from campaigning in Northern Ireland, thus encouraging the build-up of an almost exclusively sectarian party system for the decades to come.

Community relations that are based on the historic experience of inequality, deprivation, and discrimination are more likely to form the background against which inter-communal violence can develop and escalate. Yet the acceptability of violence has not only affected inter- but also intra-community relations. Feuds between rival paramilitary groups in each community, such as the Loyalist turf wars of summer 2000, and punishment beatings, intimidation, and expulsions of individuals and entire families have contributed to a deterioration of social relations, decline in trust in the effectiveness of state institutions to perform essential functions, and widespread disillusionment with the political process in Northern Ireland for several decades.

It has, therefore, been important to reduce the level of violence and "to take the gun out of politics". However, the various policies applied to do so have had different degrees of success, and have had, and will have, distinct consequences, ranging from the integration of some sections of former paramilitaries (especially the IRA and Ulster Volunteer Force) to the further alienation from the peace process of others (especially the Ulster Defence Association and a variety of Republican and Loyalist splinter groups). There is no correlation between the reduction of inequality, deprivation, and discrimination and the general downward trend in death tolls recorded in the Northern Ireland conflict over the past two decades.[10] Nevertheless, a positive correlation exists in relation to increasing residential segregation, although it is hard to say whether and where a causal relationship exists. Most probably the reduction of death tolls since the early 1970s can be attributed to a number of factors, such as improved capabilities of the security forces, better security cooperation between the British and Irish governments, and changed tactics and political agendas of the paramilitary organizations and radical political parties in both communities.[11]

The long-term impact of the conflict on Northern Irish society

The overall pattern of conflict intensity has also been affected by various (failed) attempts to settle the conflict in Northern Ireland. The most significant and instructive of these were the Sunningdale and Anglo-Irish

Agreements of 1973 and 1985 and the Good Friday Agreement of 1998. The primary changes since 1973 have been in contextual circumstances increasing the acceptability of power-sharing among some sections of the political élites in both communities and their respective constituencies, and a more consistent and cooperative effort on the part of the British and Irish governments to incentivize and pressure the political parties in Northern Ireland into an agreement and its implementation. Equally significant was the fundamental change for the better in the international context, leading to sustained positive engagement on the part of the European Union as well as successive US administrations and the Irish diaspora in the USA. These overall positive changes notwithstanding, post-agreement reconstruction in Northern Ireland faces constant challenges from the persistence of patterns of prejudice, intimidation, and fear, and their political manipulation and instrumentalization. These are among the main reasons for the difficulties that have been experienced in the implementation process of the Good Friday Agreement so far.

Although the Good Friday Agreement provides a comprehensive institutional framework for the settlement of the Northern Ireland conflict, its implementation and operation so far have been hampered by the different expectations and interpretations that exist within each of the two communities in Northern Ireland regarding the final outcome of the implementation process. In relation to security sector reform, this, in turn, has led to three key problems that have over time become the core stumbling blocks of implementation and thus of success or failure in the current peace process: decommissioning, the reform of the policing system, and the normalization of the security situation. In addition, there are a number of other issues to which the two communities attach equally high symbolic value, such as the name, oath, and badge of the police forces. While these might not have the same political significance, together with the other problems they reflect quite clearly the persisting divisions in Northern Ireland; and it is the apparent inability to overcome these divisions, not even at the élite level, that has important consequences for the process of post-agreement reconstruction as a whole.

Security sector reform in Northern Ireland so far

The Good Friday Agreement and its provisions for security sector reform

The Good Friday Agreement, concluded between eight political parties in Northern Ireland and the British and Irish governments on 10 April 1998, provides for power-sharing institutions in the province, structures of cross-border cooperation on the island of Ireland and within the wider context of the British Isles, and a variety of rights, measures, and safeguards accompanying an inclusive democratic political process.[12]

In the area of security sector reform, the agreement deals with four major issues: decommissioning, security, policing and justice, and prisoners. In relation to decommissioning the agreement provided that all political parties represented at the negotiations would continue to engage with the Independent International Commission on Decommissioning (IICD) in order to achieve "the decommissioning of illegally held arms in the possession of paramilitary groups" within two years of the 22 May 1998 referenda on the agreement. With regard to security arrangements, the agreement resolved that the British government would endeavour to return to "normal security arrangements in Northern Ireland, consistent with the level of threat", reduce the number and role of its armed forces, and remove security installations and emergency powers in Northern Ireland. In the areas of policing and justice, the agreement did not go much beyond the declaration of general principles and instead left specific arrangements to two independent commissions to be established subsequently and to undertake a comprehensive review of the situation in both areas. For "qualifying prisoners" an accelerated early release scheme was agreed.

Decommissioning

As early as June 1998, the British and Irish governments had put in place the legal and regulatory framework for the proposed IICD in a bilateral agreement that followed earlier steps taken on decommissioning since 1995.[13] However, apart from a symbolic act of decommissioning in December 1998 by the Loyalist Volunteer Force, nothing happened on the decommissioning front until 2 December 1999, when the IRA announced the appointment of a representative to liaise with the IICD, followed by similar moves on the part of the Ulster Volunteer Force (UVF) and the Ulster Freedom Fighters (UFF). After some ups and downs in the engagement with the IICD, in a statement of 6 May 2000 the IRA committed itself to put IRA weapons "completely and verifiably ... beyond use" and announced as a confidence-building measure that "contents of a number of ... arms dumps will be inspected by agreed third parties who will report that they have done so to the Independent International Commission on Decommissioning. The dumps will be re-inspected regularly to ensure that the weapons have remained silent." After the appointment of Cyril Ramaphosa and Marti Ahtisaari as weapons inspectors, several inspections took place, confirming that the weapons seen were secure and had not been used. However, even intensive discussions between the IICD and representatives from the IRA, UVF, and UFF did not manage to move the decommissioning issue any further after May 2000, when a deadline had been set by the British and Irish governments on the full implementation of the Good Friday Agreement by June 2001.

This standoff on decommissioning was characterized by mutual recriminations. The IRA claimed in a statement on 8 March 2001 that the British government had failed to "deliver on the agreement made with us on May 5th, 2000". According to an IICD report of June 2001, "the UVF will not consider decommissioning before they know the IRA's intentions and hear their declaration that the war is over", while the UFF found it "difficult to discuss decommissioning further with us while members of the UFF were continuing to be interned".[14] Among political parties the picture is similar – Unionists refused to sit in government with Sinn Féin as long as there is no move on decommissioning; Sinn Féin insists that it was in no position to dictate to the IRA and that there should be no link between individual aspects of the implementation of the Good Friday Agreement.

To make matters even worse, on 14 August 2001 the process moved back to square one. Following Ulster Unionist Party (UUP) leader David Trimble's resignation as first minister as of 1 July, there was (according to the provisions in the agreement) a six-week period in which a new first minister had to be found. Trimble's resignation, intended to put pressure on the IRA, seemed to pay off when a surprise announcement by the IRA on 9 August confirmed "that the IRA leadership has agreed a scheme with the IICD, which will put IRA arms completely and verifiably beyond use".[15] However, this was deemed insufficient by the UUP to agree to put forward a candidate for the election of first minister. Given a choice between suspension and new elections, the British government opted for a 24-hour suspension of the institutions, hoping that another six weeks of "breathing space" would provide sufficient time to facilitate an agreement between the parties that would bring the UUP back into government. The prospects for that, however, quickly faded away after the IRA announced on 14 August that, because of the renewed suspension, "the conditions therefore do not exist for progressing" on the basis of their earlier proposal for decommissioning, and that they were therefore withdrawing their proposal.

Faced with the imminent collapse of the political institutions created by the Good Friday Agreement, and under considerable national and international pressure, Sinn Féin publicly called on the IRA in October 2001 to begin decommissioning their weapons, which was followed by a subsequent announcement by the IICD that a first set of arms and other equipment had been put beyond use. While this prevented the feared collapse of the institutions in October 2001, it remains to be seen to what extent decommissioning can in fact "save" a peace process that is confronted with numerous other difficulties as well. Notwithstanding those, it is also significant, and indicative of further progress on the decommissioning front in the near future, that the British government proposed an amendment to the current decommissioning legislation, extending the amnesty period from the end of February 2002 initially until 2003, with possible further extensions until 2007. Despite Unionist and Conservative concerns that this would take the pressure off the paramilitary groups, the Northern Ireland Arms Decommissioning (Amendment) Act 2002 was passed in the House of Commons on 9 January 2002, approved by the House of Lords on 25 February 2002, and received royal assent the next day.

An alleged spy operation of the IRA at the Northern Ireland Assembly in Stormont led to the UUP threatening its walk-out and, following a well-established pattern, the pre-emptive suspension of the institutions in October 2002. Difficult back-room negotiations were meant to bring about the restoration of power-sharing by autumn 2003. A carefully crafted scenario of prenegotiated statements following another act of decommissioning, however, failed to achieve this: the UUP's understanding was that not only should the IRA decommission weapons and explosives, but also permit the chairman of the IICD to reveal the exact extent and nature of what was decommissioned. With this permission withheld, the UUP refused to rejoin the government and elections were called for 26 November 2003 without agreement among the parties generally supporting power-sharing. Unsurprisingly, hardliners and extremists in both communities carried the day.

Having lived through 30 years of troubles, both the constitutional and the paramilitary camps have had similar experiences, yet their interpretations and conclusions were fundamentally different. What complicates the issue further is the fact that it seems difficult for the hard core in each community to understand that the security of one's own group, based on the continued ability to defend oneself with arms, is very often perceived as a threat by the respective other group. Mistrust and the experience of suffering over decades are unlikely to be transformed into trust and mutual understanding in the short term. On the other hand, even if decommissioning takes place it might give a false sense of security, as it does not involve a disruption of the existing paramilitary structures or a destruction of the paramilitary's capability to rearm themselves at any time.

Police reform

Against the background of very different community experiences and levels of identification with the police forces in Northern Ireland, the is-

sue of policing has remained one of the most contentious areas of dis-
agreement, even after the two major parties in the assembly, the UUP
and the (Nationalist) Social Democratic and Labour Party (SDLP), have
agreed to nominate representatives to the Policing Board and thus ended
the impasse in the implementation of the government's plans for police
reform. The fundamental conflict here has not been, and is not, so much
over whether there should or should not be a reform of the policing system, but over the degree to which such a reform should be carried out.
While Nationalist/Republican opinion tended towards radical reform, up
to the disbanding of the Royal Ulster Constabulary (RUC), Unionist/
Loyalist attitudes, although recognizing the need for a more representative police force, favoured less decisive reforms. This difference in approach had not least to do with the widespread feeling among Unionists/
Loyalists that the RUC was "our" police force as compared to the
Nationalist/Republican perception of the RUC being "their" police force.
Clearly, from this point of view, both communities had very different expectations about the degree of reform necessary.

The Good Friday Agreement did not make any specific provisions in
relation to a reform of the police service, but left details to further negotiations and the recommendations of an independent commission. The
terms of reference for the work of this independent commission were
quite tight: Annex A of the provisions on "Policing and Justice" stipu-
lates in relation to the independent commission that "Its proposals on
policing should be designed to ensure that policing arrangements, including composition, recruitment, training, culture, ethos and symbols, are
such that in a new approach Northern Ireland has a police service that
can enjoy widespread support from, and is seen as an integral part of,
the community as a whole." It then goes on to outline in relatively great
detail how the proposals of the independent commission would contribute to enabling the RUC to do policing in a peaceful society. The recommendations of the 1999 Report of the Independent Commission on Policing for Northern Ireland sought to find an acceptable middle ground,[16]
but were not received very well in either community – Unionists and
Loyalists felt they were going too far, particularly with respect to the proposed name change (to Police Service of Northern Ireland – PSNI), while
especially Republicans had hoped for even further-reaching reforms.

Under the Police (Northern Ireland) Act 2000, which became law on
23 November 2000, and the implementation plan, the British government
committed itself to a number of deliverables suggested by the Patten Report. These included that the new Policing Board would represent both
communities; new arrangements for accountability; a new code of ethics;
a new name; a new badge and flag; a human-rights-oriented training and
development programme; and balanced recruitment to the police force in

order to achieve greater representation. The implementation of these commitments was initially at best sporadic, which further contributed to a climate of uncertainty in which the issue could be, and was, used for politicizing and polarizing Northern Irish society, which essentially played into the hands of hardliners on both sides. Nevertheless, as of 4 November 2001 all measures announced in the implementation plan had been fully implemented.

Demilitarization

As a further element of the security sector reform, the British government has undertaken a number of steps towards a normalization of the security situation in Northern Ireland. This included a reduction of the size and role of armed forces. By July 2001 the number of troops in Northern Ireland had been reduced by 3,500, military patrolling had decreased by 50 per cent since 1995, the number of army helicopter flying hours had gone down by 21 per cent, and one of the six Royal Irish Regiments had been disbanded. Following the first substantive act of decommissioning by the IRA, the army presence in Northern Ireland was further reduced, and dropped to less than 13,500 troops on 59 bases by January 2002. In addition, by July 2001 42 military installations had been closed, demolished, or vacated, and 102 cross-border roads had been re-opened between Northern Ireland and the Republic of Ireland. Furthermore, the Emergency Provisions Act was replaced by a new UK-wide Terrorism Act, and the so-called holding centres in Castlereagh and Strand Road were closed.

Other indicators

Since 1998, 444 prisoners who qualified for early release have been set free in Northern Ireland, and 57 in the Irish Republic. Reintegration has been a major problem, especially related to economic dimensions rather than in terms of political and personal aspects. The difficulties arise primarily from a lack of vocational skills, legal barriers, and personal security risks that ex-prisoners face. The relatively slow process of reconciliation in Northern Ireland has also hampered reintegration.

The overall trend of decreasing violence has been reversed since 2001, with acts of spontaneous and organized mob and paramilitary violence once again becoming a feature of Northern Irish politics. The months-long stand-off and clashes between Catholics and Protestants around the Holy Cross Girls' Primary School in the Ardoyne area in North Belfast, the murder of a Catholic postal worker, and the (subsequently withdrawn) threat by the Ulster Defence Association against Catholic school teachers and postal workers, as well as the threat by the Republican paramilitary group the "Irish National Liberation Army" against the Protestant staff at a Marks & Spencer distribution centre, testify to the persistence of sectarian divisions and mindsets in Northern Ireland. However, what is equally if not more significant is that the murder of the Catholic postal worker was not only widely condemned by representatives from all major political parties in Northern Ireland, but also led to thousands of people from both communities participating in rallies against hatred and sectarianism. By the same token, it is interesting to observe that the clashes around the Holy Cross Girls' Primary School did not spread across Northern Ireland or even lead to wider rioting in Belfast itself, as similar events did over earlier years. What this indicates is a decreasing acceptance of violence as a useful means to achieve political aims, and as such points to a change in the overall political climate in Northern Ireland over the past few years that must not be underestimated in its significance for post-agreement reconstruction.

The appointment of a human rights commissioner and the initiation of public inquiries into unresolved issues, such as Bloody Sunday and allegations of security forces' collusion in high-profile killings over the past 30 years,[17] have individually addressed specific needs of both communities.

Conclusions

Almost four years after the conclusion of the Good Friday Agreement, Northern Ireland remains a deeply divided society, shaped by over 30 years of violent interethnic conflict. The general elections on 7 June 2001, which saw the moderate Unionists and Nationalists weakened at the expense of Sinn Féin and the Democratic Unionist Party, have confirmed a trend of increasing divisions and a declining willingness to compromise and cooperate. This culminated in October 2002, when an alleged IRA spy ring at the Northern Ireland Office prompted the UUP once more to set a deadline for the expulsion from the executive of Sinn Féin, and otherwise to threaten their own withdrawal from the power-sharing institutions. Thus, faced with the imminent collapse of the institutions established under the Good Friday Agreement, then Secretary of State for Northern Ireland, John Reid, decided to suspend the institutions indefinitely. Since then a draft compromise has been hammered out in intense negotiations between the parties in Northern Ireland, which support the agreement in principle, and the British and Irish governments. Nevertheless, as no formal consensus had been achieved, the assembly elections planned for 1 May 2003 were postponed until the end of that month and then again until November 2003. Returning a majority of hardliners and extremists from both communities, a review process of the 1998 agreement was initiated in early 2004, but has not resulted in any breakthrough at the time of writing.[18]

However, the persistence of divisions and mutual suspicion in itself is not surprising – the time it takes to move a conflict-torn society away from long-established patterns of prejudice and distrust is measured in generations, not years. Table 9.3 provides a general assessment of the situation in Northern Ireland as of April 2004, in relation to individual indicators of post-agreement reconstruction.

A simple computation exercise alone reveals that with regard to 16 out of 29 indicators the current status of post-agreement reconstruction has had a negative impact, i.e. has failed to provide conditions for sustainable peace. Even more significantly, out of the 18 indicators deemed important because of the specificities of the conflict in Northern Ireland, 13 reveal a negative impact. With the exception of judicial and at least some security indicators in the area of institution building, the failure of post-agreement reconstruction to contribute to sustainable peace is resounding. The question that therefore arises is whether this failure is due to bad implementation of the Good Friday Agreement as the "founding document" of the post-agreement reconstruction process, or whether the roots for failure lie much deeper, namely in the agreement itself and its unsuitability as a framework for sustainable peace in Northern Ireland.

At a very general level, there has always been a degree of uncertainty about whether the Good Friday Agreement could really deliver on its promise: as a rigid framework for consociationalism, it required the two communities to accept a political process which essentially tried to square the circle of Nationalist and Unionist aspirations, i.e. a united Ireland and continued strong links with Great Britain. For this to be possible, it would have been necessary for both communities to drop their maximum demands and accept the proposed institutions as a compromise structure within which both groups' aspirations and concepts of national belonging could be accommodated. However, the change in attitude necessary for this acceptance to happen has not been forthcoming. It is questionable whether one could expect such a change in attitude within only a few years after entire group identities had been constructed around this Irish dimension for decades, if not centuries. Therefore, it could be argued that the agreement was fundamentally flawed from the beginning, and nothing that politicians in Belfast, Dublin, and London were doing would have prevented the inevitable failure of the implementation process. Yet this is too easy an answer and too easy a way out, especially for politicians in Northern Ireland, who bear a fair share of the responsibility for the difficulties that the implementation of the Good Friday Agreement

Table 9.3 The status of post-agreement reconstruction in Northern Ireland

Institution building

Indicator	Status
Political indicators	
Participation	Remains high, but contributes to polarization
Vote share	Increased for extremists at the expense of moderates
Performance of government institutions	Good while in operation (suspended in October 2002)
Legitimacy of government institutions	Remains low among significant sections in both communities, leading to institutional instability
Security indicators	
Violence	Has increased locally since 2000
Conduct of security forces	Fair
Decommissioning	Significant progress with the beginning of actual IRA decommissioning in October 2001, but IRA disengagement from the decommissioning body following the suspension of the institutions in October 2002
Demilitarization	Initial progress continues after the beginning of IRA decommissioning
Police reform	Progresses according to the British government's implementation plan
Judicial indicators	
Rule of law	Exists
Law enforcement	Even-handed
Prisoner release	All eligible prisoners released
Human Rights Commission	Set up, but largely inactive
Judicial inquiries into past	Set up, but contribute to polarization rather than reconciliation

Table 9.3 (cont.)

Economic recovery

Growth rates	Remain above 3% since 1998
Investment	High in 1997–1998, but remains at high levels since
Unemployment (total)	Significantly down for both communities since 1998
Unemployment (community-specific)	Employment differential remains almost unchanged
Community participation in regeneration	Apparent, but insufficient improvement for most deprived areas

Rebuilding of (civil) society

Social indicators	
Residential segregation	Remains at high levels
Integrated education	Remains at low levels
Intermarriage	Remains at low levels
Intra-communal organizations	Many and slightly increasing
Inter-communal organizations	Remain few
Inter-communal local media	Remain few
Psychological indicators	
Perception of security situation	Initial sense of improvement has given way to perception of matters turning worse
Perception of others	Significant lack of trust remains
Level of confidence in future of Good Friday Agreement	Decreases, particularly among Unionists
Significance of community-specific symbols	Remains high

Note: ░░░ indicates important issue

░░░ indicates negative impact.

has experienced so far (although they also deserve credit for the progress that has been made).

Within Northern Ireland, the emotionalization particularly of decommissioning and police reform by politicians of both communities, and a crucial lack of trust and leadership, have created a situation characterized by mutually reinforcing conceptions of resentment and entitlement among large sections of both communities. By playing to, and thereby often actually encouraging and strengthening, fears and myths among their electorates, political leaders have managed to boost self-perceptions of victimhood and perceptions of victimization at the hands of the other community. Clearly, fear and intimidation have long been features of inter-communal relations in Northern Ireland, but since 1998 politicians in both communities have done little to effect change in this respect. Nor has it helped that Unionists and Loyalists have tried to prevent any substantial reform of the police forces in Northern Ireland. Nor has the initial rejection of tabled proposals by Nationalists and Republicans contributed in any way to creating a situation of normality in which a Northern Irish police force could have been created that would have been acceptable to both communities.

By the same token, the damaging linkage between decommissioning and Unionist participation in the power-sharing government has left it to the paramilitaries to allow or block progress of the implementation process. The initially merely verbal gestures from the IRA were obviously unacceptable to Unionist leaders, who had created a "sideshow" over the decommissioning issue. It was fairly obvious that any actual decommissioning of whatever quantity of arms and explosives would be purely symbolic – exploitable as a defeat of the IRA while completely unverifiable as to the extent of paramilitary equipment actually surrendered, and certainly not sufficient to prevent rearmament. Strong leadership could have been expressed on both sides: Sinn Féin could have publicly declared its strong support for decommissioning much earlier, while the UUP should not have allowed itself to make power-sharing dependent on decommissioning. This would have made it possible for a political process in Northern Ireland to develop in which the work of the institutions created under the Good Friday Agreement would have dominated the public and political discourses, and not decommissioning. Thus, legitimate political leaders could have retained control instead of surrendering it to paramilitaries. While this changed temporarily with the beginning of IRA decommissioning as of October 2001, the damage already done to the peace process over the first three-and-a-half years of one impasse chasing another was compounded by the renewed suspension of institutions in October 2002, and will now be even more difficult to undo. It has in fact been a major reason why Unionist support for the Good Friday Agreement fell from about 55 per cent in May 2000 to 36 per cent in February 2003,[19] a result that was broadly confirmed by the November 2003 election results.

The government in London, too, is not free from blame. On the one hand, London deserves to be commended for its determination to bring a lasting peace to Northern Ireland. On the other hand, however, the strong role that the British government has retained in Northern Irish politics and its *deus ex machina*-like rescue attempts of the agreement have taken away control, and thus responsibility, from politicians in Northern Ireland. This gave the latter a convenient scapegoat in cases where they themselves should be blamed.

Thus, the prospects of the Good Friday Agreement for having a long-term positive impact on the peace process, and so on politics and society in Northern Ireland, are not bad. However, the agreement is only one step in a much longer process of transforming the ethno-national conflict that is at the heart of Northern Ireland's problems. To maintain the current positive momentum in this process will require skill and determination of all those involved in the Northern Irish peace process in London and Dublin, Brussels and Washington, and foremost in Belfast itself.

Looking back at the process of security sector reform since the conclusion of the Good Friday Agreement, it is clear that both are closely connected to each other, not just because security sector reform is one element for which the agreement makes provisions, but also because the structure of the implementation of the agreement and the operation of the institutions created by it have been crucially dependent upon the progress made by security sector reform, especially in relation to decommissioning and police reform. Underlying the ups and downs of post-agreement reconstruction so far, however, are the more fundamental dynamics of security thinking and perceptions of the two communities in Northern Ireland, both of which have experienced the past few years as a period of great uncertainty and instability regarding the status and future of their respective groups. The resulting dynamics of security thinking and perceptions are characterized by two mutually reinforcing trends that encompass Northern Irish society as a whole – the politics of fear (the hyping up of emotions about the very survival of one's own group) and the politics of intimidation (the use of verbal and physical threats and of actual violence in defence of group interests). These have become apparent in a general increase of sectarian violence since 2000 by dissident Republican paramilitary groups and their dissident and mainstream Loyalist counterparts, who use both fear and intimidation in their attempts to derail the peace process to which they are fundamentally opposed, as they see it as incompatible with their own agendas.

From this, two conclusions can be drawn that seem applicable beyond the case of Northern Ireland. First, security sector reform is only likely to succeed if the institutional structures provided in a peace agreement are acceptable to the conflict parties, and address not just their security needs but also their more fundamental political aspirations (or are able to transform the latter so that they can be accommodated within the new structures). Second, security sector reform is unlikely to succeed no matter what is on offer if the issues involved are used as proxies to destabilize and destroy a previously concluded agreement, unless there is sufficiently strong positive leadership that can create a broad consensus to marginalize maximalists and "spoilers" and prevent their reasoning from assuming a dominant position in public discourse and the political process.

Acknowledgements

Fieldwork for this chapter was supported by a research grant from the British Academy. The author would also like to thank Colin Irwin, Arthur Aughey, Antony Alcock, and Mari Fitzduff for fruitful discussions and personal insights. All shortcomings and mistakes are entirely the author's responsibility.

Notes

1. For a general overview of the state of the art in the field, see Newman, Edward and Albrecht Schnabel (eds). 2002. *Recovering from Civil Conflict: Reconciliation, Peace and Development*. London: Frank Cass.
2. On ethno-national conflicts, see, *inter alia*, Brown, Michael E. (ed.). 2001. *Nationalism and Ethnic Conflict*. Cambridge, MA: MIT Press; Diamond, Larry and Marc F. Plattner (eds). 1994. *Nationalism, Ethnic Conflict and Democracy*. Baltimore, MD: Johns Hopkins University Press; Horowitz, Donald L. 2001. *The Deadly Ethnic Riot*. Berkeley, CA: University of California Press; Horowitz, Donald L. 1985. *Ethnic Groups in Conflict*. Berkeley, CA: University of California Press; Lake, David A. and Donald Rothchild (eds). 1998. *The International Spread of Ethnic Conflict: Fear, Diffusion, and Escalation*. Princeton, NJ: Princeton University Press; Scherrer, Christian P. 2002. *Ethnicity, Nationalism and Violence: Conflict Management, Human Rights and Multilateral Regimes*. Aldershot: Ashgate; Wolff, Stefan. 2003. *Disputed Territories: The Transnational Dynamics of Ethnic Conflict Settlement*. New York and Oxford: Berghahn.
3. Harris, Peter and Ben Reilly. 1998. *Democracy and Deep-Rooted Conflict: Options for Negotiators*. Stockholm: International Institute for Democracy and Electoral Assistance.
4. Bush, Kenneth. 1998. *A Measure of Peace: Peace and Conflict Impact Assessment of Development Projects in Conflict Zones*. Ottawa: International Development Research Centre, p. 34.

5. Good overviews of the problematique are Cooper, Neil and Michael Pugh. 2002. "Security-sector transformation in post-conflict societies", CSDG Working Paper 5. London: King's College; Chanaa, Jane. 2002. *Security Sector Reform: Issues, Challenges and Prospects*, Adelphi Paper 344. London: International Institute for Strategic Studies; Rees, Edward. 2002. "Security-sector reform and transitional administrations", *Conflict, Security and Development*, Vol. 2, No. 1, pp. 151–156.

6. Bush, note 4 above, pp. 21–22.

7. Hamilton, Andrew. 1990. *Violence and Communities*. Coleraine: University of Ulster Press.

8. The political spectrum in Northern Ireland can be best imagined as divided into three political spaces: Nationalist/Republican, Unionist/Loyalist, and cross-communal. The major Nationalist/Republican parties are the Social Democratic and Labour Party (SDLP) and Sinn Féin, which seek unification between Northern Ireland and the Republic of Ireland. The SDLP has always pursued this goal with non-violent means, whereas Sinn Féin for a long time supported the armed struggle of the Irish Republican Army (IRA), the main Republican paramilitary organization. In the Unionist/Loyalist camp there are two parties which have traditionally rejected violence – the Ulster Unionist Party (UUP) and the Democratic Unionist Party (DUP). The Progressive Unionist Party (PUP) and the now dissolved Ulster Democratic Party (UDP) have, like Sinn Féin, links with paramilitary organizations – the Ulster Volunteer Force (UVF) and the Ulster Defence Association (UDA), respectively. All four parties, as well as the cross-communal Alliance Party and the Women's Coalition, are broadly supportive of the *status quo*, i.e. of Northern Ireland remaining a part of the United Kingdom. For further details, see, for example, Neuheiser, Jörg and Stefan Wolff (eds). 2002. *Peace at Last? The Impact of the Good Friday Agreement on Northern Ireland*. New York and Oxford: Berghahn.

9. For a detailed analysis of the two agreements and their impact on the Northern Ireland conflict, see Wolff, Stefan. 2001. "Context and content: Sunningdale and Belfast compared", in Rick Wilford (ed.) *Aspects of the Belfast Agreement*. Oxford: Oxford University Press.

10. McGarry, John and Brendan O'Leary. 1996. *Explaining Northern Ireland: Broken Images*. Oxford: Blackwell, pp. 288–290.

11. *Ibid.*; O'Duffy, Brendan and Brendan O'Leary. 1990. "Violence in Northern Ireland, 1969–June 1989", in John McGarry and Brendan O'Leary (eds) *The Future of Northern Ireland*. Oxford: Blackwell.

12. The full text of the Good Friday Agreement is available on the website of the Northern Ireland Office, www.nio.gov.uk/agreement.htm.

13. These included the two governments' decision on 28 November 1995 to establish an international body to provide an independent assessment of the decommissioning issue, the 1997 Decommissioning Act in the Republic of Ireland and the Northern Ireland Arms Decommissioning Act of the same year in the UK, and the joint communiqué issued on 29 July 1997 by the Irish Minister for Foreign Affairs and the British Secretary of State for Northern Ireland on completing preparations for the establishment of an independent commission on decommissioning.

14. Independent International Commission on Decommissioning (IICD). 2001. *Report of the Independent International Commission on Decommissioning*, released 30 June. Belfast: HMSO.

15. All IRA statements since 1998 are available on the BBC website, http://news.bbc.co.uk/1/hi/northern_ireland/2798801.stm.

16. Independent Commission on Policing for Northern Ireland. 1999. *A New Beginning: Policing in Northern Ireland*. Belfast: HMSO.

17. As part of the political package agreed between the UK and Irish governments in summer 2001, it was agreed to appoint an international and independent judge to investigate the following cases: Pat Finucane, Rosemary Nelson, Robert Hamill, Harry Breen and Bob Buchanan, Lord Justice and Lady Gibson, and Billy Wright.

18. The chapter covers events up to and including April 2004.

19. Personal communication from Colin Irwin. For details of Irwin's polling work in Northern Ireland since 1996, see Irwin, Colin. 2002. *The People's Peace Process in Northern Ireland*. Basingstoke: Palgrave. The data of the poll referred to here to can be accessed in full at www.peacepolls.org. Irwin's own analysis is available at www.peacepolls.org/Resources/NIPoll9A.pdf.

Part III

Experiences from Latin America: El Salvador, Guatemala, Colombia, Chile, and Haiti

10

Civil-military relations in Latin America: The post-9/11 scenario and the civil society dimension

Andrés Serbin and Andrés Fontana

When referring to Latin America, it is necessary to contextualize civil-military relations on the basis of some factors and criteria of strategic relevance for democratic objectives. In the first place, democratic transitions and (in some cases) democratic consolidation have, over the last two decades, produced a mosaic of rather heterogeneous results. The outcome of democratization has been a myriad of different and, by and large, preliminary, incomplete, and sometimes fragile attempts to build new links between the state, the military, and civil society according with democratic values and criteria.

In varying ways, a high degree of institutional autonomy of the armed forces characterizes civil-military relations in Latin American post-transition "democracies". For the most part, civil-military relations in the new democratic context have not overcome the basic (and in most cases only formal) subordination of the military to civilian authority. Thus, in order to understand the nature of civil-military relations in Latin America and its implications for security in the post-9/11 scenario, it is important to analyse the wide range of military prerogatives and the extended institutional autonomy of the armed forces.[1]

Taken together, heterogeneity and institutional autonomy of the armed forces offer a wide range of situations in which the military does not have any participation in national politics (Argentina), or may have a certain participation established by institutional norms (Chile and Brazil, each case in a different way), or has *de facto* influence and participation which varies according to the political juncture (Uruguay, Paraguay, Peru), or may become a substantial aspect of the political alliances that support (or oppose) "democratic" rule (Colombia, Venezuela, Guatemala). However, in all cases both congress and the executive have limited involvement in decisions related to national defence and military policy.

This common trait of civil-military relations in Latin American post-democratic transitions has been characterized by what Alfred Stepan calls "civilian abdication of responsibility".[2] The concept is meaningful because it refers not only to the lack of (or limited) involvement of civilian authorities in decision-making on defence and military policy, but also a tacit renunciation of building the institutional capacities (legal mechanisms, routine channels, and, particularly, civilian expertise) for effective civilian control and decision-making on defence and military policy matters.

The relevance of these common traits of Latin American post-transition civil-military relations in face of the post-Cold War scenario and, particularly, the post-9/11 scenario has not been explored sufficiently. The implications do not refer mainly to democratic stability (which depends on a wide range of factors).[3] The relevance of post-transition civil-military relations in Latin American refers to more specific aspects of the building of democracy, and also to the prospects of "hemispheric relations" – i.e. the euphemism inherited from the Cold War concern with "Western hemisphere security" used in the new context to refer to the relationship between the USA and the subregion, particularly in security matters.[4] Secondly, there is a lack of consensus regarding the major threats to security and the role of the armed forces. This lack of consensus embraces both the context of hemispheric relations and the more restricted context of the subregion, and has important security implications.[5]

It seems evident that the heterogeneity of civil-military relations in Latin America and the (varying but usually) high degree of institutional autonomy of the armed forces, together with the so-called civilian abdication of responsibility in regard to defence and military policy, are major factors determining the difficulties in building subregional and hemisphere consensus on the major threats affecting the region and the role that the armed forces should play in that context. This allows the USA to exert a larger influence on each individual country and on regional forums. However, regional weakness in security matters due to lack of consensus, limited confidence among major actors, and with regard to the policies and objectives of the USA in the region produces important costs for everyone and creates increasing risks for both subregional and hemisphere security.

With restricted civilian participation in defence and military policy, extendedly heterogeneous civil-military relations, and lack of clear definitions of the armed forces' military role, it is extremely difficult to develop a regional consensus on security matters, assume security commitments at the regional level, and develop common approaches and strategies to face the security challenges of the region.

Thus, this chapter focuses on the challenges created by varying visions of the military role and the difficulties of building a basic consensus both at the subregional and at the hemispheric levels. Furthermore, in regard to the redefinition of the military role, and also of a number of security issues (including the status of civil liberties in the political and institutional agenda) as a result of the post-9/11 international scenario, it is important to pay careful attention to the redefinition of the regional security agenda and the security priorities of individual countries – in the framework of both their respective bilateral relations with the USA and the so-called "hemispheric relations".

Finally, once the problem has been contextualized in relation to the issues mentioned above, it is conceptually and analytically necessary to underline that these relations vary in each country depending on:

- the relations established between state and civil society in the framework of the democratization processes, and the different modalities in which the military role is defined in this context
- the relations between the state and the armed forces in those cases in which, politically, civil society does not play a role as a protagonist
- the relations between civil society and the armed forces, with or without state mediation.

This dimension is related to – but different from – the diversity of civil-military relations referred to above, and which the first section of the chapter deals with in detail. The latter mainly refers to political and institutional arrangements, and the relationship between the armed forces and political power and civilian authority at the institutional level. Instead, the dimension underlined here refers to civil society and the links between the state and civil society.

In addition, it is worth noting that these three kinds of relationships (i.e. state and society in the framework of the democratization process; the state and the military, with civil society not playing a role as a protagonist; and civil society and the armed forces, with or without state mediation) are, and have been, strongly conditioned by the priorities of a regional security agenda encouraged by the USA. Changes in the regional and international context do not automatically determine the dynamics of domestic affairs in each country, even in those more exposed to, or dependent on, international factors. However, the special circumstances of the international scenario emerging from 9/11, and the way in which US foreign policy may evolve from then on, will have very specific consequences for the issues discussed in this chapter.

Military autonomy and democratic consolidation

The literature that analyses civil-military relations in the context of democratic transitions in Latin America has underlined the institutional autonomy of the armed forces and military prerogatives as two of the major factors conditioning the nature and future of emerging democracies.[6] These refer to the exercise of civil authority (armed forces' institutional autonomy), and corporate privileges of different sorts, including seats in the senate or ministries in the president's cabinet (military prerogatives). The military prerogatives and institutional autonomy of the armed forces inherited by new democracies after long periods of authoritarianism are incompatible with the full implementation of a representative system of government, and thus with the full exercise of a citizen-based sovereignty. Furthermore, they became major obstacles to the genuine participation of civil society in the definition of key issues of the emerging democratic context.

This has been a major limitation of the democratization processes in Latin America. Some of the reversals of democratization in the last few years may be linked to those restrictions. However, that is an issue pending deep analysis and empirical research, as, by and large, military prerogatives and institutional autonomy did not inhibit the continuity of democratic regimes in most Latin American countries.[7]

The problem to be analysed here is that the continuity of military prerogatives and high degrees of institutional autonomy impeded both the building of new links between civil society and the armed forces (links which otherwise could be more kindred to democratic values), and a more substantive participation of civilian authorities in defining crucial aspects of military policy, such as the role of the armed forces in a continuously changing local, regional, and global context. The fact that new democracies faced important restrictions (at both levels – the exercise of political power by civilian authorities and the participation of civil society) in the definition of major issues, such as the role and mission of the armed forces, constitutes a major problem that deserves particular attention. This is especially significant given the magnitude and the particular nature of the new threats and challenges to security (not necessarily national security, but the security of citizens and the continuity of the values and institutions of democratic societies) which emerged with the end of the Cold War and the increased acceleration of the globalization process. The current political map of Latin American democracies reveals stable situations of democratic consolidation, as well as unstable or weak democracies with shallow support from the public.[8] On this "map" we already find new versions of military political leadership, such as the Hugo

Chávez government in Venezuela and, more recently, Lucio Gutiérrez in Ecuador.

In the context of these mostly post-authoritarian democracies, civil-military relations also vary greatly. They rank from thorough subordination of the armed forces to civilian authority to situations of recurrent challenges to constitutional authority. Between these two extremes (which could be characterized by Argentina on the one hand, and Paraguay on the other), most countries dwell in a middle ground where the military does not constitute an alternative to democratic rule, maintaining a high degree of institutional autonomy. In turn, such institutional autonomy may or may not include participation in national affairs, influence in major political decisions, or involvement in partisan politics.

In the context of redemocratization and democratic consolidation processes, and with regard to the major or minor political roles that the armed forces may play in the post-authoritarian context, there are very different situations throughout Latin America. A first distinctive group is formed by Argentina, Brazil, and, to a lesser extent, Uruguay. Besides substantial differences in the nature and scope of institutional autonomy, in these countries the military does not play a major role as a political actor and, particularly, does not perceive itself nor is perceived by society as a potential alternative to civilian rule. In this framework – and with major differences in the degree of reluctance to accept either or both civil authority and lesser degrees of institutional autonomy – the military expects and accepts a civil (re)definition of its functions.

In the second group are Chile and Guatemala (as the more structured models, with several minor examples), where the military still plays a relevant political role in the framework of democracy. With varying degrees of explicitness, the military perceives itself as a political actor and is recognized as such by wide sectors of civil society.

Other countries, such as Colombia and Venezuela, cannot be easily categorized in either one of these groups. In Colombia, with an internal conflict and a fragmented national territory, the military has significant influence on the negotiations between the guerrilla organizations and the government, on relations with the paramilitary, and on foreign relations. In the latter case, the armed forces have maintained a direct link with the major regional and global power, the USA, which paves the way to varying degrees of US military presence, ranging from military assistance to direct intervention. This link has been materialized in the implementation of "Plan Colombia". In Venezuela, where on behalf of "democratic transition" a blatant militarization of public administration has taken place, the armed forces have achieved a predominant political role under the umbrella of "Bolivarianismo".[9] However, this peculiar political doctrine does not formally place the military in the role of a political actor.

In this regional context, characterized by military pressures and authoritarian regressions, Argentine civil-military relations are somehow an exception. Argentina has preserved a stable framework of institutionalization of the democratic system and, rather than being a threat or a restriction to democratic consolidation, civil-military relations have constituted a major pillar of this process. This situation is rooted in a series of drastic and profound changes in the values and perceptions of the military during the past two decades, after the defeat of the Malvinas/Falklands war in June 1982.

The social condemnation of the armed forces that followed during the first stage of the democratic transition, as information on massive violations of human rights was disclosed, produced significant tensions with both political actors and civil society. In the long run, however, the revision of the past contributed to strengthening the belief of senior and junior active-duty officers in their constructive and constitutional role in a democratic society.[10] Interviews with active-duty officers, official documents of the three service branches, and public statements of upper-rank officers suggest that the notion of the military role that currently predominates within the Argentine armed forces is characterized by the following traits.[11]

- The armed forces are an instrument that can be used at will by the government (the latter is understood as civilian authorities in the context of a democratic government, where both the executive and congress play specific and complementary roles).
- Their principal function is to deter eventual threats to the vital interests of the nation.
- Participation in peacekeeping missions and multinational forces constitutes a secondary role, but is highly valued for its implications in terms of professional training, additional income, interoperability, and interactions – especially with NATO members – and, as a result, the improvement of the local and international image of the armed forces.
- The concept of threat has been widened, now encompassing transnational phenomena and the notion of the increasing unpredictability of threats.

For different reasons, Chile is another case deserving particular attention. After 12 years of a military regime, which carried out important economic reforms and achieved significant results in that field, the armed forces left power with significant support from wide sectors of society (initially representing around 40 per cent of the public, according to official and private data gathered both during the last years of the Pinochet government and the first few years of the transition). This support from – predominantly, but not exclusively, conservative – sectors of society allowed Chile to develop a very different model and a different strategy for democratic transition *vis-à-vis* Argentina. Chile conducted an administered transition from authoritarianism, but at a huge cost for democracy in terms of military autonomy and military capacities to influence and condition national politics. That was not only a result of the success of the military regime, but also the reflection of a political style shared by the Chilean political élite. On that basis, Chile chose to privilege stability and smoothness in the unfolding of the transition. Thus, in the Chilean case the system of civil-military relations includes a large number of political and institutional prerogatives that limit the authority of the constitutional government – for example, in matters of appointments and budgetary decisions. The definition of the military's role, however, emphasizes the professional functions of the armed forces.

Reluctance to advance in regional security initiatives or to involve significant numbers of officers and non-commissioned officers in international missions has been a trait of Chile's defence and security strategies under democratic rule. Nevertheless, in 1991 Chile joined Argentina and Brazil to sign the Mendoza Agreement on Chemical Weapons. In 1992 Chile decided to join the annual meetings of the joint chiefs of staff of Argentina, Brazil, Paraguay, and Uruguay, which had taken place since 1987. Through the 1990s Chile also adopted an increasing number of confidence-building measures with regional partners, and gradually started to participate in UN peacekeeping missions. Finally, by the end of the decade, Chile signed a historical agreement that ended all pending territorial disputes with Argentina.

On the other hand, Chile has frequently expressed unfriendly attitudes towards some of its neighbours, in spite of the regional initiatives to promote cooperative security, in which Chile has been an increasingly active participant. In addition, Chile has shown no will to moderate military acquisitions. This policy deepened the military imbalance that has been growing for years in the subregion. Further, this policy has taken place not only in a framework of regional initiatives for cooperative security and an increasing military imbalance, but also in a context of social problems that affect all countries in the subregion. Those policies and attitudes are closely related to the system of civil-military relations conditioning Chilean democracy.

Brazil is also a different case, which combines high military autonomy (similarly to Chile) with a friendlier, less tense relationship with civilian authority. In democratic Brazil, the armed forces not only are not a threat to democratic stability or a hostile actor *vis-à-vis* the democratic system, but they perform different roles, both formal and informal, as a "natural" member of the political system.[12] The ministers of the army, the navy, and the air force have important decision-making capacities in their specific areas, and frequently make public statements on topics of national politics at large. A network of informal relations ties the military to the congress, the state governors, and most areas of the executive. No decisive issue of national politics can be successfully handled without the consent or support of the military. Thus, it seems understandable that during the process of democratic consolidation, Brazil did not reduce the military prerogatives inherited from authoritarianism. Furthermore, the continuity of military prerogatives and the institutional presence of the armed forces in the political system are welcomed not only by the military but by large segments of the political and business establishment and of civil society as well.

Only in recent years has President Cardoso succeeded in reducing some of the wide range of capacities and decision-making autonomy of the armed forces. Initially, the military occupied six ministries, maintained control on important sources of information, controlled the SNI (National Information System), and had preferential access to the president on a daily basis. The armed forces participated in most important issues of national politics, as these were considered matters of national security, and had complete decision-making autonomy on military matters. For more than a decade the armed forces also succeeded in opposing the creation of a defence ministry, and after President Cardoso finally did establish such an office the military successfully opposed for some time the appointment of a civilian for the position of defence minister.

As in the case of Peru, Brazil currently has a civilian appointee as defence minister. The number of ministries in military hands was reduced to four. The powerful SNI was restructured, and the traditional influence of military officers near to the president was also reduced. At the same time, the armed forces suffered a profound deterioration of income, one of the most important factors in military dissatisfaction today.

(Re)defining threats to security and the military's role

In light of authoritarian regressions in several countries of the region, the above analysis of heterogeneous civil-military relations seemed relevant. Some emphasis has been placed on the cases of Argentina, Chile, and Brazil, given the weight of these countries in the regional context and the fact that, with very different systems of civil-military relations, they all seem to enjoy a high degree of democratic stability.[13] They are good examples of civil-military relations with varying degrees and modalities of institutional autonomy and military prerogatives that do not challenge the continuity of democracy – although, in different ways, they do condition the quality and scope of democratic institutions.

Further, during the past 10 years these countries have played an important role in the process through which the region moved – however fluidly – towards the construction of some forms of collective support to democratic stability. After the so-called Santiago Commitment of 1991, democratic stability became a substantive part of the notion of security that developed in the region – confidence building and cooperative security being the complement of developing a regional consensus.[14] In fact, the emphasis on democratic stability as a substantive aspect of security reflects the priorities of a region that has suffered more from authoritarian assaults and human rights violations than from conventional wars among rival states.[15]

On the other hand, the emphasis on the differing modalities of civil-military relations that characterize the subregion does not mean to ignore other, more important, dimensions and drawbacks of democratic consolidation: for example, the quality of institutions, and the congress and the judiciary in particular. However, that emphasis responds to the relevance of civil-military relations, and the viability of new approaches to security and new definitions of the military's role.[16] From the perspective of promoting that goal among Latin American countries, it is clear that old-fashioned, quasi-democratic civil-military relations constitute a severe restriction.

For example, during the 1990s Argentina and Canada made significant efforts – with some, albeit limited, success – to persuade other countries in the region to engage in a more active commitment to global security. However, despite the significant changes that happened in both the regional and the global security environments, autonomous military establishments were effective at resisting the revision of defence policies and national security strategies in response to changes in the international environment and the standards and values of a democratic society. To some extent, they succeeded in supporting the continuity of defence policies that suffer from lack of transparency, emerge from a process that is far from being responsive to citizens' values and priorities, and promote outdated hypotheses of conflict with neighbouring countries. They have also presented unconvincing North–South conflict scenarios (which serve as hypotheses of conflict that justify substantive military budgets), and questioned, on the same grounds, the commitment of troops to global security engagements. From their perspective, those commitments would weaken national defence capacities and/or serve the interests of the USA and its stronghold on world politics.

Although such resistance and the continuity of military autonomy do not necessarily signify a threat to other countries, they do constitute an obstacle to initiatives for the coordination of political and military efforts to meet regional challenges and objectives in terms of democratic stability, human rights guarantees, regional contributions to global security, and collective action against drug cartels and organized crime. In synthesis, post-transition civil-military relations in the region combine new and old elements. At the same time, in spite of obstacles to, and even some reversals of, democratic consolidation, Latin American countries face unprecedented opportunities to update and redefine the role of the military and the security agenda of the region – which, with all these limitations, is yet an ongoing process.

One of the key elements conditioning that process is the attitude which the USA will adopt in potential scenarios, conditioned by the US concern with global terrorism after 9/11. For example, it does not seem obvious what attitude the USA will adopt in a potential scenario in which a democratic government does not support US initiatives against terrorism, and the armed forces, with or without the support of civilian sectors, destabilize democracy and immediately offer unconditional support to US antiterrorism initiatives. Or, in a different scenario, the armed forces simply destabilize a democratic government – independent from any US initiative against terrorism – while the US government is concentrating on the global war against terrorism, thus turning democracy in Latin America into a very low foreign policy priority.

However unlikely, those scenarios seem conceivable today, while they were not conceivable before the terrorist attacks of 9/11. During the 1990s the US government frequently expressed its commitment to democracy in the region and its determination not to impose any policy on Latin American countries. Among examples of a new US attitude towards Latin America are the afore-mentioned Santiago Commitment; the frequent emphasis of US diplomats on consensus and multilateralism as basic guidelines for American foreign policy in the region – e.g. during preparations for the Miami Summit of December 1994, when successive officers of the State Department emphasized that the US government was determined to base its policies towards the region on a solid consensus with Latin American countries; the initiative to create a permanent forum of defence ministers at the hemispheric level, an initiative which was preceded by many statements emphasizing consensus; support to civilian leadership on defence and military affairs; and, again, the US government's decision, in the new post-Cold War context, not to act unilaterally. After the 9/11 terrorist attacks and the resulting security policies and priorities of the USA, that attitude is likely to change.

At the same time, as already mentioned, the region lacks a consensus on its key security challenges and objectives at the regional and subregional levels. Thus, it is difficult to develop convincing security proposals that may increase the capacities for coordination and, particularly, for a fruitful dialogue with the USA on the challenges and opportunities in security matters. The task is not easy, given the heterogeneity of Latin America in regard to civil-military relations and views on regional and global security, the USA, state sovereignty, and related issues, along with the asymmetries in the consolidation (or even survival) of democracy.

In order to illustrate this wide range of views, it seems useful to summarize the differences in subregional approaches to the Brahimi Report, which resembled a comprehensive review of peacekeeping operations in all their aspects.[17] Those differences were reflected in the discussions during a regional seminar on the report.[18] By and large, there were significant differences between the Central American approaches (where there was a process of peacebuilding after the regional crisis in the 1980s of confrontation between authoritarian regimes supported by the USA and left-wing guerrilla forces), those of the Andean subregion (where the emergence of new conflict is looming), and those of the Southern Cone (characterized by the recent experience of cooperative security arrangements).

However, there was a certain consensus emerging from the Buenos Aires Brahimi Report meeting. This consensus mainly regarded the acknowledgement of a Latin American tradition of a state-based view of international policy with strong emphasis on sovereignty; a reluctance to accept multilateral or external intervention and a mistrust regarding the OAS's role, particularly in view of perceived US hegemony in this organization; and a preoccupation regarding funding for UN operations, which distracts funds from international cooperation on other priority issues of the region, such as development and poverty eradication. A strong case was made for increasing participation of NGOs and civil society organizations in developing measures to prevent conflict and engage in peacebuilding. The role of civil society in initiatives taken by the United Nations in the region, particularly with regard to the planning and implementation of peace operations, was stressed by most of the participants, including government representatives.

Southern Cone countries, the major contributors to peacekeeping operations (PKOs) from Latin America, expressed the need to have more influence on the decision-making process of PKOs. Related to that concern, there was consensus on the need for an intra-UN "democratization process", as participants felt that, while they are marginalized from UN decision-making, they carry a disproportionate share of the military burden of operations. Furthermore, participants from other countries of the region stressed the lack of effective coordination among the international agencies involved in peacebuilding activities, often leading to waste and fragmentation of human and financial resources. They also pointed to the fact that mechanisms for post-mission follow-up and continuing monitoring are unclear and fail to specify properly who is responsible for ensuring that accords not yet implemented by the mission's withdrawal are completed, and how they should proceed in this regard. They also highlighted the downsides of insufficient coordination with local actors, particularly with civil society organizations and networks.

Notwithstanding differing views and priorities on security matters, Latin American countries would benefit from making progress towards a common view on the basic questions that constitute the new security agenda of the region – particularly when there are no extraregional threats or intraregional interstate conflicts. Beyond the above-mentioned differences in civil-military relations and defence and security approaches, Latin American countries cannot continue to ignore the fact that drug cartels and organized crime, together with guerrilla warfare and terrorism, constitute the most significant threats to national and regional security, and should be placed at the highest priority level on the security agenda of subregional and hemispheric relations.

As a number of studies promoted by the United Nations in the mid-1990s have specified, emerging security threats do not threaten the state as much as they threaten societies, the individual, national identities, democratic values, public institutions, national economies, their financial institutions, and international norms and codes of conduct.[19] This calls for innovative approaches to discussing the security objectives of our societies and, therefore, the proper role that the armed forces must play in this context. However, on the other hand, we also face the challenge of building a minimum consensus among Latin American countries on what to propose to, and what to expect from, the USA in regard to these new threats. Otherwise, the USA will continue to act in isolation – thus ineffectively – and the combination of poverty, weak institutions, drug cartels, terrorism, and organized crime's increasing presence in politics, economics, and society will continue to grow and change the profile of Latin American countries, politics, and daily life, as happened throughout the past decade.

Civil society, new security challenges, and civil-military relations

Within the general framework developed in the preceding sections, there are three major issues that deserve particular attention from a civil society perspective. First, after the initial emphasis on human rights, the issues related to security and defence policies, civilian control, and the military role tend to turn into "non-issues" in the perception of civil society. Instead, social, legal, and environmental issues tend to be predominant, along with the trend to transfer responsibilities from the state to civil society, particularly with regard to social policies. However, this usually takes place without corresponding strengthening of civil society, in the framework of adjustment programmes and the "Washington consensus" and its wide predominance in the 1990s.[20]

Secondly, when (and if) there is a concern in civil society in relation to the military, it focuses on democratic stability and the prevention of a possible reappearance of the military as a political actor. However, in general, civil society tends to promote normative interpretations rather than analytical ones when it comes to issues related to the military.[21] This is probably a legacy of a very long period in which human rights issues were the predominant issue on the civil-military agenda.

Finally, once the more active stage of human-rights-related mobilization of citizens concludes, there is a tendency in civil society to assume passively the state's decisions regarding the role of the military and security agencies, and related policies and legislation. There is no movement towards the development of specific civil society mechanisms or controls to monitor executive or legislative agendas regarding military and defence issues, with only weak and very tenuous links between civil society organizations and political actors, such as political parties.

Within this context, it is important to take into account the traditional weakness of civil society organizations and their regional and international networks in Latin America *vis-à-vis* the seemingly omnipotent state. Civil society organizations in Latin America are constrained by scarce financial resources, deep and diverse problems in their management and leadership, and serious limitations in terms of their institutionalization, representation, and sustainability.[22] The priorities of civil society organizations in relation to security tend to focus on domestic and public security issues rather than on defence and military matters. The latter are perceived as largely external to the interests and concerns of civil society. On the other hand, the increase of criminality and violence throughout Latin America tends to make public security (and to some extent human rights issues) a major priority. This is particularly relevant in the case of the Central American countries, where, following the regional crises and civil conflicts of the 1980s, there was increasing civil society concern about domestic security, violence, and crime fighting, and less interest in following the development of defence issues,[23] despite increasing militarization of the police in most countries. However, similar trends are developing also in the Andean and Southern Cone countries, where citizens are increasingly concerned with crime and domestic security issues, rather than with defence matters or the definition of external security threats.

The fight against drugs takes an intermediate place, depending on how relevant it may be for civil society in each case. However, the tendency during the past few years has been that drugs, and organized crime in general, are perceived by the public as a major factor in the continuous increase of crime rates. In this context, most efforts by civil society organizations are focused on domestic issues, which are increasingly dealt with by the democratic system through links and networks established with traditional actors such as government agencies, parliaments, and political parties. However, the post-9/11 situation, characterized in essence by a transnational threat that can easily affect domestic situations, raises concerns among Latin American civil societies about threats to human rights and civil liberties.

Conclusion

The new emphasis on the war against global terrorism as a result of 11 September, and the policies and political discourse promoted by the USA after the terrorist attacks, have produced mixed reactions from different social actors in Latin America. After the initial reaction of horror and shock, civil society actors became concerned with the evolving policies of an internationally and regionally dominant USA. With regard to the regional consequences, the major concern is that US policies and, in general, the actions taken to fight terrorism may bring about new versions of the national security doctrine, with negative consequences for human rights and civil liberties (right of expression and association, among others) and the resurgence of repressive acts that could eventually undermine the basis of democracy in the region.

Within the armed forces, it is possible to identify two different reactions. On the one hand, there is resistance to assuming, as in the case of the war against drugs, an active role and to militarizing the fight against terrorism imposed by an external agenda. On the other hand, there is a revitalization of conceptions and procedures that may, retrospectively, legitimize the acts committed during the repression of "domestic terrorism" as long as they are associated with national security. Depending on the strength of the institutionalization of democracy in each case, there is only reluctant public debate on the new security demands and limitations in terms of transparency and accountability. In this framework, it is particularly important that civil society works jointly with the political leadership and the military to deepen necessary internal and external security measures to deal with new security threats, and to assess and monitor their implementation in order to avoid a negative impact on recently acquired democratic rights.

The USA's commitment to democracy and civilian control of the armed forces in the region has been an important asset for democratic stability in Latin America, or, at least, for the continuity of democratic institutions throughout the 1990s. However, the strengthening of democratic institutions, the development of effective capacities for civilian leadership in defence and military matters, and the redefinition of the role of the armed forces according to the new realities, security challenges, and emerging threats did not advance satisfactorily during the years following the end of the Cold War. This has been the case notwithstanding the fact that, throughout the 1990s, the predominant trends at the hemisphere and subregional levels seemed to favour the strengthening of democracy and the emergence or consolidation of civilian leadership and capacities in defence and military matters.

The events after 9/11 bring some uncertainty regarding initially positive trends. This follows the initial positive expressions of solidarity and support by the community of Latin American states. The preliminary announcements of the US government to fight global terrorism with the support and wide participation of the international community was followed by an increasing tendency of the US government to use military force and ignore the opinion of many actors of the international system, including some of its closest allies. That uncertainty relates to the still-feeble situation of civil-military relations *vis-à-vis* the traditional Western standards of civilian control, the pending definition of the role of the military throughout the region, and the negative impact on democratic stability of the involvement of the armed forces in national security matters, particularly in a political and institutional context of weak civilian leadership in security matters.

On the other hand, the uncertainty relates to the place that democracy and civilian control – by and large, the quality of democratic institutions – and inter-American relations in general will occupy on the American foreign policy agenda. In this regard, the inclusion of defence and security issues, both domestic and international, on the agenda of civil society organizations and networks is one of the first steps to address this problem. Secondly, there is the need to develop mechanisms of consultation and monitoring of the policies related to those issues, both among civil society organizations and state and intergovernmental agencies, and between civil society and the military. The lack of established mechanisms for civil society participation and interaction among the different sectors is one of the most relevant characteristics of the weaknesses of the institutional consolidation of democracies in Latin America. One of the most striking examples is the lack of interaction and policy coordination between civil society and citizen organizations and political parties in most Latin American countries.

Thirdly, there is the need to increase the impact of different awareness programmes among those different actors. A wider mutual knowledge, exposure, and interaction between state agencies, political actors, citizen organizations, and the military are a fundamental condition for the consolidation and development of democratic institutions. It is also important for the development of new modalities of interaction and relations between civil society, government agencies, and the military, particularly with regard to the new security challenges that will be imposed on Latin America after 9/11.

Notes

1. Augusto Varas developed this concept in several articles. A pioneer FLACSO working document of the 1980s, on military autonomy and democratic transition, began a series of analyses which made a substantive contribution to the study of civil-military relations in the region. Alfred Stepan offered another important contribution with the concept of "military prerogatives". See Stepan, Alfred. 1988. *Rethinking Military Politics*. Princeton, NJ: Princeton University Press.
2. *Ibid.*
3. The relative importance of civil-military relations, *vis-à-vis* other factors, in relation to democratic consolidation is analysed on a comparative basis in Fontana, Andrés. 1993. "Relaciones cívico-militares y agenda de seguridad en América Latina", in Adalberto Rodríguez Giavarini (ed.) *La Situación Internacional: Opciones para la Argentina*. Buenos Aires: Grupo Editor Latinoamericano.
4. Fontana, Andrés. 2001. "Re-founding hemispheric security: The community of American states in the 1990s and beyond", *Peace and Security*, Vol. 1, No. 23, pp. 41–60.
5. The literature regarding the role of the armed forces in the post-Cold War context is vast. Interesting contributions for the Latin American regional context have been made by Dominguez, Jorge I. (ed.). 1998. *International Security and Democracy: Latin America and the Caribbean in the Post-Cold War Era*. Pittsburgh: University of Pittsburgh Press; Fitch, John Samuel. 1998. *The Armed Forces and Democracy in Latin America*. Baltimore and London: Johns Hopkins University Press; Marcella, Gabriel. 1994. *Warriors in Peacetime: The Military and Democracy in Latin America*. London: Frank Cass; Millett, Richard and Michael Gold-Biss (eds). 1996. *Beyond Praetorianism: The Latin American Military in Transition*. Miami: North-South Center Press; Desch, Michael, Jorge Dominguez, and Andrés Serbin (eds). 1998. *From Pirates to Drug Lords: The Post-Cold War Caribbean Security Environment*. New York: State University of New York Press.
6. Samuel Huntington argues that restructuring civil-military relations is one of the most crucial pending tasks of new democracies. See Huntington, Samuel P. 1995. "Reforming civil-military relations", *Journal of Democracy*, Vol. 6, No. 4, pp. 9–17.
7. Converging views on this evaluation of post-authoritarian civil-military relations in Latin America can be found in Dix, Robert. 1994. "Military coups and military rule in Latin America", *Armed Forces and Society*, Vol. 20, No. 3, pp. 443–445; Escudé, Carlos and Andrés Fontana. 1998. "Argentina's security policies: Their rationale and regional context", in Dominguez, note 5 above, pp. 51–79; Fitch, note 5 above; Hunter, Wendy. 1997. *Eroding Military Influence in Brazil: Politicians against Soldiers*. Chapel Hill: University of North Carolina Press; Huntington, note 6 above. In his work *Rethinking*

Military Politics, published some years before the afore-mentioned analyses, Alfred Stepan argued that military autonomy and prerogatives, together with "civilian abdication of responsibility", might jeopardize democratic transitions. His assessment was not altogether wrong. Yet democracies, however weak and unstable, continued to survive in Latin America in spite of military autonomy, military prerogatives, and civilian abdication of responsibility. See Stepan, note 1 above.

8. See Garreton, Manuel Antonio and Edward Newman (eds). 2002. *Democracy in Latin America: (Re)Contructing Political Society*. Tokyo: United Nations University Press.

9. Inspired in the figure and role of Simón Bolívar, the military national hero who during the nineteenth century lead the war against Spanish domination in the so-called Gran Colombia (including particularly the current Andean states of Venezuela, Colombia, Peru, and Ecuador), Bolivarianismo is the official doctrine of the Chávez government. It promotes Latin American integration *vis-à-vis* US hegemony and any other external threats to the region.

10. Fontana, Andrés. 1988. "De la crisis de Malvinas a la subordinación condicionada: Conflictos intramilitares y transición política en Argentina", in Augusto Varas (ed.) *La Autonomía Militar en América Latina*. Caracas: Editorial Nueva Sociedad, pp. 33–56.

11. Field research for the project on "Military Role in Argentina: Converging and Diverging Perceptions" was conducted in 1991–1992, with support from the IDRC (International Development Research Centre) from Canada and the Fundación Simón Rodríguez from Argentina. See Fontana, Andrés and Jorge Battaglino. 1993. *Percepciones Militares del Rol de las Fuerzas Armadas en Argentina*, Serie Cuadernos Simón Rodríguez. Buenos Aires: Biblos.

12. Stepan, note 1 above; Zaverucha, Jorge. 1993. "The degree of military political autonomy during the Spanish, Argentine and Brazilian transitions", *Journal of Latin American Studies*, Vol. 25, No. 2, pp. 283–299.

13. For a comparative assessment of these three cases, see Hunter, Wendy. 1994. "Contradictions of civilian control: Argentina, Brazil and Chile in the 1990s", *Third World Quarterly*, No. 15, pp. 633–653.

14. The expression "Santiago Commitment" refers to OAS-GA Resolution 1080, signed during the OAS's General Assembly meeting that took place in Santiago de Chile in June 1991. The Santiago Commitment emphasized collective support to democratic stability in the region, together with the dismantling of violent conflict and the promotion of confidence-building measures, particularly among neighbouring states. "Resolution 1080" and "Santiago Commitment" have become alternate expressions.

15. The fact that the Santiago de Chile OAS meeting of June 1991 was the first time that every OAS member state had a democratic political system deserves to be underlined. On democracy and regional disputes and wars, see Dominguez, Jorge. 2001. "Territorial and boundary disputes in Latin America and the Caribbean", *Pensamiento Propio*, No. 14, July–December, pp. 5–29; Mares, David. 2001. "Boundary disputes in the Western hemisphere: Analyzing their relationship to democratic stability, economic integration and social welfare", *Pensamiento Propio*, No. 14, July–December, pp. 31–59.

16. See Huntington, note 6 above; Norden, Deborah L. 1996. "Redefining political-military relations in Latin America: Issues of the new democratic era", *Armed Forces and Society*, Vol. 22, No. 3, pp. 419–440.

17. See Serie Mundial de Encuentros sobre el Informe del Panel Sobre Operaciones de Mantenimiento de la Paz, *Informe Brahimi*, Seminario Regional América Latina, América Central y el Caribe, Andrés Fontana and Andrés Serbin, Coordinators, Buenos Aires, Universidad de Belgrano, 22–23 February 2001. The event was supported by the UK Department for International Development, and was organized in cooperation with

the Center on International Cooperation at New York University and the International Peace Academy.

18. See Fontana, Andrés. 2001. "Report on the Latin American regional meeting to assess the report of the Panel on UN Peace Operations (Brahimi Report)", paper presented to the international meeting Refashioning the Dialogue: Regional Perspectives on the Brahimi Report, organized by the Center on International Cooperation at New York University and the International Peace Academy, hosted by the permanent missions of Argentina, Singapore, and South Africa, and sponsored by the UK Department for International Development, New York, 12 March.

19. See *Informe de la Conferencia Ministerial Mundial sobre la Delincuencia Transnacional Organizada*, Naples (Italy), 21–23 November 1994, by Resolution 48/103 of the General Assembly, 20 December 1993; *Documento de Base: Problemas y peligros que plantea la delincuencia transnacional organizada en las distintas regiones del mundo*; General Assembly Resolution "Medidas para eliminar el terrorismo internacional" (based on the *Informe de la Sexta Comisión* (A./49/743)), 17 February 1995.

20. Jerome Booth explains that "The Washington Consensus, developed from a set of ten policy reform areas where there appeared to be some consensus in Latin America, were articulated in a conference held in Washington in 1989 and then emerged as a book." The latter refers to Williamson, J. (ed.). 1990. *Latin American Adjustment: How Much Has Happened?* Washington, DC: Institute for International Economics. Booth adds that the consensus on policy reform areas "became a set of prescriptions, [and] then became dogma. The dogma was extremely effective. It focused policy-makers across much of the globe and gave an ideological impetus to the spread of market economy." See Booth, Jerome. 2002. "Argentina: The case for a permanent end to fiscal transfers", *Cambridge Review of International Affairs*, Vol. 15, No. 3, pp. 483–497.

21. Diamint, Rut. 1999. "Estado y sociedad civil ante la cuestión cívico-militar en los 90", in Rut Diamint (ed.) *Control civil y fuerzas armadas en las nuevas democracias latinoamericanas*. Buenos Aires: Universidad Torcuato Di Tella/GEL, pp. 35–68.

22. Serbin, Andrés. 2001. "Globalifóbicos vs. globalitarios. Fortalezas y debilidades de una sociedad civil emergente", *Nueva Sociedad* (Caracas), No. 176, November–December, pp. 67–86; Association of Caribbean States. 2002. "Current and future challenges for civil society in Latin America and the Greater Caribbean: Towards a critical self-assessment", in *The Greater Caribbean, Sea of Opportunity*. Port of Spain: Association of Caribbean States.

23. Serbin, Andrés, Leticia Salomón, and Carlos Sojo. 2000. *Gobernabilidad democrática y seguridad ciudadana en Centroamérica*. Managua: CRIES.

11

The military in post-conflict societies: Lessons from Central America and prospects for Colombia

Thomas C. Bruneau

The purpose of this chapter is to analyse the relationship between post-conflict situations and democratic consolidation from the prism of civil-military relations. Civil-military relations are basically about power. They centre on the answer to the question: who is in control in a state, the military or civilians? In a democracy the answer must be that it is the democratically elected civilians who are in control, not only of the military but of all other sectors of the state apparatus. The chapter begins with a discussion of how to describe civil-military relations. It then reviews the contemporary post-conflict situations of democratic civil-military relations in El Salvador and Guatemala, and possible explanatory variables. Based upon the clarification of the framework from those two post-conflict situations, the current highly conflictive situation in Colombia is described and analysed.

Security sector reform or civil-military relations?

A main focus in this book is security sector reform (SSR), commonly defined as "the provision of security within the state in an effective and efficient manner, and in the framework of democratic civilian control".[1] Edmunds distinguishes between first- and second-generation SSR, and illustrates his discussion with examples from East and Central Europe. It seems to the present author that the distinction is arbitrary and not particularly useful, since the difference he identifies is really between the formality of laws and other documents and actual implementation. If this is the case, surely the degree of implementation must be viewed as a continuum since democratic civil-military relations, like democratic consolidation, of which they are but one crucial element, are a continuum and cannot be separated into two arbitrarily defined phases. Not much seems to be gained by the concept of SSR over civil-military relations, provided that a broad definition of the latter is employed, as is the case in this chapter. At the most basic level, civil-military relations are about power, and deal with who is in fact in control in any state at any particular time. They concern the classic question of who guards the guardians? Currently, in the third-wave and post-Cold War era, attention must also be paid to the effectiveness and efficiency of the armed forces.[2]

Finally, after more than a decade and a half of democratic transitions, and now in the consolidation phase of democratization, there is concern everywhere as to the roles and missions of the armed forces. This concern has increased tremendously after 11 September 2001 and a general concern with effective anti-terrorist operations. Specifically, the previous concern with democratic civilian control of the armed forces, largely in the author's view with the emphasis on control, has been supplemented by concern about how effective the armed forces are in fulfilling different roles and missions (from classic territorial defence to counterterrorism, counter-drugs, military support to civilian authorities, and peace support operations) and how efficient they are in the sense of achieving these roles and missions at the lowest possible cost. The broadened concept of civil-military relations is appropriate for contemporary situations, as 63 per cent of the world's countries are generally considered democracies.[3] The argument here is that a focus on civil-military relations is a necessary first step in the analysis of democratic consolidation, to be followed by a focus on other public security forces, the legal system, and all the other elements included within the concept of SSR.

Dimensions of civil-military relations

To describe civil-military relations in a democracy requires a set of variables or dimensions for comparisons. Based upon research and experience in approximately 20 new and not-so-new democracies, the author has distilled five that seem to capture most appropriately the three crucial elements of democratic civilian control, military effectiveness, and efficiency. These five variables are drawn from an inventory of some two dozen that are routinely utilized in the seminar programmes on civil-military relations offered by the Center for Civil-Military Relations (CCMR) at the Naval Postgraduate School in California, USA.

The first is the relationship between a civilian-led ministry of defence (MOD) and the command of the armed forces in a joint or general staff. If it has assumed its potential roles, an MOD is the location or platform where the democratic legitimacy of civilians meets the professional expertise of the leadership of the armed forces. It is impossible to have democratic consolidation without the former, and equally impossible to have military effectiveness without the latter. Most countries now have MODs, but they have been created for a number of reasons (including pressure by other states or organizations such as NATO), and they vary greatly in their powers and functions. It must be emphasized that for an MOD to have a significant role it requires several competencies, such as control over budgets, personnel, roles, and missions, as well as the human and financial resources actually to fulfil these competencies.[4]

The second dimension is the different roles of civilians and the military in the officer promotion and retirement process. In many countries promotion and retirement are exclusive domains of the military, except for the ultimate or final decision of a president or prime minister. This type of control, should it in fact exist, does not allow for ongoing and more detailed control by civil agencies of the composition of the armed forces. Only if civilians have the mechanisms – through promotion boards or retirement programmes – and the expertise can they in fact control the composition of the officer corps to a degree that has any significance. In the USA this process involves military and civilian decision-makers at all stages, largely ensuring civilian control and military effectiveness. In Spain during the late 1980s, for instance, civilian agencies, ultimately based in the MOD, managed to exert lasting and detailed control over the armed forces by assuming a central role in promotions to the rank of colonel and above.[5] Most new democracies have at best only rudimentary systems of civilian control of officer promotion and retirement.

The third dimension concerns the roles of the legislature, especially in a presidential system, in the formulation of security policy, control over budgets, and oversight over implementation of policies. In a presidential system the legislature can, mainly but not exclusively, play two critical roles in these three functions. It can provide a counterpoise to the executive, so that the latter, with the armed forces as its instrument, cannot establish a monopoly over power. This is what guarantees a working separation of powers. It can also broaden support for the state, including the armed forces, by providing an alternative mechanism of accountability through various territorial divisions and electoral arrangements. This becomes particularly relevant once parts of the society question why armed forces are still required in the contemporary era of democratic consolidation and despite the end of the Cold War. Obviously, a legislature will be unable to accomplish much if it is not given legally based powers, as well as structures and processes (including personnel with expertise), to participate in the formulation of policy, exercise oversight, and develop and monitor budgets.[6]

The fourth dimension concerns who defines the roles and missions of the armed forces, including the police. It is banal to state, but frequently forgotten, that somebody has to determine what to do with the state's security apparatus. After the end of the Cold War, and during the subsequent processes of democratic transition, in many countries it seemed as if the armed forces were simply left to their own devices. In Central America this was the situation in Guatemala and Nicaragua, and in South America it is the case in Paraguay. Civilians did not seem interested or qualified enough to take the initiative, and the armed forces went about their business more or less independent of the national leadership, outside the context of national and international realities. Increasingly, however, with more distance from the Cold War, the greater appeal of peacekeeping and peace support operations to civilian leaders in the context of 11 September 2001 in the USA and 11 March 2004 in Madrid, and the pressure from the USA, its allies, and international organizations such as NATO, civilian leaders are rediscovering the importance of the armed forces. The issue is, however, whether civilians are able to determine the roles and missions of the armed forces, with all that is implied in size, composition, equipment, and training, or whether the military high command retains the decision-making power and initiative.

The fifth and last dimension involves control over the intelligence system(s). In most non-democratic regimes intelligence was mainly synonymous with counterintelligence or state security. Rather than oriented towards collecting and analysing information on possible threats from abroad, the orientation was focused overwhelmingly on internal issues, to control and intimidate the population. It is extremely difficult for democratically elected civilians to become familiar with, and then control, the intelligence system. Control over the intelligence system, and the information it may have available, is highly valuable to civilian government agencies and the armed forces. After all, knowledge is power, and in many countries intelligence organizations exert close to a monopoly over this knowledge.[7]

Illustrative evidence from Central America

For the purpose of this chapter, these dimensions or variables will be illustrated with evidence from El Salvador and Guatemala. Both these Central American countries were authoritarian regimes until the 1980s. Both have seen extensive internal conflicts: a civil war in El Salvador for the decade of the 1980s, and a state of serious insurgency in Guatemala for 36 years, until the peace accords of December 1996. And in both countries the armed forces played a central role in controlling the governments and fighting the conflicts. If defined along the five dimensions discussed above, then El Salvador has experienced more progress towards working civil-military relations than Guatemala. Despite some progress, however, the institutionalization of the structures and processes remains very rudimentary in Guatemala at the time of writing (early 2004).

In El Salvador the president and his staff have taken on increasingly important roles along the four dimensions of the role of the MOD, promotions and retirements, determining roles and missions, and control over the intelligence apparatus, and the legislature is playing an increasing role in legislation and budget control. The executive and legislative branches, as well as the media and civil society, are aware of the military's role and function in society. What is still lacking, however, is the institutional basis for steady, consistent, and effective control and implementation of the powers of the democratically elected executive and legislature in controlling the armed forces. In sum, there is awareness and overall movement in the right direction of qualified civilians assuming control, but the creation of an institutional basis is difficult and slow.[8]

In Guatemala, progress is much less advanced. While there is good understanding about civilian control by a group of civilians and officers, the president continued to exercise it rather arbitrarily, and the armed forces retain the initiative in most areas. For example, while the president is the commander and chief of the armed forces, real power is exercised by the chief of the general staff of the armed forces and the minister of defence, both of whom are military officers. While there have been sporadic efforts to insert knowledgeable civilians into the decision-making process in defence, and there is currently such an initiative taking place under the authority of the MOD, until now they have not been successful. The legislature plays a minimal role in legislating policy and the budget, with virtually no oversight capability. The only area of progress is in civilian control over intelligence, where there are some initiatives. In short, despite great promises in the 1996 peace agreement in the section on "Strengthening Civilian Power and the Role of the Armed Forces in a Democratic Society", there has been very little progress. Both civilians and military officers are aware of this, and discuss it openly and with great frustration.[9] With the election of President Oscar Berger in late 2003 and his taking office in January 2004, there is a public commitment to restructure the armed forces, severely cut their budgets, and assert full civilian control. The author is working with President Berger on these initiatives.

Towards explaining variations in civil-military relations

How can one explain such significant variation in the status of civil-military relations in El Salvador and Guatemala, despite the two countries' similar backgrounds and challenges? The literature on democratic consolidation and, specifically, on civil-military relations gives great emphasis to the nature of the prior regime and the transition process.[10] These explanations might in general be useful, but in these two specific cases they are of little assistance; they are also rather dated. After all, once democracy is established (even if still in the process of consolidation), the government that is in power by virtue of elections must begin to respond to political parties, interest groups, NGOs, think-tanks, and civil society more generally. Consequently, any set of "understandings" developed prior to, or during, the democratic transition tend to be amended or renegotiated. It does not take long, therefore, for the determining factors from the past to become superseded by new realities.[11]

One must therefore complement these basic and dated variables with others that are becoming increasingly relevant. These include the role of outsiders, including states and international organizations, the coherence (for lack of a better word) of the political system, and the political learning process. Unfortunately, except for the international variables, little work has so far been done on the issues of political coherence and political learning as applied to issues of democratic consolidation.[12]

The role of outside actors

Due to the successful Sandinista revolution in Nicaragua in 1979, the ongoing insurgency in Guatemala, and the escalating conflict in El Salvador, the region became extremely important in the Cold War calculus, with much foreign involvement. With the end of the Cold War, the collapse of the USSR (and, thus, an end to Soviet assistance to Cuba, and from Cuba to Central America), and America's preference to minimize involvement, there was great pressure to encourage negotiated settlements to the conflicts. This was clearly the case in El Salvador, where the USA exercised tremendous influence through direct involvement in the armed forces and providing substantial economic assistance through grants and loans, and to a lesser extent in Guatemala, where the USA's role was less prominent. Further, both the USA and other interested parties, in the region and in Europe, agreed that the United Nations had an important role to play in these negotiations. Consequently, the United Nations, embodied in the UN Observer Mission in El Salvador

(ONUSAL) and the UN Mission in Guatemala (MINUGUA), was prominently involved in both the peace processes and in the transitions to democracy. Further, in both cases civil-military relations were a key element in the negotiations. Since the armed forces were a key element of both the authoritarian regimes and the ongoing conflicts, their past and future role loomed large in the negotiations and subsequent agreements. However, there were differences in the extent to which this "foreign factor" had an impact, in that the USA was more thoroughly and consistently engaged in El Salvador than in Guatemala. While the role of the United Nations may be very similar in both cases, the USA has been much more heavily involved in diplomatic initiatives and military engagement and training in El Salvador as compared to Guatemala.[13]

Coherence in the political system

The new democratic regimes that emerged from these dictatorships as the result of extensive negotiations are very different. In El Salvador the political system has begun to become institutionalized, and to cohere as a two-party system in which the Alianza Republicana Nacionalista (ARENA) has held the presidency and a majority in the Congress, while the Frente Farabunmdo Marti para la Liberacion Nacional (FMLN) has won the mayorship of San Salvador and served as an active opposition in the Congress. More recently, the problem has been that the FMLN has tended to split into different factions, thereby not providing the coherence that it once did. In Guatemala there has been no coherence at all. In early 2003 there were 18 political parties gearing up for elections later in the year, and politics is still totally personalized. The post-conflict presidents, President Arzu and then President Portillo, held power largely unrestricted by the Congress. Moreover, the system is so fragmented that the political system could not provide sufficient coherence to put forth a unified position on the referendum to implement the elements agreed to in the peace process. The referendum on the constitutional reforms to implement the 1996 peace accord included a section on "Strengthening Civilian Power and the Role of the Armed Forces in a Democratic Society". With the failure of the referendum in May 1999 (55 per cent voted against the propositions presented to the electorate), the lack of coherence in the government had a direct and important impact on democratic consolidation and civil-military relations.[14] The lack of political coherence was symbolized by the constitutional referendum: while it should have included some 14 items that required amending the constitution, the Congress included 54 items, many of which had little to do with the constitution and more with personal and minor political issues. The entire package failed because of its incoherence, its conflicting messages, and the political system that allowed it to be put forward.

Political learning

Political learning is a useful but poorly defined concept.[15] Politicians such as Nelson Mandela have realized that negotiations are necessary for a transition from one regime to another. On the other hand, the absence of political learning is apparent in cases such as that of Hugo Chávez in Venezuela, who apparently comes to believe his own rhetoric as he takes his country to ruin. How does political learning come into play in the cases of El Salvador and Guatemala? In El Salvador, politicians, state officials, and civil society officials have learned from the past. They want to avoid a return to the conflict and authoritarianism of previous days, and thus seek compromise and agreement. They are also very much aware that El Salvador can thrive only if it adapts and finds its niche in a globalized world of rapid change in investment opportunities, movement of labour, and communications. Consequently, the Salvadorans take advantage of every niche angle in domestic and international negotiations and adapt to changing situations. For instance, since 1992 they have been drawing on CCMR programmes, and use them to educate, involve, and reinvolve civilians and officers to continue to strengthen democratic civil-military relations. In Guatemala, in contrast, very little seems to have been understood from the past. Despite three decades of authoritarian rule and 36 years of civil war, there is little that Guatemalans are doing to avoid a return to the past. There does not seem to be any valued or institutionalized process whereby political learning is included in decision-making processes.[16] In the first three months after taking office, President Oscar Berger appeared to be committed to learning from the past and implementing new policies in the most critical areas, including SSR.

In conclusion, there is evidence that democratic civil-military relations are far more advanced in El Salvador than in Guatemala. El Salvador is making progress in this area, as in other areas of politics and economy, and prospects are good for institutionalization of the structures and processes of fully democratic civil-military relations. Guatemala is not nearly that far along, and indeed civil-military relations were extremely problematic and tentative until early 2004. When seeking to explain these differences, one is forced to go beyond the frequently cited transition and consolidation processes. The answer to the very different situations is to be found in three main factors: the different approach and level of foreign involvement and pressure; the different degree of coherence of the political system; and the relative absence of political learning in Guatemala compared to El Salvador.

The paradoxical case of Colombia

Now that the tools for description and analysis have been illustrated in El Salvador and Guatemala, one can attempt to apply them to the case of Colombia. This situation is on the one hand simpler, as Colombia is already a democracy (and has been since at least 1958). The challenge, unlike Central America, is not to achieve peace and democracy simultaneously. However, the Colombian situation is more complex, as one would expect that a system which allows democratic representation of interests would be the ideal context for peace. While representation does indeed take place, Colombia is still plagued by widespread political violence, and has been so for the last three decades. While there is some question as to whether the insurgents – on the left the Fuerzas Armadas Revolucionarias de Colombia (FARC) and Ejercito de Liberacion Nacional (ELN), and on the right the Autodefensas Unidas de Colombia (AUC) – espouse any ideology at all, they all pursue a political agenda of seeking either to control or to influence political power. The fact that Colombia is both a democracy and characterized by pervasive political violence is somewhat of a paradox. A focus on civil-military relations will allow one to begin to comprehend what is involved in this complicated situation.[17]

Despite the occasional use of the term "civil war" in references to Colombia, this is not a civil war.[18] The most credible estimates calculate that approximately 25,000 armed insurgents (from the ELN, FARC, and the AUC) are fighting each other or the government. They hold this large nation of 44 million at risk. Public opinion polls never give the guerrillas, in this case the ELN and FARC (and excluding the AUC), more than 5 per cent of popular support.[19] The issue, then, is not the strength of the insurgents, but rather the weakness of the state, and specifically in that which concerns civil-military relations. Using the five dimensions described above, the status of civil-military relations in Colombia indicates that, while Colombia is indeed a consolidated democracy, as far as the military dimension is concerned democratic control only exists on paper. However, it is important to note that with the new administration of Alvaro Uribe, who took office on 7 August 2002, improvements have become visible, as will be discussed below.

The MOD and the military

The relations between the civilian-led MOD and the joint staff have been formal, with the civilians in fact not exerting control over the armed forces. Colombia has had a civilian minister of defence since 1991. How-ever, while the MOD could potentially exercise power, this was never the case.[20] The common phrase in Colombia is that there is a civilian minis-ter of defence but not a civilian ministry of defence. That is, the MOD has lacked relevant staff not only in terms of numbers but also in terms of their preparation for the tasks of monitoring, let alone controlling, the armed forces. The last minister of defence was also the vice-president, and clearly spent more time in the latter role than in the former. Maybe most indicative, however, is that when the minister is out of the country, the military commander of the armed forces assumes authority for the MOD and the military.[21] The MOD, both the organization and the min-ister himself, have been largely formalistic, without actually exercising any power.

The officer promotion process

The officer promotion and retirement process indicates a higher level of civilian involvement and control than in the Central American cases dis-cussed above. The president, presumably with the involvement of the MOD, has been very active in promotions and retirements at the top levels of the armed forces. In Colombia this has been visible through the removal of officers for alleged human rights abuses and professional fail-ures in combat operations. A less significant role is played by civilians when it comes to the promotion of lower levels. The president has power in this area, and is willing to exercise it.

The absence of the Congress

The roles of the legislature in policy definition, budget development, and oversight are minimal. Formally, the Congress has power over policy and budgetary concerns. However, the Congress does not take initiative in policy formulation without – or even in collaboration with – the executive. The Congress as a whole, as well as individual representatives, shows no interest in these responsibilities. It receives the defence budget on a Fri-day and acts on it on the following Monday. Therefore, the potentially positive links between society and the armed forces through the role of the Congress (practising a separation of powers) simply do not exist in Colombia. In this regard Colombian democracy is weaker than would appear at first glance.[22] By default, all national issues, including national security and defence, become virtually exclusive areas of executive power.

The absence of civilians in defining roles and missions

It is in fact difficult to ascertain who decides and defines the roles of the military and the police. Again, this is formally the task of civilian agencies. However, until the election of President Uribe in mid-2002, the presidents basically decided not to decide. In private and in public, both officers and civilians point to an informal understanding in the transition from General Rojas Pinilla's military regime (1953–1958) to the National Front of 1958–1974, which created clear divisions between the world of civilians and the world of the military. The civilians would take care of government, including economic and social policy, and the military (including the police) would take care of national security and defence. Consequently, the civilians excused themselves from virtually all areas of security and defence policy to the point of absolute neglect. This might have been a useful bargain – after all, Colombia was one of only two countries in South America that avoided military rule during the 1960s and 1970s. However, this happened at a tremendous cost: the military did not focus, or was not allowed to focus, on the threat posed by the rural guerrillas of the ELN and FARC, to the point that by 2002 large sectors of the country were without any state presence, violence was rampant everywhere, and the armed insurgents – now including the AUC – carried the initiative. By the mid-1990s it was obvious to most informed observers that Colombia was facing a very serious situation of crime and insurgency that would have to be dealt with forcefully. However, all recent presidents have avoided calling upon the armed forces and the police to take forceful action. The most recent administration of President Pastrana engaged in a peace process that was, in the opinion of many, bound to fail. In essence, FARC and the ELN, with abundant resources from the drug trade, extortion, kidnapping, and other criminal activities, do not need to negotiate. They are quite content with the *status quo*. Past presidents were unwilling to counter FARC, the ELN, and the AUC with military force as a necessary step to pressure them into negotiations. This suggests that, perhaps due to their own lack of knowledge and that of the civilians around them in the MOD, they were unaware of, or due to a lack of confidence in their real ability to control they were unwilling to exercise, their legal powers to call upon the army and police to restore order. There were some instances of armed encounters between the insurgencies and the police and the armed forces. However, overall their approach was marked by conflict avoidance. In sum, formally the civilians had control over military roles and missions, but in reality they did not exercise this control; or, if they exercised it, it was to maintain an untenable *status quo* in an increasingly degenerating military, political, economic, and social environment.

Intelligence for whom?

An intelligence system should serve the executive. In Colombia, unlike other post-authoritarian governments in Latin America, including Argentina, Brazil, Chile, and Peru, the intelligence services were not used to intimidate and control the population. They were therefore not a challenge to the democratic transition process. However, Colombian intelligence services still do not support the civilian-led MOD. As in many other cases of new and not-so-new democracies, the intelligence services mainly served the president directly and themselves. They are not necessarily a threat to democracy, but are heavily autonomous and resist being brought under civilian control, and do not share information even among themselves.

In sum, civil-military relations in Colombia reflect those of a reasonably consolidated democracy. However, the degree of formalism and lack of real content are problematic. Colombia has been a democracy since at least 1958. There have been no indications of military blackmail or coups. But there are also few indications of civilian interest or engagement in military and security issues. In some countries this might not matter. It obviously does in Colombia, however, since the country has been racked by internal conflicts since the 1960s, and the impact on governance and security has become increasingly more serious. The problem was, then, less a matter of the military seeking greater autonomy and prerogatives, and more a matter of civilian disinterest and neglect. As long as civilian institutions of governance were unwilling to utilize their constitutional powers and address the country's problems with the help of the security forces, little could change in the volatile situation in Colombia.

Towards explaining Colombian civil-military relations

The role of the transition and consolidation phases

Since Colombia has long functioned as a procedural or electoral democracy with periodic and fair elections, there is little in the nature of the transition and consolidation phases that should have an impact on contemporary civil-military relations.[23] In 1958 civilian and military agencies sorted out each other's responsibilities. More than 40 years of democratic politics have offered plenty of opportunities to renegotiate this division of responsibilities, if such were perceived to be necessary. Even the 1886 constitution, the oldest continuously functioning constitution in the region, was substantially amended in 1991. At that time, or before or after, the understanding with the military could have been renegotiated. It is in the nature of democracy that issues such as the role of the military are constantly subject to political discussion and negotiation. In other countries, including Argentina, Brazil, Portugal, and Spain, divisions of responsibility and power negotiated during the transition period were renegotiated during a democratic consolidation phase. Reference to the informal agreement back in 1958 has since served as a rationale for civilian leaders to do very little in this realm. There is no indication that the military would have been prepared to launch a coup if civilian agencies had tried to assert a greater share of military decision-making. In sum, traditional civil-military relations in Colombia do not need to determine their current or future direction. The military would be prepared to share more responsibility with civilian agencies if the latter would be prepared and willing to do so.

There has been very little external influence on the evolution of civil-military relations in Colombia. Since 2000 the country has been aggressively soliciting foreign investment, loans, and military support in order to deal with the very serious problems of a lack of state presence, violence, the drug trade, and uneven development. Boasting one of the most robust economies in Latin America, Colombia was economically stable. Unlike in El Salvador or Guatemala, Colombia did not go through a transition from dictatorship to democracy, nor from war to peace. There was no need for the intervention of external actors, such as the United Nations, other international organizations, or other states. However, since 2000 there has been increased involvement of outsiders, especially the USA. This has been mainly in response to Colombian requests for funds and training.[24] Despite extensive discussion with the USA, European states, and the EU, there are no plans for UN-sponsored peace processes similar to those experienced in Central America. More critical issues in Colombian civil-military relations are the nature of the political system and political learning.

Lack of coherence of the political system

The Colombian political system is designed in such a way as to maximize the insulation and isolation of the politicians from society, including the all-pervasive domestic conflict. It is only at the presidential level, and that on the basis of a national election once every four years (exacerbated by the fact that a Colombian president cannot stand for re-election), that the issues of national security and defence, and thus of civil-military relations, might become relevant. President Pastrana was elected on a peace platform and then spent four fruitless years seeking peace, despite the fact that the armed insurgents never demonstrated serious interest in or willingness to seek peace. During that time his efforts failed to pass, let alone implement, political reforms in Congress or in the Constitutional Court. He was unable to reform the political system and make it more coherent. For example, the Constitutional Court declared his proposed armed forces law as unconstitutional, basically on a technicality. Nor did he achieve peace. This would have been difficult to achieve without a national security and defence strategy, which, in turn, would have required a different arrangement in civil-military relations. The latter, in turn, would have required political reform. Once it became clear that the peace process was a complete failure, a political outsider running as an independent candidate pursued a different course. Alvaro Uribe ran on a law and order platform. Although he sought to achieve peace, he favoured fighting the insurgents, thus forcing them and other armed elements to the negotiating table. Uribe won on the first ballot. No other organized segments in Colombia could push this agenda, including the Congress. The electoral and party systems are designed to achieve only the most limited, pork-barrel benefits for the constituents.[25] There is no incentive, and probably no means, for members of Congress to focus on a national issue, such as national security, defence, and civil-military relations. Therefore, the political system has completely neglected these issues. The armed forces are under control, and, except now at the executive level, there is no interest among politicians in focusing on civil-military relations. Alvaro Uribe was overwhelmingly elected on a law and order platform and is seeking to assert state authority over Colombia's security sector.

Absence of political learning

The Colombian élite, and this is clearly a highly élitist society even beyond what one learns to expect in other Latin American countries, have structured a system that does just fine by them individually, but fails in achieving collective outcomes. That is, Colombians often point out how segmented they are, individually, institutionally, regionally, and so forth. They have minimized the creation of institutions, be they universities, think-tanks or non-governmental organizations (NGOs), which could allow them to get together to learn from one another and basically generate political learning. There are universities, as indeed there are think-tanks and NGOs, but (until late 2003) none of them deals with security and defence or with the field of civil-military relations. One must remember that Colombia is a state at war with pervasive political violence, guerrillas claiming leftist and rightist orientations, and a state that is barely able to respond. Yet, in the whole country of 44 million people, with an extremely sophisticated society and culture, with excellent institutions of higher education and research, there was not until late 2003 a single university programme, nor a single think-tank, nor a single NGO that deals with security, defence, or civil-military relations. In sum, there is no institutional basis for political learning, and the dozen or so civilians at all interested in these themes had no institutional basis for political learning. Based upon the author's extensive meetings and discussions with Colombian civilians, including academics, journalists, and government officials, and with the military, the absence of an institutional basis for political learning is obvious to all. The most telling point, however, is that nobody seemed to think it unusual there is no place for such political learning.

Initiatives of the Uribe government

As noted above, Alvaro Uribe was elected president of Colombia on a law and order platform. He and his team have defined some of the problems described above and are seeking to have both passed and implemented constitutional and other political reforms to allow the state to respond more effectively to the serious challenges in national security and defence. So far, as of early 2004, the political reform initiatives have failed in a popular referendum. In addition, Uribe was attempting to turn the MOD into something more than a civilian minister, with the creation of two vice-ministers and the development of something of a staff. The situation, in short, has become so serious that the population elected Uribe to deal with the security problems and he is seeking to make the political and military changes to be able to deal with these problems. In the face of military pressure, however, the real versus formal powers of the MOD have not expanded. The situation as of early 2004 is something of a standoff, with the armed forces continuing to enjoy extensive autonomy but for the direct involvement of President Uribe.

Conclusion

Civil-military relations are a realm of politics that goes far beyond civilian control of the military. They are also about change and reform. Such reform requires awareness by civilian government élites of the causal factors for the necessity of reform, of how to "manage" international factors, of the relationship between the overall political system and security and defence, and of the need to create institutions where political learning can take place. This chapter has argued that in El Salvador the reforms are well on the way to becoming institutionalized. In Guatemala, despite the existence of a dynamic group of civilian experts on these issues outside of the government, the reforms have not progressed, but may with a new president as of January 2004. These two Central American countries have experienced peace and democratization at the same time with considerable, although varying, international involvement and pressure. Colombia is a very different situation, in that it has long been a democracy but is definitely not at peace. The author argues that peace, which he is convinced can only be achieved by forcing FARC in particular to the negotiating table through the government's military success, requires the renegotiation of civil-military relations. There are long-standing and difficult political obstacles to this change, and it remains to be seen whether the government of Alvaro Uribe will be successful in overcoming them – or his government will also be overcome by Colombia's legacy of violent conflict and an incoherent political system and lack of political learning.

Based on the three cases studied in this chapter, reforming civil-military relations to achieve the three goals of democratic control, effectiveness, and efficiency, or SSR in the terms of this book, is a very difficult challenge. While progress is being made in all three cases, it is extremely slow and far from being institutionalized. Further, based on the author's direct involvement in both Guatemala and Colombia, the main obstacles lie in the nature of the political system and the difficulty in political learning. Hopefully, as more is known about these issues political leaders will no longer have excuses for avoiding SSR.

Notes

1. Edmunds, Timothy. 2001. *Security Sector Reform: Concepts and Implementation*. Report for Geneva Centre for Democratic Control of Armed Forces, 20–22 November, p. 2.
2. On this concept see Huntington, Samuel P. 1991. *The Third Wave: Democratization in the Late Twentieth Century*. Norman and London: University of Oklahoma Press.
3. The current standard in quantifying democracies appears to be Freedom House. For the application of these data, and their use in analysis, see Diamond, Larry. 1999. *Developing Democracy Toward Consolidation*. Baltimore: Johns Hopkins University Press.
4. See Bruneau, Thomas C. "Ministries of defense and democratic civil-military relations", paper available on CCMR website at www.ccmr.org.
5. This observation is based on the author's interviews in Madrid in 1992–1993 with civilian officials who developed the legal bases and processes for the officer promotion process.
6. For comparative analyses of legislatures in these different functions see the series of papers by Jeanne Kinney Giraldo on the CCMR website at www.ccmr.org.
7. See Bruneau, Thomas C. 2001. "Intelligence and democracy", paper available on the CCMR website at www.ccmr.org. A slightly different version of the paper has been published as "Controlling intelligence in new democracies", *International Journal of Intelligence and Counterintelligence*, Vol. 14, pp. 323–341.
8. The author's assertions are based on annual CCMR seminar programmes in San Salvador during which he met with military and civilian leaders in security and defence as well as broad sectors of civil society. See in addition Williams, Philip J. and Knut

Walter. 1997. *Militarization and Demilitarization in El Salvador's Transition to Democracy*. Pittsburgh: University of Pittsburgh Press; Giralt Barraza, Salvador A. 1998. "On the road to democracy: Civil-military relations in El Salvador", MA thesis, Naval Postgraduate School.

9. For information on Guatemala the author draws on several CCMR research and seminar programmes in 1997–1999, 2002, and 2003, as well as de Leon, Bernardo Arevalo. 2001. *Function Military y Control Democratico*. Guatemala: Amanuense Editorial; de Leon, Bernardo Arevalo, Patricia Gonzalez, and Manolo Vela. 2002. *Seguridad democratica en Guatemal: Desavios de la transformacion*. Guatemala: FLACSO.

10. See, for example, Linz, Juan J. and Alfred Stepan. 1996. *Problems of Democratic Transition and Consolidation: Southern Europe, South America, and Post-Communist Europe*. Baltimore: Johns Hopkins University Press; Aguero, Felipe. 1995. *Soldiers, Civilians, and Democracy: Post-Franco Spain in Comparative Perspective*. Baltimore: Johns Hopkins University Press.

11. For this argument, see Hunter, Wendy. 1997. *Eroding Military Influence in Brazil: Politicians against Soldiers*. Chapel Hill: University of North Carolina Press; Bruneau, Thomas with P. Nikiforos Diamandouros, Richard Gunther, Arend Lijphart, Leonardo Morlino, and Risa Brooks. 2001. "Democracy, southern European style?", in P. Nikiforos Diamandouros and Richard Gunther (eds) *Politics in the New Southern Europe*. Baltimore: Johns Hopkins University Press.

12. In his recent writings, one of the best analysts of these topics raises the possibility of other factors in consolidating democratic civil-military relations, but he does not elaborate on these other factors. See Aguero, Felipe. 2001. "Institutions, transitions, and bargaining: Civilians and the military in shaping post-authoritarian regimes", in David Pion-Berlin (ed.) *Civil-Military Relations in Latin America: New Analytical Perspectives*. Chapel Hill: University of North Carolina Press, pp. 194–222.

13. On this important topic see, for example, Arnson, Cynthia J. (ed.). 1999. *Comparative Peace Processes in Latin America*. Stanford: Stanford University Press (with case studies and comparisons between El Salvador and Guatemala); Stedman, Stephen John, Donald Rothchild, and Elizabeth M. Cousens (eds). 2002. *Ending Civil Wars: The Implementation of Peace Agreements*. Boulder, CO: Lynne Rienner Publishers (with cases of El Salvador and Guatemala); Santiso, Carlos. 2002. "Promoting democratic governance and preventing the recurrence of conflict: The role of the United Nations Development Programme in post-conflict peace-building", *Journal of Latin American Studies*, Vol. 34, No. 3, pp. 555–586.

14. On this point see Santiso, *ibid.*, p. 563; de Leon, Bernardo Arevalo. 1999. "Demilitarization and democracy", in Cynthia J. Arnson (ed.) *The Popular Referendum (Consulta Popular) and the Future of the Peace Process in Guatemala*, Woodrow Wilson Center Latin American Program Working Paper, November, pp. 43–49.

15. For an introduction to this field see for example Leeus, Frans L., Ray C. Rist, and Richard C. Sonnichsen (eds). 1994. *Can Governments Learn? Comparative Perspectives on Evaluation and Organizational Learning*. New Brunswick: Transaction Publishers; Bennett, Andrew. 1999. *Condemned to Repetition? The Rise, Fall, and Reprise of Soviet-Russian Military Interventionism 1973–1996*. Cambridge, MA: MIT Press.

16. Guatemala is characterized by a broad and robust community of think-tanks and NGOs, many of which focus on issues of national security and defence. They hold conferences and seminars, and publish documents and books. The problem of political learning is illustrated, however, by the most recent publication. It is a multi-volume effort edited by Bernardo Arevalo de Leon, *Hacia una politica de seguridad para la democracia*, Guatemala, FLACSO, WSP-INTERNACIONAL, IGEDEP, 2002. This publication, however, has not been accepted by the armed forces or the government, despite their

involvement in its elaboration. That is, despite the efforts by Guatemalans and foreigners to reform key issues in civil-military relations, the structures and processes remain the same. It is probably worth nothing that the US government decertified Guatemala in 2003 for lack of cooperation in counter-drug programmes.

17. For a very good article on civil-military relations in Colombia, see Watson, Cynthia A. 2000. "Civil-military relations in Colombia: A workable relationship or a case for fundamental reform?", *Third World Quarterly*, Vol. 21, No. 3, pp. 529–548.

18. For an example of this misnomer, see Ruiz, Bert. 2001. *The Colombian Civil War*. Jefferson, NC: McFarland & Co.

19. Gallup poll data from January 2003, which the author obtained in March 2003, show FARC and the ELN each with a 1 per cent favourable opinion and 92 per cent negative opinion. The highest ratings they received, in September 2001, had them each at 2 per cent positive and 91 per cent negative.

20. For insights and critical comments on this point, see Lora, Mayor General Juan Salcedo. 1999. "Respuestas personalisimas de un General de la republica sobre cosas que casi todo el mundo sabe", in Maldolm Deas and Maria Victoria Llorente (eds) *Reconocer la Guerra para construir la paz*. Bogota: Grupo Editorial Norma, pp. 349–387.

21. This has been confirmed by the author's interviews and observations in Colombia. The author and the CCMR are currently working with the Colombian Ministry of Defence on a defence-restructuring project. As part of the project the author and his team conducted interviews with all of the department heads in the MOD on 5–6 February 2003.

22. There is an extensive and excellent literature on the Congress in Colombia, which demonstrates and analyses the clientelistic versus representative character of the Congress and its members. See for example Archer, Ronald P. and Matthew Soberg Shugart. 1997. "The unrealized potential of presidential dominance in Colombia", in Scott Mainwaring and Matthew Soberg Shugart (eds) *Presidentialism and Democracy in Latin America*. New York: Cambridge University Press, pp. 110–159; Crisp, Brian F. and Rachael E. Ingall. 2002. "Determinants of home style: The many incentives for going home in Colombia", unpublished manuscript; Bejarano, Ana Maria and Eduardo Pizarro Leongomez. 2002. *From "Restricted" to "Besieged": The Changing Nature of the Limits to Democracy in Colombia*, Kellogg Center Working Paper No. 296, April.

23. For a good discussion contrasting procedural, or electoral, democracy with a richer and more robust liberal democracy see Diamond, note 3 above, pp. 8–13.

24. For an excellent discussion of Plan Colombia, implications and options, see Serafino, Nina M. 2001. *Colombia: Conditions and US Policy Options*. Washington, DC: Congressional Research Service, updated 12 February.

25. *Ibid.* See also Bejarano, Ana Maria and Eduardo Pizarro. 2001. "Reforma politica despues de 1991: Que queda por reformar?", unpublished paper prepared for Kellogg Institute conference on Democracy, Human Rights, and Peace in Colombia, 26–27 March; Shugart, Matthew Soberg, Brian F. Crisp, and Erika Moreno. 2002. "Re-constituting democracy: Institutional patterns of political overhaul in Latin America", unpublished paper, 30 January.

12

Civil-military relations and national reconciliation in Chile in the aftermath of the Pinochet affair

Nibaldo H. Galleguillos

Is national reconciliation possible between a military/civilian coalition which ruled in a brutally repressive manner and the (*de juris* and *de factum*) important sectors of civil society which are excluded from meaningful democratic participation? Is national reconciliation a possibility when the military closed important avenues for human rights accountability by means of a spurious amnesty law and a series of political agreements with the democratic opposition? Is national reconciliation an attainable goal when the military/civilian coalition reserved for itself constitutional safeguards that put handcuffs on elected governments' freedom of action? Does national reconciliation have a chance when a former dictator continues at the helm of the armed forces against the wishes of a newly elected government, as General Augusto Pinochet did from 1990 until 1998? Last but not least, can reconciliation be achieved when history continues to be written and taught by those who believe that the armed forces saved democracy, even if in the process of saving it they managed to destroy it?

Implicitly and explicitly, the critical literature on Chile's transition away from military rule would tend to agree that national reconciliation would be unattainable under the above conditions. Politically, such was the strong view expressed by Patricio Aylwin (1990–1994), the first elected president to succeed the former dictator General Augusto Pinochet:

The fact that the armed forces and Carabineros commanders cannot be removed, and that the National Security Council intervenes in the make-up of the Constitutional Tribunal, grants these commanders a political role that is not proper to their functions ... All these things are traces of what the theorists of authoritari-

243

anism call *protected democracy*. They fear democracy and use these mechanisms to prevent fulfilling the people's will.[1]

The above, in turn, raises a number of seldom-asked questions, since they remain submerged in civil-military relations analyses that focus more on institutional than political issues. For example, when do the military make the qualitative jump that leads them to embrace participatory democracy? When does the conversion from deeply held undemocratic values and beliefs to genuine support for democracy take place? Is there a specific point in time when this conversion occurs? If so, is the conversion part of a process, or is it due to circumstantial events, or a combination of the two? In sum, is there a switch, somewhere, which makes it possible for individuals who have vehemently rejected democracy to turn themselves into its supporters?

In Chile's case, the May 1991 release of the report by the Commission on Truth and Reconciliation,[2] appointed by the elected government, highlighted the degree of the armed forces' arrogance and contempt for both elected officials and civil society's human rights organizations. The military not only denounced the so-called Rettig Report, but it also denied that human rights abuses were ever committed by some of its members, and that torture and assassination had been government-sponsored activities. In Aylwin's words, "an atmosphere of mutual disbelief, distrust, and reciprocal suspicion separated the large majority of civilians from the members of the security and armed forces".[3] Accordingly, under those contrasting views the prospects for national reconciliation were almost nil. The fact that General Pinochet moved on 11 March 1998 from the powerful post of commander-in-chief of the armed forces to a safe seat-for-life in the Senate further guaranteed that the model of civil-military relations would continue to be clouded by the atmosphere to which Aylwin had referred. Aylwin's sustained efforts to restore civilian supremacy were of no avail. Nor were his efforts to bring about reconciliation any more successful. His successor, President Eduardo Frei Ruiz-Tagle (1994–2000), was both cavalier and aloof about military reforms and reconciliation during his administration. His concern with the further liberalization of the economy and its integration into the capitalist world system was matched only by his desire to sweep under the carpet such irritants as unresolved human rights issues. Frei's inaction can be interpreted as an attempt to let time heal the wounds and bring about closure; it had, however, little effect on the activism of human rights organizations, which continued to press for answers and justice, thus reminding everyone that reconciliation was impossible unless the "real" truth came out.

A historic opportunity at the end of Frei's government was, however, seized by his successor, the socialist Ricardo Lagos (2000–2006). The unexpected arrest of the former dictator by British police in October 1998[4] provided the impetus for renewed efforts to reform the pattern of civil-military relations and do something meaningful about the long-sought national reconciliation. Unlike his predecessor, President Lagos stated in unambiguous terms that he would seek the reform of the institutional order enshrined in the 1980 constitution, especially those sections dealing with the re-establishment of civilian control over the armed forces. That is, the "live and let live" approach followed by the Frei administration was explicitly rejected by President Lagos. For the first time since President Aylwin, who had unsuccessfully tried to regain civilian control, the armed forces were placed in a situation where they had to recognize that serious human rights violations had occurred during the dictatorship. Until then, they had relied on the promises made by Pinochet, as commander-in-chief and their main representative in the Senate, that he would not allow any of "his men" to be touched by the courts. Now they had become orphaned, since their main protector had been rendered incapable of defending himself while held under arrest in London. The armed forces had little choice but to accept that the criminal responsibility of some of its members in the commission of human rights abuses was a distinct possibility. In addition, following the intense international scrutiny of Chile's democracy and the often-made comments about the excessive prerogatives and guardianship role of the armed forces, the military was faced with the fact that a reform of the pattern of civil-military relations enshrined in the constitution had become a true national aspiration. Chileans were reminded that there is no democracy when the armed forces have as much political power as they do in Chile. Lastly, the armed forces' day of reckoning would not be genuine unless institutional responsibility was accompanied with a sincere asking for forgiveness from victims, victims' relatives, and civil society.

This chapter shows that Pinochet's arrest became the lightning-rod that opened the way to political negotiations for the reform of civil-military relations. It also claims that although the former dictator's tribulations brought some degree of catharsis among some of his supporters, reconciliation as a national aspiration still remains an elusive goal.

The background

Conflict is a pervasive and persistent feature of societies divided by class. It has been particularly evident throughout Chile's history. In fact, the ideological, economic, social, cultural, and political project of the 17-year-long civil-military regime entrenched in a much deeper manner the class divisions that had long been part of the country's social structure.[5] The dictatorship's commitment to "end" class struggle accomplished almost exactly the opposite: its actions, legal and practical, were geared towards reinforcing the historical class divisions of the Chilean socio-economic formation. The constitutional provisions of 1980 had as their main goal to ensure that power was retained by a minority sector[6] that had no chance to win an outright victory in competitive elections through their political parties and organizations.[7]

Any discussion on reconciliation must, therefore, begin with a clear understanding of the conflict that preceded it. In the case at hand, it is important to discern whether the conflict had been resolved by the time the armed forces were forced to relinquish government to the elected political opposition. If the answer is negative, then the question must be asked of how intense the perception of the conflict was amongst the parties involved in it? Moreover, if the conflict and its root causes were not solved, what role did the armed forces assign to themselves in a post-military government? Were they to support the democratic transition constructively, or, on the contrary, constitute themselves as an obstacle to transition?

The armed forces' abrupt departure, following Pinochet's defeat in the October 1988 plebiscite, ensured that it would be up to the elected governments to deal with the pressing issue of attaining national reconciliation in order to avoid another social and political breakdown, such as the one that had led to the 1973 military intervention.

Such hopes were given a serious blow with General Pinochet's arrest in 1998. His detention brought to the forefront the painful divisions that Chilean society still endures even after more than 30 years since the 1973 military coup. To be sure, Pinochet's legal problems were of a criminal nature. However, the repercussions were eminently political, and had the potential to destabilize the process of transition away from authoritarianism by bringing back to the surface the myriad of economic, social, cultural, and political divisions that continue to run through the body politic. Standing out among them was the issue of the unresolved human rights abuses by the military/civilian dictatorship, especially the case of some 1,200 individuals who had been made to "disappear" by the dictatorship's secret police and the armed forces.[8]

Pinochet's detention created an immediate polarization within Chilean society. His supporters, including active and retired military personnel, rushed to defend him and demanded that the government brought him back. Human rights victims, human rights organizations, and some members of parliament voiced the view that Pinochet's fate should be left to the courts, and that the government should not intervene on his behalf. In a bizarre twist, the former dictator's supporters threatened to end the political transition and destroy the legal-juridical edifice erected by the dictatorship. It fell upon the elected government to defend an institutional order that it had steadily denounced since 1980. The undemocratic features of the constitution, as the above quotation by President Aylwin shows, had been firmly rejected by the political forces opposed to the dictatorship; yet the same forces have agreed to govern the country under the 1980 constitution in the name of "political realism and pragmatism". The irony was self-evident: once again, like in 1973, those who claimed to be democrats were willing to do anything to destroy *their* democracy, while those who consistently denounced democracy's shortcomings were forced to defend it as a matter of principle. Socialist President Salvador Allende died defending a bourgeois democracy he did not believe in; 30 years later, socialist President Ricardo Lagos was placed in the position of upholding the 1980 constitution that he had publicly denounced on numerous occasions.

Although fears of a military/right-wing backlash were serious enough, due to this sector's threats, such a bleak scenario failed to materialize. Gradually, the military began to realize that blind opposition and rhetorical threats against the institutional order were of no use, especially when high-profile right-wing individuals began to distance themselves from Pinochet. Eventually, the elected government, the armed forces' highest-rank officers, and important sectors of civil society (i.e. the church and human rights organizations), in a remarkable degree of political maturity, agreed to sit down to discuss and find ways to address the issues that had blocked national reconciliation. Whatever its shortcomings, and there were several, this approach would prove successful in preventing the reoccurrence of social and political conflicts similar to those that the country had faced in the early 1970s. At the very least, the government and human rights organizations denied the military and the right-wing sectors the justification for another coup. On the contrary, the healing process began with the establishment of a negotiation panel, the so-called *Mesa de Dialogo*, or Round-table for Dialogue, in August 1999.

Setting up the conditions for dialogue

Twenty-four people were chosen to be part of these negotiations. Government representatives included the under-secretaries of defence for the army, navy, air force, and *carabineros* police. Religious leaders from the Catholic Church, Protestant denominations, and the Jewish community; human rights lawyers; representatives from the four branches of the armed forces; academics (right-wing historians); scientists; and a representative of the Freemason society were also members of the panel. The panel was the first opportunity in which former ideological enemies met

to create a new atmosphere devoid of distrust and mutual recriminations. Relatives of the disappeared refused to participate, as did some re-
nowned human rights lawyers.[9] Their refusal was premised on the belief
that this ad hoc panel was purely and simply a public relations effort
to convince the UK to release the former dictator; also, much as had
been the case with the Commission on Truth and Reconciliation, the
new panel had no power to enforce its findings. It could not bring charges
against anyone. This opposition to participation in the negotiations cast a
dark cloud about the success of the panel; prospects for a true reconciliation were diminished, if not doomed, as one of the most important parties
to the negotiation chose not to get involved.

Although denials to the effect abounded, there was little doubt that the
immediate goal behind the establishment of this panel was to convince
the international community, but especially Britain and Spain, that Chile
had the legal and political mechanisms to bring Pinochet to justice, thus
preventing his extradition to Spain. A subsidiary goal was to provide an
opportunity for the armed forces to come forward and release the necessary information needed to resolve once and for all the pending cases of
the disappeared. A mediated goal was to seize this historic opportunity
and create the political correlation of forces necessary to reform the pattern of civil-military relations left behind by the dictatorship.

The workings of the *Mesa de Dialogo*

The *Mesa de Dialogo* met for the first time in August 1999, and delivered
a final report in June 2000. Each member, representing a specific consti-
uency, made written submissions, often coating them in particularistic
historical, legalistic, moral, and ethical grounds. In their presentations,
the armed forces' representatives stuck to a common script: the human
rights abuses attributed to the military government had to be examined
within a historical context that took into consideration the political excesses of the left. The latter's (or, at least, some among them) call for
armed struggle, and the ideological international support they received,
justified the repression that ensued after the 1973 coup. Additionally,
the armed forces claimed that there never was a state policy or an institutional doctrine of systematic repression of opponents to the dictatorship,
although single individuals might have taken excessive action in the pursuit of the defence of the state. Moreover, they argued that they lacked
information on the whereabouts of the disappeared. Next, they called
for the due application of the amnesty law. They told the panel that a
search for absolute justice could endanger social peace. Then they argued
that forgiveness should be asked only by those individuals found re-

sponsible for human rights abuses by the courts, but not by the institutions to which those culprits used to belong. Lastly, they claimed to have a long history of "social sensibility" and of service to the motherland, and that full responsibility lay not with the armed institutions but with the society at large.[10] This line of argument is remarkable in that it shows the armed forces' efforts to rewrite the past, demonstrates an incredible ability to foresee the future, and then uses both past and future in order to justify a brutally repressive dictatorship.[11] Neither did the past happen as described by the military, nor was there ever a real chance of the future becoming a reality. The armed forces' and right-wing historians' views of developments in Allende's Chile were and still are purely fictional.[12]

In spite of the fact that the picture which emerges from the statements made by the armed forces' representatives is far different from the way in which the military likes to portrait itself, it gradually began to acquiesce to the need to deal with the past in order to make Pinochet's return to Chile possible. Of course, references to Pinochet's battles to regain his freedom were seldom made public by the panel, which continued to pretend that its goal was to find an answer to the case of individuals who were made to disappear by the dictatorship. Some 10 months later, on 13 June 2000, the *Mesa de Dialogo* issued its final report. The armed forces were given a six-month deadline to come forward with information leading to the whereabouts or the fate of the disappeared. This agreement was accompanied with a *Mesa de Dialogo* request to the Lagos government to send a bill to Congress in order to modify the penal code and other laws regarding the principle of professional secrecy. The law aimed at preserving the confidentiality and anonymity of those individuals who would volunteer to give information leading to resolving the cases of some of the disappeared, without them having to fear retribution, legal or otherwise. Such information was to be provided to especially designated members of the armed forces and religious representatives who would be sworn to the professional secrecy oath. Another proviso in these legal amendments was assurances given to the military that the 1978 amnesty law would be enforced to its fullest once the whereabouts or date of death of the disappeared had become known. The members of the panel also accepted as *prima facie* the military's contention that it lacked information about the disappeared, although it offered to work hard at obtaining it. Lastly, the *Mesa de Dialogo*'s members made a request to the Supreme Court for the appointment of Courts of Appeal judges to devote themselves full time to the investigation of the cases involving the disappeared.

Six months later, in January 2001, the four branches of the armed forces delivered a joint report with information on about 200 individuals whose disappearances were attributed to the armed forces and the police.

The report was not even signed by the commanders-in-chief of the armed forces, but by the military chaplain. Information about hundreds of others was not provided, since the two secret agencies, the National Intelligence Directorate (DINA) and the Central National Intelligence (CNI), which were responsible for the majority of the human rights violations, were not legally under the control of the military, but of Pinochet's government. The former heads of these organizations were not part of the *Mesa de Dialogo*, nor were they summoned to appear before the panel. The fact that many military and police officers worked for these secret agencies did not seem to resonate with the military. Its unwillingness to provide much-needed information further demonstrated to those opposed to the *Mesa de Dialogo* that the negotiations between the government and the armed forces were nothing but a badly disguised attempt to obtain Pinochet's release.

Questions about the veracity of the report arose, especially regarding the information, or lack thereof, furnished by the *carabineros* police.[13] Criticisms were aimed at the fact that the cases reported by the armed forces had been chosen in a selective and strategic manner. There was second-guessing among some of the members of the *Mesa de Dialogo*, who felt that the armed forces had been less than truthful in disclosing information. For example, it was later proven that the officer representing the air force at the negotiations was married to a woman who had been a member of the secret police and had been involved in well-known cases involving some of the disappeared. Not surprisingly, human rights lawyers and relatives of the disappeared who had refused to participate in the negotiations reiterated their views that the armed forces could not be trusted to address honestly the human rights abuses committed when they were in government. Their reaction was unprecedented: they filed charges against the commanders of the armed forces for obstruction of justice. The armed forces had in the past denied repeated court requests by claiming that they did not possess any information on the disappeared; yet now they were providing the dates, locations, and circumstances under which some 200 people had been killed by military personnel. The charges were, predictably, rejected by the courts, as they have done for most of the past 30 years. Reconciliation between the armed forces and their victims' relatives seemed once again an impossible achievement.

The accomplishments of the *Mesa de Dialogo*

The success of the *Mesa de Dialogo* can be attributed to the fact that most of those involved in the negotiations were genuinely concerned with carrying out their mandate in order to bring a renewed understanding and, hopefully, reconciliation among former enemies. Everybody pitched in. The government refrained from blaming the armed forces, all the while maintaining that it was up to the courts to decide how to proceed with the investigation of the missing people. The armed forces, in turn, opened their files and provided relevant information about some of the disappeared; more importantly, they acknowledged responsibility in some of these criminal acts, as was the case with the new commander-in-chief of the navy. The parliament rushed to pass the law of confidentiality in order to protect informants. The courts not only reopened cases, but judges were assigned to investigate the cases of the disappeared on a full-time basis. Last but not least, church leaders acted as conduits for some of the informants and continued to preach about the need for forgiveness and reconciliation.

The panel's other accomplishments are also unquestionable. First, it contributed to creating the kind of climate needed to assure the British government of the need to release Pinochet and allow him to return to Chile. That is, it stressed that the courts were independent from government pressures and quite capable of investigating the charges brought against Pinochet and other high-ranking officers. Second, it made it possible to avoid a more serious confrontation between the pro- and anti-Pinochet forces. Third, it allowed a nation in denial to learn the long-suppressed truth about some of the atrocities committed by the military and secret police. Fourth, it provided a degree of closure to some of the relatives of the disappeared. Fifth, it effectively ended Pinochet's influence over the political process and the armed forces. Sixth, and also indirectly related to the work of the *Mesa de Dialogo*, a package of constitutional reforms was sent to Congress aimed at reforming the current pattern of civil-military relations.

The former dictator's legal problems did not end with his return to Chile in March 2000. Although prosecution was stayed for health reasons in July 2001, the fact that he was not acquitted of the criminal charges brought against him by the investigating judge meant that Pinochet could no longer return to his safe seat in the Senate. In 2002, after long negotiations and veiled pressures from some of his own supporters, Pinochet finally renounced his Senate seat, and thus his parliamentary immunity. This, of course, was possible because criminal charges had no future in court. However, Pinochet was not able to prove that he was innocent of the charges laid by the courts. Also, Pinochet now lacks the political platform that he often used to defend his dictatorship and threaten elected authorities. To the extent that he has been medically diagnosed with a mild form of dementia, any political statement he were to make would be in contradiction with the doctors' conclusions, and would be cause for reopening hundreds of cases before the courts.

In effect, long-held negotiations between the government, the armed forces, and the political opposition finally materialized in the bill submitted to Congress by the executive in November 2001. The proposed reforms to the institutional order created by the 1980 constitution included, among others, the end of the institution of designated senators (currently, 10 non-elected senators; including four former commanders-in-chief appointed by the armed forces). They also ended the National Security Council's prerogative of appointing some of the members of the Constitutional Court and the Senate. More important, the bill addressed the criticized pattern of civil-military relations inherited from the dictatorship. It abrogated the role of protector of the institutional order that the armed forces had arrogated for themselves. It also subjects the appointment of commanders-in-chief of the four branches to confirmation by the Senate. Lastly, it gives the incoming president the right to appoint at the beginning of his/her administration the commanders-in-chief for a period of four years, the same period as the (current) presidential tenure. The reforms, if approved, would effectively reassert greater civilian supremacy over the military by ending the constitutional prerogatives that give the armed forces greater powers than those of elected politicians, the Congress, and the courts. Conversely, accountability of the armed forces would be greatly expanded. Regretfully, none of those reforms has been approved by Congress at the time of writing this chapter (May 2004).

By 2003 another important reform of the security sector met the same fate as those indicated above. In effect, in October 2001 the civilian police and the *carabineros* police were, again, placed under the administrative and political control of the Ministry of the Interior. They were no longer dependencies within the Ministry of Defence, as had been the case under the dictatorship. This change was far from cosmetic. It restored the *carabineros'* attention to the specific task of fighting growing criminality and ensuring personal security, while abandoning their recent role as one of the most visible agents of human rights abuses. As well, the removal of the police from subordination to the Ministry of Defence reduced the strength of the armed forces, while the subordination of *carabineros* to the political authority ensured that the militarized police might again serve as a counterbalance to the other branches of the armed forces. This reform was strongly resisted by the *carabineros'* officer corps. An unprovoked attack on the building of the Communist Party by police officers was interpreted as a clear sign of rebellion. The government's reaction was to call into retirement 20 officers with the rank of general. The Lagos government's authoritative action constitutes one of the first instances of reasserting presidential prerogatives over the commanders of the armed forces. If approved by Congress, the reform would have effectively ended a pattern of civil-military relations that former President Aylwin had characterized as one in which "the restrictions on the president's rightful prerogatives in fact subject him to the decisions of his subordinates".[14] Again, these reforms were defeated in a Senate committee by right-wing politicians, including the designated military senators, in 2003.

However, a test of how much the relationship between the government and the armed forces has changed since Pinochet's arrest can be seen in the appointment of Dr Michelle Bachelet as Minister of Defence in January 2000. The new minister, a member of the more leftist faction of the Socialist Party, is the daughter of air force General Alberto Bachelet, one of several high-ranking officers tried for treason by the military government. He had been the director of the reviled National Office of Food Distribution during the Allende government, at a time when several military officers were appointed to various government posts by their institutions.[15] General Bachelet was tortured, and died in prison in 1974. The new minister herself was also arrested, tortured, and forced to live in exile during the dictatorship. Under any other circumstances, such an appointment would have been vetoed by the military. This time, however, the armed forces accepted the presidential nomination without questioning it, in a clear sign of normalization of relations between two former foes.

The subordination of the armed forces and police to civilian authority is far from complete. There still remain pockets of die-hard officers who, although not openly, continue to challenge the government. The transformation of the *carabineros* police remains an unfinished task, as reports after reports point out how even today, under a democratic government, the police continue to resort to torture against citizens.

Conclusion

The recent political history of the transition away from authoritarianism in Latin America appears to indicate that the patterns of civil-military relations in place are only tangentially shaped by the theoretical principles regulating those relations in long-standing democratic regimes. By and large, it seems that country specificity rather than democratic theory is the main factor in the establishment of a given model of civil-military relations. To be sure, references to democratic theory often made by elected civilians tend to be of the rhetorical sort; in most instances, they are simply a reflection of the frustration that is experienced by newly elected governments. Civil-military relations' analyses, therefore, cannot assume ideal conditions, since of necessity they are unfolding within an imperfectly democratic polity. These analyses must also assume that democracy is a process, a way of life, a kind of attitude and behaviour that cannot be expected from individuals who have been socialized to oppose it.

The accomplishments of the *Mesa de Dialogo* provide important lessons. First, it is a fact that, in spite of existing institutional constraints, Chile has demonstrated itself to be a politically mature society, with the legal instruments needed for successful conflict resolution. Second, prospects for national reconciliation seemed brighter due to the mutual understanding that developed among antagonistic actors. Third, it brought some humility to an otherwise self-righteous military. Fourth, the example set by the panel is now being discussed in Uruguay and Argentina as a positive initiative that could be emulated.

However, the author would argue that the successes of the *Mesa de Dialogo* are limited in their scope. Its creation, work, and results had more to do with political expediency than with a genuine commitment to justice. The *quid pro quo* between the government, the armed forces, the political class, and the judiciary demonstrated once again the pragmatism *at all costs* that has characterized Chilean politics since the last year of the military dictatorship. This political realism has, however, further entrenched an institutional order that remains profoundly undemocratic. Reforms of the undemocratic 1980 constitution confer to it a degree of legitimacy that runs counter to popular demands for the drafting of a new, publicly discussed, constitution. The architecture of constitutional reform, which elected governments have pursued since 1990, hides the fact that each reform is purely cosmetic and does not address the authoritarian enclaves created by the dictatorship. If the 1980 constitution was originally illegitimate, will piecemeal reforms eventually make it legitimate? In other words, the political system *works* in practice, even if it is founded on an illegitimate constitution. The constitution itself has been amended more than 70 times in the last 10 years; yet, as the author has argued elsewhere, its main authoritarian features and self-preservation mechanisms (appointed senators, courts stacked with judges appointed during the dictatorship, unfair electoral legislation, military autonomy, and so on) remain as firm as ever. The two pillars referred to above, the armed forces and the courts, continue to provide the defence of an institutional order that, to many a Chilean, is still profoundly undemocratic. President Lagos's commitment to make Chile a more democratic country is as stalled as was the case with President Aylwin's (1990–1994) and, although less so, President Frei's (1994–2000) commitment.

Political realism is by and large a mechanism that elected governments have been using in order to appease the armed forces and the conservative right wing. Appeasement is needed because of the fears that still linger in the body politic. Such deference is, however, not accorded to the dictatorship's victims. The elected governments have continuously toyed with the hopes of human rights organizations, the relatives of the disappeared, and the thousands who were tortured by the dictatorship's security apparatuses. Following the Commission on Truth and Reconciliation's report, monetary compensation was offered to those victims and their relatives. However, the latter's persevering demand for justice has continued in spite of the official attempts to shut the past closed. When the Chilean state failed to prosecute Pinochet, the victims and their relatives found receptive prosecutors and judges in Spain. The government's success in bringing Pinochet back to Chile was premised on its promise, finally, to prosecute the dictator. However, the appointments of higher-court judges to work full time in the investigation of the cases of the disappeared and the hundreds of files opened against the former dictator Pinochet and several high-ranking military officers seem futile when the courts continue to be staffed with Pinochet appointees. The higher courts have been quite adept at selectively finding ways to shelter high-ranking officers from justice, while dispensing some of it on to lower-rank subordinates. The government and the courts continue to play a deceptive game with the victims of repression. Even if the courts were to find some of the military officers guilty of any crime, the outcome is already known: military personnel are still covered by the 1978 amnesty law.

Since true justice is unlikely under the current legal framework and the accompanying politics of élite negotiations, is Chile ready for national reconciliation? The author believes that the answer is of necessity a negative one. National reconciliation is unlikely as long as the armed forces remain protected by the mantle of impunity embedded in the amnesty law, in the reports of the Commission on Truth and Reconciliation, the Reparation Commission, and the *Mesa de Dialogo*. Reconciliation is unlikely as long as politicians and church leaders continue to talk about the need to forgive and forget. Reconciliation is unlikely as long as many Chileans continue to prefer to be told tales rather than to look at the evidence of human rights abuses committed by the armed forces. Reconciliation will occur only when democratic equality is granted to all Chileans, and not to a few privileged ones.

In the end, needed reforms of the security sector, including the armed forces and the militarized police, have not succeeded in spite of the government's and human rights organizations' efforts. Although the political will may be present, insurmountable legal and constitutional structures still entrenched in the 1980 constitution have made these attempted reforms all but impossible to achieve until now. For the time being, the *status quo*, long heralded as undemocratic, is likely to persist.

Notes

1. President Patricio Aylwin's 1992 state of the nation address. Quoted in *FBIS-LAT-92-104*, 29 May 1992, pp. 23–24.
2. The Commission on Truth and Reconciliation was established by President Aylwin in 1990 with the specific purpose of collecting and analysing information about human rights abuses committed between 11 September 1973 and 11 March 1990. It was chaired by law professor Raul Rettig, and included individuals from academia, human rights activists, and former politicians. The final report is available as CNCTR. 1993. *Report of the Chilean National Commission on Truth and Reconciliation*, two volumes, translated by Philip Berryman. Notre Dame: University of Notre Dame Press.
3. President Patricio Aylwin's 1993 state of the nation address. Quoted in *FBIS-LAT93-099*, 25 May 1993, p. 20.
4. Former dictator Augusto Pinochet was arrested by Scotland Yard at the request of a Spanish judge investigating crimes associated with Operation Condor. Operation Condor was a coordinated effort by intelligence agencies from Argentina, Brazil, Chile, and Paraguay to track down and capture individuals deemed to be a threat to the military dictatorships that ruled those countries in the 1970s and 1980s. This government-sponsored international terrorist organization was promoted by one of Pinochet's right-hand intelligence officers, army Colonel Manuel Contreras. Contreras's greatest "success" was the car-bomb assassination of former socialist minister Orlando Letelier in the streets of Washington in September 1976.
5. The literature on this aspect of Chile's socio-economic formation is too long to list here. An excellent introductory text is Garreton, Manuel Antonio. 1989. *The Chilean Political Process*. Boston, MA: Unwin Hyman. See also Petras, James. 1970. *Politics and Social Forces in Chilean Development*. Berkeley: University of California Press; Stallings, Barbara. 1978. *Class Conflict and Development in Chile*. Stanford: Stanford University Press.
6. See, *inter alia*, Silva, Patricio. 1996. *The State and Capital in Chile: Business, Elites, Technocrats, and Market Economics*. Boulder, CO: Westview Press.
7. To understand these constitutional and electoral mechanisms which grant a parliamentary overrepresentation to the minority right-wing sectors, see Galleguillos, Nibaldo and Jorge Nef. 1992. "Chile: Redemocratization or the entrenchment of counterrevolution?", in Archibald Ritter, Maxwell Cameron, and David Pollock (eds) *Latin America to the Year 2000*. New York: Praeger.
8. The government acknowledges 1,102 disappearances, while human rights organizations number them at 1,197. See the Rettig Report, note 2 above.
9. The divisions created by the Pinochet affair even affected the human rights legal community. Human rights lawyers who agreed/disagreed with the *Mesa de Dialogo* pressed charges against each other for slandering.
10. These claims by the armed forces' representatives are extracted from their submissions, as published in the newspaper *La Tercera* and the magazine *Que Pasa* during 1999 and 2000.
11. Nowhere did the armed forces' representatives acknowledge that the 1970 assassination of General Rene Schneider, commander-in-chief of the armed forces, was the work of right-wing militants and members of the army, air force, and police, with the support of the US Central Intelligence Agency. Nor did they acknowledge that the 1973 assassination of Captain Arturo Araya was also the work of right-wing terrorists. No mention is made of the fact that of the approximately 100 people who died violently during the Allende years (1970–1973), more than 90 were Allende's supporters. The alleged threats posed by the Allende government were all manufactured by the Central Intelligence Agency, as recently declassified material in the USA demonstrates.

12. This statement is based on the author's experience as a human rights lawyer under the dictatorship. Not a single one of the dozens of political prisoners the author defended or represented was spared torture by the members of the four branches of the armed forces. Unfortunately, the government's commissions on human rights have not been given the mandate to investigate this type of abuse. Their mandate has always been limited to individuals who were assassinated or "disappeared".

13. The *carabineros* police are the largely militarized corps charged with the preservation of public order. They are recognized by their green uniforms, unlike the Investigation Police, which is a plain-clothes unit. Both are administratively under the control of the Ministry of the Interior.

14. Aylwin, note 1 above.

15. At the height of the October 1972 general strike, called by opponents to his government, President Allende shuffled his cabinet and appointed the commanders-in-chief of the armed forces to several ministerial posts. This action had an immediate effect, as the opposition called off the strike. As the mid-term congressional elections of March 1973 approached, the right-wing opposition demanded that the armed forces stay in government in order to give guarantees of a clean and fair election. General Bachelet was one among many officers who thus served under a socialist government.

13

The role of the military in democratization and peacebuilding: The experiences of Haiti and Guatemala

Chetan Kumar

This chapter[1] uses the terms "military" and "army" as referring not just to the actual armies in Haiti and Guatemala, but also to the social classes and interests that support the military. Throughout their histories, militaries in both countries have been not just political players, but have also had extensive commercial activities and interests. Hence, this chapter offers perspectives not just on the role of the military in post-conflict peacebuilding in both countries, but also on the wider trends in political and economic evolution in which the militaries' role – and that of their social backers – should be properly construed.

In both Haiti and Guatemala the army has been a major player in the conflicts and upheavals that have prompted recent international interventions. In Guatemala the army – which emerged as the tactical winner of the military conflict with the guerillas – was a central player in the subsequent peace process and continues to be an influential force in Guatemalan politics, although its public role has been greatly diminished by the defeat of the FRG (Guatemalan Republican Front) in the last presidential elections. In Haiti the army – which precipitated extensive flows of both drugs and refugees into the USA in the early 1990s – was ousted from power by a US-led invasion in 1994, and subsequently abolished. Remnants of the army were either integrated into the new national police or disbanded. However, in 2004 former soldiers armed themselves to form the core of an insurgency against incumbent President Aristide, who fled in fear of his life. These former soldiers remain largely mobilized and are an important influence on the transitional government that succeeded Aristide.

Drawing on the comparative historical experience of Haiti and Guatemala, this chapter suggests that in societies where the military has been a central element of political organization for a significant historical period, the reorganization of the polity cannot take place without the participation of the military itself or the social classes that have supported it. In Guatemala the peace process sought to enable a new coalition of élites – with only partial success – to bypass the military and its backers. In Haiti the remnants of the military leadership and the social classes that have supported them in the past have remained aloof from the country's post-conflict political process. In both Haiti and Guatemala there is a need to bring the traditional backers of the military into a wider intersectoral consensus on the broad parameters of peaceful change. In the absence of this consensus, the political process in both countries has remained largely deadlocked in recent years, despite the changes of political fortune brought about through elections or other means. The transitional Haitian government has had as little success as its predecessor in bringing its opponents as well as different social sectors around unifying themes or policies.

Given the history of military brutality in both Guatemala and Haiti, the central proposition of this chapter may appear to be counter-intuitive to observers. However, both the ranks of the Guatemalan military and the social classes that have supported the Haitian military have included a number of reformist elements that have been largely ignored by successor democratic governments as they have tried to live down the excesses and brutality that characterized recent periods of upheaval. In Haiti, in particular, the attempt by the Aristide government to transcend these excesses led to the political ostracization of entire social classes that had supported these regimes. The latter have either fled with their capital and entrepreneurial skills to North America, or continued to manipulate and influence the Haitian political process from a distance.

This chapter analyses the historical dynamics that yielded these circumstances, and then offers some recommendations for building lasting peace in Guatemala and Haiti in a manner that takes better account of the military or its remnants.

The Guatemalan conflict

Contrary to the rest of Central America, the mercantile class that settled Guatemala in the seventeenth and eighteenth centuries did not carry out an extensive commercialization of land or agriculture. Rather, they developed a political economy based upon taxation of the agricultural production of, and the extraction of forced labour and tribute from, the indigenous population.[2] In return, the indigenous communities were given a certain degree of protection.

The growth of the coffee economy in Guatemala in the nineteenth and early twentieth centuries placed great stress on this social compact, which had been guaranteed by the army and the church. The breaking point only came, however, with the entry of US commercial interests into Guatemalan agribusiness – especially bananas and coffee – in the twentieth century. The rapid expansion of the agrarian political economy soon led to considerably increased pressure on the indigenous population to offer up larger amounts of land and manpower for commercial exploitation. Land disputes erupted between commercial concerns and the indigenous peasantry. The army allied itself with US and Guatemalan agribusinesses to protect and participate in the profitable new ventures, and abandoned the upholding of traditional social compacts. This new role implied a suppression of violent peasant outbursts, and a repression of dissent from those urban elements that sought to move Guatemala away from a dependence on agriculture to further industrial and economic diversification.

In 1950 the rising influence of a small but increasingly vocal middle class led to the reformist presidency of Jacopo Arbenz, who proposed a major package of agrarian reform that alarmed both local and US mercantile interests.[3] In 1954 the US government, with the support of the coffee oligarchy, backed a coup against Arbenz.[4] The post-coup administration reversed Arbenz's reforms, and arrested and executed many reformers.

The primary outcome of the coup was to consolidate the army's growing role as the guarantor of the coffee-based political economy. Military rule, allied with commercial interests, became the primary mode of national politics. In reaction, however, by the late 1960s a significant rebellion had grown against the military and its policies. The military responded with massive human rights abuses in the periods 1970–1974 and 1978–1982 that claimed some 40,000 lives.[5] By the early 1980s the various guerrilla groups had coalesced into the URNG (Guatemalan National Revolutionary Unity).

In 1982 General Efrian Rios Montt led a coup by young reformist officers against the military oligarchy, who were seen as corrupt and therefore unable to defeat the insurgency, overthrew the government, and assumed the presidency. He then implemented a policy of blanket repression – disavowed later by the reformist officers who had supported him – that caused an estimated 100,000 civilian deaths and displacements.

The military occupied the countryside, enforcing compulsory enlistment in civil defence patrols (PAC) and setting up "model villages" of refugees.[6] Critically, these abuses discredited the Guatemalan military regime internationally and provoked an immediate change in US and international policies towards Guatemala.

In August 1983 Rios Montt was overthrown in a coup that reportedly enjoyed US sympathy. General Mejia Victores, who succeeded Rios Montt, organized an election, judged to be free and fair, for a national constituent assembly.[7] The assembly drafted a new constitution on the basis of a dialogue with all sectors and formally recognized the multiethnic composition of Guatemalan society. Subsequently, the first presidential elections in 30 years were won by Vincio Cerezo, a Christian Democrat.

While Cerezo presided over a period of renewed bloodshed, the mid-1980s brought promising regional efforts – the Contadora initiative and the Esquipulas process – to resolve conflicts in El Salvador, Nicaragua, and Guatemala, and to encourage a new US approach to Central America.[8] Also, a final attempt by the military to eliminate the remnants of the insurgency ended in a stalemate, further discrediting the "old guard" and strengthening the reformists amongst the officer class. Subsequently, the first meetings between the URNG and the new Guatemalan National Reconciliation Commission (CNR) took place in 1987[9] with the assistance of international church groups and Norway. The CNR also convened the *Gran Dialogo Nacional*, which was attended by 80 civil society organizations and provided a forum for many new civic organizations to articulate indigenous political rights.

After several rounds of talks, the CNR and the URNG signed the Basic Agreement on the Quest for Peace through Political Means in Oslo in 1990. This agreement laid out the timetable for a gradual peace process that culminated in 1996 after a series of interim accords, with each accord addressing a separate issue such as human rights or the economy. This gradual process, which was moderated by the United Nations from 1994, gave an emerging coalition of government reformers and progressive business the opportunity for effecting political and economic change that had previously been blocked by the existing institutions. The Guatemalan Congress and the political parties, under heavy oligarchic pressure, had proved unequal to the challenge of reform. Progressive members of the Guatemalan élite therefore used the peace process to bypass unworkable institutions, particularly the legislature, as well as the traditional oligarchy in an attempt to legitimize new processes and actors. For instance, the civic dialogues that were conducted parallel to the peace process fostered participation among previously marginalized groups, and the process itself formalized and regularized this participation. Several international participants in the process have informally noted that this was democracy creation through extra-institutional – albeit consensual – means.

The United Nations, which had moderated the peace process since 1994, also launched a human rights observation and verification mission – MINUGUA (UN Verification Mission in Guatemala) – in that year. Following the completion of the peace process in 1996, this mission provided assistance for the implementation of the peace accords. An important moment in the peace process was the creation of the Historical Clarification Commission in 1994.[10] This commission had no judicial authority, but was nevertheless considered an advance at a time when the military remained a strong political force. Another important step was the signing of the Agreement on the Identity and Rights of the Indigenous Peoples in 1995, which guaranteed indigenous participation in national political life.

The 1995 presidential elections reflected the growing realignment of social and economic sectors. The Guatemalan left wing formed the FDNG (New Guatemala Democratic Front) coalition, and the URNG urged voters to support this group. The new business and middle class coalesced around PAN (the National Advancement Party), which advanced the "free markets and democracy" formula. To their right, crucially, were no longer the traditional parties that had represented the oligarchy. Instead, the leading right-wing contender was former junta leader Rios Montt of the FRG, with a message that blended civic virtue and personal and social discipline with a populist anti-poverty and pro-community platform.

PAN won the 1995 elections. The formal peace process then concluded in 1996 with the Accord on a Firm and Lasting Peace that activated the timetable for implementing all previous accords. However, the PAN government was not able to deliver fully on this implementation. A general complaint was that its efforts were not implemented transparently. Relations of patronage between an earlier generation of oligarchic businessmen and their military allies were partially replicated between a new generation of businessmen and military officers.

The three areas where the greatest progress was made between 1996 and 2000 were the ones where military reformists broadly agreed with the moderates and the progressives: the demobilization of the guerillas and their reintegration into society; the return and reintegration of refugees; and the incorporation of indigenous issues and concerns into the national political agenda. On other critical issues, however – land disputes, economic reforms, the depoliticization of the army, and constitutional reform – the army and its social backers had their greatest apprehensions, and progress was limited.

The biggest challenge for Guatemala remained the non-violent resolution of the land question. As indicated earlier, a key factor driving the indigenous population to insurgency during the past three decades had been the state's failure to manage the increasing pressure exerted on them by land-and-labour-hungry coffee oligarchs. However, neither the oligarchy nor reformist business interests favoured a programme of redistribution, and they raised the spectre of a flight of foreign investment should the government start to nationalize or redistribute private property. They presented the issue of land-related violence as a legal one, and urged the government to resolve land disputes through the judicial process. This was easier said than done, since Guatemala has only the rudiments of a credible and impartial judiciary. Meanwhile, some progressive members of the business community argued for case-by-case but systematically implemented arbitration as a pragmatic method of settling local disputes.

Opposition by the private sector, and by the military and the oligarchy, also seriously retarded the reform of the tax system, and prevented Guatemala from funding employment and social welfare projects. In May 1999 the Guatemalan government held a referendum on a package of constitutional reforms that would have enshrined in law the depoliticization of the military and the formalization of the newly won rights of the indigenous population. Surprisingly, the package, comprising several complex and controversial measures, was presented to the people as a simple "yes" or "no" vote. Only 20 per cent of Guatemalans voted, and the majority rejected the package. Yet a post-referendum poll showed that nearly 84 per cent of Guatemalans continued to favour the peace process.[11] Poor referendum publicity and fear of state interventionism may explain this apparently anomalous result. Shortly after the referendum, members of both the progressive *ladino* élite and the Mayan leadership expressed their determination to institutionalize the same set of reforms through a series of smaller legislative steps.

Following the referendum, the presidential elections in 1999 were won by Alfonso Portillo of Rios Montt's FRG party. Despite its links with the military, the new government made plans to devolve key decision-making powers to provincial and community levels. Military archives, containing names of many shadowed by death squads, were declassified. Two officers were arrested and tried for the 1998 murder of Archbishop Gerardi – the first such trial in Guatemala's modern history.

Despite this promising start, however, the FRG government failed to control the growing corruption – mostly related to narco-trafficking – among the ranks of its military allies. It also failed to set a brisk pace for further economic reform. While the initial prosecutions of military officers suspected of politically motivated murders had been successful, subsequent attempts yielded death threats for court officials in some instances, and actual assassinations in others. In early 2003 the USA began to express strong displeasure at the government's failures, and to threaten a cut-off in aid.

While the jury is still out on the factors that kept the FRG government from using its links with its military allies to build a lasting national consensus, especially on reform, a key factor could have been the economic possibilities of narco-trafficking for an officer class which increasingly saw the army as being under siege from the threat of human rights prosecutions, and whose links with the mercantile élite had been sundered to a degree that they no longer saw themselves as guaranteeing, or benefiting from the profits of, coffee and agrarian production in an increasingly diversified economy. Reformist officers who considered themselves as allied with economic reformers might have found themselves caught between remnants of the old oligarchy on the one hand, and narco-traffickers in uniform on the other.

Unable to deliver even partially on the further implementation of the peace accord, as PAN had been able to do, the FRG suffered a resounding defeat in the December 2003 presidential elections, which brought back to power PAN and its allies within the Grand National Alliance (GANA). However, this reversal might have had more to do with the fact that the FRG candidate was Rios Montt rather than with any fond national memories of PAN rule in the mid-1990s. The vote conclusively demonstrated that Guatemalans were not ready for a return to rule by the military, whether in civilian garb or not, reformist or not.

The history of conflict in Haiti

Haiti is the poorest nation in the Western hemisphere. Uniquely, through 200 years of independence, its economic product has slipped steadily downwards. Like Guatemala, Haiti historically has had an economy ruled by self-serving élites who used regressive taxation to skim off of rural production in order to maintain their lifestyles, rather than invest directly in commercial development. As in Guatemala, this caused a chronic lack of investment, but also permitted rural communities some degree of autonomy.[12] However, in contrast to Guatemala, the Haitian state never organized itself to lead or facilitate a productive enterprise.[13]

In 1915 increasing instability and political violence, and the desire to protect its financial interests, led to a US intervention in Haiti. The intervention's primary objective was to marketize the country's economy. However, the previously loose relationship between government and rural districts was eroded as autonomous communities were subjected to forced marketization. The army was transformed into a tool for internal repression, which mounted after the US departure in 1934. However, the USA did leave behind basic infrastructure such as roads and communications.

US military and economic projects also spawned a small, predominantly black, middle class with nationalist views that brought Francois Duvalier to power in 1957. The hallmark of Duvalier's dictatorship was the systematic control of all aspects of Haitian society, especially through the military and a new paramilitary entity – the notorious *tontons macoutes*. Ironically, after token attempts to sideline the traditional élite, Duvalier's nationalist regime developed an understanding with them whereby their limited economic activity helped to pay for the regime's expenses. The army and its officers stood at the nexus of this accommodation as its primary guardians.

After his death in 1971, Duvalier was succeeded by his son. Given his image as a benign autocrat in comparison to his father, foreign donors conceived of a new economic strategy for Haiti that drew on its strength as a cheap labour pool for assembling consumer goods, primarily for the US market. Flourishing assembly industries were seen as an engine of wider economic growth.[14] This development strategy failed.[15] First, since it was not founded on consensus among different sectors of Haitian society, it could not mobilize the majority of Haitians.[16] Second, the Duvalier state, like its predecessors, lacked roots that reached into the economic life of the majority.[17] Third, Haitian élites who subcontracted and worked for the assembly manufacturers transferred all their earnings abroad and did not reinvest in Haiti. Most critically, unable to forge an internal consensus, the regime relied on the police and the *tontons macoutes* to enforce its diktat. The failure of this strategy underlined the need for an approach centred on the fullest possible political engagement between the state and its people, even if, economically, such an approach made only partial, short-term sense.[18]

In the early 1980s a popular movement began to seek the overthrow of the regime.[19] The state responded with violence. The USA found the anti-communist credentials of the Duvalier dictatorship less persuasive after the Cold War, and reacted by easing its exit into exile in 1986. It also did not oppose the subsequent assumption of direct power by the military. General Namphy, who took control of the government following Duvalier's exit, sought to continue the industrialization strategy supported by Haiti's donors. Given the lack of internal consensus, he did not have too much success either, and in the four years following Duvalier's departure Haiti saw a succession of coups and ineffective governments.

A critical opportunity to generate a firm internal consensus was lost in 1987, when the National Congress of Democratic Movements (CONA-

COM) was convened to assist in drafting a post-Duvalier constitution. The Congress concluded with support for a new constitution and a provisional electoral council to conduct the next elections. Unfortunately, regional and international actors largely chose to ignore the Congress, and supported General Namphy's promises to hold free elections. When those elections were held, paramilitary elements carried out a massacre at a polling station and the election results were annulled.

The failed elections of 1987 were followed by rigged elections in 1988. International monitors were then deployed to guarantee free and fair elections in 1990 – the first of their kind in Haitian history.[20] Much to the élite's chagrin, the elections were won by Jean-Bertrand Aristide, who proposed a popular upsurge or *lavalas* – literally "flood" – against corrupt governance. His promise of transformation attracted many intellectuals and technocrats who had fled Haiti during the Duvalier regime. On his election, they acquired significant positions in the new government. More conventional politicians retained control of parliament.

In the nine months of the first Aristide government in 1991, clashes between the parliament and the presidency were frequent, with street battles between government supporters and opponents. Many among Haiti's traditional élite interpreted Aristide's fiery rhetoric on uprooting the old system as a call for their assassination. However, technocrats in the Aristide government originated an economic reform plan that won the approval of international financial institutions.[21] Unfortunately, the government failed to put this plan to public debate, and thus build consensus around its key tenets. Instead, rowdy demonstrators called for compliance with the *lavalas* agenda.[22] Fearing extinction, Haiti's élite and their military allies responded with a coup in September 1991. The military regime subsequently embarked on a campaign of systematic slaughter of *lavalas* activists. The resulting outflow of refugees, and the gratuitous brutality of the military ruler, Cedras, prompted the UN Security Council to place an "oil and arms" embargo upon Haiti in 1993. Cedras then indicated a willingness to negotiate with the opposition. An agreement was signed in New York, and Cedras agreed to retire from government and allow Aristide's return to Haiti. Before the agreement could be implemented, Cedras reneged, and the Security Council rapidly reimposed the arms and oil embargo and instituted a naval blockade.[23]

By 1994 the deteriorating situation in Haiti had loosed a surge of refugees on American shores, putting domestic pressure on the Clinton administration. The USA then promoted a UN Security Council resolution authorizing the formation of a US-led "multinational force" (MNF) to facilitate the departure from Haiti of the military leadership and the restoration of the legitimate authorities.

Faced with an impending US-led invasion, the Cedras regime agreed to resign subject to an amnesty from the Haitian parliament. As a result, the MNF was able to move into Haiti on 19 September without opposition,[24] and Aristide was restored as president. In 1995 the Haitian army was abolished and replaced by the new Haitian National Police, which was to be trained by the United Nations and other international donors. The United Nations then kept peace in Haiti, and trained the police, from 1995 to 2000, when a new civilian mission, MICAH (International Civilian Support Mission), was launched with a mandate to assist Haiti in the areas of justice, security, and human rights. These roles were taken over by an OAS mission in 2002.

While international intervention restored a civilian government and replaced the repressive army with a civilian police force, it did not address Haiti's long-term political impasse. When Aristide was restored, so was the deadlock that had characterized his previous government. Part of the package for his restoration should have been the institution of a comprehensive multisectoral dialogue on key elements of political and economic reform, chaired by him as the president, but facilitated by Haitian civil society and observed by the international community. In the absence of such an effort, Haiti's weak political institutions remained deadlocked along class and factional lines. The international community did not apprehend that the real divisions in Haiti were not between political parties, but that the political process did not substantively represent or embody the country's interest groups. There were no precedents or entities for facilitating gradual change through consensus; this was neither the focus of Aristide's rhetoric nor that of his opponents in the military and the oligarchy.

Haiti's 1987 constitution bars two consecutive presidential terms. Hence, Aristide agreed to step down as president at the end of his first term in 1996. His chosen nominee, Rene Preval, was then elected president. Shortly thereafter, Haitian institutions became deadlocked.

The governments of both Aristide and Preval had agreed to implement the economic plan first conceived in 1991 with the help of international financial institutions. Aristide now argued that this plan would only benefit a small élite and would cause great suffering to the majority of the population. He did not, however, promote a multisectoral dialogue on an alternative path to economic reform that could have addressed genuine concerns regarding the stringent demands made by international financial institutions. In addition, a dispute arose over the legislative and municipal elections of 6 April 1997. The electoral process was halted before the second round of voting.[25] In June 1997 Prime Minister Rosny Smarth resigned in frustration, further paralysing the government.[26] Successive attempts to appoint a prime minister foundered over splits between the two major factions into which *lavalas* legislators in parliament had divided over Aristide's policies and persona – the anti-Aristide Organization of People in Struggle (OPL) and the pro-Aristide La Fanmi Lavalas. In March 1999, after concerted facilitation efforts by international mediators and some civic organizations, certain opposition parties reached an informal accord with the president for appointing an interim prime minister and holding new legislative elections, which were held in May and June 2000. Between 55 and 60 per cent of the electorate voted in the first round, the majority for La Fanmi Lavalas, perhaps in the hope that having the presidency and parliament under the same party would break the political deadlock. However, a dispute quickly arose over electoral procedure. International observers demanded a recount for certain seats in the Senate before the second round of voting. The Haitian government refused, saying that it could not control the decisions of the provisional electoral council. The latter defended its vote-count formula, saying that it had improvised under highly imperfect circumstances. When the second round of voting proceeded without a recount of the first round, the OAS withdrew its observer mission. Shortly thereafter, the USA suspended assistance to the country's police force.

After several failed attempts by the international community to resolve this issue, the Haitian government proceeded to conduct a presidential election in November 2000, despite international reservations. The election brought Aristide back as president. All opposition parties boycotted the election, and the international community did not recognize its results. Haiti's donors suspended official aid to the country until the political impasse was resolved. An OAS mission was deployed in 2002 to try to facilitate an end to this impasse, and to provide assistance in the areas of human rights and police reform. The mission had extremely modest success in achieving its objectives.

By mid-2003 the situation in Haiti had deteriorated to the point where the country was paralysed by almost continuous anti-Aristide demonstrations, orchestrated not just by his political opponents but also by a coalition of civic organizations that included former *lavalas* loyalists. They were soon joined by a group of former Haitian army soldiers, who re-armed themselves using resources provided by Aristide's opponents among the North American diaspora and then launched an insurgency in the north and west of the country that moved quickly towards Port-au-Prince, overwhelming the ill-equipped and demoralized Haitian National Police in the process. In January 2004 Aristide left Haiti for South Africa, fearing for his life.

In what was surely an unprecedented instance of rapid international coordination, a transitional government was installed immediately thereafter with the support of the United Nations and Haiti's major external interlocutors, particularly the USA and France. This government, headed by President Alfonso Portillo, continues in power today, with the next national elections scheduled for 2005. In mid-2004 the UN Security Council deployed another peace operation in the country, MINUSTAH (UN Stabilization Mission in Haiti), to help the transitional government to stabilize the situation.

In hindsight, when political deadlock first ensued in 1996–1997, international actors should have encouraged Haitian civil society, particularly the Catholic and Protestant Churches, to play a more active role in bridging political divides. Instead, international mediators undertook informal efforts to negotiate between Aristide and the primary breakaway *lavalas* faction, the OPL, and left aside both other political actors and key elements of civil society. These efforts did not yield significant or quick results, and often left all parties pointing at external actors as unnecessarily meddlesome in Haitian affairs.

In recognition of this factor, MINUSTAH now includes in its mandate support for a concerted national dialogue effort. Efforts to launch this dialogue have been extremely slow, however, as Haitian stakeholders have harboured differing conceptions of the objectives and format of the dialogue. These conceptions have been determined largely by a failure to reconcile narrowly defined perspectives on self-interest with those of the collective, thus pointing to an almost pervasive absence of capability and skills on the part of both official actors and civil society for constructive negotiation, consensus formation, and focused dialogue.

Analysis: Current and future roles of the militaries in post-conflict peacebuilding in Guatemala and Haiti

The Guatemalan military

In January 2003 the US State Department urged the Guatemalan government to take concrete steps to curb outlaw networks suspected as consisting primarily of former and current army officials who had moved to make Guatemala one of the primary points of transshipment of illegal drugs into the USA, and who had launched a campaign of intimidation and assassination to silence opponents.[27] Subsequently, only the autonomous human rights ombudsman took any concrete steps. He issued a request to the United Nations and the OAS to support an independent commission to look into the activities of these networks.

A number of factors may have led the Guatemalan military towards illegal activities. The report of the Catholic Church's Human Rights Commission's "Guatemala, Never Again!: Recovery of Historical Memory (REMHI)" project points to important splits within the military leadership during the war and in the post-war period that greatly enabled the onset of Guatemalan democracy. Rios Montt's coup against Garcia in 1982, and Mejia Victores's counter-coup in 1983, marked factional struggles within the armed forces between traditional and reformist elements.[28] The period preceding the 1995 election also saw an intensified power struggle between the "constitutionalist" or "reformist" army officers, allied with modernizing businessmen, and the traditional commercial and military oligarchy.

The partnership between a new class of military officers and an equally new class of businessmen was perhaps the driving factor behind Guatemala's political reform. Arguably, Guatemala has consistently been run not by its formal governmental bodies but by a military-business commercial project. Hence, to the extent that a fundamental democratic transformation took place in Guatemala in the 1980s and 1990s, it was less an institutional than an attitudinal transformation, altering the objectives of key elements of the country's power élite. An important contributory factor was the USA's altered post-Cold War attitude, whereby it did not tolerate the military's violent policies.

The subsequent shrinkage of the military's traditional economic role perhaps accounts best for the alleged engagement of some of its elements with illicit narcotics networks. Due to the country's rapid economic growth in the 1990s, the number of economic interest groups has greatly increased, thus making the economy less susceptible to oligarchic control. In addition, to the extent that the army's role in the political process has been formally reduced, it can no longer dominate the economy as publicly as it may have done in the past.

A key factor also contributing to military malaise is that many of the officer corps viewed themselves as having won the war against the URNG. They therefore saw the 1996 accords as being primarily about giving a group of upstart reformers a platform and a means for doing an end-run around the traditional power centres. While reformist officers supported the accords and their implementation, there was no wider institutional agreement – especially among the different factions in the military itself – on the proper role for the Guatemalan army once its traditional role as the militia for the coffee oligarchy was no longer economically or politically valid. While the accords did include a series of provisions on the proper subjection of the armed forces to the constitution, these did not represent a fundamental agreement with, or involve the participation of, any of the country's traditional power centres or the various factions within the military itself.

Consequently, Guatemala now faces the prospect of an increasingly disaffected but disciplined army, with little to expend its energies on except organized crime. However, given the strong hemispheric regional consensus against non-constitutional transfers of power, the army is unlikely to mount an overt challenge to Guatemalan democracy. More likely, factions within the military will continue to struggle among themselves over the extent of the government's reform programme. Hence, the degree to which Guatemala's elected civilian government can effect meaningful change will depend on the degree to which wider multisectoral consensus on the further evolution of the Guatemalan political system can be achieved. International support for Guatemala should now focus on the development of this consensus.

First, the divisive land question should be systematically addressed. Pragmatic local initiatives for resolving land disputes and encouraging micro-enterprise that have been undertaken by some in the business community, as well as some of the indigenous communities, should receive active support and encouragement from international donors.

Second, dialogues on the future of Guatemalan governance should be supported at all levels of society, and should be used as forums for building skills for peaceful dispute resolution. Several Guatemalan leaders have proposed the creation of local analogues of SEPAZ (Secretariat of Peace), the national peace secretariat created to implement the accords of 1996, in all of Guatemala's districts. These mini-peace offices could combine informal dispute resolution and arbitration with human rights monitoring and community policing functions, relieving the overstressed judicial system.[29]

It is especially critical that such dialogue and training involve elements from the military and commercial oligarchy. The increasingly negative view of them held by the USA, which continues to be the country's primary political and economic interlocutor, should help to make these hardline constituencies more amenable to such participation. In 2003, for instance, the USA had already revoked visas for a number of top military officers.

Third, Guatemala needs a significantly speeded-up programme for the reform of its justice system. International support for the training of a new national civilian police force has yielded uneven results in improving police effectiveness. The problem may be partly that policing has been conceived as a national function in Guatemala, rather than a community responsibility as in the USA. While the national format may arguably suit smaller countries such as Guatemala, the weak national institutional context of a post-conflict environment also means that such police forces are vulnerable to corruption and political manipulation. A national format may need to be supplemented. The cohesion of rural communities presents many possibilities for instituting effective policing. Community policing could be more participatory, and lead to greater public confidence in law enforcement. However nefarious their origins and purpose, the civil defence patrols created by the army in the 1980s point to the possibilities, in a less repressive environment, wherein communities could manage their own security.

The role of the USA in all of this will be critical. After the Cold War, US emphasis on maintaining both political and economic freedoms has provided an important basis for the domestic consensus that has supported Guatemala's peace process, and the USA should continue to maintain a strong position against any resort to violence by parties in Guatemala and to support dialogue and consensus building.

The Haitian army and its remnants

When the USA intervened in Haiti in the early twentieth century, it disbanded the old army and created the more interventionist Garde Nationale d'Haiti, whose primary function was to control the rural labour force. After US withdrawal, the Garde Nationale became the Forces Armée d'Haiti, a still sharper tool for internal repression. President Aristide abolished this army in 1995. Its rank and file blended into the new Haitian National Police, or into private security firms. Much of its top leadership left the country. During this entire period, however, the oligarchy that it had protected remained aloof and disengaged from the Haitian polity. Initiatives to engage these élites with the rest of the country, or to break and marginalize the economic monopolies that have sustained them, are essential to further political and economic reform.

Significantly, the transitional government has not had much success either in bringing the oligarchy into a national dialogue. In addition, due to its initial heavy-handed measures against former officials of the *lavalas* government, it has incurred the suspicion and fear of the *lavalas* followers. To complicate the situation even further, the remnants of the army, demanding a reconstitution of the armed forces, have not demobilized, and have expressed their lack of support for the transitional government.

The oligarchy continues to feel deeply threatened by the discourse on reform, and feels insufficiently secure to participate in a dialogue on political change. In part, this insecurity results from the failure of the possibly transformational interlude in Haitian politics from 1990 to 1991. Aristide was catapulted to power in the 1990 elections not on the basis of party politics but as the promised vanguard of a new regime that would fundamentally transform the polity. These expectations, reflected in Aristide's "flood" rhetoric, contradicted the gradualist approach of both those members of the *lavalas* alliance who belonged to the small but growing middle class and the few progressive elements among the traditional élite. The elected government of 1990–1991, therefore, embodied a fundamental contradiction. It sought to address popular demands for overwhelming social and economic change through the forms and institutions of electoral democracy, which traditionally postdate such change and are ill-adapted to rapid and radical transformation. This contradiction was perpetuated in 1994 when Aristide was restored to power. Haiti's small middle class remained apprehensive of runaway populism. Aristide won the popular vote in the parliamentary and presidential elections of 2000, but lacked the confidence of the business and middle classes whose entrepreneurial and managerial talent is essential for Haiti's economic revival.

The transitional government's promises to hold new national elections by the end of 2005 have not led to a new confidence among these classes. However, elections are not the central issue; the underlying problem is the different social sectors' near-total lack of confidence in each other's objectives and intentions. The transitional government has not been able to generate this confidence. The élites remain apprehensive of a populist comeback during the next elections, especially since the formerly anti-Aristide parties have not used the momentum created by Aristide's hasty departure to generate a viable political strategy, and *lavalas* remnants remain the only credibly organized political force in the country.

A starting point for confidence building would be to work towards consensus on a few pragmatic issues whereby the state can direct its limited resources and energies towards providing security and primary capital such as roads, education, and micro-credit lending. The provision of such goods should benefit all classes and sectors, and allow for real growth in the Haitian economy. Discourse centred on such public goods may also allow for Haiti's national debates to move from the divisive discourse of wealth redistribution to that of more equitable opportunities for wealth creation.

The United Nations in Haiti, especially MINUSTAH and the UN Development Programme, has recently taken some concrete steps towards assisting the transitional government in moving in this direction by supporting the establishment of a technical secretariat for the dialogue process. In addition to bringing together expertise in dialogue processes from the region and subregion, the secretariat should support national actors and the leaders of the different sectors in acquiring lasting capabilities for consensus formation and consensus negotiation. In the absence, for instance, of a national mediation commission (advocated by former Prime Minister Jacques Edouard Alexis) or a national network of mediators, practically all disagreements manifest themselves as demonstrations and counter-demonstrations, with the institutions of state serving as bystanders at best and interested parties at worst.

While Haiti lacks an indigenous population like that of Guatemala, its rural population historically has been divorced from political life. It has also borne the brunt of Haiti's political and economic mismanagement. Lack of investment and reform in agriculture means that Haiti has never had a system for adjudicating disputes over land titles or for long-term efforts to conserve the soil. Also, the state has provided no services to enable farmers to capitalize on the phenomenon of voluntary work-gangs or *konbite*,[30] which are convened by rural communities during times of particular stress, and which augur well for cooperative investing, marketing, and even profit-sharing. Appropriately targeted credit, and the conversion of informal holdings to formal titles, could lead peasants in parts of the country both to revive and to expand market production.

In the course of Aristide's departure and the formation of the transitional government, the Haitian National Police practically collapsed. Aristide loyalists as well as anti-Aristide insurgents occupied and ransacked police stations as state authority collapsed in the provinces. Many police fled or joined the insurgents. Subsequently, sufficient numbers of police have returned to work, and enough police stations have been restored with UN assistance, that the police is a viable entity once again. However, it is clearly not capable of performing its expected tasks. Given the fact that many members of the HNP (Haitian National Police) were recruited from the former army, and some fled its ranks to join the remobilized insurgents, the overall effectiveness of the HNP, and its ability to perform without political interference, could be closely linked to the success of the UN-supported national dialogue process and the development of a consensus on the place of the military, and especially its social backers, in the life of the country. In addition, several officers of the HNP have become involved in drug trafficking.[31] In fact, drug-related corruption reportedly extended through all levels of the Aristide government, and the transitional government has had only modest success in dealing with the problem.

Given the overall dereliction of the Haitian political system, the only short-term solutions to controlling the drug problem lie among Haiti's neighbours. One possibility is to engage private professional security firms from among Haiti's neighbours to perform interdiction duties immediately outside Haiti's territorial waters. Another, less politically cumbersome, proposal might involve training and resourcing Haiti's small customs force, which has reputedly performed heroically in daunting circumstances. Some have suggested creating a special security force, drawn from the police, for protecting senior government officials, leaders of political parties, and other high-profile political personalities. However, this carries the risk of becoming a "praetorian guard". One short-term tactic for combating impunity could be the revival of a domestic version of the type of human rights monitoring and observation carried out by international groups in the early 1990s. Representatives of civic organizations could accompany personalities considered at particular risk – because of their efforts to combat narco-trafficking – as a deterrent to attack.

An important step in unblocking the current political drift could be for the international community, which has rarely done so in the past, to engage the full spectrum of Haitian society so as to keep the primary political protagonists on their toes and accountable for their words and actions. To the extent that all political actors in Haiti make their claims on behalf of the Haitian population, the latter might be in a better position to call them to order than the international community alone.

In fact, the best long-term prospects for democratization in Haiti may lie with civil society. For instance, the informal 1999 accord that paved the way for elections in 2000 arose partly from small-scale efforts towards multisectoral dialogue supported by the International Peace Academy. This dialogue also assisted in the formation of an autonomous civil society group, the National Council for Electoral Observation, which successfully promoted voter education before the parliamentary elections in 2000, and then performed credibly its primary function of electoral observation. It also convened La Fanmi Lavalas and its opponents in informal meetings prior to the elections to obtain guarantees from all sides to ensure a peaceful electoral process. Given the overall level of political tension, the elections were remarkably free of violence. Subsequently, this dialogue also yielded a civic initiative to assist with the facilitation of negotiations to end the deadlock between Aristide and the opposition in January 2001 which, for the first time, involved both the mainstream Catholic and Protestant Churches in a joint facilitation role. Subsequently, as the Aristide government displayed authoritarian tendencies in 2003–2004, civic actors played a crucial role in the mass mobilization of protest against the government, and in uniting around common platforms aimed at safeguarding Haiti's fragile democracy.

In addition to a wider role for civil society, social consensus could also be built through localized schemes that bring the country's sizeable informal economy into the economic mainstream, by giving informal entrepreneurs titles to their assets and registering them so that they are eligible for assistance, such as small loans and credit, on easy terms. Prominent examples include a plan developed jointly by the Aristide government and the Center for Free Enterprise and Democracy with the assistance of economist Hernando de Soto to formalize informal property holdings; and the significant expansion of its loan portfolio by one of the country's largest commercial banks, Sogebank, to include micro-entrepreneurs.[32] The transitional government and MINUSTAH should revisit these worthwhile proposals.

In Haiti, as in Guatemala, alternative forms of political participation that aid the process of institution building are needed *until* the formal institutions acquire the desired capacity. These alternative forms of participation can be generated within the context of existing policies. For instance, the implementation of specific international initiatives to address the problems of development in Haiti could be accompanied by broad-based dialogues among the sectors most likely to be affected by them.[33] Such interaction could eventually form the basis for consensual national frameworks for social and economic action.

An important factor that constrains the potential of Haiti's civil society and its communities is the persistent tendency on the part of the political élite – both La Fanmi Lavalas and its opponents, as well as remnants of the army and the old oligarchy – to try and discredit any civic initiative or activity that they are not able to control. For instance, in 2002 the launch of a coalition of over 100 civic organizations to promote a wider national consensus around a social contract was immediately accompanied by a call for a national conference – promoted by some civic organizations opposed to Aristide – to unblock the current political deadlock, a move reportedly favoured by some of Aristide's most intransigent detractors as a means of outflanking him. Immediately, Aristide denounced the coalition as an opposition grouping aiming to overthrow a democratically elected president. Instead of moving systematically, therefore, to develop a broad-based national consensus on key and divisive issues in a manner that transcended partisan politics, the process significantly stumbled over these politics at the very start.

In the near future, the only way to ensure that future civic initiatives fare better is for international organizations to provide – in a discreet manner and through projects aimed at building local capacity for sustainable development – the types of skills required to bring together divergent views, pull together a consensus around concrete issues, and move policy discussions beyond ideological roadblocks.

Conclusion

The comparison and analysis of the current straits of Guatemala and Haiti, and of the relations between key stakeholders, provide a number of interesting conclusions.

First, the military in Guatemala and Haiti has been not just an official institution but a social sector that at times has been synonymous with the state. Democratization in Haiti and Guatemala has therefore been quite different from those situations where the military has been distinct from an otherwise authoritarian state. South Africa, where the military had always been under civilian control and in fact assisted with democratization, is an example of the latter. In the former types of situations, it takes more than a political act such as the promulgation of a new constitution or the signing of a peace accord to redefine the military's role in society and politics. In fact, even the abolition of the military may not remove its influence from politics. What is needed in such situations is a profound new national consensus that includes both the military and its social backers, and which redefines the relationships between the social sectors as well as between these sectors and the state.

Second, consensus building of the type referred to above is not an overnight task. This is because in order for such processes to be credible and successful, they have to mobilize and engage not just the élite levels of political and civic leadership, but also leaders at grassroots and community levels. Attempts to build consensus in Haiti, for instance, have only engaged the élite in Port-au-Prince, and have found little currency among common Haitians. In order to ensure that these processes are truly participatory and long-lasting, international actors should be present on the ground for the long haul. Where the United Nations is concerned, efforts to support such processes should be undertaken by the UN's day-to-day presence in the country, through its operational agencies, rather than by peace operations that are involved only for a brief period, and whose deployment may cost more on a daily basis than the entire logistical needs of such processes for a whole year.

Third, consensus-building processes are unlikely to succeed unless all key international players, and especially the donors, are united behind them. The consistent international support by all key international players for the national constitutional dialogue in South Africa has been a critical element in ensuring the longevity of its outcomes. For Guatemala and Haiti, the involvement and support of the USA will be critical for ensuring the strength and credibility of any consensus-building exercise aimed at obtaining agreement between key social sectors on national policy issues.

Fourth, such exercises require appropriate training and technical expertise on the part of both participants and facilitators. Attempts by Haitian civil society to foster dialogue and consensus have foundered, for instance, in their early stages as participants have let them be viewed as vehicles for partisan agendas. Also, without exception, promoters of these exercises could in all instances have taken significant steps early on to guarantee their inclusivity and legitimacy if they had had the proper technical and political support from the international community. In Guatemala, with the momentum from the *Gran Dialogo Nacional* and other dialogue initiatives associated with the peace process having been expended, it is time for the country's donors to support a participatory review by all sectors of the accomplishments of the past 10 years. This review should be preceded by sustained support for building the capacities of all stakeholders for constructive negotiation and consensus formation. With sufficient international backing, it should be possible to obtain the participation of the military leadership, the commercial élite, and the oligarchic remnants in such a process, as it would allow them to rearticulate a position in national life and move beyond perceptions of having been excluded from the process that led to the peace accords in 1996.

Notes

1. The author works for the Bureau for Crisis Prevention and Recovery of the UN Development Programme. The views expressed here are strictly his own and not those of the UNDP.
2. McCreery, David. 1994. *Rural Guatemala: 1760–1940*. Stanford: Stanford University Press, pp. 50–51; also p. 326.
3. Aguilera Peralta, Gabriel and Edelberto Torres-Rivas. 1998. *Del Autoritarismo a la Paz*. Guatemala: FLACSO, pp. 14–15.
4. For more on the political economy of this episode, see Bulmer-Thomas, Victor. 1994. *The Political Economy of Central America Since 1920*. Cambridge: Cambridge University Press, pp. 33–35.
5. Costello, Patrick. 1999. *The Guatemalan Peace Process: Historical Background*, available at www.c-r.org/acc_guat/background.htm.
6. Aguilera Peralta and Torres-Rivas, note 3 above, p. 81.
7. Azpuru, Dinorah. 1999. "Peace and democratization in Guatemala", in Cynthia J. Arnson (ed.) *Comparative Peace Processes in Latin America*. Stanford: Stanford University Press, p. 102.
8. Aguilera Peralta and Torres-Rivas, note 3 above, pp. 90–95.
9. On the peace process, see Dunkerley, James. 1994. *The Pacification of Central America*. London: Verso, pp. 76–88.
10. Historical Clarification Commission. 1999. *Guatemala – Memory of Silence (Tz'inil Na'tab'al): Report of the Commission for Historical Clarification, Conclusions and Recommendations*. Guatemala City: HCC, available at http://shr.aaas.org/guatemala/ceh/report/english/toc.html.
11. Jonas, Susanne. 2000. *Of Centaurs and Doves: Guatemala's Peace Process*. Boulder, CO: Westview Press, p. 210. Jonas also provides a detailed analysis of the referendum and its implications.
12. Trouillot, Michel-Rolph. 1990. *Haiti – State Against Nation: The Origins and Legacy of Duvalierism*. New York: Monthly Review Press, pp. 49–50.
13. *Ibid.*, pp. 44–48.
14. For arguments in support of an assembly-manufacturing-led growth strategy for Haiti, see Gray, Clive. 1997. "Alternative models for Haiti's economic reconstruction", in Robert Rotberg (ed.) *Haiti Renewed: Political and Economic Prospects*. Washington, DC: Brookings Institution Press; Lundahl, Mats. 1997. "The Haitian dilemma re-examined", in Robert Rotberg (ed.) *Haiti Renewed: Political and Economic Prospects*. Washington, DC: Brookings Institution Press.
15. Dupuy, Alex. 1994. "Free trade and underdevelopment in Haiti: The World Bank/USAID agenda for social change in the post-Duvalier era", in Hilbourne A.

Watson (ed.) *The Caribbean in the Global Political Economy*. Boulder, CO: Lynne Rienner.

16. According to Trouillot, "By ignoring the problems of the rural world and the relationship between it and the urban classes, the light industry strategy in the end complicated them." Trouillot, note 12 above, p. 210.

17. Maguire, Robert, Edwige Balutansky, Jacques Fomerand, Larry Minear, William G. O'Neill, Thomas C. Weiss, and Sarah Zaidi. 1996. *Haiti Held Hostage: International Responses to the Quest for Nationhood 1986–1996*, Occasional Paper No. 23. Providence, RI: Thomas J. Watson Jr Institute for International Studies, p. 8.

18. A review article by Peter M. Lewis that surveys several recent volumes which draw lessons from the experience of promoting development and economic reform in Africa points to the nature of governance in a society – the institutions of the state, the relations between these institutions and the people, and the social coalitions that engender these relations – as key variables in determining the path of economic reform. Lewis, Peter M. 1996. "Economic reform and political transition in Africa: The quest for a politics of development", *World Politics*, Vol. 49, October, pp. 92–129.

19. Dupuy, Alex. 1997. *Haiti in the New World Order: The Limits of the Democratic Revolution*. Boulder, CO: Westview Press, pp. 97–98.

20. For an account of the international community's role in these elections, see Malone, David. 1998. *Decision-Making in the UN Security Council: The Case of Haiti, 1990–1997*. Oxford: Clarendon Press, pp. 50–54.

21. Schulz, Donald E. and Gabriel Marcella. 1994. *Reconciling the Irreconcilable: The Troubled Outlook for US Policy Toward Haiti*. Carlisle, PA: Strategic Studies Institute, US Army War College, 10 March, p. 12.

22. *Ibid.*, pp. 9–11.

23. The most comprehensive and critical analysis of these sanctions and their impact is offered by Gibbons, Elizabeth D. 1999. *Sanctions in Haiti: Human Rights and Democracy Under Assault*. Westport, CT: Praeger.

24. A critical assessment of the role of the multinational force in dealing with insecurity in Haiti is provided in Shacochis, Bob. 1999. *The Immaculate Invasion*. New York: Viking Books.

25. On 19 August 1997 the United Nations suspended electoral assistance to Haiti until the provisional electoral council could establish that it was capable of holding free and fair elections. Norton, Michael. 1997. "UN suspends election aid in Haiti", Associated Press, 22 August.

26. An interesting explanation for disputes among current Haitian politicians has been offered by Andrew Reding, who suggests that Haiti's winner-take-all electoral system, as opposed to the kind of proportional representation system that prevails in South Africa, is putting heavy stress on a nascent democracy. Reding, Andrew. 1996. "Exorcising Haiti's ghosts", *World Policy Journal*, Spring, p. 21.

27. See Johnson, Tim. 2003. "Outlaw threat described: US urges Guatemala to pursue global probe of criminal bands", *Miami Herald*, 30 January.

28. See Archdiocese of Guatemala. 1999. *Guatemala – Never Again!: REMHI, Recovery of Historical Memory Project*. Maryknoll, NY/Guatemala City: Orbis Books/Human Rights Office of the Archdiocese of Guatemala, p. 269.

29. Promising models exist for this elsewhere. For a tiny fraction of its development budget, India has supported a very successful experiment called *panchayati raj* in village communities, where the reach of the formal legal system is often tenuous. Closer to Guatemala, the OAS successfully promoted a similar experiment in community-level governance in post-war Nicaragua, combining human rights monitoring and dispute resolution functions.

30. Catholic Institute for International Relations. 1996. *Haiti – Building Democracy*, CIIR Comment, February. London: Catholic Institute for International Relations, p. 23.

31. According to the US State Department's International Narcotics Control Strategy Report for 2000, "Cocaine flow through Haiti decreased from 13 per cent to 8 per cent of the total detected flow in 2000, but little of this is attributable to the efforts of the Haitian Government. Despite this decrease, Haiti's location combined with extreme poverty, corruption, and limited law enforcement and justice capability continue to make Haiti a major transshipment point for South American narcotics, especially Colombian cocaine."

32. The bank, which currently has as clients 700 street-side sellers of a variety of goods, plans to raise its roster to 10,000 by 2002, a sign of the commercial success of this programme. See Gonzalez, David. 2001. "Port-au-Prince journal: A Haitian bank takes to the streets", *New York Times*, 17 April.

33. Some USAID projects in recent years had begun to show a laudable trend towards more participatory project implementation in Haiti. See Whitfield, Mimi. 1997. "Clean water, garbage pickup slated for Cite Soleil slum", *Miami Herald*, 3 November.

Part IV

Experiences from Asia: Cambodia, East Timor, and Afghanistan

14

Security sector reform in Cambodia

Sophie Richardson and Peter Sainsbury

Cambodia is no longer at war, but it remains a long way from peace. However, its bloated, costly, and corrupt security forces are as much a part of the problem as they are part of the solution. Cambodian human rights organizations and the United Nations continue to document the regular involvement of the security forces in crimes ranging from corruption to murder, and men in uniforms continue to instil fear rather than inspire confidence. Despite the demise of the Khmer Rouge in the late 1990s, there have been few substantive discussions assessing Cambodia's national security needs and appropriate military reform. Because these forces play an integral part in propping up the regime of the ruling Cambodian People's Party (CPP), there is strong domestic resistance to any meaningful reform. Recent international efforts to trim the Cambodian military and its budget have failed utterly. Because donors were unwilling to grapple with the reality that under Cambodia's thin veneer of democracy lay a military regime, and because donors could only conceive of security sector reforms in terms of public expenditure, these efforts quickly faltered.

This chapter argues that international efforts to undertake security sector reform must begin with a realistic assessment of a country's security needs. Such an assessment must take into account a country's military and political history, and a recognition that such reform can threaten deeply entrenched interests. It also argues that is vital to involve the military in the reform process. Failure to do so will result in resistance from military commanders to change, fuelled by mistrust and fear. The advantages of a rationalized, professional institution, subordinate to civilian control, to a state like Cambodia are considerable, but efforts to create that cannot be achieved in isolation from other political reforms. As such, discussions about reforming the security sector must be included in public debates about subordinating all government institutions to genuine, democratic, civilian control.

This chapter provides a brief summary of recent Cambodian political history and a description of the current Cambodian security forces. It then critiques recent internationally driven efforts to rationalize the military and suggests improvements for similar efforts.

Background

It is important to examine the historical picture of Cambodia, if only briefly, to understand that there is no tradition of a professional, civilian-controlled military that serves the national interest, and to identify accurately the ongoing sources of violence in the country. A failure to understand the former has contributed to the failed demobilization efforts, while an inadequate grasp on the latter has led senior international officials, such as the former head of the UN's Cambodia Office of the High Commissioner for Human Rights (UNCOHCHR), to suggest that Cambodians are genetically predisposed towards violence.[1]

Cambodia achieved independence from France in 1953, at which time the then Prince Sihanouk began his official domination of the country. Sihanouk's rule is often spoken of fondly, yet that perspective ignores the reality of the violence and political oppression that characterized his regime. Sihanouk's secret police were brutal in their repression of dissent. The number of peasants killed by his army when they crushed a revolt in Battambang in 1967 has never been established, but it is estimated to be as high as 10,000, including some for whom Sihanouk quite literally paid a bounty per head.[2] His secret police's repression of the left from 1967 to 1970 was similarly brutal.

But it is not so much the violence of Sihanouk's regime that has so affected Cambodia today, but rather the concept of the "god-king" that he embodied. At independence, often a crucial time to shift state power out of the hands of individuals and into institutions such as an independent judiciary, a representative assembly, and civilian control over the security apparatus, Sihanouk instead opted to follow the lead of his royal forebears. He abused the traditional affection and respect Cambodians had for their monarch, and ran the country in a dictatorial fashion. Throughout the 1950s and 1960s, institutions that could have allowed for a degree of popular input were established, but were quickly curtailed whenever a potential challenge to Sihanouk emerged. Establishing himself as the sole arbiter of what was right for the country meant that state power and agencies, including the armed forces, remained in an individual's control. Those who did not agree with Sihanouk saw revolution as the only alternative – a path that was soon chosen.

Complicating matters was the war in neighbouring Viet Nam and its spillover into Cambodia. Sihanouk was reasonably successful in keeping Cambodia isolated from the nearby hostilities. In 1969 that isolation ended violently with the American bombing of Cambodia, which William Shawcross documented extensively in his book *Sideshow*.[3] During the four-year attack hundreds of thousands of bombs were dropped; all areas suffered except for some remote uninhabited parts of the Cardamom Mountains. Again, there has been no authoritative death toll but tens, and possibly hundreds, of thousands perished. It is hard to gauge the effect of this slaughter, but it is certainly reasonable to assume the Khmer Rouge found a number of recruits among those who suffered.

After a comprehensive bombing campaign – justified as being necessary to attack North Vietnamese military units sheltering in Cambodia – the USA backed a coup against Prince Sihanouk and installed General Lon Nol as president. This move was followed by extensive military aid to the Lon Nol regime. However, the regime was beset with corruption, and military leaders and politicians made substantial sums by selling military hardware, food, and medical supplies to the North Vietnamese and the Khmer Rouge.[4] Millions of dollars in US aid to the regime were stolen and military hardware was sold to the enemy Khmer Rouge. Reports of frontline troops being so hungry that they had turned to cannibalism were not uncommon. It did not take long for Lon Nol's forces to be overwhelmed by the more disciplined and committed Khmer Rouge.

The Khmer Rouge achieved victory on 17 April 1975. The excesses of that regime have been well documented.[5] Up to 2 million people died in the three years, eight months, and 20 days that they were in power. The entire intellectual base of the country was either exterminated or fled as pogroms destroyed anyone with an education or a government position. Other people were killed in the anarchy that surrounded the Khmer Rouge's assumption of power. The Khmer Rouge's insanity finally proved their undoing when their repeated and vicious attacks on border areas of Viet Nam prompted a swift response from Hanoi. The Khmer Rouge were no match for the battle-hardened, disciplined, and well-equipped Vietnamese army, which invaded in December 1978. Within two weeks of the Christmas assault, the Khmer Rouge had been reduced to a guerrilla force living in the hills.

Hanoi quickly established the People's Republic of Kampuchea (PRK), and for the next 10 years the country was run by a regime headed by

Cambodians but buoyed by tens of thousands of Vietnamese troops. The Khmer Rouge managed to maintain a guerrilla war from their bases in Thailand. They eventually joined with forces loyal to Sihanouk and forces loyal to Son Sann – a former prime minister. The three factions formed an uneasy alliance and managed to secure continued international recognition for their partner, the Khmer Rouge, as the official government of Cambodia at the United Nations. They also secured substantial aid from China, America, Malaysia, Singapore, and Thailand. Ostensibly, the alliance's 15,000–20,000 troops were meant to battle the Vietnamese, but they were never able to transcend their factional differences to form a cohesive fighting force. On occasion, the factions were too preoccupied fighting each other to focus on the Vietnamese.

While the PRK regime was less murderous than that of the Khmer Rouge, it was by no means benign. Unlawful detentions, forced labour, conscription into military service, brutal suppression of political dissent, and killings contributed to Cambodians' already deep resentment of the Vietnamese occupation. Throughout the 1980s the pipeline of aid from the Soviet Union to Viet Nam, and thus from Viet Nam to Cambodia, began to slow. In order to maintain its hold on power while gradually gaining more autonomy from Hanoi, staving off popular dissent, and fighting the resistance across the country, the PRK's leaders invested considerable resources in developing its own police, surveillance, and military capacity.[6] It was time and money well spent, given that the Cambodian security forces developed during this time would be key to placing – and keeping – members of the PRK leadership in power for decades to come.

In 1989 a combination of international pressure and the high financial cost of occupation led to the Vietnamese decision to pull out of Cambodia. Following this announcement, peace talks were scheduled between border-based resistance fighters, the Vietnamese-backed government in Phnom Penh, and the international community. The 1991 Paris Peace Accords led to what at the time was believed to be an end to the war. They also marked the beginning of massive assistance from the international community for Cambodia.

The UN Transitional Authority for Cambodia (UNTAC) took charge from 28 February 1991, launching a $3 billion programme of reconstruction, peacekeeping, refugee repatriation, and preparations for free and independent elections. UNTAC had laudable goals, but its success was limited, particularly with respect to the status of the security forces. Most of the international participants in the Paris peace talks appear to have grasped the importance of a unified military to the future of Cambodia's political development; the factions themselves were clearly disingenuous when they pledged to form a unified force immediately. In principle, UNTAC's mandate covered many of the important issues at stake: to implement and maintain a cease-fire, end outside assistance to the warring factions, disarm and demobilize the various factions' armies, canton weapons, reintegrate the demobilized soldiers, and establish a neutral political environment. But UNTAC had no stomach for fighting between factions resistant to disarmament and its peacekeeping troops. One of the more immediate disturbing results of this failure to implement its mandate was that the Khmer Rouge managed to increase their control from 5 per cent to 20 per cent of the country during the UNTAC period. The larger problem was that all four factions, most notably from the Khmer Rouge and the Cambodian People's Party (CPP, the post-Paris incarnation of the PRK leadership), survived the UNTAC era with their individual armies largely intact. Yet another opportunity to establish a national army under civilian control had been missed.

Hundreds of people died in political violence in advance of and following the 1993 elections. The CPP, under the leadership of Hun Sen, failed to win a clear majority. By threatening to restart the civil war, however, the party maintained its power, and although the resulting government was ostensibly a coalition, Funcinpec, the royalist party, and its leader, Prince Norodom Ranariddh, had no domestic infrastructure comparable to what the CPP had built in the 1980s. Despite pledges to unify the army and demobilize excess troops, the two parties maintained separate chains of command through the military, police, and gendarmerie. Both built up large private bodyguard units, and all manner of security forces continued to be implicated in gross human rights abuses. In March 1997 Hun Sen's bodyguards were implicated in an assassination attempt against opposition politician Sam Rainsy in which 19 bystanders were killed;[7] three months later, Hun Sen launched a successful coup against his co-prime minister Norodom Ranariddh. International observers and human rights organizations documented the administrative manipulations and intimidations that contributed to CPP victories at the polls in 1998 and 2003. Although Cambodia has had three national elections since 1993, power remains highly concentrated in CPP hands.

Thus, in several important respects, Cambodia's political structure has not changed since the mid-1980s, largely because the CPP has never been forced to relinquish control over the security forces. As a result, it is easy for the regime to stave off any and all challengers. It was a failure to acknowledge this reality – that changing the security forces could be deeply threatening to people who have enjoyed absolute and uninterrupted control over the country for 20 years – that guaranteed the failure of recent international efforts to promote demobilization.

It is equally important to bear in mind that the security forces are not the only institution that consistently fails to serve the Cambodian people. Decades of personalized and factional politics have only reinforced deeply entrenched systems of patronage instituted during the colonial era, and the majority of Cambodians are still forced to rely on individual patrons, rather than institutions, for their survival. And given the obvious connections between members of the security forces and the political hierarchy – replicated from the national to the village level – few Cambodians expect impartial defence from men in uniform, particularly if the source of their problems involves men in uniform. But neither can they expect assistance from the Ministry of Justice or state-run welfare agencies. The former is so partisan it will not challenge members of the ruling party or their subordinates, while the latter are barely functional. Until the link between the security forces and partisan interests is broken, the Cambodian state will not serve the Cambodian people. Demobilization, weapons reduction, and good governance and building civil society must go hand in hand – alone each is doomed to failure.

The current status and structure of the Cambodian security forces

The Ministries of National Defence (MOND) and of the Interior (MOI), each of which has oversight over segments of the security forces, are in principle supposed to be devoted to national, rather than individual or partisan, interests. Yet the ministries continue to be run by co-ministers, one from the CPP and the other from Funcinpec. This is meant to create a semblance of cross-party cooperation, but in practice it allows the CPP to retain almost complete dominance over the forces and for Funcinpec to share in some of the spoils of military graft.

The Cambodian security forces include the Royal Cambodian Armed Forces (RCAF), the national police force, and the gendarmerie (paramilitary police). The MOI oversees the roughly 60,000 police and 10,000 gendarmes, while the MOND manages the RCAF. The RCAF officially comprises some 130,000 troops (this number will be discussed in more detail later) across three services: the army, navy, and air force. The army is far larger than the other two services, which maintain only a handful of seaworthy patrol boats and sky-worthy helicopters, two-seater trainers, and small transport aircraft.[8] The total number of bodyguards is not currently known, but these units are in principle under the control of the MOND. The RCAF's forces are in theory under the command of a single commander-in-chief. Until recently, Hun Sen served in this position, but in 1999 he handed the position to General Ke Kim Yan. Generals Tea Banh (CPP) and Nhek Bun Chhay (Funcinpec) currently serve as the co-Ministers of Defence.

The country is divided into six military regions, each of which oversees several subdivisions. But the patronage that pervades other institutions is replicated in the military as well, and regional commanders tend to operate as individual franchises rather than as part of a truly unified national command. Appointment to a high-level position in the RCAF is often bestowed on people as a reward for cash payments or services, such as political assassinations or delivering blocks of votes, to the CPP leadership, irrespective of any ability the recipient might have as a military commander. The military has more officers than enlisted soldiers, and few of these officers have received any formal training.

Generally, the lower-level soldiers are not expected to devote all of their time to the military. Low salaries of about $20 a month, which are sometimes not paid at all, force most soldiers to spend their time making a living. Those who serve on posts near their homes typically farm to make money, but many more soldiers work for their commanders in far more lucrative and illegal endeavours such as extortion, prostitution, and trafficking in humans, narcotics, artefacts, gems, and timber. As long as these soldiers share a necessary cut with their commanders, the behaviour is not discouraged. At the same time, there are few options for ordinary soldiers to opt out if their commanding officers demand their participation in criminal activities.

Further divisions in the loyalties of Cambodia's soldiers are determined by the political affiliations of the various factions. The CPP faction of the RCAF replicates the political subdivisions of the party, dividing according to affiliations with Prime Minister Hun Sen, with former senior minister Chea Sim, or with Deputy Prime Minister Sar Kheng. Until the 1997 coup Funcinpec (the royalist political party lead by Sihanouk's son, Norodom Ranariddh) had its own troops, many of whom became disgruntled by their treatment from Prince Ranariddh, whom they saw as abandoning them after the 1997 coup. The former Khmer Rouge remain loyal to individual commanders. These affinities are somewhat fluid – for example, members of Hun Sen's personal bodyguard unit have far greater loyalty to him personally than to the CPP. The lack of allegiance to a national, non-partisan chain of command is clear.

In addition to being corrupt, untrained, ill-equipped, and unsure of their role, the security forces are also a massive drain on the Cambodian budget. Throughout the 1990s, the RCAF alone soaked up 60 per cent of the state's annual expenditures,[9] despite promises to cut back and transfer the savings to the perpetually underfunded ministries dealing with public health, education, and welfare. One analyst has also noted that the RCAF continues to benefit handsomely from access to other state resources, such as individual tax exemptions, control of lucrative tariff collection at border crossings, and the use of state land.[10]

Because there are no common standards for engaging in bilateral military assistance, the RCAF has the ability to shop around for the most friendly and least demanding donors. For example, the USA had provided assistance to the RCAF through its International Military Education and Training (IMET) programme, but this was suspended following the 1997 coup, while over the past decade aid and training from China's People's Liberation Army (PLA) have steadily increased. France has continuously provided military aid and training since 1993. The lack of common standards sends mixed messages. Some donors opted to express their displeasure with the 1997 coup by cutting off military aid, but because not all donors took this position, no serious disciplinary message was adequately conveyed. Even those that have tried to take a tougher position with respect to the Cambodian military have allowed business imperatives to soften that stance. Despite the Australian government's decision to suspend military aid to Cambodia, the Cambodian co-Defence Minister Tea Banh had no trouble making a number of visits to Australia in 2000 as the guest of the Australian oil company Woodside Petroleum, which is interested in Cambodia's oil reserves.[11]

Demobilization

The push for demobilization finally came not as a result of a consensus among the Cambodian political or military that reform was necessary, nor out of broad international concern over the security forces' involvement in human rights abuses and trafficking. In 1997 the International Monetary Fund (IMF) insisted on budgetary rationalization and identified excessive military spending as a key to reallocating scarce governmental resources. In order to meet IMF requirements that ensured continued support for the National Bank of Cambodia, the Cambodian government – in effect, the CPP – would have to agree to reduce the security forces by tens of thousands.

It was the World Bank's Post-Conflict Unit, now known as the Conflict Prevention and Reconstruction Unit, which was seeking opportunities to promote itself within the World Bank, which succeeded where others had failed. Over a series of meetings at Hun Sen's home in early 1999, the co-Prime Minister agreed to a programme that would demobilize thousands of soldiers. It is unlikely that Hun Sen had experienced a revelation about the gross excesses the security forces cost his country. Rather, it is more plausible he and his senior advisers, having heard the initial description of the programme, spotted an extraordinarily simple opportunity to bilk money from an aid project.

In addition to the questionable imperatives of the financial institutions and equally suspect Cambodian government commitment, the very premise of a bloated military was deeply faulty. First, despite ample evidence to the contrary, donors believed that excess military spending was a result of an excess of soldiers – not an excess of corruption. The Cambodian government has continued to claim that it has a force of at least 130,000 soldiers, yet its own commanders admitted that the numbers are probably no greater than 40,000. As noted above, many of the soldiers who would in principle be demobilized had, in effect, already done so of their own volition. Not only would a demobilization programme not solve the problem, it was likely in effect to reward the corrupt practices that created the situation. Moreover, project designers believed that a direct reduction in the numbers in the military would yield a corresponding benefit in savings to the national budget, and that this matter was simply one of budgetary policy. Those who pushed for demobilization saw it merely as another exercise in reducing a bloated roster of public servants. They did not see it as a challenge to the ruling party's primary means of retaining power, a remarkable oversight given experiences of trying to slash rosters of civilian public servants elsewhere. Few seemed to foresee opportunities that the project itself presented for ongoing corruption in the security sector. Finally, the programme's initial architect had no military experience, dismissing such expertise as "unnecessary".

Nevertheless, the World Bank, which had been charged by the IMF to finance and manage the project, though not implement it, offered up its first three-step proposal in early 1999. Because the RCAF had no central roster, the first step was to create a comprehensive registration system. All soldiers would be issued with a new identity card and their information would be entered into a database. Second, 55,000 troops were to be demobilized over three years. Third, each demobilized solider would receive $1,200 worth of tangible assistance. Other aid agencies, such as GTZ and the World Food Programme, would actually implement different phases of the project.

The RCAF's leadership, which had not to date demonstrated any enthusiasm for the project, became considerably more interested at the prospect of being put in charge of disbursing over $60 million of cash and goods. Men across Cambodia began paying regional commanders to get on the lists of those to be demobilized so that they too could benefit. The World Bank later denied that such an approach was ever considered, yet the project's designer articulated precisely such a plan at a large conference in Phnom Penh in May 1999. Donors quickly quashed this approach.

The next incarnation of the project retained the idea of creating a central registry but revised what would be given to demobilized soldiers. Each soldier would receive approximately $240 cash, a "basic needs" package of food and household utensils, and the choice of a motorcycle, sewing machine, water pump, or house. Soldiers were also to receive a medical examination and referral to other state agencies for further treatment if required, and assistance in settling into their new lives, including job training. The revised approach would be tested through a pilot programme.

This plan appeared to be an improvement on the past one, and a total budget of $42 million was agreed upon. The Cambodian government would borrow $7 million to finance its part of the programme, $18 million of IDA credits would be extended, and the governments of Japan, the Netherlands, and Sweden pledged approximately $14 million, with local and international NGOs making up the balance. The Cambodian government established a general secretariat as its implementing agency. It appointed Sok An, the chairman of the Council of Ministers (Cambodia's cabinet), and Svay Sitha, a senior adviser to Sok An, to run the office. Neither man had served in the security forces. No RCAF officials were involved.

But as the project got under way in 2000, it proved to be riddled with errors, corruption, and a lack of transparency – much of which had been predicted by participants in the May 1999 conference. The registration that took place over the course of 2000 was surreal to some observers. At no point did the World Bank or its partners put in place mechanisms to verify whether the RCAF's numbers of soldiers were accurate. The process that was meant to weed out the "ghosts" from the RCAF's archaic lists of 140,693 service people simply took that number as a starting point. This number was reduced by about 10,000 when about 8,000 widows and children were transferred to the jurisdiction of the Ministry of Women's and Veterans' Affairs and 1,500 were demobilized in pilot programmes. Yet there was no reliable way to verify whether the 130,000 soldiers – or those on the lists submitted by regional commanders to be demobilized – had ever actually existed. It was similarly impossible to verify whether the 15,000 people who went through the pilot programmes had ever in fact actually been soldiers. It remained perfectly plausible that individuals at the general secretariat or the MOND could simply draft lists of names, organize men to register under those names, and thus make them eligible to be demobilized. The general secretariat resisted World Bank suggestions to audit the database, but resistance did not stop the forward march of the project throughout 2001.

The pilot programmes also revealed important flaws in the larger project. Not all soldiers got full health screenings, and few were required – as a result of a failure to designate to which agency this responsibility would fall – to hand in their weapons. Over the coming 18 months, increasing complaints were heard that the sewing machines, bicycles, and water pumps were either of poor quality or had failed to materialize at all. While job training was well intentioned, it could not do much given the disastrous state of the Cambodian economy. Questions persisted about why none of the more expensive, Phnom Penh-based troops were being demobilized, which should have been obvious given their political role. Similarly, analysts wondered why the leadership and staff members at the general secretariat were not suffering from the same resource shortages as provincial soldiers. Although the World Bank was presented with clear evidence of corruption related to goods procurement within the project in June 2002, it failed to act on this. It also failed to act on recommendations to make the project more transparent to local non-governmental organizations.

An internal review by the World Bank of the demobilization project in 2002 finally questioned the number of soldiers on the military roll. There were also concerns raised about procurement procedures and the transparency of the entire process. Until those matters were dealt with, the World Bank was increasingly unwilling to release funding, though these hesitations were never made public. The remainder of 2002 was devoted to World Bank and demobilization secretariat staff members arguing over auditing the programme's finances and the database. According to a World Bank staff member, an agreement was finally reached in late 2002 or early 2003 to a more transparent selection process of soldiers to be demobilized, but no headway was made on the issue of verifying the numbers and the database.

By this point, campaigns for the July 2003 national elections were getting under way. Although the World Bank managed to keep its other projects moving forward, and although only the most senior Cambodian official involved in the project was actually running for office, the World Bank accepted the government's explanation that it was too busy with the elections to address demobilization properly at that time.

Shortly before the elections, the World Bank finally publicly acknowledged corruption within the demobilization programme and demanded that the government pay back about $2.8 million it had improperly contracted and cancelled $6.3 million of credits. The specific charges revolved around events of precisely a year earlier, about which it had done nothing. Since that time the project has remained in limbo, supposedly as a result of the Cambodians' year-long political stalemate.

World Bank reports and officials' speeches in 2003 and 2004 continued to excoriate the Cambodian government for corruption, poor planning, and low capacity. Yet no references are made, even in the ubiquitous "lessons learned" sections of these documents, to comparable failings on the World Bank's part. Even after the Cambodian government announced in September 2004 that it planned to return to mandatory military service without completing any kind of demobilization process – a policy that makes commitments to reducing the military appear all the more tenuous – a $12 million loan still remains available. The only entity known to have been definitively demobilized was the general secretariat.

Envisioning demobilization

Successful security sector reform in Cambodia was and is undoubtedly a great challenge. There are few other state agencies with such national infrastructural reach, and it is not in the CPP's interest to allow that power to be eroded. Yet the World Bank's efforts represented yet another missed opportunity, one in which an accurate diagnosis of the problem, understood in the context of the country's recent history and broadly supported by a variety of international donors and agencies, might have been able to begin the slow process of transforming the Cambodian security forces.

First, approaching the issue as a matter of public expenditure created an inappropriate and inaccurate emphasis. Making the Cambodian national budget acceptable on paper to the IMF could have been achieved with a few strokes of a pen, and that approach would not have been any less effective than the demobilization programme. Moreover, it would have been less costly.

Rather, the appropriate first step in Cambodia's security sector reform should have involved a thorough assessment of the country's security needs, one that included Cambodian and international military experts. A defence white paper was drafted in 2000 with help from the Australian defence attaché to Cambodia, but World Bank officials, who insisted the demobilization project was not about military reform, refused to discuss the document. Ironically, the strongest backer for military reform appears to be General Ke Kim Yan, who wishes to transform the RCAF into a sufficiently professional force such that it could take part in future peacekeeping missions. Unfortunately, General Ke was not involved in any of the discussions regarding demobilization. Had there been a thorough security assessment, as well as an accurate inventory of troops and equipment, the groundwork could have been laid for a fundamental transformation of Cambodia's security forces.

Second, the failure to acknowledge adequately the context compromised the project's ability to succeed. Insufficient attention was paid, for example, to whether the large majority of lower-level soldiers needed to be "demobilized" at all, given their individual reintegration into communities. At the same time, the typical relationship of the security forces to the population – usually one of domination and fear – was not factored in at all. Equally as important, the political and partisan roles of the security forces were never discussed, such that it is impossible to tell whether project designers were simply unaware of this status or whether they found it too difficult to address. But by failing to do so, the project endorsed the ongoing unconstitutional and profoundly undemocratic use of a national institution by a political party. The failure to help break that link is arguably worse than the failure to reduce the cost of the security forces to the Cambodian people.

Finally, for all of the resources the international financial institutions devote to assessing, quantifying, and making dire predictions about corruption in Cambodia, the IMF's and World Bank's failure to design and implement a transparent programme is the height of hypocrisy. From the beginning of the project there were signs of serious corruption – the debate over the number of soldiers perhaps the most prominent – yet World Bank officials ignored or denied them. The World Bank's Cambodia country director took refuge in bureaucratic distinctions when he denied any obligation to verify the figures;[12] its key financial officer for the programme opined that funds would be released if about 60 per cent of them could be accounted for. By failing to obtain accurate information and uphold high standards, one wonders what analytical or moral right entitles the World Bank to judge others' capacity for "good governance". Had the government not lost interest in the project over the course of 2003 and 2004, it is not impossible that it would still be going on.

Should similar projects be envisioned elsewhere, it is crucial first to achieve an informed consensus regarding the country's collective security needs. The consequences of approaching security sector reform almost entirely as a means to rationalizing public expenditure are clear. Moreover, without an understanding of whether the security forces remain an instrument of particular interests, advocates of reform run the risk of further entrenching interests that do not serve the nation as a whole. It is equally important to understand whether the country's recent history offers any tradition of, aspirations for, or objections to a unified national force. Until international institutions are able to answer these questions and design appropriate programmes to answer them, their efforts are unlikely to succeed.

Notes

1. Sainsbury, Peter. 2000. "UN Human Rights Center gets new chief", *Phnom Penh Post*, Vol. 9, No. 6, 17–30 March.

2. Osborne, Milton. 1994. *Sihanouk – Prince of Light, Prince of Darkness*. Sydney: Unwin and Allen, p. 192.

3. Shawcross, William. 1979. *Sideshow: Kissinger, Nixon, and the Destruction of Cambodia*. New York: Pocket Books.

4. Kiernan, Ben. 1985. *How Pol Pot Came to Power*. London: Verso, p. 347.

5. See, among others, Chandler, David. 1991. *The Pol Pot Regime: Brother No. 1*. Boulder, CO: Westview Press.

6. For an excellent discussion of the PRK's security forces, see Gottesman, Evan. 2003. *Cambodia After the Khmer Rouge: Inside the Politics of Nation Building*. New Haven and London: Yale University Press.

7. Bainbridge, Bill and Lon Nara. 2002. "Grenade attack five years on", *Phnom Penh Post*, Vol. 11, No. 7, 29 March–11 April.

8. Sainsbury, Peter and Bou Sarouen. 1998. "The mouse is mightier than the MiG", *Phnom Penh Post*, Vol. 7, No. 7, 10–23 April.

9. International Crisis Group. 2000. "Cambodia: The elusive peace dividend", *ICG Asia Report*, No. 8, 11 August, p. 20.

10. Adams, Brad. 2001. "Demobilization's house of mirrors", *Phnom Penh Post*, Vol. 10, No. 24, 23 November–6 December.

11. Author's interview with Australian diplomatic staff.

12. Adams, note 10 above.

15

International force and political reconstruction: Cambodia, East Timor, and Afghanistan

William Maley

The fall of the Afghan capital Kabul to forces of the "Islamic State of Afghanistan" on 13 November 2001 among other things focused attention on ways in which an international force might contribute to political reconstruction in war-torn societies. On the same day, the UN special representative for Afghanistan, Ambassador Lakhdar Brahimi, provided a detailed briefing to the UN Security Council in which he outlined a model for political transition in Afghanistan, which the Security Council unanimously endorsed the following day. Doubtless as a result of his own experience as chair of the UN Panel on Peace Operations, Brahimi put forward a cautious proposal for the deployment of a "robust security force" which would not be a classic "blue helmet" peacekeeping force, but a melding of contingents supplied by a "coalition of the willing". Following the Bonn Agreement of 5 December 2001 and the installation of a new Afghan interim administration on 22 December 2001, an International Security Assistance Force (ISAF) was deployed in the Kabul area, very much along the lines which Brahimi had proposed. Yet despite strongly worded calls from both the United Nations and the interim administration for the force to be expanded and deployed in Afghanistan's other main cities, the USA in March 2002 effectively blocked such moves,[1] arguing instead that it was preferable to concentrate on the rebuilding of an Afghan national army. Only on 12 October 2003 did UN Security Council Resolution 1510 finally authorize the expansion of ISAF throughout Afghanistan, but by then major security problems had reemerged and a great deal of momentum had been lost.[2]

The interconnections between security sector form and the wider tides of international politics deserve more attention than they historically have received, and the aim in this chapter is to examine two notable Asian deployments undertaken in the context of UN operations – those in Cambodia and East Timor – and to draw out some of the implications for Afghanistan of the events in these theatres of operation. The comparison is useful, for each of the three has suffered the ravages of uninvited and unauthorized foreign invasions, both overt and "creeping", which to some degree have structured the attitudes to external force of key actors; and the United Nations has been handed a role in all three to try to restore stability and reasonable living conditions for the local population.[3] An examination of Cambodia, East Timor, and Afghanistan highlights the differences in these various cases, and the perils of believing that one model of security sector reform can fit all situations. The wider character of the state, the nature of the conflict which led to international action, and the character of local actors will need to be taken into account in designing assistance measures. Specifically, the chapter highlights a number of ongoing difficulties in Afghanistan, namely the resurgence of warlords, low levels of trust, the threat from "spoilers",[4] the need for first-rate intelligence, and the need to balance properly the maintenance of security with the provision of policing services and "law and order".

Cambodia

The genesis of the UN's Cambodian experience lies in the pathologies of the Cambodian state, and in the complex politics of South-East Asia in the 1960s and 1970s. The war in Viet Nam posed major challenges for the regime of Prince Norodom Sihanouk, who had ascended the throne of Cambodia as early as 1941, but left it in 1955 to become actively involved in day-to-day politics. His manipulative, divide-and-rule tactics led to an erosion of his support at the level of the political élite, and his ideological eccentricity alienated important US policy-makers. His overthrow in a 1970 coup by General Lon Nol was hardly unexpected. However, it did not lead to a renewal of political vigour in Phnom Penh. Lon Nol proved ineffectual, and his years in office were marked by escalating corruption and an erosion of the capacity of the armed forces, which increasingly existed only on paper. Confronted with an active communist insurgency and a legitimacy crisis, the regime collapsed in April 1975, leading to the inauguration of the so-called Khmer Rouge period.

These "Red Khmers", ultra-radicals inspired by Maoism and Fanonist ideas of the purifying value of violence, plunged Cambodia into an era of totalitarian killings, regional isolation, and tension with neighbouring states, especially Viet Nam.[5] In December 1978, after a series of border clashes, Viet Nam had had enough. Its forces invaded Cambodia, and drove the Khmer Rouge from the capital. The surviving Khmer Rouge leadership was displaced to the north-west of the country, but not eliminated as a military force: it received cross-border supplies from circles in Thailand alarmed at the expansion of Vietnamese power. In addition, a non-communist resistance group, the Khmer People's National Liberation Front (KPNLF), took up arms against the new regime in Phnom Penh. This regime was headed initially by Heng Samrin and then by Hun Sen, and, while at first dependent upon Vietnamese military backing, managed to develop significant conventional forces (the Cambodian People's Armed Forces, or CPAF).

Conflict dogged Cambodia for most of the 1980s, with Viet Nam remaining firm in its support for the Phnom Penh regime, China supporting the Khmer Rouge, and Western and regional states for the most part declining to accept the legitimacy of the Hun Sen regime. However, changes in the international environment, and especially the normalization of party-to-party relations between the Chinese Communist Party and the Communist Party of the Soviet Union in 1989, set the scene for progress over Cambodia. The Paris Accords of October 1991,[6] endorsed in enabling resolutions of the Security Council, paved the way for the most ambitious "peacekeeping" operation attempted by the United Nations up to that time, and confronted the military component of the UN Transitional Authority in Cambodia (UNTAC) with a range of complex tasks.[7] From the author's point of view, the most important were the conduct of a free and fair election, and, in order to secure a neutral political environment for that election, the disarming and cantonment of forces of the various factions. The latter were very much the responsibility of UNTAC's military component, headed by the force commander, Lieutenant-General John Sanderson. General Sanderson performed his tasks with great dexterity, but things did not proceed according to plan. By September 1992 over 42,000 regime troops had been cantoned, but the Khmer Rouge had declined to discharge their responsibilities to canton their forces. The military component of UNTAC was therefore given a new mandate, namely to create a secure environment for the conduct of the election. This it did, and the election was conducted peacefully in May 1993. However, subsequent events did throw into sharp focus just how limited the thrust of UNTAC's peacebuilding strategy had been.

First, the *reluctant* and *insincere* character of the internal parties proved a barrier to progress. With hindsight, their signatures on the Paris Accords owed more to pressure from their outside patrons than to a sudden surge of democratic or pluralist instinct. As time passed, the concerns of the patrons drifted elsewhere, and the parties began to look for ways either of extracting themselves altogether from the commitments they had made, or of minimizing the limitations which those commitments imposed. While the Khmer Rouge were the first and in some respects the worst offenders, Hun Sen's Cambodian People's Party (CPP) was not far behind, and it used a number of the instrumentalities of the state of Cambodia (SOC) to lethal effect against its opponents, particularly in the early months of 1993. This augured poorly for what would happen after the election. The CPP secured only 38 per cent of the vote at the election (compared with the 45 per cent secured by the royalist Funcinpec party). Hun Sen was clearly not prepared for this outcome, and an orchestrated threat of secession (the so-called Chakrapong rebellion) proved sufficient to win Hun Sen the paradoxical position of "second prime minister", from which he was then able to use the unreformed security sector organs to pursue his own agenda despite having failed at the polls. The CPP was interested in retaining power, not in sharing it.

Second, security sector reform had not been given the prominence in UNTAC's mandate that it deserved. The focus of those who crafted the settlement was on securing a new government in Cambodia which would enjoy both internal legitimacy (as a result of free and fair elections) and external legitimacy (through the acceptance of the credentials of the new government by the UN General Assembly). While the Paris Accords anticipated demobilization and cantonment, the future character of the coercive instrumentalities of the state was treated as a matter to be resolved as a matter of sovereign authority by the new authorities constituted by the transition process. Thus, while the force commander and a number of senior UNTAC figures were fully aware of the perils that lay in wait, they were not mandated to address those problems directly.

Third, the commitment of the regional powers, although ostensibly to the "democratization" of Cambodia, proved with time to be more to the elimination of Cambodia as a "regional problem". This had the effect of diminishing the significance not simply of free and fair electoral processes, but also of the package of measures, including security sector reform, which form part of the process of developing a consolidated democracy. The dimensions of failure in this respect became clear as the democratic expectations of those who voted in the 1993 election were frustrated by the emergence of neo-authoritarian rule.[8] Hun Sen used classic "salami tactics" (to use an expression coined by the Hungarian communist dictator Mátyás Rákosi) to slice away at his opponents through a series of incremental measures that ultimately left them profoundly weakened. These included the removal of the Finance Minister, Sam Rainsy, in October 1994; the arrest of the Foreign Minister, Prince Norodom Sirivudh, in November 1995; and the 5–6 July 1997 coup by Hun Sen, which forced the First Prime Minister, Prince Norodom Ranariddh, out of the country. The 26 July 1998 election was a pale shadow of the 1993 election, and high levels of pre-poll intimidation deprived it of any reasonable claim to be free and fair.[9] Yet neighbouring states, which had felt obliged to isolate Cambodia after the July 1997 coup, raced to endorse a flawed exercise in "democracy" because it suited their own interests to do so.

Ultimately, security sector reform in Cambodia was blocked by the sad reality, as Sue Downie has put it, that "the party (CPP), the government (SOC), the administration (SOC) and the armed forces (CPAF) were one".[10] The role of the security sector was to maintain this complex of forces in power, and inclusiveness and professionalism did not figure in its job description.[11] The Royal Cambodian Armed Forces, created in the aftermath of the 1993 election, were an uneasy combination of forces from the different pre-poll factions, with the CPAF elements playing a dominant role and answering to Hun Sen. The 1997 coup eliminated even the vestigial elements of diversity within those forces: former Funcinpec generals were particularly targeted in an outbreak of slaughter. Where government and the security sector are distinct, and norms have evolved which dictate the subordination of the latter to the former, then reform may be possible. It will not be possible where to promote security sector reform is in effect to invite a dominant power to cooperate in its own dismemberment.

East Timor

East Timor presented a quite different challenge: not that of integrating different combatant forces while taming a potential hegemon in their midst, but rather of developing (with very substantial UN involvement) the appropriate form of security sector as part of a process of developing new state instrumentalities in a putative UN member.

East Timor's recent history stands as an indicator of how decolonization can go wrong. After centuries of Portuguese rule, East Timor in 1974 felt the seismic effects of the revolutionary changes in Lisbon following the retirement and then death of António de Oliveira Salazar, who had ruled Portugal as an autocrat from 1932 until 1968. New political parties emerged in Dili and its surrounds – notably the traditionalist União Democratica Timorense (UDT), the pro-Indonesian Associacão Popular Democratica Timorense (Apodeti), and the radical pro-independence Frente Revolusionaria de Timor Leste Independente (Fretilin). A large number of East Timorese entertained the hope that this ferment would lead to the emergence of their territory as a distinct state, but these hopes were crushed when Indonesia invaded East Timor on 7 December 1975. Over two decades of high-level repression were to follow, but the Indonesian occupation and purported absorption of East Timor (in flagrant violation of UN Security Council Resolution 384 of 22 December 1975, which called on Indonesia "to withdraw without delay all its forces from the Territory") did not go uncontested on the ground. An armed offshoot of Fretilin and the subsequent Conselho Nacional da Resistencia Timorense (CNRT), known as the Forças Armadas de Libertação de Timor Leste, or Falintil, controlled the bulk of the territory for the first three years after the Indonesian invasion. However, Falintil was gradually driven from much of the country by the sustained application of Indonesian pressure from 1978, and by the late 1990s, according to one estimate, was down to about 600 fighters, working in bands of about 20.[12] These forces were led by Nicolau Lobato, who was killed in 1979; and subsequently by José Alexandre ("Xanana") Gusmão, who was captured by Indonesian forces in 1992 and subsequently imprisoned, but secured recognition as the embodiment of the aspirations of the East Timorese people.

The Asian financial crisis and the fall of President Soeharto of Indonesia in May 1998 created space for progress over the East Timor issue, and the United Nations found itself directly involved. On 27 January 1999 President B. J. Habibie of Indonesia proposed that a popular consultation be held in the territory to determine whether the people of East Timor wished to opt for independence or autonomy within the Indonesian republic. On 5 May 1999 a set of agreements was signed between Portugal and Indonesia which provided for a poll to be held. As far as security was concerned, the agreements were very loosely worded.[13] The third agreement provided in paragraph 1 that a "secure environment devoid of violence or other forms of intimidation is a prerequisite for the holding of a free and fair ballot in East Timor. Responsibility to ensure such an environment as well as for the general maintenance of law and order rests with the appropriate Indonesian security authorities." Paragraph 4, however, provided that the "police will be solely responsible for the maintenance of law and order". In violation of a basic requirement for such operations,[14] there was no neutral security force deployed for the consultation, and the UN Mission in East Timor (UNAMET) instead contained merely a civilian police component to liaise with the Indonesian police (PolRI). The security environment proved anything but secure: militias associated with the Indonesian military (TNI) used violence and intimidation to seek to shape the outcome of the consultation. According to UNAMET's head, Ian Martin, "UNAMET observed that Falintil exercised great discipline in the face of militia violence".[15] Gusmão ordered a unilateral cantonment of Falintil's forces, and this was completed by 12 August 1999.

The May 1999 agreements were premised on the assumption, which proved to be preposterous and which was manifestly preposterous at the time, that the TNI could and would act as a neutral source of security before, during, and after the "popular consultation". The results of the vote were announced by the UN Secretary-General, Kofi Annan, at a meeting of the UN Security Council on Friday 3 September. Fully 78.5 per cent of voters had favoured independence. At this point the pro-Indonesian militias embarked on a rampage which UNAMET was utterly unable to control.[16] This assault on people and property forced states such as Australia to scramble to put together a "coalition of the willing" which could be deployed into the territory once pressure on Jakarta elicited what key states saw as a necessary invitation. The INTERFET deployment, commanded by Major-General Peter Cosgrove, proved highly effective and set the scene for the handover to a UN peace operation (UNTAET) which culminated in the conduct of legislative elections in August 2001, paving the way for East Timor's presidential vote in April 2002 and independence the following month.[17]

The unexpected processes in which the United Nations found itself involved after the INTERFET deployment had implications for security sector reform as well. Rather than peacefully transforming the existing bureaucratic structures into those of an embryonic independent state, UNTAET was confronted with total state collapse and the need to rebuild institutions from scratch. In the security sector, a Timorese police force was the focus of activity of civilian police deployed to East Timor under UNTAET auspices. This reflected the reality that East Timor's security would not be based on the ability of an East Timorese army to fight off the Indonesian military, but rather on the continued commitment of key states such as Australia, and key institutions such as the United Nations, to bringing the territory safely to membership of the international community of states. While Falintil had played a key role in resisting the Indonesian occupation, the new armed forces and police were not designed to supply sinecures for former Falintil fighters, but rather to provide professionals who could aid a new government in discharging appropriate state functions, namely the maintenance of a secure law and order environment for citizens. The effective victory of the interests that Falintil served meant that its fighters could return to their homes and accept the authority of the new state.

Dreadful as the events of September 1999 were, they actually provided an opportunity for reconstruction of a security sector appropriate to the new state's needs and resource base. In September 2000 the "East Timor transitional cabinet" took the decision to establish an "East Timor defence force" of 1,500 regular infantry, with a reserve of the same size. The responsibilities of the force, trained by both Portugal and Australia, include deterrence of aggression and aid to the civil authority in the event of natural disasters (where the logistical capabilities of a well-trained military force can be of inestimable value even if the force is not especially large). At a donor conference in June 2001, a number of Asian and lusophone states, together with Australia, the USA, and the UK, offered support for specific areas of future development. This embeddedness of the new force in a network of responsible states might have been thought to augur well for the future path of security sector development as far as the military is concerned, although, as Desmond Ball has pointed out, the opportunity costs of sustaining such a force are considerable.[18] However, progress proved slow, and in April 2004 the UN Secretary-General reported to the Security Council that the army, known as Falintil-Force Defence Timor-Leste (F-FDTL), was confronted with a number of serious institutional problems, "including a poorly understood definition of its role, low morale, uncertain respect for discipline and authority, insufficient training of personnel, and unresolved relations with former combatants".[19] This was highlighted by a confrontation in January 2004 in Los Palos between F-FDTL personnel and the new police force, the Policia Nacional de Timor-Leste (PNTL).

Where policing is concerned the story is more complex, for progress here is intimately connected with the issue of reconstitution of the rule of law and institutions to give effect to it. In the absence of a judiciary of high integrity, transparent criminal law, and a well-designed penal system, it is naive to expect that civilian policing will be able to maintain the legitimacy that is central to its efficient operation. Nurturing positive developments in these spheres is an important element of the work of the UN Mission of Support in East Timor (UNMISET), established on 20 May 2002.

This case highlights the importance of member states' flexibility in the face of rapidly changing circumstances. An INTERFET-type deployment was one contingency for which Australia had *not* planned: its planning (and pre-positioning) had focused instead on an emergency extraction of UN personnel from Dili, or a more serene post-ballot peacekeeping deployment without the need for a Chapter VII mandate.[20] Yet given the constructive roles played by Australian troops and Australian police, the spin-off benefits of an essentially unanticipated deployment may prove to have been considerable. But of course, only time will tell how effectively the task of reconstruction has been performed.

Afghanistan

The task of moving forward in Afghanistan is daunting and has a number of significant elements.[21] It involves nothing less than the rebuilding of the state from scratch, but without the large-scale international presence that has assisted the process in East Timor, and in the face of schisms within the Afghan population on a scale and of a depth that East Timor was mercifully spared. These challenges are a direct product of the events that have brought Afghanistan to its present condition. As part of a successful reconstruction process, Afghanistan must redevelop political structures, find ways of legitimating them, maintain élite unity, and offer security for its people from both external danger and internal attack. The reconstruction of a functioning and legitimate security sector is necessary to underpin all these processes.

The Afghan state's monopoly on the legitimate use of the means of violence was lost in the late 1970s, when a communist coup and the Soviet invasion of Afghanistan delegitimized state power and prompted the emergence of a range of opposition forces (*mujahedin*). With the collapse of the communist regime of Dr Najibullah in 1992, the Afghan army splintered as well.[22] Afghanistan lapsed into a mosaic of power holders, with the Islamic State of Afghanistan, led by Burhanuddin Rabbani and Ahmad Shah Massoud, under attack from the Pakistan-backed Hezb-e Islami of Gulbuddin Hekmatyar, whose forces reduced southern Kabul to rubble in a sustained assault from mid-1992 to early 1995.[23] However, Hekmatyar proved incapable of holding territory, and from 1994 Pakistan focused instead on promoting the Taliban movement, a pathogenic, ethnically Pushtun, anti-modernist force made up of former *mujahedin*, students from religious *madrassa* schools, and relics of the Khalq communist faction who joined either opportunistically or for reasons of ethnic solidarity.[24] With financial help from Osama bin Laden's Al Qaeda organization, the Taliban took Kabul in September 1996. However, they did not succeed in eliminating Massoud, who executed a dexterous retreat which kept his forces intact and provided the leadership for anti-Taliban resistance to continue in the north-east of the country. Although Massoud was assassinated on 9 September 2001 by Al Qaeda suicide bombers, the structures which he had put in place were to play a key role in the collapse of Taliban rule between October and November 2001 following America's attack on the Taliban and Al Qaeda (Operation Enduring Freedom) in response to the terrorist strikes in Washington and New York on 11 September 2001.

The Bonn Agreement of 5 December 2001 sketched an outline for security sector reform in Annex I, in which the participants in the talks requested "the assistance of the international community in helping the new Afghan authorities in the establishment and training of new Afghan security and armed forces", and also requested the Security Council "to consider authorizing the early deployment to Afghanistan of a United Nations mandated force" to "assist in the maintenance of security for

Kabul and its surrounding areas". They anticipated that such a force "could, as appropriate, be progressively expanded to other urban centers and other areas". On 20 December, two days before a new Afghan interim administration was sworn in, the UN Security Council in Resolution 1386 authorized the establishment of the International Security Assistance Force, with a Chapter VII enforcement mandate. It was not a peacekeeping force under direct UN authority, but a security *assistance* force, to secure Kabul and assist the process of developing a unified national army. Its expenses were to be met by the participating member states. ISAF was initially led by the UK, followed by Turkey, and then Germany and the Netherlands jointly; command of ISAF was finally transferred to NATO on 11 August 2003. Once deployed, ISAF set to work immediately, and on 3 April 2002 a graduation ceremony was held for the first battalion of the Afghan National Guard. On 1 December 2002 President Karzai issued a decree providing for a national army of 70,000 troops, which would be largely American-trained.[25] However, despite this symbolic achievement, many hazards litter the path towards security sector reform.

One is warlordism. The problem of predatory warlordism re-emerged as a significant challenge to the state in the immediate aftermath of Operation Enduring Freedom. This was to a significant degree a product of the US strategy of cooperating with various predatory anti-Taliban armed formations,[26] as well as arming the Pushtun tribes that most rapidly "reflagged" themselves as anti-Taliban forces. Very little thought seems to have been given to the long-term consequences of such a policy, even though the indiscriminate arming of extremist groups within the *mujahedin* had contributed significantly to the traumas of the 1990s. Warlords differ in their strategies – some have extremely ambitious objectives, whereas others are interested simply in maximizing their cut of available resources – and the strategies to deal with them also need to be appropriately nuanced.[27] The problem of warlordism can be confronted in various ways: by combating warlords directly, by undercutting their support base, by purchasing their loyalty, by incorporating them into the state, or, in the long run, by promoting norms of behaviour which prohibit predatory extraction. A blend of these approaches is probably required, depending upon the exact nature of the warlord involved, but at the very least it is necessary to reconstitute a national army. Yet warlords rightly view this as a threat to their interests, and may well seek to act as spoilers in order to prevent their interests being compromised. The consequence of recrudescent warlordism has been marked insecurity outside Kabul, and sometimes even within the capital itself, and the consequences for ordinary Afghans have on occasion been quite hideous. Too often, a climate of impunity has poisoned the post-Taliban atmosphere.[28]

In addition, levels of trust between different power holders in the new Afghanistan remain low. There are considerable difficulties in rebuilding the military and police in such circumstances, for those who have little prospect of controlling the new coercive instrumentalities of the state are likely to be suspicious about how those who *do* control them will use them. Even before the April 1978 coup, the Afghan military was divided by the corrosive effects of nepotism,[29] which contributed to the staging of the coup itself. What residual professional norms may have sustained the vestiges of a national military are now gone. There is one significant organized force, namely the Panjsheri groups led by Massoud and now by Defence Minister Muhammad Qasim Fahim. These groups rightly regard themselves as having contributed crucially to the rapid ousting of the Taliban, but tend to regard with a certain scorn the claims to similar status made by Pushtun warlords who supported the Taliban until the US bombing campaign began. Some tensions naturally exist between those who spent years struggling against the Taliban in difficult circumstances, and émigrés who spent the war years abroad but rightly regard themselves as superior administrators. There are also tensions between different visions of Afghanistan's future that different groups entertain. While there was initially some evidence that within upper echelons of the interim administration the degree of cooperation between different groups was unexpectedly high,[30] this eroded over time, with major tensions surfacing during the work of the Constitutional Loya Jirga in December 2003 and January 2004.[31] In any case, it is another task altogether to replicate similar cooperation in large-scale organizations such as the armed forces or the police.

This is why it is important that the process of rebuilding be lubricated by the deployment of a force such as ISAF, which is politically neutral *between* different forces within the Afghan government, even if it must play a role in affirming the dominance of the Afghan government over warlords. As Barnett R. Rubin wrote in 2002, the "position of the United States and its coalition partners – that they will train Afghan national forces rather than use international forces to maintain security – is disingenuous. An expanded international force is needed precisely to provide security during the reorganization of irregulars into a smaller, more disciplined force that will maintain security."[32] Some see the US position as reflecting an American desire to be able to pursue remaining pockets of Al Qaeda terrorists without the risk of being impeded by the presence in the vicinity of other international forces; to others it simply points to a hostility in Washington to an agenda of "nation building". However, the net effect is to leave a raft of potential responsibilities for a new force that could well overwhelm it.

In the light of the obvious security vacuum in the countryside, the USA and its coalition allies have moved vigorously to promote the idea of "provincial reconstruction teams" (PRTs) as an alternative to either an expanded ISAF or a fully deployed Afghan national army. Such teams, comprising armed troops together with a relatively small number of civil affairs specialists, have been deployed in Bamyan, Mazar-e Sharif, Gardez, Herat, Kandahar, and Kunduz. They have involved not just American troops, but also personnel from the UK, Germany, and New Zealand. The fusion of military and civil tasks has engendered a degree of controversy, since aid workers are often reluctant to be seen hand in hand with those whose standard operating procedures ("rules of engagement") may encompass the use of lethal force; but a more serious criticism of PRTs is that they have been largely deployed in areas of relative stability (such as Herat and Kunduz), rather than in the many danger zones that could profit from a demonstration of international resolve, and therefore have made little contribution to ambient security.

Even with an effective ISAF, the reconstitution of the Afghan national army would be a top priority. There is no doubt that this is an essential long-term objective, and since the long term begins in the short, it was appropriate that the transitional authority – which succeeded the interim administration in June 2002 – opted to pursue this path. However, it is necessary to be realistic about the pitfalls in building new militaries from scratch. Some observations made by Sir Robert Thompson more than 35 years ago about capacity building in South Viet Nam remain pertinent: he warned that if, "because demands are urgent and impatience wins the day, training is reduced and short crash programs are instituted, there will be a constant supply of inexperienced, incompetent, useless officials who will be incapable of implementing any policy and who will merely add to the prevailing confusion".[33] Furthermore, it is one thing to put soldiers through basic training in which they practise drill, learn how to use weapons, and study rules of engagement. It is another thing altogether to inculcate an *ultimate* sense of loyalty to the new institution they have joined, rather than to other identities they may consider salient. The test for the Afghan national army will come when its members are called upon to obey commands which oblige them to act in ways they would not otherwise adopt; and it is only once the new army has passed this test (rather than fragment in a moment of crisis) that it can be expected to enjoy widespread confidence. This obvious point was made painfully clear in Iraq in April 2004 when Iraqi recruits balked at fighting fellow Iraqis.[34]

Finally, any security force in Afghanistan – Afghan or international – will need access to high-quality intelligence, not only to thwart the activities of potential spoilers, both internal and external, but to anticipate tensions between different Afghan groups into which the military could inadvertently be drawn. The past claim that the United Nations has no need for intelligence because it has no enemies cannot be a guide to action in Afghanistan: the United Nations, and states acting under UN Security Council authority, are playing inescapably political roles, which will just as inescapably win them the enmity of some forces. This cannot be wished away, but with due care can be managed.[35]

In a country in which power has long originated from the barrel of a gun, political actors will be understandably reluctant to consent to an irreversible decommissioning process from which perfidious opponents might benefit. Defining spheres for which different groups may exercise responsibility in terms of the maintenance of order may be a useful first step towards reintegrating combatants into civil society. But this should be only part of a process of building policing capacities by which order in different parts of the country can be reinforced. At the end of the day, Afghanistan does not need a large army: for its external security it will essentially depend on the renewed interest of the international community in pressuring Afghanistan's neighbours not to meddle in its affairs. What it does need is a significant policing capacity, so that the notion of the rule of law can begin to replace the notion of the rule of men.[36] This cannot happen overnight, but there will never be a better moment to start building in this direction.

Conclusion

The cases of Cambodia, East Timor, and Afghanistan militate against any simple "one-size-fits-all" approach to the promotion of security sector reform as part of UN peace operations. In Cambodia the CPAF proved untamable: where this is the case, the UN's prospects of bringing about major change through anything short of a Chapter VII peace operation will be poor. In East Timor the United Nations was confronted with a task of facilitating the building of a new national army, but in surprisingly propitious circumstances – with reputable member states ready to help, and a relatively high degree of élite consensus over how to proceed. In Afghanistan the United Nations faces much more troubling circumstances, with dangers from warlords, low levels of trust, and at least the potential for the international community to abandon Afghanistan yet again. What all cases of this type fundamentally require is *commitment*. If the wider world is serious about breaking cycles of autocracy or conflict, it has the capacity to make a difference. Whether it has the will is much more questionable.[37]

Notes

1. Sipress, Alan. 2002. "Peacekeepers won't go beyond Kabul, Cheney says", *Washington Post*, 20 March.
2. See Rubin, Barnett R. 2004. "(Re)building Afghanistan: The folly of stateless democracy", *Current History*, Vol. 103, No. 672, pp. 165–170.
3. See Maley, William. 1993. "Regional conflicts: Afghanistan and Cambodia", in Ramesh Thakur and Carlyle A. Thayer (eds) *Rethinking Regional Relations: Asia Pacific and the Former Soviet Union*. Boulder, CO: Westview Press, pp. 183–200; Maley, William. 2000. "The UN and East Timor", *Pacifica Review*, Vol. 12, No. 1, pp. 63–76; Maley, William. 2002. "The reconstruction of Afghanistan", in Ken Booth and Tim Dunne (eds) *Worlds in Collision: Terror and the Future of Global Order*. London: Palgrave Macmillan, pp. 184–193.
4. See, generally, Stedman, Stephen John. 1997. "Spoiler problems in peace processes", *International Security*, Vol. 22, No. 2, pp. 5–53.
5. See Jackson, Karl D. (ed.). 1989. *Cambodia 1975–1978: Rendezvous with Death*. Princeton: Princeton University Press; Kiernan, Ben. 1996. *The Pol Pot Regime: Race, Power and Genocide in Cambodia under the Khmer Rouge, 1975–1979*. New Haven: Yale University Press.
6. For the text of the agreements, see United Nations. 1995. *The United Nations and Cambodia 1991–1995*. New York: Department of Public Information, United Nations, pp. 132–148.
7. On the Cambodian mission, see *ibid.*; Doyle, Michael W. 1995. *UN Peacekeeping in Cambodia: UNTAC's Civilian Mandate*. Boulder, CO: Lynne Rienner; Findlay, Trevor. 1995. *Cambodia: The Legacy and Lessons of UNTAC*. Oxford: Oxford University Press; Doyle, Michael W., Ian Johnstone, and Robert C. Orr (eds). 1997. *Keeping the Peace: Multilateral UN Operations in Cambodia and El Salvador*. Cambridge: Cambridge University Press; Peou, Sorpong. 1997. *Conflict Neutralization in the Cambodia War: From Battlefield to Ballot-Box*. Kuala Lumpur: Oxford University Press; Brown, MacAlister and Joseph J. Zasloff. 1998. *Cambodia Confounds the Peacemakers 1979–1998*. Ithaca: Cornell University Press.
8. See Heder, Steve. 1995. "Cambodia's democratic transition to neoauthoritarianism", *Current History*, Vol. 94, No. 596, pp. 425–429.
9. Sanderson, John M. and Michael Maley. 1998. "Elections and liberal democracy in Cambodia", *Australian Journal of International Affairs*, Vol. 52, No. 3, pp. 241–253.
10. Downie, Sue. 2000. "Cambodia's 1998 election: Understanding why it was not a 'miracle on the Mekong'", *Australian Journal of International Affairs*, Vol. 54, No. 1, p. 46.
11. See Hendrickson, Dylan. 2001. "Cambodia's security-sector reforms: Limits of a downsizing strategy", *Conflict, Security and Development*, Vol. 1, No. 1, pp. 67–82.
12. Martinkus, John. 2001. *A Dirty Little War*. Sydney: Random House, p. 14.
13. For the terms of the agreements, see United Nations. 1999. *Question of East Timor: Report of the Secretary-General*, A/53/951, S/1999/513, 5 May, Annexes I–III. New York: United Nations.
14. See Walter, Barbara F. 2002. *Committing to Peace: The Successful Settlement of Civil Wars*. Princeton: Princeton University Press.
15. Martin, Ian. 2001. *Self-Determination in East Timor: The United Nations, the Ballot, and International Intervention*. Boulder, CO: Lynne Rienner, p. 72.
16. See Kingsbury, Damien (ed.). 2000. *Guns and Ballot Boxes: East Timor's Vote for Independence*. Clayton: Monash Asia Institute.
17. See Smith, Michael G. with Moreen Dee. 2003. *Peacekeeping in East Timor: The Path to Independence*. Boulder, CO: Lynne Rienner.

18. Ball, Desmond. 2002. "The defence of East Timor: A recipe for disaster?", *Pacifica Review*, Vol. 14, No. 3, p. 189.
19. United Nations. 2004. *Report of the Secretary-General on the United Nations Mission of Support in East Timor*, S/2004/333, 19 April. New York: United Nations, para. 7.
20. See Cotton, James. 2004. *East Timor, Australia and Regional Order: Intervention and its Aftermath in Southeast Asia*. London: RoutledgeCurzon, p. 116. For a critical discussion of Australia's role, see Maley, William. 2000. "Australia and the East Timor crisis: Some critical comments", *Australian Journal of International Affairs*, Vol. 54, No. 2, pp. 151–161.
21. For more detailed discussion of transition complexities, see Rubin, Barnett R., Ashraf Ghani, William Maley, Ahmed Rashid, and Olivier Roy. 2001. *Afghanistan: Reconstruction and Peacemaking in a Regional Framework*, KOFF Peacebuilding Reports 1/2001. Bern: Centre for Peacebuilding, Swiss Peace Foundation; Maley, William. 2001. "Moving forward in Afghanistan", in Stuart Harris, William Maley, Richard Price, Christian Reus-Smit, and Amin Saikal *The Day the World Changed? Terrorism and World Order*, Keynotes No. 1. Canberra: Department of International Relations, Research School of Pacific and Asian Studies, Australian National University, pp. 18–24.
22. See Davis, Anthony. 1993. "The Afghan army", *Jane's Intelligence Review*, Vol. 5, No. 3, pp. 134–139; Jalili, Ali A. 2002. "Rebuilding Afghanistan's national army", *Parameters*, Vol. 32, No. 3, pp. 72–86.
23. See Maley, William. 2002. *The Afghanistan Wars*. London: Palgrave Macmillan, pp. 194–217.
24. See Maley, William. 1998. "Introduction: Interpreting the Taliban", in William Maley (ed.) *Fundamentalism Reborn? Afghanistan and the Taliban*. New York: New York University Press, pp. 1–28; Rashid, Ahmed. 2000. *Taliban: Militant Islam, Oil and Fundamentalism in Central Asia*. New Haven: Yale University Press; Dorronsoro, Gilles. 2000. *La révolution afghane: Des communistes aux tâlebân*. Paris: Karthala; Maley, William. 2000. *The Foreign Policy of the Taliban*. New York: Council on Foreign Relations; Goodson, Larry P. 2001. *Afghanistan's Endless War: State Failure, Regional Politics, and the Rise of the Taliban*. Seattle: University of Washington Press; Nojumi, Neamatollah. 2002. *The Rise of the Taliban in Afghanistan; Mass Mobilization, Civil War, and the Future of the Region*. New York: Palgrave Macmillan.
25. Landler, Mark. 2002. "Afghans plan a new army of 70,000", *New York Times*, 3 December.
26. The word "predatory" is used because not all armed anti-Taliban forces engaged in the extractive activities which lie at the heart of warlordism; on the contrary, some enjoyed high levels of local legitimacy.
27. See Giustozzi, Antonio. 2003. *Respectable Warlords? The Politics of State-Building in Post-Taleban Afghanistan*, Working Papers Series No. 1, Crisis States Programme. London: Development Research Centre, London School of Economics and Political Science.
28. See Human Rights Watch. 2003. *"Killing You Is A Very Easy Thing For Us": Human Rights Abuses In Southeast Afghanistan*. New York: Human Rights Watch; Niland, Norah. 2004. "Justice postponed: The marginalization of human rights in Afghanistan", in Antonio Donini, Norah Niland, and Karin Wermester (eds) *Nation-Building Unraveled? Aid, Peace and Justice in Afghanistan*. Bloomfield: Kumarian Press, pp. 61–82.
29. See Magnus, Ralph. 1986. "The military and politics in Afghanistan: Before and after the revolution", in Edward A. Olsen and Stephen Jurika Jr (eds) *The Armed Forces in Contemporary Asian Societies*. Boulder, CO: Westview Press, pp. 325–344.
30. Constable, Pamela. 2002. "Afghanistan's rebirth imperilled by its past: Security, aid remain key weaknesses", *Washington Post*, 8 April.

31. Gall, Carlotta. 2004. "Afghan talks adjourn, deeply divided on ethnic lines," *New York Times*, 2 January.
32. Rubin, Barnett R. 2002. "Is America abandoning Afghanistan?", *New York Times*, 10 April.
33. Pfeffer, Richard M. (ed.). 1968. *No More Vietnams? The War and the Future of American Foreign Policy*. New York: Harper & Row, p. 163.
34. See Ricks, Thomas E. 2004. "Iraqi battalion refuses to 'fight Iraqis'", *Washington Post*, 11 April.
35. See Smith, Hugh. 1994. "Intelligence and United Nations peacekeeping", *Survival*, Vol. 36, No. 3, pp. 174–192.
36. See McFarlane, John and William Maley. 2001. "Civilian police in United Nations peace operations: Some lessons from recent Australian experience", in Ramesh Thakur and Albrecht Schnabel (eds) *United Nations Peacekeeping Operations: Ad Hoc Missions, Permanent Engagement*. Tokyo: United Nations University Press, pp. 182–211.
37. See Maley, William. 2002. "Twelve theses on the impact of humanitarian intervention", *Security Dialogue*, Vol. 33, No. 3, p. 274.

Conclusion

16

Post-conflict societies and the military: Recommendations for security sector reform

Hans-Georg Ehrhart and Albrecht Schnabel

Post-conflict environments tend to be highly fragile and unsafe for both the normal citizen and those organizations – internal and external – actively involved in the slow process of consolidating a sense of physical security, political stabilization, and economic development. As has been argued throughout this book, international military engagement in conflict and post-conflict theatres has usually been marked by good intentions and honest concern about the security of post-war societies. Yet all too often these engagements have not been blessed with much success. Some recent reform proposals for more effective and meaningful military interventions to facilitate reconstruction, reconciliation, and conflict resolution have been offered to the academic and policy communities. Two such studies in particular carry the potential to be of great assistance in this process – the so-called Brahimi Report (initiated by the UN Secretary-General to address and stimulate rapid reform of the UN's capacity to undertake peace support operations), and the 2002 Swedish report *Challenges of Peace Operations*, drawing on an impressive international effort to study in great detail, and with the help of numerous experienced peacekeepers, the theoretical and operational challenges of today's peace operations.[1] Particularly the former has been noted by various contributions throughout this volume. Based on the various case studies in this book, a number of issues emerge which could improve security sector reform efforts by international, national, and non-state actors. As a conclusion to this book these suggestions will be summarized in the following pages.[2]

General recommendations: Towards sustainable security sector reform

The involvement of international peace support operations in post-conflict reconstruction, and their security, economic, and political peace-building tasks more generally, are only one side of the coin. The other concerns the post-conflict role of the internal security apparatus, including – but not exclusively – former combatants. Without a lasting transformation of a post-war society's security sector, little long-term stability can be achieved. Security sector reform is generally regarded as the policy framework through which a growing number of donors address security problems in post-conflict societies. Security sector reform must be understood as an integral part of the overall process of post-conflict peace-building. By the same token, developments in security sector reform depend on, and shape, the wider dynamics of the reconstruction process.

The overall aim of security sector reform is to enable states to ensure national defence and protect citizens within policy and budgetary constraints that are consistent with national development goals. Besides its military-driven goals, security sector reform should maximize the capacity of all security actors so that they actively contribute to social, economic, and political development.[3] Among others, security sector reform needs to consider the following issues: the transition from military regimes; the challenge of divided societies; size and budget of security forces; disarmament, demobilization, and reintegration of former combatants; democratization; and issues of good governance.[4]

The restructuring of the security sector is inextricably determined by the specific context within which such initiatives occur. It is therefore difficult to advocate a general strategy that can be adopted by different governments in the restructuring of civil-military relations in their own countries. It is possible, however, to provide a generic set of principles, criteria, and methodological assumptions that will be applicable to all transformation processes regardless of historical, political, and cultural peculiarities.

Any attempt to engage in a process of security sector transformation should explicitly outline those principles on which security sector reform will be based. The following broad principles draw on the arguments presented in this book. They should ideally find reflection in the appropriate constitutional provisions, legislative frameworks, standard operating procedures, and institutional culture of the armed forces themselves.

- The principle of civil supremacy entails four key principles which should be respected by both the civil authorities and the armed forces in the execution of their respective responsibilities; namely the principles of the separation of powers, legality, accountability, and transparency.

- Decisions on the roles, responsibilities, tasks, organizational features, and personnel requirements of the security forces should be made in accordance with the circumstances of a developing country engaged in a difficult and complex transition.
- The determination of the roles, responsibilities, tasks, organizational features, resource requirements, and personnel requirements of the security forces should be done in a manner that is affordable to the country concerned, particularly in light of a limited resource base and pressing demands on its budget from all sectors of society.
- The roles and responsibilities of the security sector should be enshrined in the constitution. The constitution should ensure that the security sector would respect human rights as reflected in the constitution and domestic and international law, and will understand and operate within the framework of the democratic process within the country concerned.
- Security forces should be non-partisan in their political behaviour and should not further the interests of and/or involve themselves in political activities.
- The conduct of security policy and the management of security matters should be handled in a consultative and transparent manner, and should encourage a high level of parliamentary and public participation without endangering the lives of personnel and without prejudicing the ability of the security forces to conduct legal and legitimate operations.
- National security should be sought primarily through efforts to meet the political, economic, social, and cultural rights of the country's people; and the activities of the security sector should be subordinate to and supportive of these efforts.
- Both the political authorities and the leadership of the armed forces and other security sector actors should strive to build and maintain high levels of dialogue and partnership in all their dealings with one another. Such collaboration should be predicated on regular and continuous interaction between these interlinked communities, and should occur within the hierarchy of authority and oversight as established in the country concerned.

Main challenges

Many transition societies continue to face threats and challenges to their national interests, sovereignty, and internal stability that will continue to require the presence of external security forces for medium- to long-term periods. Based on the country's strategic environment, typically these forces need to execute a wide variety of secondary and "non-traditional" operations (peace missions, internal law and order responsibilities, and, in some cases, reconstruction and development tasks).

In this context, internal and external actors face – and should respond to – the following challenges.

- The armed forces' traditional role of external defence alone is no longer suitable to address today's needs for participation in the complex spectrum of peace support operations. These additional roles have to be incorporated into armed forces' doctrine, organization, and training.
- In a post-conflict settlement setting, peacekeeping functions have been modified and expanded to such areas as maintaining public order and providing logistical support for political and social transition. International security forces need to be prepared to respond to these additional tasks.
- The extent to which the military can get involved in reconstruction and rehabilitation should be considered in terms of available civilian skills and expertise. A proper division of roles and functions between the military units and civilian agencies should be negotiated in a local operational context.
- Dealing with unarmed civilians requires restraints of force and conciliatory measures based on dialogue and mediation. The integration of peacekeeping roles into community building requires partnerships with the local population.
- Reform of the military/police education system requires an emphasis on human rights issues and democratic oversight of the security sector.

General recommendations

Drawing on suggestions voiced throughout this volume, the international community should consider the implementation of the following actions to assist in the process of security sector reform.

- Security sector reform is likely to succeed if the institutional structures provided in a peace agreement are acceptable to the warring parties and supporting élites, and they respond not just to their security needs but also to their more fundamental political aspirations. At a minimum, these aspirations should be transformed, so that they can be accommodated within the new structures.
- In order to be successful, security sector reform requires the presence of strong leadership that can create a broad consensus to marginalize "spoilers" and prevent their agenda from assuming a dominant position in the public discourse and the political process.
- International criminals and terrorists exploit states with poorly functioning security sectors to harbour their activities. This should provide increased incentive to regional and international actors to assist such states to reform their security sectors on an urgent and comprehensive basis to prevent the spread of cross-border crime and international ter-

rorism. Increased focus on terrorism should not, however, lead to misguided support for further centralized and empowered, yet unaccountable and oppressive, security structures, in the belief that strong security structures are required to fight terrorism.

- Security sector reform should include the military, security intelligence, border control, and financial control functions along with the usual law enforcement, judicial, and corrections functions as an integrated system based on the principles of rule of law and civilian control.
- The reform process should go beyond institutional reform and include the transformation of public security attitudes from ones of fear, disrespect, or disinterest to ones of trust, cooperation, and voluntary compliance.
- International and regional peacekeeping and peace support forces that are often deployed as surrogate security institutions to states characterized by political, legal, and security vacuums should be used more effectively. They should support the broader aims of security sector reform, without compromise to their security role and their requirements for force protection. The positive model of a functioning security institution, which an international force typically represents, should be exploited as a benchmark for the local reform process.
- International forces should be encouraged, and resources provided, to engage more fully with the local population. Their specialized personnel (e.g. legal, medical, religious, engineering, communications, public affairs, logistics, education, and administrative officers) should be encouraged to engage with their local counterparts.[5]
- An overall reconciliation process should serve as the foundation for restructuring the security forces as legitimate and democratically directed institutions.
- Coordination should be improved among all armed forces (among international actors, and between them and local actors), and a lead actor (or force contributor/component) who will be perceived as unbiased by *all* conflict parties should be identified.
- Media and other opinion-makers should advocate the need for improving interethnic relations and eventually equal ethnic and minority representation among the security forces.

The role of the donor community

Most donors focus on narrow security sector reform objectives and face real dilemmas in providing focused and effective assistance in response to the wide agenda and multifaceted needs of national capacity building in the formulation and implementation of reformed security policies. On the one hand, this reflects the immense difficulties of working in post-war environments, which lends itself to "crisis management" approaches. On the other hand, it stems from the lack of a shared understanding within the donor community of what security sector reform means, from conflicting donor objectives, and from weak internal capacity in this area.

With the aim of developing more coherent and sustainable programmes of assistance for security sector reform, the following recommendations should be embraced by donors.

- It is crucial to develop a shared understanding among national and international partners of what security sector reform means, the objectives of external assistance, and how these can be achieved.
- In countries with weak institutions and persisting tensions, greater emphasis should be placed on preparing the political terrain for security sector reform before encouraging ambitious and sensitive institutional reforms.
- Prior to designing appropriate steps of security sector reform, thorough needs assessments are necessary, preferably done by teams that combine international and local actors (and stakeholders).
- Appropriate timeframes and normative frameworks for security sector reform should be developed which allow local norms and conceptions of security to adapt to international standards of security sector governance.
- Security sector reform assistance should be integrated more effectively into wider post-conflict reconstruction strategies, particularly with respect to macro-economic stabilization and adjustment programmes.
- Strategic coordination on security sector reform issues should be enhanced by building an "up-stream" culture of cooperation through political dialogue and joint policy-making initiatives.
- Strategic reform efforts should be facilitated at the national level by prioritizing activities that develop and enhance human resources. An appropriate balance should be negotiated between external "models" of security sector reform and local interests and capacity.

Issues for future enquiry

The role of force to bring about and consolidate peace is a delicate issue. Is the use and display of military force able to stop violence, suppress the resurgence of violence, and perhaps even transform destructive, violent interaction into non-violent, constructive behaviour? This volume attempts to show that the security sector plays an important and indispensable role in helping post-conflict societies to secure a transition to a more productive and peaceful life. While creating the conditions for successful political, economic, and social transitions, the latter are also prerequisites for sustainable security sector reform. This is where external assistance, such as in the form of international peace operations, becomes a driving force in creating a secure environment and facilitating security sector reform, which, as an important factor among many others, spurs the wider transition process and creates a solid foundation for sustainable peace. By doing so, external military forces can lead by example. They display the constructive role that security forces can play in adding stability and legitimacy to the transformation of political, economic, and social processes. If affected societies and their political, economic, and security élites are committed to peace, stability, and development, there is a fair chance for success. In the broadest sense possible such success could be defined as a context in which, first, external actors (be they individual states, regional groupings, or larger international players, military and non-military) are able and willing to stay the course and support an irrevocable process towards security consolidation and security sector reform, and, second, where national and local authorities are committed and able to sustain such progress once external actors retreat.

Many critical issues and questions remain unresolved and call for future studies. It would be helpful if future work would examine issues such as the role of armed forces in deterring peace spoilers during the reconstruction period; the nature, sources, and moral and legal legitimacy of external military "intervention"; the extent to which the international community is responsible for post-conflict assistance; and the division of labour between local, national, regional, and international actors in post-conflict settings. There are numerous issues of a more practical nature that require further enquiry – in general terms, but also in the context of very specific peacebuilding theatres. These include the collection, analysis, and sharing of best practices, and systematic cross-case study evaluations of past and ongoing peacebuilding efforts. The lessons learned from the practical implementation of security sector reform efforts would help greatly in identifying better strategies for effective multi-actor cooperation. The task of nation building in post-conflict societies has received much attention, in particular in the contexts of Bosnia, Kosovo, East Timor, Afghanistan, and, as an evolving case study, Iraq. More has to be learned about the interplay between external and local actors, and methods to support and, most importantly, assure sustainable transfer to local and national stakeholders.

Notes

1. United Nations. 2000. *Report of the Panel on United Nations Peace Operations*, A/55/305-S/2000/809, 21 August. New York: UN General Assembly/Security Council; The Chal-

lenges Project. 2002. *Challenges of Peace Operations: Into the 21st Century – Concluding Report 1997–2003*. Stockholm: Elanders Gotab.

2. For additional insight in the requirements for, and challenges of, effective security sector reform, see the findings of a series of workshops organized by the Geneva Centre for the Democratic Control of Armed Forces (DCAF) in Karkoszka, Andrzej. 2003. "Security sector reform – The concept, its political usefulness and growing importance: A summary of the DCAF tracks at the 5th ISF", in Alan Bryden and Philipp Fluri (eds) *Security Sector Reform: Institutions, Society and Good Governance*. Baden-Baden: Nomos, pp. 313–321.

3. The following recommendations were among those previously disseminated as part of an interim project report. See Ehrhart, Hans-Georg, Albrecht Schnabel, and Monica Blagescu. 2002. *Towards More Effective Assistance in Security Sector Reform – Policy Brief*, Hamburger Informationen zur Friedensforschung und Sicherheitspolitik No. 34. Hamburg: Institute for Peace Research and Security Policy at the University of Hamburg.

4. Please consult the first two chapters in this volume for detailed discussions of the key tasks of security sector reform efforts.

5. In this context it is particularly important that security sector reform efforts become more sensitive to gender issues, particularly the role of women. As Vanessa A. Farr argues, "for those who have historically been excluded from engagement with any aspect of the security sector, nothing short of its *transformation* will help them take their rightful place as democratic co-owners of control over the forces and institutions that are intended to ensure the safety of all". See Farr, Vanessa A. 2004. "Voices from the margins", in Clem McCartney, Martina Fischer, and Oliver Wils (eds) *Security Sector Reform: Potentials and Challenges for Conflict Transformation*, Berghof Handbook Dialogue Series No. 2. Berlin: Berghof Research Center for Constructive Conflict Management, p. 69 (emphasis in the original).

Index